DALCROZE TODAY

It is important—and would be imprudent ever to forget—that Eurhythmics is to be considered a form of education through *music and* into *music*.

Emile Jaques-Dalcroze,
'La Grammaire de la rythmique (préparation corporelle aux exercices de la méthode).'

DEDICATION

I affectionately dedicate this book to my earliest guides along the Dalcrozian way:

Jeanne-Alice Bachmann-Borel, my mother, my first teacher of piano and improvisation;

André Bourquin, who introduced me to the joys of group singing and polyphony;

Christiane Montandon;

Irène Boghossian-Reichel;

Monique Petitpierre-Rochat—my most delightful rhythmics teachers.

And may all their successors rest assured of the faithful gratitude I bear them and to the memory of

Fernande Peyrot

Dalcroze Today

*An Education through
and into Music*

MARIE-LAURE BACHMANN

Translated by
DAVID PARLETT

Translation edited by
Ruth Stewart

Preface by Jack P. B. Dobbs

CLARENDON PRESS · OXFORD

This book has been printed digitally and produced in a standard specification in order to ensure its continuing availability

OXFORD
UNIVERSITY PRESS

Great Clarendon Street, Oxford OX2 6DP

Oxford University Press is a department of the University of Oxford.
It furthers the University's objective of excellence in research, scholarship,
and education by publishing worldwide in

Oxford New York

Auckland Bangkok Buenos Aires Cape Town Chennai
Dar es Salaam Delhi Hong Kong Istanbul Karachi Kolkata
Kuala Lumpur Madrid Melbourne Mexico City Mumbai Nairobi
São Paulo Shanghai Singapore Taipei Tokyo Toronto

with an associated company in Berlin

Oxford is a registered trade mark of Oxford University Press
in the UK and in certain other countries

Published in the United States
by Oxford University Press Inc., New York

© Oxford University Press, 1991

The moral rights of the author have been asserted
Database right Oxford University Press (maker)

Reprinted 2002

ISBN 0-19-816400-9

PREFACE

For too long the teachings and pioneer work of Emile Jaques-Dalcroze have been neglected by educationists in this country. It is our hope that this book will help to change that position. Not only does it give a lucid exposition of teachings which deserve greater recognition from all involved in education, but it also contains a wealth of practical, imaginative suggestions for ways in which those teachings can be adapted to meet current needs.

It is particularly appropriate that it should appear at this time when our concentration on technology threatens to push to the periphery of education those aspects which nurture the feelings and the spirit. This situation is not too dissimilar from the one which Dalcroze faced as Professor of Harmony at the Geneva Conservatoire. There he realized that the accepted method of training was so geared to the intellect that it failed to give students the first-hand aural and physical *experience* of music which was essential to their growth as musicians. Aware that musical experience depends on the power and quality of physical sensation (the kinaesthetic sense), he decided to focus attention on two of music's basic elements—rhythm and dynamic intensity—with the students using their bodies as their instruments of expression. From the experiments which followed this decision, several principles emerged which remain of lasting value. He saw clearly that theory should always follow practice, that rules should be introduced only after the facts which give rise to them have been experienced, that students should be creators themselves as well as responders to the creation of others, and that before anything else they should learn to know themselves. Apart from these general principles, he gradually devised a total programme for developing musicianship—based on the interrelation of aural training, rhythmics, movement study, improvisation, and keyboard harmony. Such a programme which breaks down compartmental thinking in musicians warrants serious attention today.

Although his work was at first directed towards music students, he soon recognized that it was applicable to all—especially to children whose responses were delightfully uncluttered. Through the experiences he initiated he enabled the development of powers of observation, apperception, analysis, understanding, and memory, and helped pupils to become responsive, flexible, and vital personalities.

His system has not remained static. Whilst holding firmly to its original principles, exponents have always left room for spontaneity and a fresh response to new educational situations. This is splendidly demonstrated by Marie-Laure Bachmann in her book which stakes out so clearly the tenets of Dalcroze's position, and affirms how integral the underlying principles are, not just to music education and education in general, but indeed to life as a whole, for they are directly related to that rhythmic energy which is fundamental to all our living.

Jack P. B. Dobbs

NOTE ON THE NAME JAQUES-DALCROZE

Emile Jaques was, early in his career, asked by his publishers to make his name more distinctive, and so added to his surname the name Dalcroze. He was, however, known affectionately to his students in Geneva as 'Monsieur Jaques', whereas overseas he and his work have come to be connected simply with the name Dalcroze, the name he gave to himself.

ACKNOWLEDGEMENTS

I thank the Collège de l'Institut Jaques-Dalcroze de Genève and its President, Mᵉ Gabriel Jaques-Dalcroze, for entrusting me with the responsibility of preparing this work.

I thank also the Director of the Institute, M. Dominique Porte, for its original conception and for having unreservedly placed his confidence in me.

The kind understanding of the *Conseil de Fondation*, of the Institute's Board of Directors and Governors, and of rhythmicians in Switzerland and abroad who have so willingly shared their experiences with me, has afforded me the most congenial of circumstances in which to complete the present work.

My deep gratitude is extended to all those friends who have so unstintingly given me help and encouragement: especially to Martine Labarthe and Christiane Gillièron, who painstakingly read the manuscript section by section as I worked on it; to my sister Lise Meier, who took upon herself the task of making it presentable; and to my friend Professor Pierre Hirsch, who rendered me assistance with the correction of proofs.

The following people have kindly contributed to this book by allowing me to attend their classes and/or granting me extended interviews:

Frances Aronoff, New York University;
Monique Bosshard, Atelier Monique Bosshard, Lausanne;
Liliane Favre-Bulle, École de Rythmique Jacques-Dalcroze de Nyon;
Ruth Gianadda, École primaire de la Gradelle, Geneva;
Barbara Gincel, Écoles primaires de Vincennes, Paris;
Monica Jaquet, Cours de Rythmique Monica Jaquet, Geneva;
Esther Messmer-Hirt, Conservatoire de Bâle, Basle;
Lisa Parker, Longy School of Music, Boston;
Valéry Roth, Cours de Rythme Valéry Roth, Paris;
Marta Sanchez, Carnegie Mellon University, Pittsburgh;
Elisabeth Vanderspar, Dalcroze Society Incorporated, London.

M.-L. B.
Geneva, August 1984

ACKNOWLEDGEMENTS FOR THE ENGLISH TRANSLATION

I would like to extend my whole-hearted thanks to the Dalcroze Society UK, for having decided that my book should be translated into English and for undertaking responsibility for the cost thereof; to the translator, David Parlett, whose taste and sensitivity allowed the translation to be most faithful in all respects; to my friend and colleague, Ruth Stewart, who spent many hours in reading the translation and the printed proofs, and with whom I was lucky to share fruitful discussions relating to many points of issue in the book; finally, to Jack Dobbs, President of the Dalcroze Society UK, for his kind hospitality when we met, his unfailing interest and practical help, and for having agreed to write a Preface to the present edition.

Marie-Laure Bachmann

CONTENTS

PART I

PART II

PART III

PART I

I

INTRODUCTION

Et presque tout cela se passait aujourd'hui
c'est-à-dire, comme toujours, dans le temps.
Et tous suivaient celui qui criait "En avant!"
Et puis, soudain, ce ne fut ni n'était aujourd'hui,
hier soir ou demain matin, on entendit un autre cri:
"En après!"
C'était, venant d'une autre espèce d'impasse d'espace,
une voix d'enfant, la voix joyeuse et folle d'un
hors-la-loi du temps.

Jacques Prévert, *En ce temps las*

*(And nearly all of that took place today—in other words, as always, within
time. And everyone fell in behind him who shouted 'Forward!'. And then,
at once—it wasn't, never was today, or last night or tomorrow morning—
they heard another cry: 'And beyond!'. Coming from some quite different
and neglected piece of space, it was a child's voice—the happy, silly voice
of one of time's outlaws.)*

By way of preamble to my presentation of the work and thought of
Emile Jaques-Dalcroze in the following pages—my aim being to draw
out every possible implication for the present day—I invite the reader
to eavesdrop on an imaginary conversation between the creator of
Eurhythmics and two personalities of our own time: Jean Piaget
and Alvin Toffler. Perhaps—who knows—some such conversation
actually has been held in 'some quite different and neglected piece of
space' . . .

These names are chosen chiefly for the symbolic dimension they
bring to bear on the resultant trio: in effect, the three speakers
respectively represent—under one title or another—the Past, the
Present, and the Future. The first, Dalcroze himself, lived from 1865
to 1950; the second, Piaget, lives on in the relevance of his theories to
modern society and in the attention they continue to enjoy; and the

third is characterized by the way in which he directs himself specifically to the future of humanity.

From Toffler I borrow several passages from his masterpiece *Future Shock*, in which he describes the nature and effect of the increasing rate of change exhibited by the evolution of western society. The comments attributed to Piaget are taken from *Psychologie et Pédagogie*, a work comprising two essays written respectively in 1965 and 1935. These display their author under a little-known light, and one of minor importance relative to his work as a whole; namely, that of an educational philosopher concerned about the way in which schools succeed—or fail, as the case may be—in making full and proper use of genetic psychology.

As to the quotations from Dalcroze, they derive from a small selection of many written works distinguishing a career of over forty years. Though inevitably limited in number, they strike me as ideally illustrating not only how faithfully the Dalcroze of 1942 (aged 77) clung to the fertile and uncompromising impulses of youth, but also his breadth of vision and depth of insight—qualities which all, in my view, justify his being classed as 'one of time's outlaws'! Should the reader remain to be convinced, I invite him to indulge in a little game. It involves no more than covering up the names attached to the following quotations and then attributing them to their respective authors. This may not prove an astoundingly difficult task—but the occasional hesitation might be permitted, just in case . . .

Three Conversation Pieces over the Wall of Time

I

Modern educational theory has made great strides, of course. Yet all its engaging ideas, its subtle analyses and thought-provoking tests, are still inspired by yesterday's mentality . . .

D. 1942: 57[1]

[You don't have to convince me!] It's frightening to see how great a gap there still exists today, no less than in 1935, between the great advances that have been made and the complete absence of any fundamental rethinking about methods or courses, or even about the

---

[1] The speakers are indicated by initials, with D. for Dalcroze.

nature of the problem—in short, about education as a whole, both in its own right and as a crucial discipline.

P. 1965: 11

Is it really, [do you think,] necessary for so many different branches of study to remain so traditional in outlook? Are there not indeed some traditions which actually do more harm than good? Aren't we lucky that so many young and adventurous teachers are now blazing a trail out of all that dusty rigmarole of old-fashioned doctrine?

D. 1942: 58

[This much is certain:] child psychology can yield more and more data on the mechanism of development and constantly increase our understanding of it, but such facts and knowledge will never spread through schools if teachers haven't absorbed them thoroughly enough to make original use of them.

P. 1965: 181

In our drive towards progress and liberty, 'tradition', more often than not, is only responsible for holding us back. There are some ideas and some beliefs that everybody takes for granted. For lack of thought and character, we rely on propositions no longer soundly based and follow particular practices merely out of deference to our 'elders and betters'— who for their part made them up as and when the need arose.

D. 1942: 58

[Gentlemen, believe you me:] the Reversionist sticks to his previously programmed decisions and habits with dogmatic desperation. The more change threatens from without, the more meticulously he repeats past modes of action. His social outlook is regressive. Shocked by the arrival of the future, he . . . demands, in one masked form or another, a return to the glories of yesteryear.

T. 1970: 320

[I'm afraid] people will baulk at any novel venture so long as previous experience continues to satisfy them in any way and they remain temperamentally incapable of questioning its usefulness. Any little liberating concession they deign to make will strike them as definitive and immutable: to them, any concept of 'how it will be tomorrow' today seems nothing less than a lie.

D. 1898: 12

[Will they never realize that] it is ridiculous to see the future as nothing more than an extension of the present [?] . . . Change is not merely necessary to life; it *is* life.

T. 1970: 304

How sad it is that so many people do not wish to dream, but only to sleep!

D. 1907: 45

II

[I have always felt that] imitating other people's experiences is a nonsensical and often self-deluding practice. Our own experiences work only for ourselves, and it is wrong to hold them up as a model to people who are built on different lines from ourselves and feel things differently from us, and whose thoughts and feelings need to be guided, not distorted.

D. 1942: 61

If there is any real desire—and the existence of a real *need* is becoming increasingly obvious—to produce individuals capable of making new discoveries and helping tomorrow's society along its forward path, an education based on active discovery of the truth is clearly superior to one that merely conditions its subjects to want things by reference to predetermined wants and know things through the acceptance of ready-made truths.

P. 1965: 45

[Exactly!] The trouble with most educational practice is that children are not made to experience things for themselves until the very point at which they are expected to learn from what they do, instead of having active experience encouraged right at the start of their studies, when body and brain are developing in parallel and are constantly communicating their impressions and feelings to each other.

D. 1919*a*: 5

[It is a misleading approach too, since] whenever a concept is thought to have been definitively formed from an observation, the action itself is forgotten. Now what constitutes the common source both of concepts and of their corresponding observations is the sensory-motor function. This is a general and fundamental truth which education cannot afford to underestimate.

P. 1965: 57–8

[Yet educationalists consistently underestimate it. Will they never learn that] individual progress is not entirely synonymous with the maturing of one's intellectual faculties? . . . The important thing is that each new mental conquest should be accompanied by an improvement in the physical process which led to its achievement.

D. 1942: 126

[To which I would add that time is pressing. My friends,] one thing becomes starkly clear: to be able to make these increasingly numerous and rapid on–off clicks in our interpersonal lives we must be able to operate at a level of adaptability never before asked of human beings.

T. 1970: 110

[I'll go along with that. For I have long maintained that,] throughout childhood, children should not only *have* good muscles but also know how to use them and how to ring the changes on their use . . . What is more, they must learn immediately and unhesitatingly to resist any muscular action that serves no particular purpose.

D. 1942: 63

[You're absolutely right—especially since] the problem for anyone faced with rapid change is to keep within their limits of adaptability and then to establish an optimal rhythm allowing them to live life to the full . . . To survive, to avert what we have termed future shock, the individual must become infinitely more adaptable and capable than ever before.

T. 1970: 34

[That's all very well, but if] sighting our aims is one thing, reaching them is another. For we must consider the question of ways and means, which relates more to psychology than to sociology, yet at the same time has a bearing on our choice of aims.

P. 1965: 33

III

[Gentlemen, a question to which I have long addressed myself is this:] Would it not be possible to establish a more direct line of communication between the senses and the mind—between experiences which inform the intellect and feelings which inspire the sensory means of expression? *Every thought is the interpretation of a deed*, [I think you will agree?].

D. 1898: 11–12

It is universally accepted that intelligence starts off in a practical or sensory–motor form, only little by little internalizing itself into thought in the true sense of the word, and that this is a continuous process.

P. 1935: 231

[In other words,] the child only becomes aware of the development of thought after the experience of physical sensations . . .

D. 1942: 164

[That's one way of putting it . . . Perhaps more precisely,] a given notion may appear on the practical or sensory–motor scene well before it submits itself to the grasp of ideation or reflection . . . Childhood, in the view of new-wave theoreticians, is not a necessary evil: it is a biologically useful phase characterized by a progressive adaptation to physical and social surroundings . . . The primary functions of intelligence are to understand and to invent—in other words, to construct structures by structuring reality.

P. 1935: 251, 224; 1965: 47

[It seems to me from what you say—and I am delighted to hear it!—that] the wider and more varied the child's physical experiences, the greater the number of different facets, so to speak, from which his child's imagination may be reflected. This will undoubtedly result in the refinement of his intelligence, not to mention his excellent physical development. That in turn is what will best enable him to benefit from experience. [Another thing I always like to stress is that] the child's natural curiosity concentrates—naturally enough—chiefly on those acts which he is capable of executing himself. Nothing excites him more than the discovery of his own physical abilities. The child engages with delight in all those exercises which his body can take part in. Let us now harness that engagement and put it to good use in our future educational projects.

D. 1942: 56, 54; 1905: 35

[Let's also bear in mind that] we must search for our objectives and methods in the future, rather than the past. . . . For education the lesson is clear: its prime objective must be to increase the individual's 'cope-ability'—the speed and economy with which he can adapt to continual change.

T. 1970: 354, 357

[I'm not entirely sure I'm with you there, for] only one technique strikes me as suited to the job—and that's the one that seeks to liberate the body and the mind from all the antagonisms forged by nature as well as by nurture.

D. 1942: 151–2

Historical Overview

On looking at the dates involved it is noticeable that at least as much time elapsed between Dalcroze's first and last writings as between himself and the present day. That he took advantage of ideas which were 'in the air' at the time, as and when they passed his way, there can be no doubt: his thoughts and way of describing things bear witness to them, even if he did not systematically acknowledge his sources. He was interested in everything and everybody, as indicated by the books he read and the people he met.[2] He had especially, as few before him, the knack of seizing on the wing, so to speak, everything capable of lending weight to his beliefs or opening up new fields of exploration. 'I lack the scientific outlook and make things up as I go along—but a single word will sometimes be enough to foment nothing less than a revolution within me', he wrote in a letter to E. Claparède (see Berchtold 1965: 81).

But we come after him in point of time. Further discoveries and experiments and other circumstances of life have replaced those to which he was accustomed. We not only *ought* to bear this in mind in order to assess the value of Eurhythmics today, but very probably we shall *want* to do so: for just as Dalcroze himself was, at least in part, the product of his time, so are we of ours. Someone discovering Eurhythmics[3] for the first time today necessarily differs from one who might have discovered it in 1920 or 1940, whether or not they are up to date with contemporary thought on education and music.

The birth of Eurhythmics at the start of the century coincided with a renewal of emphasis on human individuality. In becoming a new-

---

[2] Cf. Berchtold's abundant documentation (1965), in particular as to fruitful exchanges between Dalcroze on the one hand and E. Claparède, T. Flournoy and O.-L. Forel on the other, all of whom admired his researches and gave him every encouragement.

[3] Throughout this book the word *Eurhythmics* is capitalized whenever it specifically denotes the *rhythmic* or *Dalcrozian–rhythmic* method of teaching.

found focus of philosophical interest, human beings, with their real-
life problems, inevitably became central to the blossoming of education,
psychology and sociology.[4] These disciplines have continued to
attract new insights ever since. And this is the second of my reasons
for prefacing the subject-matter of this book with the three-way
conversation introduced above. In an allegorical sense, since they are
by no means uniquely representative of their respective disciplines,
our interlocutors put before us three distinctive points of view of man
and his relationship with the world about him. And no educational
method of the present day, especially that associated with Dalcroze,
can afford to ignore this threefold point of view.

MAN IN HIS RELATION TO THE WORLD

Toffler, for his part, focuses particular attention on the *outside world*.
He analyses both sudden changes and those that come about gradually,
asserting that they follow upon one another with accelerating pace. He
examines the impact on western society of the ceaseless growth in
science and technology. Far from deploring this evolutionary process
he considers it entirely natural, certainly inevitable and in many ways
quite fascinating. But in his view this entails important consequences
for the individual: the need on one hand to develop his capacity for
adaptation to the full, and on the other to strengthen his capacity for
self-realization. In effect, man must feel that he has some active part to
play within this world of movement; but he must at the same time
resist his natural ascendancy over it, and find some means of change
concordant with his own rhythm of life and individual needs. In this
condition, Toffler believes—though his optimism seems to disregard
a number of underlying threats—'The people of the future enjoy
greater opportunities for self-realization than any other group in
history.' (1971: 320)

Piaget, applying himself to the means and mechanisms by which all
forms of human knowledge are developed, focuses his attention on the
interface between the human subject and his world of experience.
What he studies is therefore a *relationship*—more precisely, the
successive forms adopted by this relationship throughout the period
of the child's development, culminating in its final stage of adult
understanding and scientific thought. It is by the actions of his
moving body and the exploratory activities of his organs of sense that

---

[4] Cf. Bochenski 1962: 17–40.

the baby gradually learns to distinguish himself from the surrounding world. It is through actions exerted upon objects which sometimes yield to and sometimes resist his efforts that the world acquires, in his eyes, a real and coherent identity. By constantly having to adapt his actions to the natures of different objects, and by an awareness of new possibilities opened up by his physical growth, the child finds himself in possession of faculties increasing in both number and refinement. He thereby succeeds in establishing an increasingly enriched network of relationships between himself and the world. Space that he can move about in, things and places that can be rediscovered after he has left them, come to acquire for him the characteristics of stability and permanence, a real existence independent of himself. From that point on he is able to evoke in its absence both the mental image of an object and its verbal representation by means of language. This newly acquired faculty of representation enables him to imagine his own movements, acts and actions (or those of others), instead of having to re-perform the action as was formerly the case. It also enables him to establish relationships between objects themselves, and, in time, to make abstractions of their properties for such purposes as comparison, measurement, reasoning and analysis. Thus it is that Piaget defines thought as 'internalized action', from which proceed those forms of reasoning, generalization, and abstraction characteristic of the adult mind, but whose roots go deep into the baby's first efforts at co-ordinating movement and perception. Man will nevertheless continue to have recourse to one or other of them throughout his life; for these acquisitions do not disappear but become mutually integrated and complement one another, thus producing the best possible adaptation to the current situation.

For Dalcroze, stamped with the ideas of his day, what counts is *Man* himself, and the avowed aim of his work will be to enable that being to achieve fulfilment. No human faculty must be left hiding its light under a bushel: they are all capable of helping one another, of pulling together with a view to affirming that functional balance and harmony which is the source of all well-being.

After that, the individual must be put in full possession of all his powers of action and reaction. He must be enabled to face up to every kind of situation, so that at any given moment he may select from the whole gamut of possibilities that which strikes him as the most appropriate. On that depends his 'freedom of the man of thought and action' (1919c: 163). Well-being and self-determination will often be invoked by Dalcroze as obvious and natural benefits accruing from the sustained practice of his Eurhythmic method.

Although addressing themselves to different questions, our three authors are clearly in accord in stressing the individual's capacity for *adaptation*. For Toffler, it is the very essence of survival. In examining what end it serves and where its enemies lie, the author of *Future Shock* bases his 'philosophy of anticipation' on the results of recent research in the fields of economics, sociology, and neurophysiology.

For Piaget, who found in the study of biology a point of departure for his constructivist epistemology, adaptability is the primary function of intelligence. In other words, intelligence is the goal achieved in human evolution by that drive to adaptation which characterizes every living creature.

As an educationalist, Dalcroze is concerned with the *how* of adaptation. He sees it as a faculty which does not merely develop of its own accord but is capable—a point to which he will devote himself—of being improved and refined until it assures the individual of maximum autonomy. He was to find his own model in music, which 'only acquired rhythms of its own by originally borrowing from those of the human body' (1910: 19).

WHY MUSIC?

A man of his time, Dalcroze found himself in debt to a restricting philosophical heritage which, if it allowed his own ideas to see the light of day, at the same time stamped its own mark on their actual formulation. It has been noted that in his aspirations no less than in his explanations he reverts constantly to the old principle of duality, with *mind* on one side (intelligence, imagination, emotions, the soul), and *matter* on the other (the body, the senses, actions, instincts). These two long-standing adversaries he will undertake to bring together, not to say fuse together, 'so that "thinking man" shall from now onwards be no longer a separate person from "physical man" ' (1919c: 163).

The idea of union or fusion takes for granted the existence of two such entities. At the same time it necessarily implies the existence of some unifying agent suited to the task of bringing about the desired conjunction. This middle term—this 'medium', in fact—is something Dalcroze has ready-made to hand(s)! Furthermore, it is something that existed before he started developing his ideas, a something *for* which he lived as well as *from* which he made his living—and that was Music. To this he would assign the reconciling role.

Why music? Why, because she is the Muse we dance and dream our dreams to, who beguiles or assails our ears as readily as our thoughts, who guides our sentiments and lays our instincts bare . . . Not one human faculty is capable of resisting her appeal. Born from the exercise of faculties which she plays upon in countless combinations, created by Man and addressing herself to him, music, of all human products, is the one which remains most intimately bound up with life. 'None of the arts is closer to life than music. It may be spoken of as life itself.' (1905: 20–1).

Music, too, for Dalcroze, is the only art capable 'of drawing into a single law, as into a single power, all forms of energy and scattered laws' (1942: 114). In other words, music already exercises the synthesis he is looking for: while drawing together the components of personality, it acts as an ever-present model of that final synthesis. For it is in music that tones, timbres, and rhythms, nuances, pauses, accents, tempi, and all the physical and dynamic phenomena of the world of sound, find themselves brought into conjunction, arranged, super-imposed, measured, and shaped by the power of creative thought. It is this that brings to them that property of *sense* in both meanings of the word—direction and significance—which constitutes the individuality of any given musical work.

But where to site the meeting-point between mind and matter and the music chosen to unite them? In other words—what does each one have in common with the other two?

Music, says Dalcroze (1907: 43), 'is composed of sound and movement, and sound [itself] is a form of movement'. The body, for its part, is composed of bones and organs and muscles—and 'muscles were made for movement' (p. 39). As to *mind*, whether taken to imply emotions (which literally means 'movements'), or whether it refers to the mobility of thought itself—mind is also movement, and capable of being moved:

> Je ne sais pourquoi
> Mon esprit amer
> D'une aile inquiète et folle vole sur la mer . . .
> Mouette à l'essor mélancolique
> Elle suit la vague, ma pensée,
> A tous les vents du ciel balancée
> Paul Verlaine, 'Je ne sais pourquoi' (1978: 94)

(How can I say how my so bitter soul on silly trembling wing flies oversea . . . A
seagull borne on melancholy flight, my mind skims over waves, buffeted by every
sky-blown wind)

Now the type of movement used must be such as to comply with both
the requirements of the mind and the capabilities of the body. For
Dalcroze, this role can only be fulfilled by *rhythm*, that 'compromise
between force and resistance'.[5] For rhythm—which, he says,
consists of movements and breaks in movement, and is characterized
by continuity and repetition—rhythm lies at the root of all manifestations of the life force, from the most primitive to the most highly
evolved. Above all, and this is what chiefly interests him, rhythm is an
expression of individuality. Thus the same action performed by two
different people will differ in length, breadth, and significance,
according to each one's underlying rhythmic personality. Similarly,
the organization of one's working day, the written expression of a
given thought, and, in general, any human activity of a practical,
aesthetic, or intellectual nature, will bear the subject's individual
rhythmic marks:

Rhythm is at one and the same time order and pace in movement and a
personal way of performing that movement. The study of rhythm should
therefore lead us to bear ourselves, in every aspect of everyday life, in an
individual manner. (1915*b*: 89).

To allow everyone to become truly themselves and to attain full
mastery of their potential—such should be the aim of the fusion
sought for. As Dalcroze neatly puts it, 'Scientific man should be able
to turn himself into sporting man whenever he feels like it'. (1919*c*:
163).

   So now a model has been perfected which relates to the duality in
question. 'What brings them together is *rhythm*,' he writes again in
1942 (p. 138); and: 'It is for others to systematize my ideas and to
bring under rigorous control that eminently desirable partnership
between mind and matter'.

Although in the theoretical formulation of his ideas the thinking of
Dalcroze remained firmly rooted in nineteenth-century philosophy,
in reality—or rather, in some other reality—it overspills that framework to a considerable extent. Artist, poet, and creative thinker,

   [5] This definition, due to the German theoretician Schleich, was adopted by Dalcroze
and taken up by Ansermet (1924: 6).

Dalcroze shares with his peers the role of herald of things to come. Like the poet, he expresses through his pen, often before reasoning it out in his mind, something which is sooner or later universally accepted and made the subject of *ad hoc* theorizing. Like him, he draws the elements of his creative work from wells sunk deep into the future—from dreams and intuitions, from the inner senses and open-minded interest with which he surveys the world. And so: 'I have begun to envisage a musical type of education', he writes at the outset of his career, 'in which the *body* itself would act as *intermediary* between sounds and thought, and would become the direct instrument of our feelings (1898: 12). (My italics—M.-L.B.) Convinced thereafter that 'every thought is the interpretation of a deed' (1898: 11–12), he would not be slow to offer, through the formulation and practical development of his rhythmic methods, a partial preview of a theory soon to be put on a solid footing by advances in the psychology of growth: namely, that the body—or, more precisely, the *moving* body—is at once the source, the medium, and the essential condition of all subsequent understanding. He is amongst the first to realise that 'the basic nature of the rhythmic sense is of a motor kind' (Teplov 1966: 338).

THE MOTOR ORIGIN OF THE SENSE OF RHYTHM

At the time when Dalcroze was making his first discoveries, teaching at the Conservatory and motivated by his twin concerns to bring his lessons to life and to find both cause and cure for his music students' persistent difficulties, psychologists and other researchers in America and Germany were busy highlighting the fundamentally motor nature of the sense of rhythm. From Teplov's *Psychology of Musical Ability* (1966: 339–42) we learn for instance of Bolton's conclusion (1894) that the involuntary movements which accompany the perception of rhythm do not merely stem from but are indeed the very essence of the rhythmic experience. We learn, too, how Meumann (1894) came to show that movement plays a primordial role in the appreciation of 'musical time'.

Some years later, the Dalcroze method was already sufficiently well developed to have become the subject of regular courses, conferences and demonstrations, and soon of written articles surveying the progress made. With his first intuitive ideas corroborated by practical experience, the creator of Eurhythmics could affirm that 'Not a single musician hindered by some fault in his expression of musical rhythm fails to demonstrate that fault in a *bodily* way', and that 'some instinctive connection exists between *rhythm*, in all its varieties, and *gesture*' (1907: 41). He was already maintaining that

Once rhythmic awareness has been formed through the experiencing of movement, a constant alternation may be observed between the influence of the rhythmic act on representation, and of representation on the act . . . The representation of rhythm, the image reflected by the rhythmic act, finds a life of its own in every one of our muscles. Conversely, every rhythmic movement is a visible manifestation of rhythmic awareness (1907: 41–2).

Meanwhile, researchers in other countries were continuing their work. Koffka (1909) brings out the role of motor representations in the experience of rhythm; Rückmich (1913) affirms that motor sensations are essential to the 'catching' of a rhythm, as much as for maintaining it once caught; and Seashore (1919) credits the perception of musical time to physical movements, which may be imaginary no less than real (Teplov 1966: 340–2). The following year, 1920, sees the first appearance of *Le Rythme, La Musique et l'Education*, a comprehensive collection of the most important articles charting Dalcroze's discoveries up to 1919. A notable extract states that

the appreciation of musical rhythms always evokes some degree of motor image in the listener's ear, as well as instinctive motor actions in his body. Muscular sensations eventually come to be associated with aural sensations, and these, so reinforced, impose even greater significance on the business of appreciation and analysis (1919c: 170).

Although a somewhat static model may be suggested by his use of an outmoded philosophical vocabulary, we can see that we are in fact directed to a highly dynamic model by the practicality, first-hand observation, and accumulated experience of one who had recourse to but a single guide—namely, his deep and intimate understanding of music. It was by practising it in every form, analysing the works of the great masters and losing no opportunity to listen to the music of his contemporaries, by experiencing it for himself and studying its effect on others, that Dalcroze became convinced of the primary, not to say primordial, role of movement in the appreciation of music. 'It is interesting to note', Professor Claparède wrote to him as early as 1906, 'that you have arrived, albeit by routes entirely different from those of physiological psychology, at the same conception of the psychological importance of movement as a *support* for intellectual and affective phenomena' ('Opinions et Critiques', 1924: 41). (My italics—M.-L.B.)

Dalcroze seems to have been unaware of the discoveries of German and English-speaking researchers, despite their relevance to his own observations. Probably, had he known of them, he would often have been only too pleased to press them into service rather than pass them by in silence. Having on more than one occasion been wrong-footed by over-scrupulous or ultra-conservative adversaries, he was always careful to ensure that his insights and practical results were solidly underpinned.

We must repeat, however, that these ideas were 'in the air' at the time. They could have reached him from a variety of sources without his stopping long enough to work out where they came from. As we have seen, he was the sort of person who could find grist to his mill in everything. Methodical at heart, he was driven harder by his creative spirit than may have been proper for the detailed verification of all his pronouncements, and he attached particular validity to his own personal observations. In this respect he showed himself faithful to his assertion (1898: 9) that 'Any rule not forced upon one by necessity and by observations drawn directly from nature is false and arbitrary.' Only such a temperament, that of pioneering settler coupled with meticulous observer, could have put an educational method of so broad a scope on so firm a footing, and this at a time when scientific researchers in the same field were by no means yielding concrete results worthy of their practical or educational implications.

EDUCATION THROUGH MUSIC AND EDUCATION INTO MUSIC

We have to thank the educationalist within him for examining the basic constituents of music and demonstrating that 'music is not heard by ear alone but by the whole of the body' (Mothersole 1920: 23); hence the ability to sense and imagine the movement embodied by music must be regarded as fundamental to musical training.

But it is the artist in him we must thank for never losing sight of music in his endeavour to 'transform the whole organism into what might be called an *inner ear*' (Dalcroze 1898: 10). Music, in which the simple and the complex coexist, is also a construct of the mind. It implies an ability to organize movements in time and the world of sound, and thereby calls upon one's powers of reflection and analysis. It requires a development of the aesthetic sense suited to the formation of qualitative judgements and reasoned appreciation. These qualities, moreover, are not restricted to the realm of music, but are equally vital to any activity of an intellectual, artistic, or practical nature.

In assigning to musical rhythm the twin functions of drawing out individual potential and drawing one into the subtle world of music, Dalcroze would turn Eurhythmics not only into an invaluable resource for education in general, but also into a vital and peculiarly rich device for music education in particular.

Aims and Thesis of the Present Work

If Dalcroze Eurhythmics occupies a unique position in relation to more recent teaching methods involving the practice and mastery of bodily rhythms, the reason, I think, is twofold:

1. Dalcroze Eurhythmics is rooted in the nineteenth-century concept of two opposing sides of the human constitution, mind and body, its purpose being to bring the two into harmony;

2. It involves music in its entirety, applying its most primitive as well as its most advanced aspects to the functioning of our essential humanity.

In each case it focuses equal and simultaneous attention on both mind and body. Eurhythmics makes no prejudgement as to their relative value but sets itself the task of initiating efficient and unbroken lines of communication between the two. In other words, it lays no claim to being an end in itself, but rather demands to be regarded as the means to an end—specifically, as a *way of forging links*.

From this derives a working method as distinctive in its effects as in its field of application. Specifically, Eurhythmics draws out the instinctive and spontaneous expression of an individual's bodily rhythms, at the same time bringing into play all his physical abilities, whether simple or complex, related or unrelated. For this purpose it makes use of music, *from* which it draws its powers, and *to* which, in return, it offers access. It also makes use of the spatial environment, which gives scope to bodily movements and progressions in space.[6]

---

[6] *Mouvement(s) et déplacement(s)*: both mean 'movement', the first implying movement on the spot, the second movement from one place to another. 'Progression' or 'locomotion' will suffice for the latter whenever it is vital to draw a distinction, though neither English word sounds as natural in context as *déplacement* does in French. (Translator's note)

Eurhythmics thereby facilitates the discovery of the laws governing relations between space, time, and energy. This constant and simultaneous combination of the spontaneous and the calculated, of the impulsive and the controlled, comes to establish what Dalcroze liked to call a 'current of consciousness' between an individual's various component parts. It leads to the re-creation of a personal unity by responding to its twin desires for freedom and structure.

Mastery of the relations unifying space, time, and energy is, at root, of equal importance to every one of us. In so many different walks of life such mastery represents both an economy and an asset. Hence, at least in theory, there are no bounds to the range of possible applications for Eurhythmics.

Furthermore, the breadth of the field it explores and the very nature of its aims make of Eurhythmics an essentially adaptable tool. This requires that those who are to teach it be provided with a highly developed and multivalent personality, so as to afford them complete freedom of choice as to their particular field of activity. All these points will be amply illustrated throughout. The primary function of this book, however, will be to relate the concepts of Eurhythmics to the context of the present day.

FREEDOM AND STRUCTURE

In Dalcroze's day the most striking aspect of Eurhythmics must have been its liberating character. What was then the novel practice of encouraging pupils to work with bare feet and arms was a particularly concrete manifestation of such a liberty, and one vigorously condemned by many a right-thinking person![7] Today, the word 'liberating' figures prominently in courses, methods, claims, and publicity slogans: one might almost be led to believe that it responds to some innate public desire that is never really far below the surface.[8] As a Dalcrozian colleague of mine once said: 'It used to be outrageous to go barefoot; we've got over that problem now, and people go around in bikinis . . . But their minds are just as skimpy as they ever were before.'[9]

[7] On this point, cf Dutoit-Carlier 1965: 326–31.
[8] A comparable buzz-word in the English-speaking world is 'educational'. Any product likely to be used or enjoyed by children, especially in the field of leisure, is liable to be promoted as 'educational' as if the term implied some built-in property lacking from related or competitive products. The fact that toys, games, and indeed anything used by children is more or less educational by definition is conveniently overlooked—often ignorantly, and sometimes dishonestly. (Translator's note)
[9] M. Bosshard, in a recorded discussion, 8 Nov. 1979.

Less attention has been paid, however, to the need for form and structure in this new-found sense of freedom. There is a reluctance to point such things out as desirable in a course seeking to put the best light upon itself, as if they were somehow incompatible with the idea of enjoying oneself. Once mention structure, it seems, and everyone starts confusing it with intolerable restriction. Even so, we find experiments in liberation all too often fizzling out. Thus, being expressive for its own sake, or playing musical games for the fun of it, though offering both exercise and achievement when properly carried out, are generally fated to collapse under their own weight when practised in a sort of vacuum.

What also needs to be taken into account is that everyday life is increasingly gripped in a vicious straitjacket of timekeeping. The individual finds himself deprived of any need to organize his own activity—even, sometimes, of the need to think. He therefore finds himself without resource when he has a moment to himself. 'There was a time', the same colleague remarked, 'when people reacted against order. But nowadays there simply *is* no order: society has broken down; the family has been split up. As far as I'm concerned, reverting to one's body is to return to one's own home; it is an attempt to relive one's alternations of relaxation and activity, and thereby to recreate rhythm. Rhythm springs from rest and activity and all the subtle gradations we go through from one to the other . . . It's trying to "live in one's own house" that I find so interesting, because that takes *time*—and time, these days, is constantly being hijacked!'

The Dalcrozian approach, suited as it is to respond to this double need for freedom and structure, strikes me as providing a particularly felicitous and probably unrivalled means of education into art and life today—as I hope to show the reader, in a more concrete way, in the following chapters.

As far as education *into music* is concerned, Eurhythmics from the outset is a doorway into the living subject, as opposed to the purely academic, book-bound approach to music teaching. Its originality lies in transmitting through the body, by means of movement, concepts which hitherto were only acquired in the course of an intellectual or technical training.

The idea of living life and undergoing experiences at first hand is nowadays universally approved, and a lot of research has been carried out in this direction, often with considerable success. Even so, one cannot but be conscious of a persistent gap between the traditional activities and methods still in use today and the aspirations of modern education. All may agree on the need for music-teaching 'from the life', as it were, and suited to the requirements of the present day, but there is not always unanimity as to exactly what it should consist of. In particular, exponents of contemporary music often rail against adherents to the music of the past: the latter condemn the former for following a path where 'anything goes', and are themselves accused of turning the world of music into a 'dusty old museum'. Eurhythmics can claim to be acquitted of both charges. That this is not always granted may be put down to circumstances to which we shall address ourselves in due course. Whatever the reason, my purpose is to demonstrate that Eurhythmics as originally conceived may be considered as a form of education into music as a whole (*LA musique*), as opposed to the traditional approach which is directed towards a particular type of music (*UNE musique*).[10] Furthermore, we shall have occasion to show that the resources available to Eurhythmics do not limit it to the simple role of initiating or acclimatizing, but in fact provide the necessary tools for a musical education in its entirety.

APPLICATIONS—MANY AND VARIED

Eurhythmics is based on the joint mobilization of mind and body— specifically, on those faculties which enable us to act, react, and adapt to the surrounding world in order to cope with it to best advantage. It can therefore work for anyone, at any time or place, regardless of their age or ability, or of their personal problems, whether known or unknown. In other words, it demands no particular *a priori* talent on the part of anyone approaching it, except of those who are studying it in order to teach it to others.

Although Eurhythmics was originally tailored to the musical training of young students at the Conservatoire, it not surprisingly came to overspill its borders. Even in 1910, Dalcroze was advocating the teaching of Eurhythmics to children from the age of 6, and he soon found that it could be profitably employed as early as infant school. Nor was he slow to promote the practical application of his ideas to the education of the blind and the mentally handicapped.[11] At the same time, and despite his chosen specialization in the field of childhood, he did not drop the idea of the 'perfectible adult', but became increasingly conscious of the need to impart to teachers,

[10] A contrast brought out by Maneveau (1977: 184).
[11] Cf. Dutoit-Carlier 1965: 386 ff.

lecturers, musicians, or specialists in movement a means of mastering and absorbing into their respective domains the principles in which he believed.

Those who have been sufficiently persuaded of the value of Dalcroze Eurhythmics to regard it as indispensable to the development of their own work, or to encourage its adoption in the circles they move in or share their enthusiasm for it with others, will be found in every walk of life. They include theatre people—actors and producers, opera directors and ballet masters, dancers and choreographers; painters, architects and designers, musicians, conductors, composers, singers and instrumentalists; writers, critics, and poets; scientists, doctors, psychiatrists, educationists . . . the list is endless.[12]

Following Dalcroze, his former pupils and their own successors have continued to expand Eurhythmics' field of application, pushing the age limit further forward, increasing the resources of therapy, and discovering countless opportunities for disseminating the experiences thereby acquired. Eurhythmics has consequently found itself sited at the crossroads of the most varied human activities. Whether in the teaching of techniques, the acquisition of knowledge, or the practice of different branches of the arts, it sets out to facilitate the discovery and use of those abilities proper to their accomplishment. Not surprisingly, it is often said of Eurhythmics, with some degree of emphasis, that it has its starting-point in everyone and leads on to everything.

This depth and variety, this ability to respond to the needs of such diverse groups of people, constitute at once the strength and the weakness of the Dalcrozian approach—or, if not a weakness, at least its Achilles' heel. Vulnerable it certainly is, for this is inevitable in any person or system which keeps nothing hidden and holds nothing back, and yet, being necessarily unable to reveal all its facets at once to any single observer, cannot be grasped from one point of view without being misunderstood or misrepresented as a whole. This explains why we sometimes hear comments betokening a fragmentary and often muddled conception of the facts. 'Dalcroze's method might be worth looking into if it weren't exclusively designed for children!', I was recently told by a conductor friend of mine. 'Eurhythmics is for girls!' we are often assured by supposedly well-informed persons. It would

---

[12] For instance: Copeau, Dullin, Stanislavski, Pitoëff, Diaghilev, Appia, Hodler, Ansermet, Bloch, Martin, Cortot, Claudel, G. B. Shaw, Cocteau, Flournoy, Claparède. For a fuller list, see Berchtold 1965.

be wrong to underestimate the significance of observations like these on the ground that they have no substance in fact: for they soon acquire substance, albeit falsely, if only by virtue of obtaining general currency. In the face of such assertions, parents for example put their boys down for activities they think of as 'more manly', or else they pull their children out of Eurhythmic courses when they consider them 'too old for that sort of thing'. They consequently tend to build up the very image they set out to knock down. It is a fact of life that the most heavily subscribed courses at the Geneva Institute (at least in 1980) are those for young children, while those for 'older children' are invariably for 'older girls'! How can anyone expect a school so governed by the law of supply and demand to remain true to the principles that brought it into being? To what extent should we expect it to remain so? Or does some much deeper reason underlie such a state of affairs? The reader must be left to draw his or her own conclusions.

Those who are not content to explore a single facet of Eurhythmics but decide to go all the way into the subject very soon fall prey to contradictory impressions. One minute they find it impossible to reconcile additional aspects of it with their first impression of the subject—('How may one expect a way of teaching sol-fa to be of any use to therapy?' I was once asked by the headmistress of a school in Paris, convinced of her facts and with mind closed to any further discussion of the point); the next, they find themselves forced into a relentless series of mental readjustments. They cling to all their past experience as a cosy protection against the disturbing thought of a system which, like a Jack of all trades, is master of none. Eurhythmics therefore finds itself first assimilated into dance, gymnastics, or free movement, then reduced into a way of developing perceptions or encouraging music appreciation, then confused with one or more known teaching methods, most of which have the advantage of a more narrowly defined field of application or a relatively restricted content. Such misunderstandings strike me as unavoidable. They always have been there. And they have become even more prominent today; for our present rate of change has encouraged over-specialization to the point of absurdity, and no one has much time for a field of study whose horizons are not all immediately visible to the naked eye.

The strength of Eurhythmics, its inherent structural consistency, becomes obvious to all who approach it from within. They will soon discover that what we are talking about is above all a *personal experience*. Dalcroze never ceased to emphasize this concept, thus denying anyone the right to judge Eurhythmics without first trying it out for themselves (a demand we must perhaps acknowledge as being more than a little Utopian!); and if he steadfastly refused to allow his method to be reduced to a formula, it is because the very fact of doing so would by definition have resulted in its own contradiction.

THE DALCROZIAN IDENTITY

Can we even apply the term 'method' to a way of thinking which does not prescribe a path to follow so much as provide a means of following it, whatever it may be? Dalcroze himself occasionally used the term: 'The method I devised and which bears my name', he would say, as if to emphasize, perhaps for want of a better word, the essential unity underlying the superficial diversity of his creation.

I myself prefer such terms as *process*, or *approach*, or *experience*. Being less regimented, more flexible, they strike me now as more descriptive of the essential Dalcrozian process. For it offers many paths to follow, every one of them shaped by its own particular landscape. It was a felicitous notion on the part of that admirer who, at the end of a demonstration given by *Monsieur Jaques* in 1932, extolled the importance of his method*s* (Berchtold 1965: 36). Dalcroze may have spoken of it in the singular, and his ideas may have passed into history under the title *Méthode Jaques-Dalcroze*, but those who saw them practised by their author were under no illusions: 'Nothing dogmatic about this,' wrote Jacques Copeau, the great theatrical producer. 'It's an incessant invention, a perpetual outpouring. Nothing is fixed, nothing set solid, nothing but constant experience and discovery. He even seeks instruction from his own pupils. He questions and consults them . . .' (Berchtold 1965: 114).

Dalcrozians will do well to remind themselves from time to time of this basic flexibility, this lack of dogma, as the two essential qualities underlying the practice of their chosen profession. For in their distinctive capacity as specialists in Eurhythmics they sometimes feel threatened on observing to what extent they differ amongst themselves. It has to be said that they are pushed this way by the example of so many other methods, some of them admirable and many quite consistent, which do not inhibit themselves from having their contents and programmes set out ready-made in practical handbooks.

More recent methods also have the advantage of not being current fifty years after the deaths of their originators! To explain: any new idea depends for its conception and development on techniques and practices current at its date of birth. In fact, it is partly because of them that it sees the light of day at all, and only on them can it build its own foundations. This is a fact of life, and one which in my view gives rise to two major difficulties.

The first is that of separating an idea, after its initial appearance, from the form it took when first put into practice. It really does take time and sensitivity to tease out the essence of a principle from the constraints of its particular embodiments. And these for their part tend to take on durable forms lasting well beyond their proper time. It is a risk run especially by any self-sufficient system, or one of sufficient richness to engender its own evolution without recourse to external props. Dalcroze Eurhythmics, whose value lies in its capacity to forge an immediate and long-term tool from the ensemble of human faculties, owes it to itself to escape from this pitfall, to which its very self-sufficiency lays it open.

The second difficulty is that of finding new applications for the idea, once it has been perfected, which are of a piece with those already tried. For 'You cannot think up a new development without in some way modifying the original idea' (Dalcroze 1948: 53). Thus the adoption of new uses may be inhibited as much by a concern for orthodoxy as by mere laziness or lack of imagination. In this connection a friend of mine once pointed out what depths of inertia are sometimes instigated by innovators themselves: 'It remains a powerful motor for as long as they survive, but once they die it becomes an equally powerful brake'.[13] The problem for anyone wishing to call themselves 'Dalcrozian' today is to escape that force of inertia without at the same time shooting off into space. It isn't easy to maintain a balance between these two extremes. On one hand, the threat of crashing to earth afflicts those who are themselves 'prevented from flying by a giant's wings' (!)[14]—a threat which particularly assails Eurhythmics practitioners, who feel themselves to be the heirs, the agents, and the guardians of a work whose perpetuation has been entrusted to them. On the other (but does this really count?), the point of no return, of disappearance into space, that threatens the independents, the isolationists, the freelances—those who forge methods of their own which threaten to lose touch with their origins,

---

[13] A. Meutémédian: private communication, 1980.
[14] *ceux que les ailes d'un géant empêchent de voler*: a slightly modified reference to Baudelaire's poem 'The Albatross', whose *ailes de géant l'empêchent de marcher* when the poor bird is being tortured by sailors. (Translator's note)

or who are content to throw into the melting-pot everything they happen to rub up against in the course of their travels.

Here again we must let the creator speak for himself. He too occasionally (1948: 24) entertained the dismal prospect of his work's being 'made a travesty of by incompetents', while at the same time counting himself blessed to see his successors 'seeking to find out new ways'; for he had long held that 'the finest achievements come not from movements but from individuals' (1900a: 15). One of his pupils, Claire-Lise Dutoit, happily encapsulated a thought conducive to reconciliation between various different tendencies by remarking: 'Jaques-Dalcroze still leaves everyone behind!'[15] This observation often comes to mind, and I have found it to be a significant factor in determining my approach to the present book.

The 1927 edition of the review *Le Rythme* pointed out that 'from the moment Jaques-Dalcroze first put his ideas into practice far too many people have been ready to exploit his name to bolster experiments bearing only the vaguest and most superficial resemblances to his method' (Ed. C. 1927: 18). The reverse is true today: many other methods have made a name for themselves without realizing that they owe him many of their best ideas. Herein, I believe, lies the measure of the success of the ideas which he professed; it is itself the mark of their long-term value.[16]

Far be it from me to play such methods down in favour of the one and only first-born. A particular method should not be granted pride of place or held superior to another just because it is older. What counts is that it remains a living force today and addresses itself to the future of the individual as much as to his present. My purpose in the following exposition of Dalcroze Eurhythmics is to show that it contains all these potentials for enlightenment, and at the same time to render homage to its founder; for, as he said himself (1942: 59), 'The people who command respect are those who have communicated useful experiences to those around them, and sown the seeds of original and beneficent ideas'.

---

[15] C.-L. Dutoit; private communication, c.1970.
[16] A similar fate has befallen many a song of his which has passed into the anonymous repertoire of international folklore!

2

INITIATIONS

Time—Space—Energy

That all movement requires space and time is beyond question. Any given movement, whether long or short, firm or feeble, fast or slow, human or mechanical, depends upon some minimum of space and time for its very existence.

For proof of this principle we need only look at the evidence of our own eyes. The first thing we notice about bodily movement is how it relates to space—a property that has to do with its energy, with its very plasticity. We may say, 'What a fine movement that is! How disorganized it is! Such stiffness!' Whether seen through the eyes or experienced through the body, movement is automatically analysed by reference to its actual displacements (changes of position, use of space, orientation) and to the manner in which they are executed (lightly or weightily, supply or stiffly, slowly or briskly). On the other hand its sense of duration, the order and rhythm with which it unfolds, the extent to which its component parts run concurrently or consecutively—in short, those aspects of movement related essentially to *time*—pass often unremarked, to the great advantage of its spatial aspect.

Let's do an exercise. Specialists in movement nowadays attach particular importance to points of departure and completion. Thus a movement of the arm initiated by flexing the shoulder backwards and progressively stretching the muscles right down to the fingertips produces an entirely different feeling and effect from a movement in the same direction begun by flexing the elbow! Try this, and you will notice, amongst other things, that the second naturally results in a different position of the hand.

Did you also notice that although in describing this movement we emphasized its localization and direction, we could not entirely dispense with terms relating essentially to the element of time? Such words as *initiate, progressively, effect, result,* demonstrate that movement is not just a matter of *here-and-there* but is equally possessed of a *now-and-then* dimension. You might now repeat one or other of these movements, concentrating this time on moments of departure and completion. You will become aware that by varying the lapse of time between them, and occupying that period with a total immobilization—or continued progression—of the gesture, you can produce a variety of results. According to context, these will influence the expressiveness or aesthetic of your movement, and hence of the meaning one may seek to attach to it.

A sense of timing is crucial to many situations occurring in everyday life. Two examples will suffice.

1. When you have to catch a moving object before it hits you—or misses you, or escapes from your grasp—your own movement must comply with two temporal imperatives: first, it must foresee the point and moment of contact, otherwise it will not synchronize with the travel involved and will fail to get there in time; secondly, the very act of grasping must be carried out with a degree of precision which increases with the speed of the object concerned: too soon or too late, and it is ineffectual.

2. When you find yourself having to react instantaneously to some kind of danger or other urgent stimulus, the outcome may well be determined by your capacity to adapt your movement to a sudden hesitation or change of direction.

In these two examples, the outcome of the movement (hit or miss) is brought about by a space–time combination which has to adapt itself to circumstances. The lack of control sometimes observed in this respect has given rise to such expressions as 'blind panic', or 'out of the frying-pan into the fire'—which, I think, nicely illustrate how a sense of spatial control can be upset by a badly organized sense of timing.

Situations in which time clearly plays an overriding role in bodily movement are legion—notably those requiring fast reflexes and rapid responses, as well as those that call for endurance or presuppose a plan of campaign. Any action demanding anticipation, organization, co-ordination, or following through call as much upon the temporal as on the spatial aspect of movement. It may not always be easy to estimate their relative importance, but at least there can be no doubt that neither is exercised without reference to the other.

Now it is to the temporal aspect of movement that music particularly

addresses itself, if only because it does not directly engage the eyes.
There is the time music takes to unfold itself, the duration of notes
and silences: periodicity, simultaneity, alternation; repetitions, evocations, halts; barlines, tempi, accelerandos, rallentandos; anticipations,
pauses, and delays; the procession of phrases . . . the list is endless!
And if music has been described as 'the art, *par excellence*, of time', it
is precisely because its effect is entirely contained within the time
required for its performance. While a picture can be looked at free
from most constraints of time, no piece of music can be listened to
faster or slower than the speed at which it is performed.

We therefore see that any teacher of bodily movement who happens
also to be a musician will be better placed than most for access to *bodily
time*. Such teachers will have recourse to music as an aid to underlining,
bringing into relief, to 'isolating', as required, that temporal aspect of
movement which is all too often swamped by its spatial aspects.

By a neat circularity of events, the student able to rely on music to
monitor and improve the timing of his movements will discover for
himself that 'that ultimate musical instrument, the whole human
body, is more capable than any other of appreciating sounds in all
their possible shades and nuances of duration' (Dalcroze 1919*b*: 143).
He thereby gradually develops an awareness of musical organization
in its own right; for 'muscular sensations eventually combine with
auditory sensations, which, thus reinforced, bring more weight to
bear on the sense of appreciation and analysis' (1919*c*: 170). On these
grounds, too, Dalcroze could say (1907: 40) that 'the perfection of
movements within time secures complete *consciousness* of musical
rhythm'.

But it would be equally true to describe Music as *movement in space*.
In case we are tempted to forget that space is not restricted to what we
can see, the example of blind people will remind us that there are other
senses through which it may be perceived. In much the same way,
anyone who has noticed with what difficulty the deaf move around in
the dark will appreciate how important the sense of hearing is to those
who can hear. These are extreme examples, of course: they do not
imply that one must perforce be blind in order to hear well. But it is
certainly noticeable that the importance attached to visible phenomena
often eclipses, and may even diminish, the sense of hearing. How
many television addicts, for example, declare themselves quite incapable of following a radio broadcast properly!

That music is a spatial phenomenon is often confirmed in a visible way. Thus the arrangement of instruments in an orchestra did not arise by chance but is perfectly designed for effective listening. Moreover, modern composers increasingly tend to modify the classical arrangement for their particular needs, thereby turning instrumental space into an integral part of their creation. Even the choice of concert halls and the distance between players and audience—everything, in fact, normally associated with the realm of sound—proves that music, the art of time, cannot do without space. So vital is the element of space that it often has to be simulated, as demonstrated by the development of stereophony in recorded music.

Technical terms suggesting the spatial aspects of music are almost as common as those relating to time. We talk of space being filled with waves of sound, of the localization of sound in the body of an instrument or the vocal apparatus, of orchestral density and the weight of sound. We speak of range and pitch, of the conjunction or overlapping of sounds, of rising and falling lines, of movement in parallel, converging or diverging. Notes go in clusters or series, or are separated by intervals; we recognize motifs, lines, development, form, symmetry, breadth.

The development of twentieth-century music from Debussy onwards has largely consisted in the often systematic exploitation of the spatial resources of the world of sound. Now, more than ever before, Time and Space each define themselves by reference to the other. This has renewed and enriched our appreciation of the music of the past; for it is only when considered in its entirety that music reveals itself for what it has always been—namely, the art of space and time *together*.

An area particularly capable of benefiting from this renewal of interest in sound–space is undoubtedly that of musical education. Here, amongst other developments, increasing importance has been attached to listening to music: the time when reading, writing, dictation, and counting were the sole constituents of so-called 'musical' instruction, at least in some schools, now seems to have been swept away. Instead, teachers are moved to facilitate access to the world of music by methods of active comprehension. The most important of these include musical composition and *bodily movement and gesture*.

Now bodily movement not only underlies the way we appear to the outside world in how we express ourselves and relate to others: it also means our personal and individual way of occupying space. In Poincaré's words (*Le Rythme*, 1916: 29): 'We should be quite incapable of . . . realizing space if it were not for the fact that we possess an instrument to measure it by. As it happens, this instrument to which we submit everything, and which we use instinctively, is nothing less than our own body'. It is to our bodily experience that we owe our ability to grasp spatial concepts such as inside and outside, near-to and far-from; positional relations such as above, below, beside, between; the dimensions of height, width, and depth; distances and lines of travel; shapes and contours; straights and curves, surface and volume.

No music teacher wishing his pupils to comprehend music in all its 'spatiality' could therefore hope to find a better medium than that of bodily movement. And if he is not content to induce it in his pupils but starts sharing in the experience himself, he will become even more aware that

Every human body contains within itself more orchestral possibilities (in the concatenation, juxtaposition, and contrast of gestures and attitudes, . . . by positional changes both at rest and in movement) than the most complex of symphonic bodies. (Dalcroze 1916*b*: 111)

At the same time, adds Dalcroze (1916*b*: 116): 'A gesture is nothing in itself: its value lies entirely in the feeling that inspires it.' More recently, Antonin Artaud (1948: 133) would bequeath us this poem:

> Ce matin
> moi qui ai tout inventé
> j'ai pour la première fois compris
> la différence
> entre une sensation
> et un sentiment
> dans la sensation
> on prend ce qui vient
> dans le sentiment
> on intervient

(*This morning / I who have discovered everything / I for the first time have grasped / the difference / between sensation / and sentiment: / in sensation / you take what comes / in sentiment / you come between.*)

'You come between' . . . You *intervene* . . . The idea of subjective intervention seems more meaningful to me than the term 'sentiment', which has been so roundly abused that one can hardly be sure of grasping whatever truth it is supposed to contain.

One's own intervention may be gratuitous or deliberate, instinctive or thought out. Upon it will depend the expressive or aesthetic significance of the gesture or work of art; for significance subsists not only in the product of the creator but also in the hearing of the listener, in the entire organism of whoever is involved. It may be reacted to or reasoned out, spontaneous or willed, sustained, momentary, or developed at length. It stamps upon movement—whether bodily or musical—the mark of its own energy, its rhythm, its direction, its driving force. It endows a gesture with its strength and substance, its nuances and elements of plasticity. It also has an impact on the interplay between the particular time and space in which it is contained.

The great wealth of relationships between time and space is best discovered by practical experience followed by an analysis of the energy by which they are motivated and controlled. The basic objective of Dalcroze Eurhythmics is to facilitate this discovery. This is based on the exercise of bodily movement in relation to music, 'which combines so many natural juxtapositions of intervals, so many thrusts and accentuations, as to furnish our movements with an infinite number of rhythmic models', and which is, 'of all the arts, that which best teaches us to balance the weight and lightness, the length, sequence, and termination of our motor acts' (Dalcroze 1942: 115, 138). Hence, with few exceptions, the exponent of Dalcroze Eurhythmics is neither a specialist in movement as such nor a specialist in music as such, if either is regarded as an entirely self-contained discipline. On the other hand, his particular training may entitle him to be considered a specialist in body–time and musical space, and in rhythm, 'whose two basic elements, space and time, are absolutely inseparable' (Dalcroze 1919c: 163).

What a vast domain! And how ambitious the programme! The scope of the project is matched only by the difficulty of deciding whereabouts to make a start on it. 'Start from the inside, then!', Dalcrozians will say. Fair enough; but in this instance the problem lies in trying to give some idea of it through the medium of words and sentences, while knowing in advance—and with good reason—that there is no substitute for real-life experience.

Initial Exercises

It sometimes happens that a number of adults come together to take the first steps in Dalcroze Eurhythmics. They may be united by some common interest—perhaps they are all musicians, for example, or teachers; alternatively, they may come from various places and various different backgrounds, and have nothing more in common than an interest in this introductory stage. The main thing, however, is to give them all, in a limited period of time (two or three days, perhaps; better still, a fortnight) the opportunity of enjoying as complete an experience as possible. That this in fact is generally achieved goes right to the purposive heart of Eurhythmics. The active discovery of the bonds uniting energy to time and space demands a degree of personal investment on everybody's part, and consequently would not be adequately met by a programme that kept saying 'To be continued . . .' until the list of exercises had been worked right through. On the contrary, what it does require is a course that expands concentrically around a constant 'here-and-now' and simultaneously takes into account the personality of the teacher, the group of people under instruction, and the time available for the purpose. Only from these initial ideas can a teaching programme be developed which will constitute a complete unit at each level of its implementation. Depending on the scale envisaged, *level* may mean a single lesson, a working day, a week-long training period, or a year of study.

As far as each student is concerned, each level, regardless of its individual subject, invariably consists in an *exploration of his personal potential in several directions*. At the same time, it offers everyone the chance to discover their own limits and to seek how best either to push them further out or to come to terms with them. Furthermore, each of these levels will help to deepen those preceding it—partly by recapitulation, but largely by repeating earlier exercises in a different format and by taking the skills already acquired and applying them to different subjects. In this way it promotes the necessary *degree of awareness* essential to the work to be done. Finally, although each level starts off as a personal experience, it is at the same time a *collective* one. For Eurhythmics uses exercises requiring group collaboration no less than individual exercises; and even in the latter— given that most of them take place in space, and that space belongs to everyone (!)—there are few occasions on which the presence of others does not have to be taken more or less into account.

Every level, then, as defined above, will include a musical and a physical content in proportion to its particular place in the course as a whole. From all of which it will be readily understood that no particular Eurhythmic exercise may be singled out as 'Lesson One' *par*

excellence. On the contrary, there are at least as many 'Lessons One' as
there are Dalcrozian tutors to propose them—perhaps even more!
Thus, for instance, one tutor may wish to begin her course or work-
shop by getting everyone to listen to a passage from a musical
composition. She could ask her subjects to concentrate on points of
repose, on length of phrasing, or perhaps on the overall mood of the
piece, and invite them to express their reactions to it by making some
movement or changing their position.

Another may prefer to engage immediately his pupils' capacity for
rapid response. He might, for example, get them to react to alternations
of motion and immobility suggested by some music which he will
improvise. The suggested movement might consist in beating time or
walking in time to a given tempo; or it might be a continuous
movement whereby they trace out a design in space with the hand, the
elbow, the whole body, etc., right up to a point at which it is suddenly
broken off.

Another teacher will start with a relaxation exercise in which each
participant will concentrate on his or her own pulse with a view to
communicating its rate to the others, whether vocally or by means of
gestures.

The starting-point of Lesson One might well be centred on a single
note, held for a longer or shorter time, which requires the pupils to
keep absolutely still until they can no longer hear it (or, alternatively,
to freeze into immobility as soon as it ceases to be audible).

Yet again, one might start by inviting pupils to make free use of any
available materials (scarves, ropes, balls, etc.), then think of various
ways of getting them to discover the dynamic and plastic resources of
these objects with a view to making use of them for the invention or
imitation of given rhythms.

Quite often (but there is no obligation!) 'Lesson One' will consist in
moving about in time to various speeds and simple rhythms picked
out by the teacher on a piano, who for her part will match her
improvisations to her pupils' natural abilities. Thus a suitable tempo
for comfortably moving about to, whether walking or running, will
tend to be faster for children—their legs being short—than for adults.
Children will also generally be capable of running for longer periods of
time than adults without getting tired; on the other hand, though,
they will need relatively frequent changes of pace in order to keep
their attention held.

It will be noted from this last example that it is distinctly advant-

ageous to have recourse to some sort of *improvised* music as opposed
either to a recording, which unilaterally demands compliance with an
unchanging tempo or rhythmic line, or to a printed score, which
cannot with integrity be submitted to all the modifications (fragment-
ation, repetition, accentuation, variations in speed and shading, etc.)
imposed by such an exercise. This two-way adaptive process enables
pupils to be aware from the outset of the sense of *complicity* existing
between their personal movement and the music that brings it out.
For such complicity, helpful as much in the refinement of bodily
movement as in musical training as such, will prove to be the
cornerstone of the entire educational process of Eurhythmics.

Three Cases Analysed

To give further examples of 'Lesson One' I will expand on the ones
I know best from personal experience. The three following situations
will help put in context those aspects which I have already referred
to as the 'here-and-now' of the Eurhythmics lesson. They involve
respectively a group of 'lay' adults, one of young children, and one of
adult specialists.

NON-PROFESSIONAL ADULTS

I will quite often ask a group of adults whom I don't yet know—and
who generally don't know one another either—to walk around the
room at their own individual speeds, taking no notice of anyone else
except to avoid bumping into them, and concentrating on the feelings
induced in them by their particular style of walking. They should,
while doing so, seek to make that style as even and as comfortable
as possible.

This obviously takes place without music, and gives me the advantage, as I see it, of being able from the outset to encourage each
individual to perform a quite ordinary and uncompromising activity
in an entirely personal way.

Next, I invite them to look all around (without relaxing their
motion or speed) and notice which others are walking faster or slower
than themselves. Do they, perhaps, walk faster than everyone else?—
or more slowly, if it comes to that?

Then I will ask them to try and adjust their walking all to the same
speed, which necessarily involves their making mutual concessions to

one another. Not until such consensus is attained will I begin to use music, at the piano, to give expression to their common speed.

I have been known to substitute for improvisation a recording of the Andante from Bach's *Italian Concerto*.[1] On more than one occasion the natural tempo of the harpsichord has been found to coincide exactly with the common walking speed—thus allowing us to clear up a common misunderstanding about the word *andante*, which is all too often taken to mean 'slowly' when in fact it means 'moving along'. It also led us to suspect that the idea of a fairly clear-cut 'average tempo' can probably be extended beyond our particular group of individuals, and that certain 'human constants'—such as pulse, respiration, and associated movements—could well be cast in the role of yardstick for it.

Sometimes, when the floor is particularly reverberant, the discovery of a common tempo may derive from auditory sensations. In this case the exercise will be fortunate in incorporating its own corrective measures! Even so, when I continue by asking them to repeat the exercise (its eventual purpose now known in advance) by each starting off with an individual tempo different from what it was before—either faster or slower—the participants regularly claim that it is much harder to settle on a slower common pace than a faster one; and this applies regardless of the means (auditory or visual) by which they arrive at it. How to continue such an exercise depends on several factors. In my own experience I don't think it has ever gone the same way twice. This can be explained by the fact that the exercise is so rich in possibilities:

One might choose to go further into the realm of space utilization: experience has already been gained in the need to be able to move around freely amongst others who are also moving about.

One might proceed from the time dimension to that of rhythm: both share a common origin in the muscular sensations which have already been experienced.

One might try to detect the common tempo underlying several different pieces of music which have been proposed: this will be much easier to achieve if one has already tried it out for oneself.

One might undertake some exercises requiring the collaboration of several participants: we have already called upon every member of the

---

[1] To me, this piece nicely demonstrates how *tempo giusto*, corresponding as it does to the most natural and balanced walking pace, simultaneously sustains and liberates the imagination, which then gives free rein to all the fantasy inherent in Bach's extremely lovely melody.

group to enter into an agreement, and the group is now beginning to take shape in its own right.

One might even . . . But everyone must discover a method for themselves; in any case, the various possibilities are not mutually exclusive, and often will combine in advantageous ways. Choosing between them may be regarded as the responsibility of the teacher, who, while certainly guided first and foremost by the general plan of campaign proposed, will also take into account such observations as will have been made, so far, of wishes expressed by the participants, for example, or of a novel idea that might have originated with them. It is for the teacher to judge to what extent he might depart from his initial plan without losing sight of it altogether.

YOUNG CHILDREN

They are 4 or 5 years of age and arrive in a group for the first time at the place where I shall be taking them. The surroundings are unfamiliar: a large, empty space full of unknown objects. It is a question of 'house-training' them, so to speak, so that they come to feel themselves entirely at home there. We had better start with the peripheral objects; for 4-year-olds can only come to terms with space step by step and little by little.

The first attraction is always the long bench fixed to the wall. All of a sudden, the boldest of them will be perched on it. It's just right! Then everyone has to prove they can jump off again. Can they land safely on their feet? That's rather more tricky! Let's just have another go on this . . .

Here is the marble fireplace, where no fire burns. But you can all get in it one at a time (nice and dirty!); or you can blow on the imaginary fire to keep it going, and the resultant *puff, puff*! soon draws everyone in.

There is a wall with a perpendicular piece jutting out at the top. One of the children, immediately followed by the others, throws himself into this enclosure. The last one in uses little building blocks to secure the equivalent of a door to this *ad hoc* hidey-hole. Is it possible to get in and out of their hide without making the slightest noise? They carefully tiptoe over the blocks. Can they all fit comfortably in it together? That takes a few more goes to achieve!

Then there's the old green ceramic stove, no longer in use. What can that be? I explain that people used to be able to warm themselves on it without getting burnt. They finger its shiny surface, feel it with their cheeks. It's cold! Imagine when it was warm . . .

We'll spend the whole hour here. Already much experience has been gained unconsciously. We have exercised our muscles and our sense of balance; raised our voices, blown things and overcome various obstacles; we've experienced silence and tried squeezing ourselves all into a confined space; we've touched a surface to feel its temperature, imagined things that were not really there.

What we have to do now is to make contacts between different places. It isn't hard to remember every little thing we've done, but were we fully aware of each? Where exactly did we do the jumping? Where do we go noiselessly? What is it we do at the fireplace?

We walk confidently towards the stove; we rush across the room to be the first to jump; we tiptoe along to our hiding-place again. I improvise a piano accompaniment for these various walking speeds: and all the lines that join these different points together begin to take on an existence of their own—*because music directs towards the action it underscores some portion of the attention which was previously concentrated on the goal to be attained.*

I could equally well have begun by using music to bring out the rhythms appropriate to each change of place. Or, at first with words and the help of gestures, and then at the piano, I could have accompanied the jumps, the puffing and blowing, the tactile surface-testing, and then drawn the children's attention to the music itself: is the piano saying *jump!*—or is this 'going-on-tiptoe' music?

In this example, my overall object of helping children to structure new-found space dictated that music should be used in the first exercise as means rather than end—a case of *par la musique* rather than *pour la musique.*

THE PROFESSIONALS

As part of a two-day session bringing choral directors together, thus involving people with musical or at least vocal training and in possession of a repertoire, I started off with an exercise in *internal singing.*

Everyone thought of a song well known to themselves (and to everyone else, if possible), which they liked well enough to keep repeating should it become necessary to do so. No one should let anyone in on the song they had chosen, but should sing the first verse of it internally, to themselves, two or three times in succession, without skipping a note or a word, and without letting a sound escape their lips. This turned out to be a novel experience for most of them, and required no little concentration on their part.

After a series of progressive instructions, I eventually asked them to
let the song 'move' them—literally—until the whole song was welling
up inside them, and lacked nothing in its expression but the actual
words and sounds! While repeating their song, they had to do this by
concentrating at first on its musical nature, as well as its subject matter
and general atmosphere; then on its rhythmic qualities, or phrasing,
or cadences, as the case may be; and on the sense of particular words
which evoked a movement or image, a tone or an attitude.

From almost imperceptible beginnings, movement found itself
achieving greater and greater expression, *without ever leaving its point
of departure within the body of each individual*. In other words, at any
given moment there was never any question of simply *miming* songs.
Nothing of the sort was seen; yet many of them were clearly sketched
out, some indeed—as far as I can tell—quite unmistakably so.

Underestimating not the breadth of their repertoire so much as
their diversity of tastes, I had anticipated that many of my participants
would have chosen the same song. Acting on this assumption, I had
reckoned on continuing the exercise as follows: Several of them at a
time circulate amongst the performers with a view to discovering
which of them has or have chosen the same song as themselves. This
would result in the formation of little groups. Each group would
then—out loud at last—have sung its chosen song (or *songs*, should
any have found themselves wrongly grouped together!). Then the
movements evoked by the song could have served as the basis of a
communal dance, in which the other participants could have joined.
This activity would have enabled us to graduate from *personal* to
communal space.

Alas! This observer found herself quite unable to sort out any two
matching interpretations. I recognized certain resemblances, but not
with absolute conviction. Could all the songs possibly have been
different? (there were a good forty or so taking part.) But then if such
disparity were due to personal differences—differing degrees of
sensitivity, or shortcomings in the various interpretations—how could
the participants have been expected to recognize *their* particular song
in such distorting mirrors? No; I had to find some other way of
proceeding.

Taking care to pick on those who seemed most confident of what
they were doing and whose movements displayed distinctive characteristics, I asked if they would be willing to perform solo in front of the
group. One or two assented to this proposition, thus permitting ten or

so participants to congregate around each one. Each of these four or
five groups had now to try and recognize the song it was 'looking at'.

One of the songs was picked out almost immediately, though it was
by no means the best known. Even before its first performance was at
an end, the whole group was singing it, having (so to speak) hauled
themselves aboard the moving train!

The others took longer to identify. There were several cases of
mistaken identity involving songs with marked similarities to the one
being demonstrated—which was rather a good sign for a first attempt.
Some, however, could eventually only be guessed at, being found out
by a series of probing assertions such as 'this one has a rocking
movement: it has something heavy about it: its phrases are short . . .';
and so on, until its eventual discovery (though not by those who had
by this time lost their tongues!).

Ah—I nearly forgot! It turned out, in the final analysis, that all the
chosen songs were in fact different, with one exception, if I remember
aright. Dalcroze himself would have been delighted, bearing in mind
his complaint (1905: 19) about the 'deplorable decline in French
choral singing'. For my part, I could only regret that my lack of
foresight forced me to divorce my exercise from that discovery of
space which was supposed to be its crowning achievement! This
naturally impinged on the rest of my course, and I was obliged to
make some necessary adjustments to it.

By the end of this exercise various parallels had been established
between this form of musical expression and the directing of a choir,
which relies on certain conventions. We sought out what bearing the
former had upon the latter, in what respects it fell short of it, and so
on. At the same time we tried to describe the relationships between
words and music, prosody and melody, the rhythm of a song and the
character of a text.

I found it time-saving, in a two-day course, to start with an exercise
involving everyone in a rather obvious way. This was designed to
encourage them, in the following exercises—which at first sight had
nothing to do with directing choirs—to observe or to discover what
links *ought* to exist between Eurhythmics and their own particular
sphere of activity.

For this same course I had planned to illustrate that sentence of
Dalcroze's (1898: 10) about seeking to 'transform the whole organism
into what might be called an *internal ear*'. More than any other, this
subject struck me as likely to make an immediate impact on the people

I was involved with, and this particular 'Lesson One' seemed to be an ideal choice from this point of view.

It may seem surprising that on this occasion I had not seen fit to describe Eurhythmics in terms more consistent with the way in which it is generally understood; after all, these people were mostly beginners. It may seem surprising that I did not begin with a simpler exercise involving more movement and being easier to correct—an exercise which would have made greater demands upon their active motor functions and have enabled me to contribute to the proceedings in a more distinctly audible way. This would not have prevented me from following my plan through, for I could still have gone on to the same 'Lesson One' in due course. There is something in that: and if anyone other than myself had done so, it would have been for perfectly good reasons, relating to their own particular intention.

Personally, I felt more inclined to spend two days on giving more than a general view or simple 'image' of Eurhythmics. Even if such an image is inevitable, let us at least delay it as long as possible: that way it will have more chance of being accurate. It seemed to me that the best means to this end would be to offer an initial exercise which could not possibly reinforce any preconceived notions that may already exist in the minds of the participants.

In any case, I was anxious to leave my trainee choral directors in no doubt from the outset that, in this context, it was *they themselves* who were the musicians. By deliberately forgoing the exercise of any real control over their actions, and restricting myself to the most general of directions, I managed to give them confidence in this respect. I have since discovered that Stanislavski's remarkable book,[2] known in English as *An Actor Prepares*, has a rather different title in Russian: it translates, apparently, as *The actor's work upon himself*. I shall probably have occasion to refer to it again.

The examples given above furnish us with material relating to the first of three components of what I have called the 'here-and-now' of Dalcrozian instruction: the actual *instructor*, the *group of people* under instruction, and the proposed *duration* of that instruction. In point of fact, all three of them have been much in evidence, whether individually or in conjunction with one another, throughout these detailed illustrations. We are now in a position to embark upon them more systematically.

[2] New York: Theater Arts, 1936.

The Dalcroze Teacher

If I put the Dalcroze teacher at the head of the list it is because on that one personality everything else will hinge. It will be objected that it is in the nature of every kind of teaching to be stamped with the quality of its dispenser—at least, when it is either of good quality or else remarkably bad. In the present case it must be borne in mind that for the Eurhythmics teacher there is absolutely no manual pointing the way to follow in any given instance, day after day or week after week. Nor is there a list of exercises which might be held up as a blueprint of the method. Not only does he organize his own personal course of work, he will also have invented for himself—and will continue this creative work as and when the needs arise—most of the exercises that he sets in motion.

How then, it will be asked, can you be sure of receiving a truly *Dalcrozian* instruction from the teacher facing you? There are others who create and invent things, other people who organize their work ad lib. How can you be sure of anything any more? Nevertheless, I think elements of confirmation may be usefully sought in two different directions. The first lies to some extent in the 'guarantee' implicit in the formation of the Dalcrozian himself. The second involves applying a number of criteria for testing the Dalcrozian quality of a given exercise, a lesson, or a whole course. The examples we have looked at so far should enable us to identify one or two of these. However, apart from the fact that such a list would be incomplete, I prefer to wait a while so that the reader may have every opportunity to form some idea of them for himself.

When the Eurhythmics teacher ventures to describe his work as 'Dalcrozian', you can generally take it that he possesses something more than the abstract idea normally covered by the term. He has, to this end, freely committed himself to three or four years of full-time Dalcrozian instruction, and must, even before being allowed to pursue these studies, have been able to furnish satisfactory evidence of good bodily control and a musical accomplishment proper to the development of his future professional skills.

The main object of the instruction he has received would have been to make him experience for himself that 'one of the first fruits of exercises designed . . . to establish rapid and efficient

communications between the two poles of our being . . . is to teach
[the pupil] to know himself, to govern himself, to take possession of
his personality' (Dalcroze 1914: 59). For, as Dalcroze was to put it
again (1924: 7):

no one can claim to understand the whys and wherefores of 'Eurhythmics'
until he has realized that it is above all a way of opening ourselves up, of saying
'I know and think, *simply because* I feel and experience'.

The second goal of the studies he has pursued, and this contingent
upon the first, would have been to put the future instructor in
possession of a number of practical and theoretical methods and
insights in the realm of music and body movement. He will so deeply
have studied the ways in which music and movement interact as to be
'in a position to impose upon his pupils no exercise which he would
not be easily capable of performing himself' (Dalcroze 1922*b*: 7),
whether spatially with the whole of his body, or at the piano, where his
powers of improvisation should be a match for all the movement and
musicality in the exercise. But he will have immersed himself as much
in their actual contents as in their interactions. For it is well known
that, in order to teach the most basic elements of any discipline at all,
it is vital for them to be possessed in so much greater measure by the
teacher. Even more important for anyone intending to go further than
an elementary introduction is the teacher's need for a margin of safety
sufficient to put into perspective each phase in the progress of the
pupils entrusted to us. Each phase must in fact be envisaged not only
as the continuation of those preceding it but also as preparation
for those to come. From this point of view it is therefore necessary
in some degree to be able to see beyond one's immediate horizons.
Furthermore, the rhythmician may find himself confronted—especially
at the outset of his career, though this may continue indefinitely—
with unexpected difficulties on the part of his pupils, whose abilities
he may have overestimated, or, conversely, who may perform with an
equally unforeseen degree of facility. In either case, it is by his broad
perspective of the areas covered by the exercise in question that he will
be led to effect appropriate modifications on this particular exercise,
or perhaps to abandon it in favour of another, so that he may bring to
his pupils an experience as tractable as it is satisfying. And it is self-
evidently by his own experience that he will be led to acquire the
necessary perspective. Given, however, the range and variety of skills
which Eurhythmics demands on the part of its instructors, it is

important for them to emerge from their training in possession of as wide and well-founded a repertoire as possible.

Finally, the Eurhythmics practitioner will, in the last stages of his training, have had many opportunities of taking the knowledge he has acquired and putting his personal experiences to the test in teaching practice pursued under the control of different experts. Such practice may be expected, if not to have led him into a 'profession' in the strict sense of the word, at least to have acquainted him with the ground rules of all good teaching, as well as a deepened understanding of Dalcrozian methodology. It should also be able to strengthen his desire to make the teaching of Eurhythmics his future vocation.

A Series of Choices

Once initiated into his own responsibilities, the Eurhythmics teacher will have to select from the means at his disposal those he considers most appropriate to his current situation. It is first and foremost in respect of his own development (i.e., that 'working upon himself' that he has carried out, as well as of the various areas which he ought to have mastered) that he must be *up to the task of making a certain number of choices*.

I, for example, had the practical ability to make good use of improvisation at the piano in the three instances quoted above. As it happens, in the first two cases this was exercised only late in the proceedings, and very modestly at that, while in the third the question of using it didn't even arise. In the choral directors' lesson I could have made myself acquainted with a sufficient number of songs to have appreciated in advance the range of choices open to the participants. (In some ways, as we have seen, this would have been a helpful thing to do!) Or again, I had access to a sufficient quantity of objects in my teaching-room and a sufficient quantity of ideas in my head to have conducted the children's lesson along quite different lines had I *chosen* to do so.

But it is the variety of his practical methods that will enable the Eurhythmics teacher to *seize every opportunity to make one choice or another*. Thus I was at liberty either to engage the adult choral directors in exactly the same way as the adult non-specialists, or to take account, as in the event I did, of their presumed differences. I could have decided to begin any of my three lessons with a ball game, for instance, or a floor exercise; and have indeed done so on other occasions.

As only a few children, some half-dozen, were present in this instance, I was able to take advantage of their number by concentrating on individual exercises (e.g. jumping off the bench one by one), or on communal exercises which only with great difficulty could have been used as a first lesson for a larger number without degenerating into an uncontrollable riot (e.g. walking around at speed, squeezing into a tight corner). But I should not have felt any obligation to do so, even then.

By contrast, my choice of exercises had to take into account that the adults, whether or not they were specialists, were beginners but not children; that the non-specialist adults were not acquainted with one another; and that the choral directors were only there for a couple of days!

His preferences and personal characteristics, as well as his particular aptitudes (or inaptitudes), *will naturally predispose the Eurhythmics teacher towards making some choices and avoiding certain others.*

It will be noticed, for example, that the exercises used with the two adult groups were of one and the same type. For all their differences, both immediately plunge the participants into an essentially personal performance, and evolve in parallel towards the establishment of an understanding—be it in the passage from an individual to a collective walking speed, or from the individual expression of a silent song to its recognition by the whole group.

The fact that when I took a small group of children I made use of their limited number to bring out their individual forms of self-expression may lend support to those who have already come to think of me as a 'sociable individualist'! Still, even though I may secretly agree with them, those who are not themselves expert in Eurhythmics should watch other instructors giving lessons before correctly identifying as an individual characteristic something which they might have thought common to all. It will then become apparent that there are hundreds of ways of applying that basic rule of Eurhythmics which requires one to proceed 'from the particular to the general, and not from the general to the particular' (Dalcroze 1924: 7).

It will also be found that 'those laws particular to a given temperament which justify the bending of rules form the substance of truly original teaching, in which the teacher's personality ought properly to be revealed' (Dalcroze 1900a: 38–9). No one will have too many opportunities—(I hope, since I make a point of avoiding them!)—to observe that my inclination to favour personal experimentation and collective creativity is the other side of the coin of my distinct lack of enthusiasm for having to deal with large groups! 'It would be wrong', as Dalcroze said, 'to believe that any given Eurhythmics teacher can *imagine* and *direct* exercises of a choreographic nature in a spirit of complete originality . . .' On the contrary, it is essential that he 'make a serious assessment of himself and avoid specialising in any branch that clashes with his temperament' (1924: 2–3).

In the final analysis it is his own experience (and often his 'intuition', if not even his very *in*experience) that *dictates to the Eurhythmics teacher a particular choice from amongst all those at his disposal.*

Having worked with children for many years, I knew that most of their interest centres on their environment so long as it remains unusual, and that any exercise that failed to take the environment into account would have relatively little chance of capturing their imagination. That is why, rather than starting them off on an exercise based on an exploration of their motor capabilities (running, walking, ad lib rhythmic movements), I preferred to lay stress on things and happenings *outside* themselves, leaving such motor abilities to be discovered as one of many possible consequences.

As to adults, I knew from experience that right from the start they are rarely keen to be put under the spotlight or to indulge themselves in movements requiring them to externalize themselves in a manner to which they have not yet become accustomed. That is why, in the 'lay' group, I involved them in so humdrum an activity as just walking about while concentrating on themselves, and with the choral directors decided to start off with a well-known song (i.e. a reassuring point of reference), and one individually chosen (thereby not giving rise to the threat of comparisons).

It is for precisely the same reason that I chose to develop the two exercises by giving the most general of instructions (as in merely determining whether one person's walk was faster or slower than another, or when we got round to translating the musical content of a song in more 'physical' terms). With more advanced students, it would have been possible, for the same purpose, to have recourse to personal examples or comments which might have led them to accept a closer involvement.

It was the same reason again that led me to choose those of the choral directors who seemed most sure of themselves, even though I allowed them the option of not having to perform in front of the others. In this group, on the other hand, it was my very *in*experience (or perhaps experience of a different sort acquired in other circumstances) which led me to assume that the chosen songs would be few in number, and that I would therefore be able to make the exercise more communal in form.

The nature of one's training, diversity of practice, personal inclinations, and experience: this is the order in which I place the various factors leading an instructor to the selection of a particular exercise. But if this order describes the way in which selection factors are developed in the Eurhythmics trainee, it is nevertheless clearly the *content* which the expert plans to furnish in his teaching, as well as the physical material to which he has recourse (surroundings, objects, etc.), which will in practice ultimately control the selection of a given exercise.

Pupils in Rhythmics

The need to take account of the nature, characteristics, and personalities of those being taught is of the essence to any system of *education* in the true sense of the word, as opposed to the sort of instruction which merely consists in transmitting information to or instilling a technique within a group of people permitted to receive it.

Thus Eurhythmics, which is based on the principle of *personal experience*, and which (apart from those occasions on which a more didactic approach is followed) has been defined as 'education through music as well as into it', finds itself doubly motivated by this imperative. Specifically, it takes account of it by definition, since the efficacy of its procedures rests precisely upon its ability to make use of any individual's spontaneous movements, then make him conscious of those movements so that he may achieve mastery and freedom of use over them according to his particular needs.

Consequently, it would be both artificial and presumptuous to carve rhythmics up into convenient slices so as to fit it into pre-defined categories. There is no such thing as 'rhythmics *for* adults', 'rhythmics *for* children, *for* the very young, *for* dancers', and so on: rather, there is rhythmics *and* there are *certain* adults, *certain* children, *certain* dancers, etc., for whom it acts as a means of personal development.

It is important that this distinction be fully understood, as well by those who teach rhythmics as by those who watch it being taught. For the former, it constitutes an invaluable economic factor whilst at the same time proving that they exercise true mastery of their domain. 'What I do with four-year-olds and what I do with adults are one and the same thing!', said Valéry Roth, a Paris-based Eurhythmics teacher. 'The only difference is that one lot are four years old and the others aren't . . . Which is no good reason for restricting 'irregular rhythms' to the latter!'[3] And Marta Sanchez, visiting professor at Geneva, profited from the visit of a little girl in her course for future professional rhythmicians by demonstrating to them how she introduces youngsters to the rhythmic feature known as 'syncope', which just happened to have been the topic of her lesson.[4] As to non-specialist observers, once they have grasped this distinction they will be able to appreciate the unity underlying the apparent diversity, and to recognize variety where they had expected to find conformity.

This further entails in both groups the ability to grasp that the number of possible Eurhythmics exercises is unlimited, and that greater insight into the essence of Eurhythmics will be gained not by simply *collecting as many exercises as possible* but by *making every effort to absorb the basic mechanisms and principles that underlie them*. For these enable one most economically and efficiently to find ways of devising and applying all the exercises one wants.

FIRST EXAMPLE

Imagine you have taken part in the three following exercises, on which you may have been making notes:

Exercise 1. 9-year-olds have been running behind one another and jumping over sticks so placed and spaced on the floor that it takes just three steps to get from one to the other (Fig. 2.1). At the piano, the teacher has been emphasizing the pace with a lively 3/4, not without such embellishments as variations in the rhythm, pauses, etc., though with repeated references to the time signature as and when necessary, it being important that each jump finish on the first beat of a bar.

Exercise 2. In another class, 5-year-olds have been running around ad lib over a floor randomly strewn with sticks, their task being to

---

[3] Interview recorded 23 Oct. 1979.
[4] Private communication, 1980.

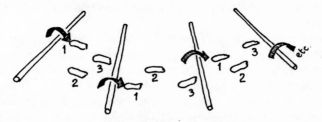

Fig. 2.1

jump like foals over all the sticks they happen to come across. The piano plays running-music, accompanying now one child and now another in their own particular jumps.

Exercise 3. The same 5-year-olds, on a different occasion, have each been bouncing a ball on the ground to match each sudden emphasis on the piano, at which now one and now another sequence of bars is played—perhaps in common time for a while, then at five to the bar, then two, and three, and so on. The children pick it up as they go along; the ball invariably bounces on the first beat, and they do this without having to count, but only by sensing points of emphasis succeeding one another at regular intervals.

Beware of thinking of the first exercise 'Now that's an exercise *for* 9-year-olds!'. Think, rather, how well-trained these children must be to exercise control at such speed over an area littered with objects, to regulate their strides in spite of running speed, to have automatically achieved the necessary alternation of left and right foot when jumping over the sticks, to catch up with themselves in the following bar should they have lost step with the one before, without letting themselves get carried away with their running, and all the time keeping an ear on the musical beats. Without such training, neither adults nor even older children achieve as much without difficulty, if at all! On the other hand, expert rhythmicians can, with no trouble at all, vary the rhythms of a passage without losing the beat, or alternate different time signatures (e.g. three to a bar, two, three, four etc.)—all of which points to an accurate assessment of the space to be sectioned, and recall of the training received in muscular sensations.

You might also appreciate that, whether the subjects are 30 years old or just 7, such an exercise carried out in slower tempo and varying time signatures is particularly useful to trainee musicians who have not yet come to realize that in the reading of a text the *bar line* is itself a sort of stick—to be jumped over without hesitation but at exactly the right moment!

When I described the 9-year-old children as 'well-trained', I did not mean to imply that that they had practised this particular exercise on a number of occasions—rather, that in the course of practising a variety of exercises they had acquired all the skills necessary for its successful execution. For example, they will have done exercises of the second type described above (Exercise 2), from which they will have learned not to collide with obstacles through inattention or faulty spatial evaluation. The obstacles might have been sticks, but could equally well have been anything else, including the splayed legs of their comrades.

They will also have done exercises of the types described in the third illustration (Exercise 3), which would have enabled them to make an instinctive correspondence between a musical stress and a movement requiring a particular amount of effort. They might have used balls for this, or sticks, tambourines, whole body movements, hand-beats, or walking.

They will have had occasion to note how bars containing an odd number of beats come to contradict the binary nature of walking rhythm by making the down-beat coincide first with one foot and then with the other.

They will not necessarily have done all these preparatory exercises at the age of 5—perhaps not till they were 7, or even only at the start of their current year. And the same exercises, or some just like them, may well form part of lessons for older children or adult beginners.

SECOND EXAMPLE

Some time ago, with an adult group—they were school music teachers —I devised an exercise called 'body-awareness' (*prise de conscience corporelle*), following an inspiration suggested recently beforehand while working with 6-year-olds. It went as follows:

> Pupils work in threes. Two of each trio sit or kneel a few metres apart and roll a ball across from one to another. The third lies at full length on his or her back (or stomach) about half way between them, at right-angles to the passage of the ball (Fig. 2.2). This constitutes an obstacle, except in so far as the body may be partially lifted off the ground to form an archway. The object of the exercise is to raise just that part of the body directly 'attacked' by the ball.

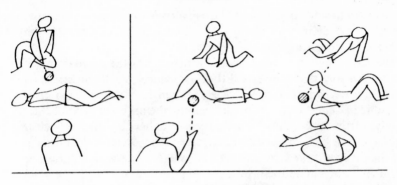

Fig. 2.2   Fig. 2.3

The ball-rollers, needless to say, try to aim for a different part of the
body each time—shoulders, knees, ankles, neck, etc. (Fig. 2.3).

Piggy-in-the-middle, of course, must make full use of head
movement by turning from one side to the other to see where the
ball is coming from, thus gaining a few valuable seconds in which to
anticipate its point of impact with an appropriate 'reaction in
advance'.

The adults enjoyed this exercise as much as the children did, and
I think I can safely say that it would have appealed equally to professional
Eurhythmics students. But the nature of that appeal would vary, since
the exercise bears with it different importance and significance to each
of the three groups. Yet didn't I do 'exactly the same thing' with each
one? Of course I did—but we have to recognize that in each of the
three situations I was working with a different end in view. Let's see
what this was for each of the three groups.

The children's group

I mentioned that I was inspired towards this exercise by 6-year-olds.
This is how it came about. In the middle of a relaxation exercise, I was
walking around between the pupils, who were lying at full length on
the floor, and gently bouncing a ball against them, its purpose being to
'check whether they were really nice and relaxed'. If they managed to
avoid making any sort of movement, contraction, or smile, which
would give away the fact that they had felt the ball, then the answer
was yes! Then I asked them which part of the body it had touched, and
they had to tell me without moving it. Just for fun, one of the children

tried hard to avoid being hit by the ball by moving his whole body out of the way, though he was not quick enough, or sufficiently well placed, to get entirely out of its way.

Perhaps, then, it would be possible to combine these two exercises in such a way that the second (ball-avoidance) would lay stress on maximum *economy of effort*. The children had shown themselves capable of being conscious of and naming the different parts of their body; furthermore, most of them seemed to have a sufficiently clear grasp of their body to make it unnecessary to support their identification of the part concerned, by moving it as well. Now, would this grasp be firm enough, should the need arise, to *precede* contact with the ball?

This is how I arrived at the exercise described above, first rolling the ball myself, then getting the children to do it, after I had noticed that the difficulty lay not at the level of body awareness but at that of following through the path of the ball and consequently of *anticipating* its point of contact. By rolling the ball themselves, the children would learn to adjust their movements to the point of contact they had in view. At first, I asked them to specify the point in advance by shouting it out before rolling the ball, thereby at the same time alerting the pupil lying down. After that, I got them to decide it 'in their heads' so that their comrade would have to 'guess' whereabouts the ball would try to make contact next. And it was the latter's job to say just where the other had been aiming, at the same time making the necessary movement to avoid being struck. Then they changed places.

As to economy of movement, this took some time to acquire. It is, you see, one thing to envisage the body occupying a particular position, but quite another to imagine the appropriate movement involving just one part of the body. The child *knows*, for instance, that he will be struck on the knee, but he raises both legs right up to the hips; he *knows* that shoulders are being aimed at, but he sits himself bolt upright instead of just pushing himself up on his elbows. This global approach to movement, with such lack of autonomy displayed by different parts of the body, is characteristic of the young child, and it would be pointless (or at least not very helpful) to undertake any detailed scheme of work centring on the differentiation of body movements in one who is too young or has built up only a hazy picture of his body. With this group of 6-year-olds, however, such work was already feasible, though it took place bit by bit, in response to such questions as 'Can you make even less of a movement than that and still let the ball get through?'.

Adult group

With the group of adult music teachers, there was no problem about the ball's line of flight or anticipating its point of contact. There was hardly any about economy of movement either—what they found most difficulty in attaining here was to *get themselves moving*! Hitherto little used to paying any conscious attention to the various muscles involved in their everyday movements, these adults found themselves suddenly faced with the necessity of making an *immediate choice* from amongst a large number of unknown muscles. Is it arms? Righto!— but the torso, finding itself in line of fire once the arms are lifted, stays glued to the ground! Hips? OK!—but the legs fall back as far as possible behind, and the hip is mercilessly smitten by the ball!

But when I said 'Now think, and take your time; the hips were raised correctly, and the torso was not ignored. It was evidently the *slowness* of their representation that held them up. So then we 'played with time': for example with the timing of the ball, at first rolled very slowly, then slightly faster, then all of a sudden, after a moment's pause; with the timing of the body, the ball being passed from one to the other in strict time, but always from a different direction, with 'piggy in the middle' successfully avoiding the ball. Now it was a question of equalizing one's physical acts; not falling into facile reactions, working through without delay towards more difficult acts of imagination, maintaining a fluid degree of attention sufficient to pass readily from one part of the body to another, and well enough sustained not to wander off course on the way.

This exercise, which started off as a jolly little achievement test, finished up as a source of pleasure in representation and sensory control.

Rhythmics students group

The enjoyment to be had from using well-controlled muscles will serve for advanced students not as the end but as the point of departure of the following exercise, which we may therefore refer to as an *exercise in control*. It is in any case vital at all levels to revert frequently to exercises easily mastered and designed for enjoyment, for these enable the pupil both to assess the progress he has made and to feel at ease in the work he is doing. Now, what better way could there be of focusing on one's progress than by successfully completing an exercise requiring total participation? Such a one is the following;

for, however easily it may be carried out, it neither entirely dispenses with the need for attention nor can be made a test-piece in automatic response, since it contains a continuous element of surprise.

On the other hand, it can be a source of countless opportunities for perfecting particular skills with the overall aim of pushing back the limits of ability required for its successful execution:

> We might, for example, decide to test their *powers of concentration* by making the exercise last as long as possible, with the ball being rolled at great speed;
>
> Or we might test *muscular control* by delaying bodily movement to the last possible moment, so that it will then have to be extremely fast and precise;
>
> Or we might test *body awareness* by reacting to two balls aimed at two different parts of the body simultaneously, etc. The students themselves will undoubtedly come up with the best ideas, as they know better than anyone else what areas of ability are most in need of developing.

These examples will leave the reader convinced, I hope, that from a Dalcrozian point of view Eurhythmics exercises cannot really be designed in advance *for* one group or another, or one purpose or another, without being reduced to the lowest possible levels of usefulness, if not deprived of all significance whatever. In which case, dear reader, you will now be happy to abandon all hope (if indeed you entertained it in the first place) of finding in this book a catalogue of graded exercises or a classical hierarchy of 'model lessons'.

The Instructor's Standpoint

Following this same train of ideas, I should now like to return to the ball-game described above (Exercise 3). We have seen that such an exercise may prepare the ground for a more complex one in which the child is led to make a movement corresponding in energy to an emphasis in the music. But it is equally possible, once it is put into effect, for this exercise to have as its primary aim that of teaching the child so to regulate his movements as to simply catch his ball with confidence and precision. In this case the teacher's role at the piano will not be to *instigate* rhythmic changes in order to check that the basic tempo has been properly grasped, but to *select* certain rhythms with a view to matching the movement which will be most comfortable and most suited to enabling the child to catch his ball, followed then, when that goal has been achieved, by some bars of music underlining his consequent sense of satisfaction. Given this way of prolonging the ball game, changes of time signature may be introduced to test the newly acquired technique by speeding the movement up or slowing it down—not with the injunction 'Follow the music!', but rather 'Now let's see if we can bounce the ball a little more slowly, and then a little faster'.

I once knew a 7-year-old who, whenever we began the ball game, invariably said 'Play the piano—I can't do it if you don't!' It goes without saying that his greatest achievement was made the day the piano stayed shut! In another version of the same exercise, ultimate achievement consisted in responding immediately to the slightest musical variation. In both cases, the relationship between music and movement will have played a vital role. These two exercises may well have looked virtually identical on the surface, but the underlying *intention*—that which shaped their internal organization—was by no means the same.

Again, it is possible—perhaps even probable—that the children given this exercise with a view to increasing musical sensitivity may at the same time have improved their ability to catch the ball, and in much the same way those who did it as an exercise in the development of technique may simultaneously have increased their awareness of the close relations between music and movement (as indeed suggested by the 7-year-old boy's remark as quoted above).

It is on reciprocal influences such as these, on that element of the work in question carried out more or less unconsciously, that Eurhythmics partly depends for its success and in which the secret of its economy to some extent resides. Which, however, does not justify any inference or implicit belief to the effect that one thing leads to another, and vice versa (!). On the contrary, one must have very clear intentions in order to be ready to seize upon anything in the exercise which may be of immediate help to them, or on another occasion to take advantage of any abilities which the exercise may have improved as an added bonus.

In one of his earliest writings, Dalcroze—'who considered nothing alien to him if of human origin' (!),[5] and whose patriotism was

---

[5] Cf. Homo sum: humani nil a me alienum puto'—'I am a human being, and consider nothing alien that is of human origin. (Terence, *Heauton Timorumenos*, 77). (Translator's note)

matched only by his sense of humour—encouraged drill-sergeants to march their men in time to shifting key signatures (3/4, common time, etc.) and varying tempi, as a counter to the invariable 'one, two; one, two' which inevitably favours the left foot and right arm. Quite apart from the fact that by being less mechanical the march would also, in his view, become springier and less tiring, he declared himself ready to prove that soldiers exposed to this sort of exercise would have developed a sense of musical rhythm *as an added bonus* (1905: 34)!

It must be doubted (surely?) whether a programme aimed at softening up the conditions of military training while at the same time promoting artistic awareness would have held any appeal for the appropriate authorities. After all, the intention by which he was motivated here can hardly be considered interchangeable with that of, say, identifying the elements of military music designed to stimulate battlefield enthusiasm . . .

Thanks to the psychology of personal growth, we are today better informed than ever before on the way in which concepts develop and on the general mechanisms underlying different types of training. Those areas in particular to which Eurhythmics has the most to offer—space, time, and the relations between them—have been the subject of advanced studies by which we are better enabled to understand the child's viewpoint at different ages, the way in which he thinks and behaves, and the steps by which he reaches the stage of adult thought.[6] Rhythmicians find such information invaluable on two counts: it steers them clear of trial-and-error methods and guards against sudden surprises in their work with children, especially when there is no formal programme of education to guide them in their choice of content; and it enables them (whether dealing with adults or children) to break a complex problem down into simpler components calling upon skills already mastered in earlier stages.

Generally speaking, it is helpful for a teacher to know how to identify the cause of any difficulty encountered, and especially to be able to distinguish between those that may be overcome with more training and those suggesting that the exercise is not rightly matched to students' current level of accomplishment. Rhythmicians are, however, fairly well insured against these risks, so long as they bear in mind that, following Dalcrozian theory, the progress of the exercises

---

[6] See, for further details, Part 3 (Ch. 5).

they set should by definition be subordinated to their students' *demonstrated* attainments as well as to their *potential for personal expressiveness*. The latter in any case was the subject of special attention on the part of Dalcroze. Noting to what extent adults differed from children in this respect, he went on to insist on the need for a difference of approach between the two. He expatiated on this subject with such insight that I cannot resist quoting him here. It is important, he says (1926*b*: 12),

to respect constantly the child's spontaneity by adapting exercises to it, be they physical or musical. In adult lessons, however, the teacher has the difficult task of arousing motor instincts which have been lying dormant, of imparting a joyful freedom to limbs hitherto bound and held in the frozen prison of conventionality, and to release into real life organisms too long held in thrall to the lifestyle of the ultra-civilized.

Even if reality admits to some exceptions, and we now have more numerous and sophisticated ways of differentiating children from adults and children from one another, even so, such thoughts as 'respecting spontaneity' or 'arousing dormant instincts' still head the list of prominent concerns to the rhythmician. And if our words have changed, if the beneficiaries, whether children or adults, are no longer rigorously sorted on the basis of their self-expressive potential, we are daily able to verify that this double imperative has lost none of its *raison d'être*.

The Period of Instruction

A course of instruction normally reaches a self-defined end. In theory, you follow an instruction course in swimming until you have learnt to swim, in painting or a foreign language until you feel you can get by without the instructor's help, in an academic or scholarly subject until you pass a qualifying examination in it. The planned length of such a course will be based on the level of achievement you are expected to attain plus various associated factors such as seasonal considerations, the length of the academic year, and how many hours per week or day can be devoted to the subject in view of your other commitments and physical stamina.

More often than not, the instructor in any given branch of study is only concerned with one of these functions, or very few of them at most. His course will be given over a one- or two-year period; or he may be involved with the same pupils for ten days in a row, or for an hour a week over three months; or whatever. And the teaching in question hardly lends itself to more than one or two such possible formats. Rhythmics, on the other hand, is accustomed to them all, and the same rhythmics teacher is liable to have to work within a large number of them either successively or simultaneously.

Thus for any given circumstance it should be possible to devise an appropriate rhythmics instruction period by asking oneself the following questions:

What are the pupils there for—just information, or 'formation'?

If the former, how long is the instruction to take—two days or two weeks? And how long in each day—two hours?—a whole morning? —longer?

If the latter, are we talking about a general extension of personal development, or something complementary to a given aspect, or something specifically professional? Is it to be regarded as a discipline in its own right or as an auxiliary subject? Will the pupils be following it at the rate of one day per month? One hour? Two or more hours per week?

Has no particular time limit been set on the period in which we shall be working together? Or are we in fact restricted to a single academic year? Or is the course expected to extend over two or three years?

Is this period of time to culminate in some sort of final examination? Or will it be punctuated by periodic assessments? Or will it be entirely free of such constraints?

Such questions will give rise to various combinations of answers depending on the level involved, on whether instruction is given privately or institutionally, on the type of establishment incorporating rhythmics in the structure of its syllabus, and whether it is there treated as a subject in its own right or as part of a more wide-ranging course. We will survey some of these possible formats in the following pages and see what practical or educational consequences they may entail.

STATE SCHOOLS

The rhythmics teacher in a state school can generally count upon at least one academic year in which to set his work up. The subject may in fact be taught over a period of two or more years—this is becoming increasingly common in parts of Switzerland—but it doesn't follow that the same class will consist of the same pupils at each higher grade, nor that the same teacher will continue to take them.

He will see his pupils once a week for a period of anything from 20 to 45 minutes.[7] Thus it will be seen that rhythmics has a very small part to play in state education, its part being reckoned the 'minimum indispensable' by the heads or teachers of those schools which have taken it up. In fact, its role in the school syllabus is largely regarded, in the secondary and later primary stages, as more of a complement to either musical or physical education, while in nursery schools and reception classes it is perceived, rather, as providing a basis for the acquisition of skills relating to spatio-temporal perception and structurization. These different functions become more obvious to the extent that greater collaboration is achieved between rhythmics teachers and those in other areas of the school syllabus.

In Switzerland—where, however, its teaching is by no means widespread—it remains one of the few subjects entirely free from the constraints of an official examination. This distinction has the advantage of giving the teacher a free hand in the planning of his course, with the notable result that he can take account of the 'group personality' of each particular class. Thus the teacher is confronted with various possible ways of achieving the aim he will have set himself, as illustrated by the following plan (from Ruth Gianadda):

To enable me to form some idea of each class I generally put a variety of exercises into effect over the first few lessons, and then, on the basis of what I observe in them, try to go forward in the direction that seems to open itself up. One class may respond very favourably to the physical side of the exercises and express itself quite easily. Another may be more 'academic', or evince greater powers of reasoning. In every case I try to enable the children to achieve as great a level of autonomy as possible in the time they are to spend with me: primarily in the sense of motor control, but also in the social sense, in their dealings with one another, and in a creative sense, in their dealing with themselves. This last-named aspect strikes me as the most interesting one to concentrate on in school rhythmics, as it is the one to which by far the least attention is paid during the rest of the week.[8]

This statement of a personal point of view helps underline this important fact: that when a school decides to incorporate rhythmics in

[7] Here, as elsewhere, certain details and illustrations of continental timetabling are simplified, summarized, or omitted from the English translation where they do not add significantly to the point at issue, and may in any case now be out of date. (Translator's note)

[8] Ruth Gianadda (Geneva), interview recorded 31 Oct. 1979.

its syllabus it is not so much a subject as a *person* which it is welcoming aboard. The very broad margin of individual freedom encouraged by rhythmics on the part of its teachers necessarily means that the continuance of rhythmics instruction throughout the school rests more often than not entirely upon their shoulders, for its existence depends upon the goodwill of the directors, who in turn will judge it by the image it presents in the person of the teacher they engage.

Although rhythmics may be released from statutory evaluation in the corpus of academic work, it nevertheless has an important part to play in community functions (demonstrations, exhibitions, etc.) such as take place on open days and similar public occasions. Performance, though, is only one facet of school rhythmics. It is not an end itself but only one possible achievement arising from a year of work. It usually takes but very few lessons to put together a presentation based on the training and the skills acquired in the months immediately preceding. This means that only one hour a week over a year or two is already likely to produce appreciable results, bearing in mind that there are often more than twenty pupils to a class, and that they will certainly not all have started off with the same degree of aptitude.

UNIVERSITIES AND HIGHER EDUCATION

At this level, there are two main branches of activity. One is the training of rhythmics teachers as in Geneva, and the other is the instruction in rhythmics at university level, as, for example, in North America and Germany, where it is incorporated into a general curriculum as a separate discipline. In the former case it is the bedrock of the syllabus; in the latter, it is part of the music course, where it may be expected to produce a level of achievement appropriate to that of the further education of which it forms a part. The rhythmics teacher will therefore have to bear these considerations in mind when devising his particular course. Equally, he will have to keep abreast of what goes on in related subjects with a view to making such reference to this as may be appropriate to his own course at any given time. He will therefore be putting to immediate use the *raison d'être* of rhythmics as it applies at this level—namely, his ability to show the relationships between all the various musical studies, including movement, and different activities of the individuals concerned.

After each year of study (in which the student will generally have had several rhythmics lessons each week) there will be an examination or some other form of evaluation to assess the level he has reached and, if so warranted, to sanction his admission to the next higher level.

Long-term Projects

TERTIARY LEVEL

Here it will be appropriate to remind ourselves that Eurhythmics was originally conceived as being *for adults*. It was with his students at the Geneva Conservatory that Dalcroze first put his original insights to the test. This gave him the advantage of a clear-cut vision of the goals attainable at the very highest level, thus implying the degree of access to all the concepts and techniques (musical ones, in this instance) which the mature individual is capable of mastering. Dalcroze himself (1916*a*: 11) asserted the conviction that his experiments 'would be of benefit to the most cultivated of intellects and the most accomplished of talents, and could lead composers into entirely novel forms of expression'.

Among the current long-term projects in Dalcroze education for adults, the main course for the training of teachers is the full time three or four year course involving rhythmics, *solfège*, piano improvisation, practical teaching, with other related branches. This course, which exists in Geneva, aims to provide teachers of sufficient skill to train not only children and amateurs but also other teachers or advanced students. Such a course is not practical in other countries, for a variety of reasons. Consequently, a large variety of courses has been developed according to the appropriate conditions: foundation courses (full time, or part of a general foundation course), short full-time courses, short or long part-time courses, the latter being continued over the period of tertiary level training. Such courses can also be devised for postgraduates to enhance either teaching skills or the skills of professional musicians. Courses might also be devised for artists in other fields (such as dance, drama, the visual arts, and architecture). Within the field of professional musicians there are possibilities for many specific courses—for example, for singers, conductors, and students in opera schools.

EURHYTHMICS IN MUSIC SCHOOLS AND CONSERVATOIRES

Thus we see that Dalcroze was always thinking of the adult musician, and was concerned to spare him tiring efforts at an age when his physical development was in course of being completed—and when he would therefore be finding it very difficult to acquire new habits. It was to this end that he put forward the hypothesis that the sooner the student was put in contact with the principles he recommended, the sooner would his skills as a musician blossom and flourish. From then on he continued to promote the idea of the *long-term project* working side by side with his own ideas of musical instruction, so that it would be impossible to dispense with this notion without cutting Eurhythmics off from one of its major dimensions, namely, the development of musical capabilities.

It is under this rubric that Eurhythmics has been put into practice by those conservatoires and music schools which have taken it up. Within this framework rhythmics first precedes, then completes and deepens the study of an instrument. At the same time, it develops the student's creative and expressive powers by means of an original approach to harmony and ear training, especially through the medium of improvisation in all its forms, this being pivotal to the Dalcrozian method. It thereby affords a favourable introduction both to modern music and to that of other times and cultures.

It follows that the rhythmics instructor in a music school will see his work as a continued progression, as a form of training that may go on being pursued for as long as his pupils continue to attend it. Thus even what might be called the 'initiation period' sets in train, from a pre-cognitive level, a Dalcrozian education destined to be extended year after year by the acquisition of all the basic essentials for the development of a musical ear as well as for musical practice. Initiation, as the word implies, is therefore a *beginning*, and not, as is widely believed, a sort of pre-preparation to which the pupil must be subjected while 'waiting' until he is old enough to do something else (such as learning music by traditional methods!). 'I really have to do battle against this idea of rhythmics as nothing but a *basis* for something if I want parents to entrust their children to me from the age of 7,' says Esther Messmer, who teaches rhythmics at a German-Swiss conservatoire.[9] And she is not alone in this. Perhaps in the attitude of some parents we have to recognize an element of distrust as to the effectiveness, beyond a certain age, of a form of teaching which looks more like fun than what they have come to think of as 'proper work'! Such prejudice is

[9] Interview recorded 10 Oct. 1979.

not new, nor is it restricted to music education. Dalcroze himself observed in 1916:

A chasm yawns between primary education, as prescribed by Fröbel and Pestalozzi as a logical consequence of their thinking, and the instruction imposed upon adolescents by an age-old routine. It would seem that no sooner does a child get into secondary education than the school curriculum sets out to make him forget his own existence as a child. (1916a: 12)

It often happens that the Dalcroze instructor teaching rhythmics in a school of music is at the same time charged with the teaching of basic musical skills (*solfège*)[10] as such—and of harmony, in higher classes—such topics being subject to regular examination. At the Conservatoire de La Chaux-de-Fonds, for instance, Mathilde Reymond-Sauvain, herself a former pupil of Dalcroze, has long been teaching all of these, spreading her instruction over the whole period of study from beginners' classes to the gaining of a diploma in a given instrument. The results of a unified musical education afforded throughout the curriculum from childhood to adulthood will be readily appreciated: in a related field, the spectacular results of the Kodály method, which in Hungary has been applied on a national scale with unflagging enthusiasm throughout the child's schooling, bear striking witness to this fact.[11]

At the Institut Jaques-Dalcroze in Geneva, rhythmics and *solfège* are generally taught by the same teacher and integrated one with another, rhythmics being incorporated into *solfège* lessons and vice versa. And music benefits from this; for the pupil sees it from the outset as something relevant to him, something he can experiment with, which helps him progress in motor exercises, and into which he finds himself drawn by the pleasantest and most enjoyable of means.

RHYTHMICS AND PRIVATE TUITION

Equally long-term will be the plan of campaign encompassed by those who elect to teach privately.

---

[10] *Solfège* encompasses all the activities relating to pitch, aural and vocal training, as well as reading and writing musical scores. In the Latin countries, emphasis is placed on developing the ability to name notes while singing. For all these diverse activities the Dalcroze approach uses an original set of techniques (as described in this book), and aims above all to develop *inward listening* and mental representations of musical elements through the internalization of physical awareness. It is in this sense that the word *solfège* should be understood throughout this book.

[11] See Szönyi 1976.

Having moved on from the idea of reforming musical education, Dalcroze was able from an early date to make claims for the positive effect of Eurhythmics, whatever the age range to which it was applied, on one's personal attitude and behaviour, accompanied by an improvement in powers of attention and concentration, an increase in the speed of adaptation, and a mastery of physical reactions and movements—not to mention a greater alertness in mental powers, memory improvement, and greater ease of expression both of oneself and of one's relations with the world. This discovery, which led him so often to describe his method not just as an 'education into rhythm' but also as an 'education by means of rhythm', underlies so many private courses and schools of Eurhythmics where everyone, whether child or adult, may be expected to experience personal development of a type that will continue to make itself felt for the rest of their life. In this case no examination, in theory, is necessary to determine a pupil's suitability for admission or for promotion to the next higher level, nor is any level of final attainment set which might otherwise restrict the abilities to be acquired. The pupil is there for pleasure, and remains there as long as he likes.

Anyone who takes an interest in children's extracurricular activities knows how difficult it is nowadays to engage their full attention (or that of their parents!). So many options are open to them in this area that the temptation is great to try them all out one by one, whether 'to keep up with the Joneses', or 'just to give it a whirl', or simply 'for the sake of doing something', with a consequent readiness to switch to something else at a moment's notice. Eurhythmics is not immune to this customary fate. Even so, however, there are Eurhythmics specialists who achieve the miracle of retaining many of their pupils for a very long time. Such, for example, is the case with Liliane Favre-Bulle, director of the School of Eurhythmics at Nyon (Vaud, Switzerland). 'Many are the children', she says, 'who have worked their way through the whole course from the age of 4 to the brink of adulthood.'[12] If one thing strikes her as important for the continuing viability of the private school it is the obvious delight taken by the pupils themselves in the annual end-of-year public display which they always put on:

Children just *love* getting ready for something. Doing exercises for their own sake is not what counts for them; but once you start building a whole

---

[12] Interview recorded 6 Nov. 1979.

experience *based on* the exercises they have done, they feel themselves really committed. I don't think I have ever seen a single one refuse to dress up! Each class involves itself in other classes' work, and sometimes several classes will collaborate. This spurs them on and gives them ideas for what they want to be doing next year. 'What are we going to do next time?'—that's the thought in everybody's mind at the beginning of the autumn term!

If the prospect of a combined-effort public performance undoubtedly encourages both them and their parents to continue the course, it is equally certain that what keeps their interest up throughout the year is the enjoyment they get out of each and every lesson: 'If there's one thing I cannot bear, it's reading boredom in my pupils' eyes!' says Valéry Roth of Paris. 'So every lesson has to be for them an opportunity to discover, to invent, to give of one's personal best.[13] To which Monique Bosshard of Lausanne adds: 'What makes a lesson successful is not the number of activities they have carried out or notions they have acquired—rather, it is the extent to which each session has enabled the child to blossom out and simply *feel good*. A line of work for the whole year sketches itself out little by little at the same time as technical requirements appear.'[14] For her part, Liliane Favre-Bulle also emphasises the inherent call to *happiness* in the Dalcrozian approach. This is apparently a hackneyed term nowadays, and the currently preferred term is 'a feeling of well-being', which seems somewhat modest. But none of this detracts from the generally accepted fact that any Eurhythmics lesson devoid of any sense of *joy* (of which Dalcroze observed (1915*b*: 93) that 'it makes its appearance on the very day when we are conscious of having made some progress within ourselves') would be deprived of one of its most basic Dalcrozian qualities.

As for adults who do it for pleasure, they can continue with a course for as long as they find Eurhythmics helpful to them in their daily lives. It is with this in view that the instructor will from session to session endeavour to 'enable the pupil to find his own potential deep within himself'.[15] Nor is it unusual to find that Eurhythmics so becomes a part of their life that adults once embarked upon a course continue to renew their subscription year after year almost automatically—perhaps on the model of those faithful members of a choir for whom communal singing once a week is something that

---

[13] Interview recorded 24 Oct. 1979.
[14] Interview recorded 8 Nov. 1979.
[15] M. Bosshard, interview recorded 8 Nov. 1979.

happens of its own accord! Thus such Dalcrozians as Monica Jaquet in her Geneva courses, Valéry Roth (died 1988) at her Paris studio, Jeanne-A. Bachmann at the School of Music at Le Locle, Edith Naef at the Institut Jaques-Dalcroze—to name but a few—count amongst their pupils adults who have been with them for eight years, or ten, fifteen, twenty, and sometimes even more, and still with unflagging enthusiasm! This of course implies that even though some topics are encountered time after time, and even if the same exercise is repeated later in one guise or another, the instructor must be committed to continuous creation, unbounded imagination, and the constant renewal within himself of the well-springs of living lessons. I shall hardly be accused of exaggeration if I maintain that for this reason the Dalcrozian is well insured against ageing even when well advanced in years!

Medium-term Projects

There remain other plans of action, which we might refer to as medium-term projects, whose aim is to reach a point at which the pupil can dispense with the aid of Eurhythmics in getting on with his everyday life. Such are cases in which the Eurhythmics expert has a therapeutic role to play.

THERAPEUTIC EURHYTHMICS

The variety of fields impinged upon by Eurhythmics, coupled with the range of abilities it is capable of developing, make of it a notably flexible and economical instrument in the hands of one who undertakes to be of help to a person experiencing difficulty in realizing—or rediscovering—his latent capabilities.

At a very early date Dalcroze's own followers could see what part Eurhythmics had to play in the then little-explored field of education, or re-education, for those afflicted with mental, sensory, and motor handicaps. Even before the end of the first quarter of the twentieth century such people as Juan Llonguerras of Barcelona and Mimi Scheiblauer of Zurich—to quote but the best-known examples— were starting up courses designed for the blind and for children either deaf or mentally handicapped. The latter, indeed, founded in her home town a professional school which remains even today one of the most important in Switzerland. Similar projects have been undertaken by Dalcrozians in virtually every European country, and in Geneva the value of Eurhythmics as a method of 'psycho-motor re-education' was already recognized by the medical profession, thanks to the work of, notably, Angèle Porta and Jo Baeriswyl, and thanks, too, to the support accorded Jaques-Dalcroze by Dr Weber-Bauler and Professors Flournoy and Claparède.[16]

The therapeutic application of Dalcrozian Eurhythmics is nowadays one of several recognized practices referred to in French under the general term *thérapie psychomotrice*, and it will be encountered wherever the need is felt for such a facility:

State schools: In German-speaking Switzerland, for instance, Leni Reinhard's successors work with children of certain special classes. In the French-speaking cantons, many development classes benefit from Eurhythmics lessons. Within this framework, the teacher's planned course will necessarily be influenced by the length of the school year; but this is a less important consideration than that of furnishing the pupils from week to week with an indispensable means of opening up and supporting the harmony of their everyday lives.

Specialist institutions for retarded children or those exhibiting serious maladjustment problems, sensory restrictions, or physical handicaps: The number of Dalcrozians engaged in work of this type throughout the world is practically uncountable. All the same, we ought to mention, in England, the pioneer work carried out until recently by Priscilla Barclay in a hospital for severely handicapped children and young adults, some even bedridden, who were unable to profit from the most basic level of educational structure. Long-term work is needed here, though of varying degrees according to the severity of the handicaps encountered and the resources and principles of the particular institutions ready to open their doors to this type of treatment. Throughout the period allotted, the aim of the Eurhythmics teacher will be—whether working with patients individually or taking them in small groups—to encourage the child (or adult) to discover his or her personal capacities and to learn how to make full use of them.

Private establishments: We mention here, in French-speaking Switzerland, the *Atelier Monique Bosshard*, Lausanne, and the Geneva-based *Centre d'Expression psychomotrice* directed by Micheline Duchosal and

[16] For further information, see Dutoit-Carlier 1965: 386 ff.

the present author, both pupils of Claire-Lise Lombard-Dutoit.[17]
It is in this context that the psycho-motor therapist will be confronted
by the widest and most varied spectrum of problems. In the normal
course of a week's work she will turn her attention from the slightest
physical handicap to the most crippling infirmity: from the young lad
who, albeit top of his class, is agonizing over his omission from the
football team, to the young autistic adult incapable of verbal communication; from the mentally handicapped child of three who cannot
yet walk, to the university scholar experiencing problems with spatial
orientation. But whatever the problem is, whatever the impetus
behind the fact of seeking treatment (whether by private initiative or
medical recommendation), the therapist's plan can be summarized in
two sentences: (1) work with this person right up to the time when, if
possible, he or she can dispense with your help, and only up till then;
(2) consequently, direct all your work in pursuit of the greatest
possible autonomy, not just in the limited field of the handicap itself,
but in all other areas of activity which it either impedes, or, at least, is
felt to do so.

How long it will take for such a scheme to achieve its ends of course
varies with the severity of the case. Speaking for myself, I have seen
such schemes 'completed' in everything from four months to eight
years. One might reasonably say, however, that so long as no external
hindrance is put in the way of a therapeutic charge an optimum
average length would be about two to three years. Generally, in
accordance with a phenomenon well known to specialists, the child
makes enormous strides in the first year of psychomotor therapy,
sometimes even within the first few weeks. Such spectacular progress,
by its very nature, induces the parents into a premature declaration of
their satisfaction. All the same, an extra year will allow the child to
consolidate what he has acquired and reliably transfer to his social
surroundings the progress which has so far been exhibited only in the
family circle and under therapy. In very severe cases associated with
irreversible handicap it is often right to plan for the long term with an
individual, in the interests of affording permanent support and
encouragement. In such cases the therapist will generally be wise
enough to 'pass the torch on' to one of her colleagues after three or

---

[17] The latter is also equipped to function as a training centre for Dalcrozians hoping
to specialize in therapy.

more years, in order to allow a period of renewal on either side—
always provided, of course, that it is possible to do so.

Psycho-motor therapy centres engaging one or more Eurhythmics
specialists are not particularly common. Many Dalcrozians, however
—not just in Europe but in many other countries throughout the
world—include in their private curricula a specially designed course
for children or adults with psycho-motor problems, and it is by no
means rare for doctors or specialists in childhood malformations to be
sufficiently interested in their work to send them patients for treatment.

Short-term Schemes

TRAINING PERIODS

Short-term schemes, finally, are those which come into operation
when the teacher conducts a *re-training* or an *introductory* course in
Eurhythmics. This may involve a very brief and compressed period of
work, or perhaps several encounters more widely spaced over a period
of time. In either case the teacher will have to make a choice: whether
to offer a general survey by using as many exercises as possible, or to
concentrate on one or two aspects which can then be dealt with at
greater depth.

The danger in the first case is that of imparting only a superficial
idea of Eurhythmics, thereby losing the possibility of properly understanding it. On the other hand, this approach is capable of opening up
broader horizons to the trainees. In the second case, the opposite
danger is that of conveying the impression that Eurhythmics is
restricted to the particular subjects covered. But these subjects will
have the advantage of being grasped from within, and the limited
experience gained by the trainees will then be more easily extended
into the running of their everyday lives.

These risks are considerably reduced when the training session
brings together Eurhythmics specialists or those who are already
widely experienced in it. Generally, the object of the exercise will be to
deepen one or another of its aspects in the knowledge that everyone
can be expected to relate it to a wider context. Sometimes the other
approach will be preferred, in which case the aim will be to enable the
participants to broaden their horizons while refreshing their ideas.
But when the course involves trainees who may be learning about

Eurythmics for the first time, it is well worth while taking the trouble to examine these options carefully.

Adopting the first method, that of a broad and varied general survey, presupposes on the part of the participants an ability to synthesize, to come to terms less with the letter than with the spirit of the thing—qualities often lacking in novices, especially when they are just itching to get into 'experimental methods'! Any Dalcrozian who has had occasion to conduct introductory classes will at some time or another have come up against the obstinacy of trainees who would much rather remain sitting down, pencil in hand, than risk letting a single exercise escape the clutches of their collectomania. Anne Fischer (France), with considerable experience in this field, enjoyed a notable success the day when she was able to persuade one of the participants to let go of her pencil: 'If you actually *take part* in the exercises from now till the end of the morning, I promise you will have not the slightest difficulty in remembering everything when you eventually come to write your notes up. And if I'm wrong about that, I also promise I will give you as much of my time as you may need in order to get your notes straightened out.'[18] Not only did the teacher gain from this deal, but so also did the participant; for the exercises she was able to remember after doing them have truly become part of herself: she knows precisely to what *personal experience* each of her particular notes refers, whereas, if she had remained glued to her chair, they would soon have become a dead letter to her.

This working method therefore makes it essential for the Eurhythmics teacher to plan ahead so as to allow sufficient time to return to exercises already practised, either by inviting trainees to take notes and make free use of them later, or by seeking to establish with them an appropriate synthesis by which to illuminate the meaning of each particular exercise.

The Dalcrozian who opts for the second solution and sets himself the task of exploring a limited range of fields in greater depth will, for his part, have faith in the power of Eurhythmics to establish very quickly a 'line of communication' between the individual's opposite poles. Furthermore, he will trust in his own ability to make the trainees realize that they are dealing with a general mechanism capable of being adapted from their single experience of it to a wide range of situations. And yet, for the same reasons as quoted above,

[18] Anne Fischer, private communication, 1979.

this 'faith' alone is not enough. I can remember dolefully hearing the remark of a former pupil of mine (a remark which she evidently regarded as a compliment) by which she informed me that an exercise in piano improvisation which I formerly used to illustrate a particular principle was still being used by her in its original form, without her ever having thought to change its musical content.

The Eurhythmics teacher who proceeds in this centrifugal fashion should first assure himself that the heightened personal experience which he seeks to instill into his trainees is actually matched by their ability to assimilate it. There, too, a minute spent on discussion with a view to establishing together what different avenues of application are opened up by a given exercise will help to widen the field of information while at the same time defining it more clearly.

Imagine that you have it in mind to 'discover' Italian painting. What will you do—traipse around after a guide who will give you a one-hour tour of the Uffizi Gallery?—or spend the same amount of time in the company of a connoisseur, looking only at his two or three favourite paintings? Trick question? Don't let it fool you: there do exist some very good guides and some quite mediocre connoisseurs! Either way, the visit will have succeeded in its aim if it gives you the urge to make an early return visit on your own account!

Initiation . . . In our sphere of interest we understand the word 'initiation' in both its meanings (limiting its reference to time): that of 'giving or receiving the basic principles' of a type of education (in a science, a discipline, an art, etc.), or that of 'affording or obtaining a greater or lesser overall view'. Both cases imply the beginning of something, an *introduction* to a study which can be followed through to the point at which one may describe oneself as truly 'initiated', this time in the strictest sense of the word.

Hence *initiation* means any teaching addressed to beginners in the subject. Some pedagogues have devoted all their attention to making this initiation the bedrock on which all future training may be built. Their approaches, individually recognised as such, sometimes betray their object by the very title they go under. Thus we have the *Bon Départ* ('Flying Start') method, the purpose of which is to establish a good basis for subsequent acquisitions in reading, writing, and academic skills;[19] also the Willems musical initiation designed for children

[19] An illustration of this method appears in the course of the film *Yvon, Yvonne* (1968), by Claude Champion and Agnès Contat.

as well as adults, whose underlying philosophy additionally enables it to be studied as 'initiation' in the full sense of the word.[20]

Besides acting as a means of initiation into music for young children and beginners (its strong point being to impart all the elements of a musical training together with the art of putting them to use) Dalcrozian Eurhythmics is essentially, and especially in introductory courses, a form of initiation into itself—that is, into the discovery of the bonds uniting music to bodily movement, and of the influence which these two activities may bring to bear upon our various aptitudes.

The fact that Dalcroze's ideas took their point of departure from the higher levels of musical study, combined with their workability with younger and younger children—which therefore makes them better trained in the long run—enables us to account for the existence of so many highly sophisticated exercises in Eurhythmics. These are designed for the mastery of often quite complex musical concepts and presuppose a high degree of technical performance. We may mention, for those familiar with such terms, canons based on bars of alternating simple and compound time, the immediate apprehension of doubling or tripling the speed of a given rhythm, and metrical dissociations ('five in the time of four', etc.) calling for a corresponding physical dissociation. It is hard enough to appreciate the level of attainment implied by such exercises by simply watching the education of children in it; what is more, the very real ease with which well-trained students succeed in performing them tends to veil their inherent difficulty from the eyes of the untrained observer. Eurhythmics, therefore, in its creator's mind, is essentially a long-term experience. But in foreseeing very early on its wide range of possible applications, Dalcroze himself was inevitably obliged to open the door to relatively brief practical encounters. Can we therefore really be surprised today to see how often the latter take precedence over his original conception?

The rhythm of modern life does not encourage people to pursue a freely chosen course for more than a few years at a time. We seek so much and find so little; though it is equally true that we seek in all directions at once, for fear of passing the essential by, even if it thereby runs the risk of even more certainly evading our grasp. In these circumstances Eurhythmics cannot reasonably impose on those who are interested in it such long and intensive studies as would require some sort of 'act of faith' or commitment on their part. It

[20] Cf. *inter alia*, Willems 1976 and 1954.

would indeed be letting itself down if it withdrew from a society which failed to provide the sort of conditions most favourable to its proper expansion, or if it reserved its riches only to a few 'initiates'—for was it not born of the very desire to open up to everyone what was previously accessible only to a few?

It was perhaps a clairvoyance of our present time that led Dalcroze to observe (1916a: 15):

I consider that in matters of art and social endeavour, the amount of time that one devotes to it does not play as important a part as is generally supposed. *Sustained application* throughout that period is the real requirement! . . . What makes a dilettante is his lack of utter devotion to the studies he undertakes over a greater or lesser period of time, his simple assumption that the fact of enrolling for such a course is equivalent to making progress in it!

PART II

3

EURHYTHMICS:
ENDS AND MEANS

Returning to Sources

By 1910 Jaques-Dalcroze had clearly defined not only the aim of
Eurhythmics and the results it could claim to achieve, but also, in
general terms, the working methods available for such achievements.
Two articles published at this time (in 1909 and 1910) yield an
essential resumé of his thoughts in this direction. They were to
undergo no substantial modification as a result of later developments;
on the contrary, the latter, while further clarifying the Dalcrozian
approach, would more often than not confirm it by subsequent
experience. On the other hand, Eurhythmics was to enjoy considerable
enrichment from the enlargement of its horizons due to its many
inevitable bifurcations at the hands of practitioners with a variety of
personalities, and for this reason it is necessary for us to look back to
their common sources. From several points of view it would in fact be
difficult to follow through the original Dalcrozian train of thought by
simply extrapolating backwards from observations of current practice,
for which purpose we should also have to take into account our
recognition of several lines of evolution—in education, in the arts
of movement, and in present-day music. But in familiarizing ourselves with the original concept as first expounded by the creator
of Eurhythmics, we shall have at our disposal a suitable frame
of reference for enabling us to come to grips with the essential
unity of Dalcrozian thought which underlies current applications of
Eurhythmics in spite of their variations—or even of their (real or
imagined) differences. This return to sources will provide modern
Dalcrozian practitioners with a valuable opportunity for rediscovering
those basic principles central to their own development, thus enabling
them to assess what portion of that inheritance remains of greatest
value to them in their everyday work.

Like the great majority of educational innovators, it was by focusing on faults and failures that Dalcroze managed little by little to construct the edifice of his sytem, thereby opening up entirely new horizons. As analysed by Dalcroze, such faults and failures were manifest in three areas: in music education as such, in the limited accomplishment of future professional musicians, and in the motor abilities of the first students of Eurhythmics.

Gaps in Music Education

As to music education, Dalcroze started from the following observation. Hitherto, the study of music had been the prerogative of only a small number of individuals who were so to speak 'predestined' for it by a natural aptitude and a favourable environment, which would have resulted in their early recognition by the experts charged with their instruction in the realm of music. Nowadays, of course, music is, in principle, accessible to each and every pupil: it forms part of every school curriculum, and clearly is no longer restricted to pupils of manifest ability in this specialized field.

What qualities should be considered indispensable to all prospective professional musicians? Dalcroze summarised them as follows:

refinement of hearing, nervous sensitivity (*sensibilité nerveuse*), a feeling for rhythm—i.e. an accurate sense of the relationships between movement in time and movement in space—and, lastly, the faculty of spontaneously *externalizing* their inward sensations (1909: 64).

He adds:

Only if all these qualities are found together, each and every one, albeit at the embryonic stage, in the make-up of the future musician—only then will modern musical studies be able to produce a true artist, for they prove that music *lies within him*, is an essential ingredient of his constitution, and can be developed by the very exercise of these faculties. But suppose such faculties do not exist—how then can learning an instrument be expected to develop them . . .? (ibid.)

He subsequently enlarges on the point as follows (1912*a*: 47):

What constitutes a good ear is generally thought to be no more than the ability to name and recognize the relations between the notes one hears. This is wrong. The sounding of notes exhibits other qualities than mere differences of pitch. The ear ought also to appreciate different degrees of sound intensity, of dynamics, of the greater or lesser speed at which sounds succeed one another, of timbre, of everything about the *expressive* quality of music which goes under the name of 'colour'. In my view it is this quality which must be a child's natural possession before one can begin to think positively about a musical future for him.

But, he insists, 'it is the job of education to bring out the child's musical nature' (1912*a*: 46).

In other words, teaching methods which succeeded in the past, when the musical qualities listed above were assumed present in every pupil even before he started 'learning music', are incapable of calling forth aptitudes of which there is no evidence at the outset. This is a significant gap which music education absolutely must fill, otherwise it will be meaningless to make claims for the accessibility of music to everyone. In laying itself open to all, such education may no longer take for granted any specifically musical abilities on the part of its pupils. It must therefore find some way of awaking then developing them in those who have not so far shown natural talent.[1]

In passing, it is remarkable that Dalcroze should have taken such a line at a period when 'musical talent', and especially the sense of rhythm, were still largely considered unteachable—an opinion which has long persisted (cf. Teplov 1966: 358)—even if, paradoxically, everyone paid lip-service to an innate 'right to music'. Dalcroze had to draw particular attention to this contradictory attitude on his contemporaries' part—an attitude which he criticized as leading them to fill music colleges and conservatories with people who were not really suited to them, and for whom instrumental virtuosity was to become an end in itself at the expense of other qualities which remained forever out of their reach. Therefore, as he put it:

it was when I realized that about nine-tenths of the virtuoso students in my class liked music little and understood it less . . . that I conceived the notion of devoting my life to developing the musical abilities of the child, so that they might subsequently be released for instrumental studies in a condition enabling them to turn technique into a way of externalizing and fulfilling themselves . . . instead of devoting it obsequiously to the pursuit of second-hand thoughts and feelings (1909: 65).

[1] These proposals and concerns are of particular relevance in the 1990s in the light of the well-nigh explosive interest in pre-instrumental musical education and the realization of the need for preparation and then assessment and appropriate development of the seeds of musical talent. (Translator's note)

This first aim which he fixed upon—that of plugging the gaps in traditional music education—would remain at the forefront of Dalcroze's ideals throughout all the later refinements of his Eurhythmic method, and every one of its constituent exercises will be seen to contribute towards one or more of those basic musical qualities of which we may remind ourselves as follows:

a refined ear;
nervous sensitivity;
a sense of rhythm;
a spontaneous ability to externalize inward sensations.

As an example, let us consider the following exercise (though many another would do as well), which will lend itself to all the above-mentioned properties if one only takes the trouble to envisage it from different points of view:

The rhythmic figure played at the piano is given in Example 3.1.):

Ex. 3.1.

The pupils each have a ball in their hands. From the piano we hear only the first bar—the four-quaver *anacrusis* of the figure. The pupils then throw their balls in the air on the first crotchet that follows so as to catch them on the second. This means they can make use of the four-quaver interval to get ready for their action and to estimate the exact moment at which the ball must be thrown—i.e., after a period of time equal to that separating each quaver from the one before. Now, the teacher, at the piano, may from time to time vary the tempo of the four-quaver phrase, thereby simultaneously forcing each pupil to evaluate not only the moment at which the ball must be thrown but also the strength that must be imparted to it so that it stays in the air for just the time needed to enable it to be caught not a split second earlier or later than the second crotchet in the bar.

Having to adapt oneself to a spatio-temporal situation which may vary at any moment, and at the same time to maintain, come what may, one's consciousness of the equation $\quad \downarrow = \sqcap \quad$ in the context of the unity of the whole rhythmic phrase, are requirements ideally suited to developing the pupil's *nervous sensitivity* as well as reinforcing his *sense of rhythm*.

If I may add a little aside on this subject: everyone knows how nervous excitement and stage fright may work their effect on the tempo of a performer—instrumentalist, dancer, singer, etc., generally in the direction of greater speed, possibly not unconnected with the faster breathing and pulse-rate experienced in any such situation. Whenever an instructor needs to be assured that a song or a dance will 'keep to the beat' in a public performance, he will do well to get his pupils to practise it beforehand in various different tempi, both faster and slower than the ideal, so that its performance speed may be appreciated as something relative—i.e. by the instinctive comparison of its component parts and passages—rather than as something absolute and automatic, more or less rigidly determined by prior instruction.[2]

Let's go back to the ball-throwing exercise. The teacher may further use it as a way of developing a *refined ear* by adapting it to one or other of the following procedures:

If the four-quaver phrase is played at the piano in ascending scale the pupil has to throw his ball in the air; if it is played in descending scale he must bounce it on the ground. Variation may then be introduced into the actual pitch register and pitch intervals between notes to oblige the ear to make an immediate analysis without benefit of any prior assumption.

Or again: if the first two quavers are sounded a perfect fifth apart (or at any other chosen inverval), the pupils, being arranged in pairs, must exchange balls; if not, they throw them for themselves to catch.

Or even: if the four quavers correspond exactly to the first tetrachord of the major scale then the ball must actually be thrown in the air; if of the *minor* scale, only a pretence of throwing is to take place.

Finally, this exercise can be used as a way of *externalizing the emotive faculties* by being made to take any of the following forms (the pupils now being without their balls):

The four introductory quavers are to be interpreted as expressing either a challenge or an invitation, and on the subsequent two

[2] I am grateful to my mother, herself a rhythmician, for drawing my attention to this point in the course of a round dance with her pupils.

crotchets each pupil must perform some sort of expressive movement reflecting the character and the nuance of what he has just
heard (reaction against an aggressive noise, response to an appeal,
etc.). This also provides a good opportunity for replacing the
pianist with one of the pupils, who during the four-quaver phrase
will initiate some sort of expressive stimulus—physical or vocal—
to which the others will respond either by allowing themselves to be
influenced by him (imitation), or by reacting in contrast against
him.

Awareness of sound cannot be formed except by repeated experiences of the
ear and the voice, nor awareness or rhythm other than by repeated experiences
of movements of the whole body (Dalcroze 1907: 38).

But:

it is not enough to be able to recognize and distinguish sounds in order to lay
claim to a good ear for music. It also requires that external auditory sensations
should create an inner state of consciousness and feeling (1912*a*: 46–7).

Defects in Musical Performance

If it was the deficiencies of music education which clearly pointed out
the aims to be pursued, it was by identifying the defects exhibited by
his trainees for prospective musicianship that Dalcroze was able to
define the field of action which would soon reveal itself as Eurhythmics.
All inadequacies of musical performance, he maintained, whether
vocal or instrumental, exhibit their weakness at the level of rhythmic
understanding or expression. These weaknesses are to be observed in,
for example, speeding natural movements up or slowing them down,
in fudging or blurring the articulation, in failing to follow adequately
as an accompanist, in accentuating too brusquely or not precisely
enough, in an inability to achieve the right proportions in phrasing
and shading, and so on (cf. 1909: 66). 'What is remarkable', he wrote
in 1907 (p. 41), 'is the existence of an instinctive connection between
rhythm, in all its nuances, and *gesture*.' Now there are certain subjects
for whom this connection is realized badly, or with difficulty. Dalcroze
listed these various faults under the general heading *arhythmism*
(cf. 1910: 20–1):[3]

[3] The reader interested in musical arhythmism is directed to the remarkable
chapter of *Souvenirs* which Dalcroze entitled 'Reflections on arhythmism' (1942:
71–84).

inability to maintain a movement for the whole of its natural duration in performance;

. quickening or dragging a movement which should be uniformly maintained;

inability to increase or decrease the speed of movement when necessary;

tendency to jerkiness or 'bittiness' when the movement should be flowing, and vice versa;

starting or finishing too early or too late;

inability to integrate two movements of a different type (fast/slow, supple/rigid, forceful/gentle, etc.);

inability to execute simultaneously two or more contrary types of movement;

inability to shade a movement by continuous gradations (from *piano* to *forte* or vice versa);

inability to match the rhythmic or metric accentuation of a movement to the requirements of musical logic.

'It was in seeking to determine the specific cause of each musical failing, and in finding the means to its correction, that piece by piece I built up my system of rhythmic gymnastics' (1909: 66). Having established the hypothesis that 'all the causes of arhythmism are *physical in nature*' (1910: 20), Dalcroze soon went on to sort them into three categories (which are not unreminiscent of certain major lines of classification nowadays employed in pathological neurophysiology):

1. 'Inability of the brain to convey orders fast enough to the muscles required to execute the movement.' In other words, malfunction is sited at the level of *emission*. This is linked, according to Dalcroze, to the subjects' inability to represent clearly the orders to be transmitted in the available time, and proceeds from a lack of their rhythmic education.

2. 'Inability of the nervous system to transmit these orders faithfully and smoothly, and with complete accuracy of address. 'Malfunction in this case is sited at the level of *transmission*. In these subjects, 'the brain grasps the rhythms properly . . . but the limbs, albeit capable of executing them, fail to do so because the nervous system is in disarray'.

3. 'Inability of the muscles to execute [the movements] accurately.' In these subjects, 'the limbs are incapable . . . of executing orders clearly transmitted from the brain, and nervous impulses [have] no

effect'. Within the system it is here the *carriers out* that fail to perform their task adequately, through weakness or lack of training.

Whatever the cause, Dalcroze evidently regards arhythmism as proceeding from 'lack of harmony and co-ordination between the conceptualization and execution of movement' (1910: 21).

Thus the way is pointed to several broad categories of exercises designed to remedy these deficiencies. Some will need to contribute to the improvement of muscular suppleness and an accurate appreciation of bodily movements; others will aim to improve conceptualization and speed of comprehension; yet others will focus on reducing the length of time taken to react to various types of stimulus and improving the quality of control exercised on the limbs involved, or will seek to eliminate functionless gestures while instigating improved economy of movement. All will thereby contribute 'towards the creation of a swift and unlaboured internal communications system between all the organs of movement and thought' (1909: 67). For:

before committing one's body to service in any art, it is right to perfect the mechanisms of this body, to develop all its faculties and correct its faults. Nor is it even sufficient that such faculties should normally operate instinctively, as is the case with many gifted individuals. For it is also necessary that they operate consciously, so as not to be dependent upon a momentary nervous excitement (1916b: 106).

Dalcroze clearly keeps his musician's aims in sight. His exercise categories, which I list below under his own headings (1910: 21–2), relate particularly to musical performance, whether instrumental, vocal, or even the conductor's actions:

'Exercises which constrain the muscles towards accurate execution of the brain's instructions, whether these orders be of incitement or of inhibition (an interruption or slowing down of the movement);

exercises which seek to automatize series of movements in their many combinations;

exercises teaching how to co-ordinate automatic and voluntary movements;

exercises aiming to eliminate all motor actions resulting from any irrelevant nervous response;

exercises seeking to individualize and discriminate muscular sensations and to improve the sense of body attitude.

The aim of all these exercises, Dalcroze adds, will be:

the improvement of mental concentration, an accurate appreciation of physical economy, a blossoming of personality; and, in addition—through the progressive education of the nervous system—the development of sensitivity in those who have little or none already, or, as the case may be, the harmonization of nervous reactions on the part of those who are highly strung or over-excitable (1910: 22).

It will be observed that such aims are designed to serve other ends, notably those of music education as outlined above. But what will not fail to be noticed also (and Dalcroze would be the first to recognize it) is that, thus articulated and systematized, neither his observations nor his ambitions could be restricted solely to the realm of music. For the latter is but one particular element (even if he himself regards it as being of primordial importance) of a greater whole comprising all those activities capable of being affected with dysfunction at some stage or other of their development. This opens the door to so vast and bewildering an array of possibilities that you would have to rack your brains to think up any possible exceptions to the rule! Might we then not say that the deficiencies here categorized as examples of arhythmism must find their counterparts in many other walks of life? It is not altogether rare to find oneself incapable of, for example, breaking a movement off at just the right moment, or performing two or three different actions at the same time. And such occasions surely lay us open to a charge—whether of physical clumsiness, of slow reaction speed, or of simple inattention.[4]

Inequality in Motor Aptitudes

Jaques-Dalcroze was not slow to realize that the deficiencies he had observed overstepped the boundaries of music alone. In 1907 he had actually noted that 'not a single musician who commits some fault in the expression of musical rhythm fails to exhibit that fault in his own *bodily* make-up' (1907: 41). He had indeed already taken it upon himself to get his pupils to practise with the whole of their body (and not just those parts of it linked to the playing of an instrument). In so doing, he found himself persuaded that the models of rhythmic movement presented by the body—itself so rich in possibilities—ought properly, given adequate training, 'to evoke in pupils' minds

[4] The reader will later come across many descriptions of exercises which could have been inserted at this point, but which I prefer to set in a more concrete context.

clear-cut rhythmical images ranging the whole gamut of dynamic and temporal gradations' (1910: 20). This is exactly what happens in the field of writing, he later pointed out:

A child at school learns to make written marks on a page all the sooner if he has previously been led to practise, with the whole of his body, the spatial movements and dynamic shadings which any line may take in any plane . . . (1932*a*: 4)

On the other hand, he observes, the specialization of any particular part of the body with a view to musical performance lays the ground-work for a limited number of dissociations, and those who have been subjected to such a partial type of education are as embarrassed as anybody else when prompted into dissociations of a different nature. In other words, his working hypothesis was as follows:

Practising a particular rhythm with a particular part of the body does not impart eurhythmic grace to the body as a whole, whereas rhythmic exercises of a general nature may well be readily adapted to particular manifestations of rhythmic activity . . .; for once a person has familiarized himself with fundamental dynamic possibilities in both time and space he will familiarize himself all the more readily with their application to the most diverse of particular purposes (ibid.).

However, he went on, it is a long and arduous task to achieve rhythmical practice of this generalized nature on the part of adults, because their specalized training, combined with their lack of training in other areas, leaves them anchored to motor habits which they can only be trained out of with great difficulty. From this point of view it will therefore be more economical to undertake rhythmic training with children, in whom motor habits have not yet been firmly fixed. In fact, Dalcroze showed himself over-optimistic in imagining that the task would be that much easier with children, and he was not slow to admit it. He had been under the impression that Eurhythmics would lead them smoothly into aptitudes that were crying out to be revealed, and in which traditional education mistakenly failed to take sufficient interest. But it wasn't quite as simple as that, and he was forced to observe (1909: 65) that many children 'do not enjoy an instinctive appreciation of tempo, nor of intervals of time, nor of physical poise', and eventually to conclude that 'as far as motor faculties are concerned, all men are not born equal'. We know today that many motor habits take hold very early on, well before the age of the children Dalcroze

led into rhythmic exercises, and that they depend on several factors—
on their earliest educational experiences, certainly, but also on their
individual characteristics as well as on what some authors, notably
M. Stambak (1963), refer to as their 'motor type'.

Consequently, as Dalcroze remarks (1909: 66), 'this child will
always be running a little slow, that one always fast; one will take
uneven steps, another display no sense of balance . . .'. At the same
time, these observations confirm him in his conviction that rhythmic
education should be undertaken from childhood, for 'all these failings
will, if not corrected in these early years, come out again much later in
the performance of music'.

In particular, he has great expectations of Eurhythmics instruction
in schools, provided that it is regular and comprehensive:

Rhythm plays as important a part in music as sound, and I know from
experience that one benefit of an education which develops natural bodily
rhythms will be the ability to induce a love of music even in those for whom its
sound has little meaning . . . I maintain that practically all those children who
dislike music because they have no ear for it will inevitably come to appreciate
it if their rhythmical faculties are actively developed . . . They will like it *for the
very experience of movement* which it reinforces, and because, for them,
movement is a natural and familiar thing. (1910: 24)

And he adds, maliciously:

You will tell me that it only diminishes music to make it enjoyable to people
who can only appreciate one in two of its properties. And I will tell you that
what really diminishes music is the practice of teaching no more of it than that
single element: virtuosity!

Such laying of groundwork for the arts, however, and such development of the aesthetic sensibilities are merely an additional consequence
by way of bonus, for the goals Eurhythmics sets out to achieve will
naturally be of primary interest to schools. Judge for yourself:

ability to act rapidly, as well as to refrain from acting too rapidly;
ability to act slowly, as well as to refrain from acting too slowly;
ability to pick up a habit fast, and to drop it again with equal
rapidity;
ability to make a rapid response to a question;
ability to concentrate at length.

All these will result from the lively study (enlivened by music which
constantly adapts itself both to the physical abilities of the students

and to the requirements of particular exercises) of the relationships between speed and restraint, strength and flexibility, mobility and immobility, sounds and silences, work and rest, 'in accordance with the laws of balance and alternation which are the laws of Rhythm' (1910: 23).

When it comes to working out the consequences of what has been described above it will be seen that either of two approaches may be adopted. The first—a 'centrifugal' approach—will consist in meeting on their own ground the various domains touched on by the Eurhythmic mode of education, with a view to applying the various exercises to them by ensuring that their content relates to the objectives of each particular domain. As we have seen, each type of exercise developed by Dalcroze is so flexibly defined as to be readily adaptable to the needs of the most varied of domains. I have already enlarged on their range and variety. Clearly, if the most immediate of them involve music education, the expressive potential of the body and the stage, it is because the raw materials of Eurhythmics—music and movement —relate most fundamentally to them. But there are also those who have come to apply exercises based on the same principle to areas as far removed (apparently) from music and movement as the teaching of geography, arithmetic, spelling, and elocution, not to mention the many therapeutic uses mentioned above, which I need not expand on here.

The other approach will be the opposite one of turning Eurhythmics into a separate discipline in its own right, in which the successful completion of each exercise will be an end in itself for the time being, and whose main objective (enough to constitute a whole course in itself!) will be to enable each individual to draw the maximum benefit from all his various faculties, whatever the field of application that may subsequently be envisaged.

For Dalcroze, there was no question of having to choose between these approaches: both impressed themselves upon him with equal intensity. By nature, he was more inclined towards the first, for it was his earnest desire that his discoveries should be of particular benefit to all those disciplines relating more or less to music—not just music education and instrument studies, for which he devised hundreds if not thousands of exercises, but also dance, ballet, the vocal arts, theatre, in all of which he had innumerable contacts and about which he often expressed himself. But by vocation (if I may so describe the acute consciousness he had of his duty, almost of his mission), he devoted to the second approach at least as much time, and probably even more energy, than to the first. He was always looking to the future, and had high hopes of it—the word 'hope' was one to which his pen had frequent recourse in his books as well as in his songs. (Though it must be added that he wrote much in the aftermaths of two world wars: for all that he was a Swiss national, he was sufficiently a *citizen of the world* to experience them as events which touched him personally.) He was conscious of having made discoveries and set in train appropriate ways of enabling people to develop themselves, whether as individuals or in groups, and firmly believed that the desire to realize one's full potential, if sufficiently widespread and recognized by those who possessed it, could not but have a beneficial influence on society as a whole. It was therefore towards society as a whole, towards future generations (and not just future generations of musicians), that he was directing his aspirations when he opted for children as his field of specialization, writing (1910: 22):

I think I may claim in all honesty that *healthy* children, if exposed to the specialized education which I envisage, invariably become rhythmic creatures after three or four years, by which I mean released from all nervous and muscular disorders: in them the cerebral and physical functions are fully harmonized, and they will have developed a true appreciation of the relationships between movements in time and space.

Also (1910: 25):

If I firmly believe in the possibility of developing an artistic sense as well as will, personality, and mental concentration in children exposed to education into and by means of Eurhythmics, I also believe that art itself . . . cannot fail to be both benefited and sustained by such an education.

There is that of modesty, of delight, of not a little hope, in yet another sentence, dating from 1919: 'I really believe I have created an indispensable complement to children's education, both here and for all countries' (1919c: 173).

Piano Improvisation, the Primary Tool of the Eurhythmics Lesson

One thing that never fails to strike even the most unmusical newcomer to an international congress of Eurhythmics at Geneva—thereby benefiting from an opportunity to witness in a limited period of time a large number of lessons given by teachers of wide-ranging provenance and varying temperaments—is the dominant role played in most of these lessons by piano improvisation. Such an experience not unusually constitutes a major discovery. Whether he previously knew of Dalcroze Eurhythmics only by hearsay, or had delved into the literature of the subject, or even attended a few one-off lessons, he would probably have had little conception, in advance of any direct, sustained personal experience of it, of the extent to which the teacher makes use of piano improvisation as an integral part of his lessons.

Let us suppose that the newcomer, wishing to plunge into the essentials of Dalcrozian instruction, had gone to the international congress held in summer, 1981. He might perhaps have taken part in the first exercise offered by Lisa Parker (USA). To enable participants to make contact with one another and with their surroundings, she elected to draw from the outset on their power of auditory discrimination. The playing of a single melodic line at the piano was a signal for them each to wend a solitary path among their neighbours; two lines called on them to take hold of the nearest person within reach and move around as a pair; while the playing of three or more contrapuntal lines meant they were to congregate in little groups. They were thus required to switch from one mode to another upon distinguishing a change in the number of melodic strands. As it happens, the practised ears of the musicians among them readily caught the signal, even before they knew exactly what the next instruction was to be, by the actual shape of the musical phrases—by the very fact that a phrase ended in a way proclaiming 'this is a point (or pause) suitable for a change of instruction'. And they were delighted to see that they had got it right, especially towards the end of the exercise when they noticed that the teacher, at the piano, was exercising her right to take them by surprise by making rapid changes of instruction, or sometimes teasing their sense of anticipation by prolonging certain phrases beyond the span that might naturally be expected of them.

Alternatively, he might have taken part in the first exercise given by Françoise Füri of Switzerland. Her topic being that of musical accents, she decided to start off with words, and to underline the international nature of the congress by reference to ways of greeting one another in various different languages. Getting her participants to observe that the main stress falls in a different place depending on

whether the phrase is *Buon giorno!* or *Guten Tag!*, for example, and
that *Hello!* is pronounced differently from the first two as to both
intonation and rhythm, she took these distinctive verbal rhythms and
adapted them into equally contrasting rhythmic fragments suited to
the needs of her exercise (Ex. 3.2).

Ex. 3.2

Hel - lo!

Gut-en Tag!

Buon - gior-no!

To each one of these fragments there corresponded a distinctive
mode of locomotion which brought out its particular expressive
quality (linear advance, gyration, a sudden jump). It was up to the
participants to sort out which of these rhythms (or concatenation of
several) they were having to deal with, and to adapt the movement
of their bodies to it, while the teacher was making her musical
interpretation of it at the piano. It was also their task to reconstitute
the rhythm when the piano proposed no more than a regular pulse.
Finally, acting without the teacher's support, and having absorbed
each of these rhythms together with its expressive and metrical
characteristics, they could freely develop among themselves games of
guessing, question and answer, or quick reaction.

Our visitor would also have been able to watch an exhibition
exercise conducted by Dominique Porte of Geneva, involving children
of about 8 years old. Even sitting in the audience, he might have found
himself playing this game on his own account, paying at least as much
attention to what the piano was doing as to what was going on before
his eyes. To a piano accompaniment, the children were walking
around a number of hoops placed at random on the ground. When
warned by a signal (the insistent repetition of a single note) that the
passage of music was nearing its end they were to start moving
towards a hoop of their choice, but were not to stand in it unless the
final cadence reached an actual conclusion. In any other event—such

as the cadence being avoided or the piece ending on an inconclusive note—they were to reach a halt while still outside the hoop. The moral of this, of course, is that not everything that stops has necessarily been completed . . . On another occasion, it was on the *initiation* of musical phrases that their attention would be brought to bear. For this, the children were seated in a circle. Each in turn had to try to recognize the leitmotiv of a given theme, thereby earning the right to join up with the friends who had got there before him in this enjoyable race. But it was important not to lose one's turn, for the teacher continued playing without a break, and the theme could appear in any register of the piano and after a longer or shorter period of time; furthermore, it could be more or less disguised by the presence of simultaneous melodic strands, as commonly happens in fugues and two- or three-part inventions. They therefore had to be able to recognize a single tone-pattern appearing in a number of different disguises.

Then again, our congress participant might have been one of those who sought to capture from life, and to express physically in a thousand instinctive ways, rhythms with unequal beats played by Valéry Roth of France, who at the piano made light of what appear to be the most intractable rhythmic complications. Or one of those whom Edith Naef of Geneva led to explore the sometimes alternating, sometimes simultaneous bars of 6/8 and 3/4 in Bach's *Little Prelude in D minor*,[5] eventually proceeding—this time following her piano improvisation—to express with feet and hands (i.e. by walking and gesticulating) that well-known 'two against three' exercise in which success demonstrates the perfect independence of limbs from one another. Or even, on another occasion, the participant may have been one of those whom Lisa Parker's piano improvisations helped to grasp, in every variation of speed, the essential nature of the rhythmic device of syncopation. This was followed by the idea of either doubling or halving the speed, so that the group could finally appreciate and perform a Gershwin song that so happened to contain these diverse elements.

It may have been (why not?) the same delegate who was led by these and related experiences to exclaim, as a pianist friend of mine did: 'I have come to realize in these few days just how indispensable piano improvisation can be to a lesson in rhythm and movement, and that a teacher who is good at improvisation has the advantage of a quite

---

[5] In J. S. Bach, *Preludes and Fughetti* (BWV 926).

invaluable tool!'.[6] At the same time, he might well have taken into account the degree of mastery and flexibility that piano improvisation requires of those who practise it in a Dalcrozian context. For such people must not only be expert enough to employ suitable pianistic means to illustrate all the intricacies to be found scattered throughout the realm of written music—rhythmic or metric, melodic or harmonic, dynamic or agogic as the case may be: but they must also be capable of bringing out and emphasizing bodily movement, of stimulating spontaneous reactions and knowing exactly at what rate to increase the level of their demands, of introducing variations without giving way to irrelevances, of breathing expressive quality into a gesture, of imparting form and consistency to an impulse that comes from the heart.

Valéry Roth liked to point out that, generally speaking, the rhythmics teacher improvising at the piano is not 'music-making' in the usual, communal sense of the word. Very few real-life musical situations actually call for such things as the endless repetition of a single motif or rhythmic figure, the progressive curtailment of a theme by lopping off another note each time it comes round, a sequence of bars of which every other one repeats the rhythm of its predecessor twice, at double speed, the unrelieved alternation of crescendo with decrescendo, an accelerando based on a mathematical progression, or a melodic or harmonic theme repeated several times with a new variation at each repetition, etc. This is not to say that such particulars are completely lacking in musical literature; nor, in suitable circumstances, would anyone fail to put them to use or quote them by way of example;[7] but the proper purpose of piano improvisation will be precisely to pick out these various musical dimensions—economically and appropriately to the needs of the moment—so as to present them in a repeated form in such a way as to impress them on the pupils' bodies and awareness (their movements being in any case naturally inclined towards repetition and automatic response). It also serves to enable them to vary their responses—impulsively or systematically as the case may be, and whether with a view to teaching something new or to freeing the pupil from undesirable habits—by making increasing demands on his powers of concentration.

[6] Sylviane Lentin, private communication, 1981.

[7] Dalcroze himself, with a didactic end in view, composed any number of small pieces of this type. But he was not alone (cf. for example Bartok's inexhaustible *Microcosmos*, S. Heller's *Etudes*, Op. 47, numerous sketches and short pieces by B. Reichel, etc.).

· Given the requirement of soliciting pupils' responses and getting them to appreciate from the outset the relationship between the feel of a movement and a musical feature, the repertoire of already composed music would hardly provide a wide enough range of suitable possibilities without making enormous demands of time and energy on those who would seek to comb the literature for a sufficiency of relevant passages. The Dalcrozian improviser, by contrast, being first and foremost an expert in rhythm, is able to draw on his own powers of expression, precision, imagination, and controlled spontaneity—qualities indispensable to creative music-making at the piano if it is to bring out all relevant associations between auditory sensations and physical movements. Any properly trained rhythmics instructor may be expected to demonstrate these powers. All the more fortunate will he be, too, if he can compose spontaneously (or even after putting a little time into it) authentic pieces of music—such as dances and songs—worthy of illustrating, at the end of an exercise, what obstacle has been overcome, or likely to arouse pupils' anticipation of delights to come. A goodly number of rhythmics teachers can do so unerringly. Some attain remarkable heights in this field. But it does not follow that every rhythmics teacher automatically doubles as an all-round artist, and none, indeed, need feel demeaned by trying to supplement his weak points by drawing on music from any period. In fact, he can hardly do without it, be he never so brilliant at improvisation, for much the same reason that no one would expect to teach literature or poetry by concentrating solely on grammar or on the works of a single author.

Unfortunately—alas!—it is not always the least competent improvisers who turn most readily to the best of other composers' music. Far from it: they often have little interest in exploring it, or are put off by the pianistic demands it threatens to make on them. And it is not necessarily those who improvise with great facility, for they are inclined to use their talent as a way of cushioning themselves against the need to work. It is in fact above all those who *love the piano*, and it is impossible to insist too strongly on this fundamental requirement of all prospective new candidates for admission to the profession of rhythmics studies. At the same time, let us not run away with the idea that piano music is the only music worth considering in these respects. We shall see elsewhere (Ch. 5) just why the piano remains the rhythmic expert's most favoured instrument; but the same goes for any instrument which the rhythmic teacher may prefer, knowing how to play it well and having learnt to improvise on it—violin, flute, voice, guitar, or whatever: he must love that instrument, and not suppose that the dilettante's approach will suffice. For his role as teacher demands that he be as expert in a particular instrument as in rhythm itself. And the use he may be expected to make of his instrument forbids him to play it indifferently.

Luisa Di Segni is a Dalcrozian teacher in Rome, who, rather than remain at the piano, devotes much of her lessons to exploring and experimenting with the voice and the sound characteristics of various instruments. From a conversation I had with her recently, I learnt to what extent the opportunity of demonstrating her work at a Eurhythmics congress—where one inevitably encounters extremes of tradition and liberalization and a whole variety of interactions between them—enabled her to bring out the true Dalcrozian essence of her work. In such a context one is indeed able to recognize correspondences between this type of approach and other forms of instruction closer to their sources, whereas when this same work is presented in other contexts and set against other current forms of inculcating musical or physical sensitivity, it is often harder to distinguish its specific purpose and underlying principles.

In this respect I think it important to point out that the training in piano improvisation received by the prospective rhythmics teacher— first as a pupil responding to his teachers' improvisations, then as a trainee seeking to master keyboard improvisation on his own account—is likely to have a far from negligible effect on his eventual professionalism. This still applies whether he elects to make less use of the piano than he actually could, or abandons it in favour of some other instrument, or even if he makes greater use of words and silence in his lessons. For, as a branch of study in itself, piano improvisation stands at the centre of every other sort of teaching he has received, in rhythm, harmony, counterpoint, physical expressiveness, traditional dances, forms and styles, piano. It is the ultimate test of his ability in these various fields, and in itself the most favourable ground on which to make syntheses, effect choices, question things and generally discover his own personality. Speaking for myself, I have yet to meet the student, good or bad, on whom it has not had a profound effect, or who claims not to have enjoyed studying it.

Some Objections and Misunderstandings

If there is one thing that may be set against Dalcroze—especially by a Dalcrozian!—it is the fact that throughout his career he remained considerably less than explicit about just how much use he made of piano improvisation in carrying out his rhythmic exercises. We may, in retrospect, be able to understand the reasons for this deficiency; but there is no doubt in my mind that it lies at the root of certain erroneous interpretations or defective applications that people have been able to make of his ideas. As it happens, he did eventually rectify this omission, but more often than not this was at the instance of his pupils, and, occasionally, when pushed to do so by the very mis- understandings of those who had drawn their inspiration from him.

One may well see in this an illustration of Claparède's 'Law of Consciousness', which postulates that the events most deeply ingrained in us are the ones that we experienced the earliest and have only become aware of at a considerably later date![8] This is surely how we should explain such a gap in his earliest writings. For Dalcroze, the use of music was the most natural thing in the world. Music was an essential part of his make-up; it was his language, his reason for living. He could cite it as one of his goals because he was a music teacher, because it would have been his earnest desire that everyone should be led to know and love it. Nor did he fail to nominate it as the most desirable—indeed the only—means of enabling everyone to live in harmony with him- or herself. He therefore said much about the role of music; but to describe in detail exactly how he introduced it into his lessons, or, in practical terms, how he used it to enliven, inspire, or control his physical exercises, is an idea that never seems to have entered his head. He would have regarded such a thing as a form of talking to himself, or indulging in self-analysis. In any case, at that time he was fascinated by the way the body moved, and by the prospect of uniting, for the benefit both of individuals and of art, 'Rhythm, Word, and Gesture'—a union which he described as 'Music in the Greek sense of the term'. What he therefore set out to do in his early writings was to exalt the possibilities and expectations of bodily movement rather than go into, so to speak, descriptions of how the workman used his tools. This is how he himself expressed it by

[8] Claparède 1918: 72, cited in Gillièron 1979: 47.

imagining the example of a gymnastics instructor who had decided to counteract an excessively metrical approach and turned to music with a view to discovering interesting rhythms for his pupils to practise:

I, a music teacher, have trodden the path in an opposite direction to that which I have just described to you, and, having set out from music, have now arrived at gymnastics . . . Struck as I am by the inability of so many pupils to absorb the elements of musical rhythm through the mind, I have required the body to furnish me with model rhythmic movements (1910: 20).

It was this discovery—in other words, what had struck him as novel—that he most wanted to talk about in his first articles. Nevertheless, for anyone who knows the way he thinks, there can be no doubt that whenever he talks of rhythm (usually with a capital *R*), whenever he refers to a performance of movement, music—and especially musical improvisation—forms an implicit part of it. Yet it would not be right to point the finger of scorn at all those readers of his who did not find it easy to grasp his point. At one period, when he was wrestling with the proposition that 'rhythm is not the same as metre', only a handful of his pupils and one or two professional musicians were able to grasp what he was getting at. Nor, indeed, is it at the hands of musicians that he has most suffered from being misunderstood.

Music, Rhythm, Sound

Confronted with such misunderstanding, Dalcroze more than once sought refuge behind his explanation that 'Eurhythmics is essentially personal experience'. He was undoubtedly right, if only because the permanent presence of music and the part played by the teacher's improvisation at the piano cannot come but as a revelation to the one-off participant or spectator at a demonstration! Still, had he then been able to prevent one of the most fundamentally original aspects of his method from—albeit unintentionally—hiding its light under a bushel, it seems quite likely that a number of misapprehensions could have been avoided—given that it is sometimes hard to tell which mis-apprehensions are involuntary and which deliberately concocted. In this connection I can give an example of a so-called 'misapprehension'. I owe the discovery of this deception to some background reading done in connection with the present book, specifically in Teplov's *Psychology of Musical Aptitude*. In an important chapter on rhythm,

the author twice refers to Dalcroze by name. The first occasion is one
for paying tribute to the pedagogue who so brilliantly grasped the
active, motor nature of the sense of musical rhythm (p. 345); the
second constitutes a criticism which to my mind is most unsoundly
based, but which it will perhaps be not without interest to examine
here.

One of Teplov's theses runs as follows:

The sense of musical rhythm is of a kind not only motor in nature but also
affective; it rests on a perception of the expressive quality of music. It is for
this reason that a sense of musical rhythm can be neither aroused nor
developed outside the confines of music (p. 353).

To which, supposes Teplov, it may be objected:

Certainly, outside the realm of music no one can develop a sense of *musical*
rhythm. But all one has to do is to work first at developing a sense of rhythm in
general. Once this point is reached, developing the sense of musical rhythm
becomes a very simple matter and is easily achieved. (ibid.)

Teplov continues:

This objection could find support in the authority of Dalcroze himself, who
urged that one ought first to study rhythm and music separately, thus giving
rise to the following prescription: 'A sense of rhythm will never be fully
developed nor become part of the pupil's flesh and blood unless rhythm has
first been perceived in isolation, as something entirely independent of any
relation to music. Rhythm must present itself to the tender soul of the young
musician as having an independent existence, and not as one component of an
art form which itself is indivisible.'

And in Teplov's own conclusion (ibid.):

However great the authority of this eminent specialist in rhythm may be, and
however noteworthy his success in teaching, this proposition must be accounted
utterly erroneous. It strikingly reflects the basic vice of a concept of rhythm
nowadays widespread in science and gravely prejudicial to musical education.

This crushing and apparently irrefutable reproach will nevertheless
be found quite unacceptable by anyone with the slenderest grasp of
Dalcroze's thinking, especially as it appears with not the slightest
gloss to modify its tenor. But let's just look at the facts, for something
here demands more careful thought.

In the first place, the quotation attributed to Dalcroze is taken from
Der Rhythmus als Erziehungsmittel, a work published at Basle in 1907

under the aegis of Paul Boepple and consisting of a series of six discussion papers which Dalcroze initiated in Geneva one summer. The publisher specifically states in his preface that he has 'decided to gather together and print the text of these papers' (p. iv).[9] He goes on to seek the reader's indulgence for the German edition, since

it has not been possible to acquire a copy of the French original in its entirety and I have been obliged to refer, in part, to translations made by some who are unfamiliar with the Method[10] (p. v).

Now, this somewhat suspect work is the only one to which Teplov has been willing (or competent) to refer: it is the only title listed under the name of Dalcroze[11] in the otherwise extensive bibliography of over 200 titles provided by him at the end of the book (pp. 412 ff). Did he then, at time of writing (the first edition, in Russian, appeared in 1947[12]) not have access to the German edition of *Le Rythme, la musique et l'éducation*, which appeared in 1921 (Dalcroze 1921b)? Had he in fact consulted it (and I have the feeling that he could hardly have been unaware of this book, which in some respects has some bearing on theories of his own), he could not have failed to turn up statements such as this:

The mechanism of the body is useless unless pressed into the service of a practised sensitivity. Studying the translation of musical rhythms into physical movements cannot but lead to the development of sensitivity (1916b: 108);

or this:

I consider that it is on the sense of hearing that the whole of musical education should be based, or, at least, on the perception of musical phenomena; for the ear gradually accustoms itself to recognize relationships between notes, between tonalities, between chords, and the whole body begins—with the help of specific exercises—to perceive nuances of a rhythmic, dynamic, and agogic nature in music. (1912a: 55)

---

[9] '[Der allgemeine Wunsch der Kursteilnehmer] . . . bewog den Unterzeichneten zur Ueberarbeitung und Drucklegung dieser Vorträge.'

[10] 'da es nicht möglich war, das französische Original im ganzen Umfang zur Verfügung zu erhalten und ich mich zum Teil auf die Uebersetzungen durch der Methode fernstehende Personen verlassen musste'.

[11] Tibor Dénes, who amongst others compiled a complete catalogue of Dalcroze's pedagogical and literary works in French and other languages, does not include this item, referring it rather to the bibliography on the Dalcroze Method, under the name of Paul Boepple (cf. F. Martin *et al.* 1965: 574).

[12] Date indicated by Eric Emery (1975: 514).

Or again:

There is only one way to get the body to realise its full gamut of expressive possibilities, and that is to subject it to a thoroughgoing musical regime (1919*b*: 141).

And finally, to bring an inexhaustible list to an end:

Any teaching method designed to develop an awareness of the relationships between musical movement and that of the muscular and nervous systems ought to be pressed not only upon dancers, but also upon all artists and performers especially involved with rhythm.

How, after that, can music possibly be thought to be lacking from such a declaration as the following?

We have said elsewhere, and often enough, that movement lies at the root of all the arts, and that it is impossible to be artistically cultivated in any area without some study of form in movement and without a complete education of the tactile–motor functions. It is this realization that impels us to ensure that the study of *solfège* be preceded by the education of the nervous and muscular system, following the laws of metrics and rhythm . . . (1919*b*: 134).

Does not all this demonstrate that for Dalcroze, and contrary to Teplov's objection, *music is the very condition which renders possible* 'the development of a sense of rhythm in general', and that there is consequently no question of developing it 'outside the realm of music'?

As to the way in which music should be translated:

a gesture means nothing in itself: its value subsists entirely within the feeling that motivates it . . . For any attempt at expressiveness on the part of those completely unaffected by music and entirely deaf to its imperatives is nothing but a pipe-dream (1919*b*: 126–7).

Does this sentence not curiously pre-echo Teplov's thesis described above? In any case, in the following passage Dalcroze does not fear to play the visionary:

Ah! It will surely be possible one day, when music has settled down within the heart of man and lives as one with him . . . to dance dances without having them accompanied by sounds. The body will prove sufficient unto itself for the expression of all the joys and sorrows of humanity: it will no longer need the aid of instruments to pace those rhythms out, for all those rhythms will . . . lie within itself . . . Until then, however, we must urge the body to accept the intimate collaboration of music . . . (1919*b*: 131)

As a second step, let us now more closely examine the Dalcrozian 'quotation' proffered by Teplov. This has undergone several modifications, perhaps through successive translations (?); but it remains sufficiently recognizable for us to relate it unhesitatingly to its original, which runs as follows:

yet a sense of rhythm will only become the spiritual possession [of the pupil] when he has been granted access to persistent experiences of it as an independent unity, rather than as one component of an art which strikes him as indivisible, and whose breaking down into separate compartments offends his musical sensitivity (Boepple 1907: 5).[13]

To inaugurate the musical education of a child destined to become a musician by baldly proclaiming 'music is composed of rhythm and sound' would be much like 'yielding the art of his soul to the vivisectionist', as may be read on the page preceding that from which Teplov drew his quotation. And if it is true that 'one should study rhythm and sound separately', it is possible to do so 'without drawing the pupil's attention to the dichotomy deliberately effected by the pedagogue . . . (Boepple 1907: 4).[14]

To put it another way, it is only after getting the child to see that music is essentially a form of movement (movement in space and movement in time)—the child, that is, who finds movement the most familiar and natural thing in the world—that one can set him on a course of instruction into music as such. For the purpose of this study it will then be possible to point out, in the movement of music, what things relate to the realm of time, of metre and of the arrangement of rhythmic values, and what to sounds and their relative positions in tonal space, without running the risk of disembowelling an art whose various components derive their significances one from another.

What we quarrel with, for it would have struck him as nonsensical, is the idea that Dalcroze could ever have urged, here or anywhere else, that anyone *should study rhythm and music separately.* Yet there can be no smoke without fire: it is from the phrase 'to study rhythm and

---

[13] 'Jedoch wird dieselbe die Empfindung des Rhythmus nur dann Vollständig zu ihrem geistigen Eigentume machen, wenn ihr Gelegenheit geboten wird zu dauernden Empfindungen, als unabhängige Einheit und nicht als Teil einer Kunst, die ihr unteilbar scheint und deren Zerstückelung ihre empfindsame musikalische Seele nicht ertragen kann'.

[14] 'Und dennoch muß man den Rhythmus vom Tone getrennt studieren lassen, aber ohne daß, das Kind die vom Pädagogischen beabsichtigte Zerlegung der Kunst inne wird.'

sound separately' that some of the particular misunderstandings mentioned above have sprung. The many and various definitions attached to the word 'rhythm' by no means all agree with one another, sometimes going so far as to flatly contradict one another. The term 'rhythm' is in fact an unfortunate one, in so far as it can be applied irregularly, and indifferently, to the part or to the whole. Now in Dalcroze's world it is obvious that no musical rhythm can exist without associated sound, as it is equally obvious that sounds do not constitute music in themselves. Thus to have rhythm *studied* separately from sounds is by no means the same thing as seeing to it that they be *experienced or heard* in isolation from one another. And the weight of evidence as to lessons given by Dalcroze would surely confirm that when his pupils were being encouraged to grasp a rhythm—whether for the usual purpose of translating it into physical movements or for that of notation in terms of crotchets and quavers and barlines—it was always a *musical* rhythm that he presented them with, full and rich in its melodic line, its accents and harmonic landmarks. In much the same way, when they were required to indicate by body movements (or to write down) the rising or falling line of a tune, its modulations or intervals, they were accorded the assistance of musical rhythm, which attaches significance to strands of sound, helping to foretell their closing cadences, to locate repeated sequences, and to identify the basic chord progressions in which the tune finds its rest or support.

The only thing is that Dalcroze did not say enough about all that, or say it loud enough. He all too often made the error of assuming that the word 'rhythm' as it emanated from his pen would mean the same to his readers as to himself, the error of not consistently attaching the adjective 'musical' to it whenever the context so required, the error of not constantly referring to his own definition and the practical methods he used for 'advancing the study of rhythm', bearing in mind that in his lessons rhythm and sound were always closely linked by virtue of his improvisation at the piano. It is beyond doubt that each of these elements contributes to the intelligibility of the other, even if only one of the two is subjected to analysis.

Rights of Priority

I can understand that certain individuals are unable to assert the musical equivalence of rhythm and of sound, but, all the same, it seems to me that a musician entering a room where machinery is moving at full swing is no true musician if he fails to be carried away with admiration at hearing such a fabulous symphony creating the magic of parallel and contrasting rhythms, nor if he does not immediately set to work on serious research into the task of learning the secrets of that animated, shuddering life that simultaneously quickens nature, man, and all his works. (Dalcroze 1915a: 76)

Let us now return to the context of that music teaching of his day which Dalcroze countered by making himself the herald of rhythm. This type of teaching consisted primarily in training pupils to identify the pitch of sounds and to attach names to notes, to keys, to chords. Sight often played a greater part than hearing in this sort of training. The next (or concurrent) step would undoubtedly be to measure the length of musical values and to arrange them in proper succession; but these were essentially intellectual exercises chiefly based on counting. Rhythm—in the sense implied by von Bülow's 'In the beginning was Rhythm'—was never taught as such. Left out of account, it remained more or less subsumed within the mysterious manifestations of musical talent.[15] Now, says Dalcroze (1915a: 84), 'In music, it is nothing but rhythm, created by the emotions, which most frequently gives birth and life to the melodic line'.

Whether we think, for example, of the endlessly repeated little chants of children at play, or catch ourselves muttering when obsessed with a word or thought—aren't such things more than ready to pass from articulation to chanting, and from chant to melody?

Think for a moment of a tune you know well and tap its rhythm out, without singing. You will hear it echoing inside yourself as clearly as if you were singing it out loud, and anyone watching you could quite easily, if they knew it too, guess exactly which song you were thinking of. But now deprive it of its rhythm—and guessing it will not then be so easy, especially if you also omit the words. After about the third or fourth note the song becomes as unrecognizable to you as it would for anyone who may be listening. Only by the lucky off chance of a distinctive interval would it be possible to recognize it in spite of such treatment. Whatever it is, it will no longer be of any musical interest.

Considerations of this order alone would suffice to show that if either topic should have priority over the other in the study of rhythm and sound, this honour should certainly be accorded to rhythm. That said, is it in fact obligatory that the two should be studied one after the

---

[15] In this connection see Lussy 1884: p. iii.

other? Could not these aspects of training be put into effect simultaneously? Yes, says Dalcroze, in cases where we are dealing with
children whose musical potential is beyond doubt even before they
begin lessons, and who have only to learn what names to attach to
things they already know and feel in depth. But experience showed
him that in the majority of cases 'the child has difficulty in grasping at
one and the same time a melodic line and the rhythm that breathes
spirit into it' (1909: 65). Those familiar with music teaching would do
well to remember how, in notating a piece of musical dictation, the
need to note the rhythm and pitch of sounds simultaneously is often
such as to induce errors which the pupil easily avoids when required to
concentrate only on one thing or the other.

It seems to follow naturally (though it wasn't obvious at the time,
and who knows whether it is even now universally understood?) that,
just as no one teaches a child to read and write before it has learned to
speak, so there is no point in teaching it music until it has reached the
stage of feeling its effects. As Dalcroze points out (ibid.):

there are two biological structures by which we are enabled to appreciate,
understand, live, and experience music: these two structures are the ear, in
respect of sound, and the entire nervous system in respect of rhythm.

The entire nervous system, that is, *including* the auditory function,
which here operates in conjunction with the other senses (visual,
kinaesthetic). These mutually reinforce and collaborate with one
another in various combinations whenever the motor function happens
to be mobilized. Further observation forces one to the conclusion that
in order to be a good musician one needs, first, an ear capable of
distinguishing and comparing sounds themselves as well as their
duration, and, second, a body capable of reproducing such sounds
(whether vocally or instrumentally), and that in a way which accurately
reflects their distribution in time with the required dynamics (cf.
Boepple 1907: 5). Dalcroze draws certain conclusions from these two
observations, based on the principle that actions should precede
analysis and personal evaluation:

If . . . we compare the functions of the ear with those of the musculature, we
are led to affirm that in deciding which comes first in elementary music studies
the ear must cede pride of place to the musculature.

And:

It will [first of all] be necessary for the child to insert durations between the
movements to be performed to a rhythm or time-beat, so as to increase his

awareness of his own powers of rhythmic representation . . . He should then be taught to appreciate the sonority with the rhythm, and to distinguish between that which is movement and that which is sound; and thence to transpose movements into sounds and sounds into physical gestures.

This type of approach will be equally suitable, our author says, for musically gifted pupils as well as for those less well endowed. In either case, a truly educational instruction will be carefully designed to start from the most concrete and accessible experiences and then progress towards increasingly abstract or complex ideas. And what the young musician most enjoys about music, what he finds most immediately accessible, is its movement, and all the feelings and experiences excited within him by this movement of sound and rhythm. What's more, the same thing surely applies to any music lover, whether child or adult.

In a statement which was subsequently to cause him many an embarrassment (and which, unfortunately for him, is repeated in many of his early writings), Dalcroze articulated as follows his conviction that music studies should begin with the motor experience of music itself:

Sonority is obviously of secondary importance since it does not find its origin or model within ourselves, whereas movement, being instinctive to the human being, is consequently of primary importance. (1909: 65)

One can certainly dispute the point that sonority, unlike rhythm, 'does not find its origin or model within ourselves'. As we have seen, Dalcroze began by advancing other reasons for justifying the priority of rhythm at the outset of musical studies. At that period it seemed to him perfectly in order to seek to argue rationally for what had come to him through intuition and experience. But anyone lifting one of these assertions out of context could easily make him appear to say what in fact he did not say, either to do him down (as in the case of Teplov; see above), or to elevate him (even to guru status) in a sense which actually ran counter to everything he stood for—as witness the following example.

In 1920, when Dalcroze gave a series of papers and demonstrations in Great Britain, a number of articles appeared in the British press, testifying to the remarkable impression he had made. These articles were translated and published in an edition of the journal *Le Rythme*. Amongst them may be found, in particular, a piece from the pen of a journalist on the *Glasgow Evening Times* under the heading 'La musique vivante' (*Le Rythme*, 5 (June 1920), 27–8). This article, which is highly enthusiastic and in general well researched, includes the following information (p. 28):

His disenchantment with normal educational methods has led Dalcroze to study the origins of the musical experience, and to conclude that movement (or rhythm) is the primary component of music, given that it is a component of every human being. Sound need therefore occupy only a secondary position. [*sic*][16]

At this point reference is made to a footnote by Dalcroze himself, stating:

No such analysis appears either in my articles or in any of my books. I have stated quite simply that the element of movement is *just as important* as that of sound in musical expression.

Could it be that he did not in fact say it quite as simply as he claims? To say that movement comes before sound in the human make-up is certainly not to say that sound is a matter of secondary significance in music; to set rhythm and *sound* in opposition for the sake of music training is not to oppose rhythm and *music* for the same reason. We may well suppose that the layman gets lost in distinctions too subtle for him to grasp; or that some teachers, less than enthusiastic about music, interpret misunderstandings to their own advantage, and turn music into the poor relation—indeed, the deaf mute relation—of physical (or even of musical) education. In the event, one cannot but regret that someone like Teplov—an informed musician, and far from being a layman—could have fallen headlong into such an easily avoidable trap and made such categorical judgements out of what he found there. And such regret is only aggravated when the same author, several pages later, acknowledges the power of rhythmics to develop the sense of musical rhythm, and goes on to elaborate—in lines from which the name Dalcroze is noticeable by its absence—his view that 'this procedure is only valid to the extent that rhythmic exercises are musical exercises and music remains pivotal to them' (Teplov 1966: 356). A point of which the creator of Eurhythmics would warmly have approved!

---

[16] This passage is translated from the French. (Translator's note)

Learning to Improvise

'Improvisation is the art of expressing one's thoughts off the cuff as rapidly as they pass through the mind', wrote Dalcroze in an article (1932*b*: 4) expressing amazement that improvisation should receive so little encouragement in instrumental studies. He himself was of the opinion that it could only be of enormous help, its role beging to

develop students' *speed of decision-making*, of instrumental execution, of effortless concentration and immediate plan-formation, and to establish *direct* communications between the spirit that pulses, the brain which represents and co-ordinates, and the arms and hands which put into execution (p. 3)

The improviser has an obligation to

put rhythms and harmonies together, to absorb combinations of note lengths with as brief a delay as possible, to foresee and prepare for pauses and reprises of movement (p. 3),

which can only benefit his playing and his sensitivity to the instrument. It is also to be observed that

the tactile sense often has a marked influence on the musician . . . The hand is the most intelligent and sensitive of our organs. Its sensitivity is so refined that it often responds to flights of imagination more rapidly than the ear itself, which, more often than not, confines itself to controlling the dictates of musical gesture (p. 8)

And while Dalcroze forcefully asserted (p. 12) that 'any child musical enough to pursue a piano lesson is capable of improvising', neither did he deny this capacity in adults who wielded sufficient mastery of their instrument:

To turn a pianist[17] into a good improviser one must engage his *attention*, his readiness to adapt and vary, [in other words his] *intelligence plastique*—'sense of plasticity'—*which result from his personal memory and from impressions in his brain. We have to develop instinctive automatic responses*, which are the product of countless repetitions of our thoughts and feelings. (p. 14)

The translation into pianistic terms of diverse rhythmic exercises which have first been experienced in a physical way makes it easier for the apprentice rhythmician to develop an ability of considerable value

---

[17] This applies equally to any instrumentalist.

to him—nothing less, in fact, than a finely honed tool for his chosen profession of rhythmics teacher. It therefore comes as no surprise to find that Dalcroze's plan for a course of improvisation includes study subjects which are often the same, but expressed in terms of piano, as those encountered in rhythmics courses. I will quote a few of them by way of example, they being taken from a 17-point list drawn up by Dalcroze (1932*b*: 14) and accompanied by several descriptions of exercises or by commentaries designed to put flesh on the bones:

RAPID PERCEPTION OF TIME SIGNATURE BY SIGHT AND EAR (POINT 4)

For example, the student at the piano plays while keeping his eyes firmly fixed on another student positioned a few steps away from him, who is beating the time out—sometimes three-time, sometimes two- or four-time, as the fancy takes him. The pianist's object is to provide an immediate musical sense (using the resources of phrasing, repetitions, melodic inflexions, and harmonic structures in his playing) of the changes of measure, which he does to some extent under constraint, and with no prior knowledge of what is going to come next. At the same time, the student who is doing the conducting must keep one ear on the piano, with a view not to blindly imposing his will, but to seeking to choose the most favourable moment for a change in time signature or the repetition of a sequence. The whole thing should ultimately result in a shared creation, whose structural integrity will be a measure of the understanding existing between the two collaborators.

STUDY OF RHYTHMS IN SPACE WITH THE HELP OF MUSCULAR AWARENESS (POINT 5)

A given rhythm, whether beaten, tapped, or written out, is capable of becoming a musical motif according to how it is embodied in a matrix of sound which imposes its own trajectory and plastic quality upon it.

For example, a motif such as $\,\gamma\,\sfrac{}{}\,\Box\Box\,|\,\sfrac{}{}\,$ will appear musically different in character depending on whether it is played in a chromatically rising progression (Ex. 3.3), or the same note is sounded three times and followed by a minim a major third below it (Ex. 3.4).

If we now attach no significance at all to the exact intervals, we will still find that any fragment based on this rhythm played on the keyboard in equal steps from left to right will recall the first example

Ex. 3.3

Ex. 3.4

rather than the second—whereas, if played with a repeated note followed by another one 'a little lower', it is still likely to put us in mind of Beethoven's Fifth Symphony!

This overall sense of the spatial organization of a given rhythmic movement should be capable of reappearing at the slightest prompting, otherwise no musical structuring is possible. The possibilities of repetition, transposition, cross-reference, transformation, deformation, etc., all depend on the individual's ability to recreate an image from a particular impression in his auditory and muscular memory, even if other impressions have since come and attached themselves to the first. This ability assumes a particular importance for the rhythmician whenever he wishes to translate into terms of sound a physical rhythm suggested by one of his students, or to arouse in them the recollection of a movement they have carried out before.

EXERCISES ENCOURAGING THE ACQUISITION OF MANY AUTOMATIC RESPONSES, AND FOR THEIR COMBINATION AND ALTERNATION IN ACCORDANCE WITH SPONTANEOUS ACTS OF WILL (POINT 9)

In some ways, learning to improvise is rather similar to learning a foreign language: you can only speak it fluently when you reach the stage of not having to think about each and every word you have to enunciate. Note, too, that the very structure of the language (word order in sentences, use of connectives, agreement of tenses, etc.) must have become so thoroughly absorbed that you can concentrate entirely on the content of the communication, whose quality of articulation will be all the greater the richer the vocabulary you have at your disposal.

Similarly, in diatonic language, all possible arrangements of tonal functions must be capable of instantaneous recall, and this through the internalization and automatic recollection of the auditory and tactile sense-experiences associated with them. It then becomes a matter of conscious decision-making how to determine their arrangement in time and sound.

It will also be possible to seek the automatic recall of particular audio-tactile sensations in their own right (intervals, concords, clusters, examples of parallel or contrary motion) to facilitate their cogent deployment in the language selected for use, whether diatonic or not. For example, consistent use of the whole-tone scale requires that the pianist's fingers pick out augmented fourths without hesitation whilst automatically avoiding chromatic features as well as perfect fourths and fifths.

Such exercises can very well be done with eyes shut: the sense of sight will not then take charge of anything capable of being controlled by the ear and muscles alone. In any case, playing without looking at the keyboard (or looking at it as little as possible) is absolutely essential for the rhythmician, who, whilst playing, will have to keep a close eye on what his students are doing.

Improvising may in some way be likened to devoting oneself to rapid composition. Dalcroze says, in this respect, 'rapid creation does not mean non-serious creation: meditations lasting a few minutes can be just as deep as meditations carried out at length' (1932*b*: 5). An improviser may well have complete grasp in advance of what he intends to say at the piano, of how much time he will spend on it and the paths that he will follow. It is highly desirable that he should succeed in this, otherwise, under pressure, he will all too often lose his way, spin out and dilute his ideas, or offer his hearer a piece that lacks both tail and head. The moments he will spend in mentally clarifying his intentions before starting to play are certainly not without value.[18]

Improvisation differs from composition, however, at least to the extent that it lives in a permanent state of development, and remains at the mercy of the unexpected, even at the hands of the cleverest improviser. It is impossible to rub anything out, impossible to demolish anything that has been constructed. Thus learning to improvise is to a large extent learning to cope with the unexpected and to take advantage of one's mistakes! A chord may suddenly appear at one's fingertips which bears no relation to what had been expected and wanders off the path originally embarked upon; nothing for it but to

---

[18] Oswald Russell, improvisation instructor at the Institut Jaques-Dalcroze at Geneva, rightly insists on the saving of time and energy afforded by the brief interval before playing in which to sketch out mentally the path to be followed. I myself invariably insist that, to make any such performance possible, the student start playing in full knowledge of what he *wishes* to say, this being in my view a necessary (if not always sufficient) condition to his finding the *means* of saying it.

change one's plans: either follow the detour till it joins up with the main route, or else adopt the newly opened route and change the intended continuation. This, in any case, is the way to make happy discoveries—discoveries that might otherwise not have been thought of, and which will serve to increase the improviser's resources. At the same time it is a way of making something of mistakes by trying to disguise them. Has a particular note turned out different from what it should have been? No point in holding things up to replace it with another: it has already been heard, and irrecoverable time would be wasted in seeking to correct the fault. But might it not be used as an appoggiatura to the simpler chord originally intended? Could it be taken as an excuse for modulating into a new passage? If not, let's not worry about it. Let the wrong note be: we'll make a better job of it next time round! Or—more subtly—let's repeat it more insistently, so as to give the impression that it was intended, and then try to fit it in to the continuation of the piece! An error may therefore prove a source of enrichment and novelty. One can only hear in advance—surely?— what one already knows. Every creative act, indeed, requires its fair share of the unpredictable.

EXERCISES IN DISSOCIATION OF MOVEMENTS (POINT II)

If it is relatively easy for the trained pianist to interpret scores in which both hands are required to execute differing rhythmic movements, it is quite a different matter when he himself has to create the music he is playing. Very often the left hand, being less developed than the other, limits itself to picking out the beats (or just the first beats) in each bar, or allows itself to be influenced by the right hand when it is supposed to be maintaining a rhythm of its own. Amongst a number of exercises enabling beginners to develop improved dissociative ability between the two hands is the following example: one hand plays at twice the speed of the other; at a given signal, their roles are reversed. Or again: the left hand automatically keeps up a rhythmic ostinato based on a few notes, or on repetitions of the same interval, while the right hand plays a tune at first in slow time values, then in progressively faster ones, until it arrives at the tune played in its proper rhythms, which must neither upset the left-hand's ostinato nor get entangled with it.

In rhythmics lessons, there are many occasions on which the teacher should be able to test dissociative ability, whether by getting the students to perform different rhythms as between feet and hands, or by getting two or more groups to circle about in different ways at the same time—himself meanwhile accompanying them at the piano.

EXERCISES IN CONCENTRATION; LISTENING WITH THE INNER EAR (POINT 7)

It takes training to be able to hear in advance, with any degree of precision, what one is going to play. But such aptitude is required of the rhythmician when, for example, he wants to make an exact translation of a repeated movement created by one of his students. One such exercise that more advanced students may practise to this end is as follows: without moving, the student imagines a movement which he is doing internally, trying to get into the sensation of its length, its direction, its points of support. While doing so, he listens to the music which this imaginary movement induces within himself, then makes a pretence of playing at the keyboard in such a way as to evoke the sounds to which he is listening. Finally, he actually plays it, and the others then try and discover the movement he had been thinking of. After that, everyone shares their impressions and criticisms.

In another exercise, a student invents a short passage in two voices and repeats it several times. While doing so, he must concentrate his listening now on the right hand, now on the left, until he is sufficiently sure of them both to be able to change them over—i.e., to play the left-hand line an octave higher with the right hand and vice versa.[19] Gradually, the student will require only a small number of repetitions before he is able to change the voices over.

In other exercises in the rhythmics lesson the teacher will want to make the bass imitate the upper voice, when, for example, playing two or more voices in imitation or in canon. These exercises train the polyrhythmic and the polyphonic senses.

STUDY OF ANACRUSES, PAUSES, AND PHRASING; . . . IN NUANCES AND RULES OF EXPRESSION; . . . IN 'READING' AND TRANSPOSING MOVEMENT INTO MUSICAL RHYTHMS (POINTS 12, 15, 16)

Here I group together a number of items of which each alone might form the subject of one or several sessions, in order to emphasise how

[19] I owe this exercise to Bernard Reichel, who has always made a point of getting his pupils to appreciate how the voices in harmonic or polyphonic play preserve their own identities, and thus are each in turn able to exert their influence on the subsequent course of the music.

closely linked are the various subject components of music and movement. It would undoubtedly be possible—in fact desirable, in a didactic context—to lay stress on one subject rather than another; but there is no absolute criterion by which to judge, in the abstract, whether any particular exercise would prove more or less successful for any given student. To guarantee the quality of the final result, it will not suffice to pursue the contents of any exercise exactly to the letter. One student, for example, may achieve perfect mastery over his movements and piano-playing by the exercise of a series of phrasings, yet his harmonic support points will be out of tune with the rhythm they are supposed to be helping to underline; another may perfectly master the principle of modulating into neighbouring keys, but will forget to take suitable expression and phrasing into account. Yet another will play with so many different nuances of expression that one will be at a loss to follow his melodic or harmonic intentions. Thus the instructions or suggestions which the instructor will feel moved to give will vary from one student to another and one circumstance to another. But there do remain two inexhaustible sources of inspiration and mastery to which the teacher may wish to direct the student's attention.

The first makes call upon his internal feelings and his power of mental representation. For example, the student can learn to bring a 'human dimension' to his phrasing by basing it on the pattern of his own breathing; he may succeed in endowing his piano-playing with an unwavering crescendo—or in keeping up an unfaltering tempo—by concentrating on the need to renew constantly the necessary energy within himself. He can learn to bring the piece he has started to its logical conclusion, without interruptions or irrelevant detours, by foreseeing the whole of its course in his mind's eye as if it were a visible line of progression in space. Or again, when trying to express a particular impression or state of mind at the piano, he can learn to assign to his own body (by getting it to adopt a muscle tone and posture suited to the sentiment expressed) the task of finding himself the required sound combinations at the keyboard and the appropriate time structures and dynamics; after which he can readopt the role of pianist–improviser in order to create with this initial expressive material a composition responding to the demands of his own musicianship. In other exercises he may seek to interpret expressive movements performed by others, or, again, to draw impressions from the form or content of graphic, plastic, or other visual works with a view to translating them into terms of sound.

The second source of inspiration and technical device obviously resides in musical works as such. It isn't a question of copying or performing them slavishly, but rather of analysing some of their components in order to use them as a model or canvas for the achievement of original work.

A given piece of music may lie at the root of many others: one might think of retaining just its form, its succession of tonalities, or its time signature and quality of movement; or perhaps only one or two of its rhythmic motifs or chord progressions may be taken as the starting-point of a piece which, far from sounding like a pastiche of the original composer, will bear the stamp of its new creator.[20]

Exercises in all these areas, allied to those more specifically designed for the mastery of a multiplicity of rhythmic movements and combinations, ought ideally to lead the future rhythmician to the point at which all Dalcroze's warnings to teachers of his method become superfluous! Here, however, are some of them, taken from a long list of which a good half relate to piano improvisation (1926b: 11 ff). These are offered to rhythmicians who recognize, with Dalcroze, that 'in our somewhat complicated teaching we are often led into bad habits which our educational ardour and altruistic zeal prevent us from noticing' [!]:

Seek at all times to suppress any muscular contraction likely to harden your playing and compromise its suppleness. Don't *bang* the keys; but give every *ff* as much power as possible without damaging your eardrums or frightening the students (Point 3).

Avoid excessive use of the pedals (4).

Guard against an unintended *rubato*; on the other hand, *vary the tempi* . . . (5).

In polyrhythmic exercises, make each line melodically interesting— do not be content with the simple repetition of notes and chords (7).

Vary your registers: don't stick to the piano's middle range or any other fixed position (8).

---

[20] Christiane Montandon first drew my attention to the importance of this type of exercise, being predisposed towards them by her extensive knowledge of the piano repertoire and the care with which she constantly nourishes her students' musical imagination by getting them to discover the treasures of existing music.

Avoid excessive use of the chord of the dominant seventh (10).

Take a breath between each rhythm and each sentence (11).

Do not improvise all the music needed in a lesson, but select some interesting rhythms from the works of the masters (13).

Do not keep the tune going without a break: students must get used to following a rhythm through without the support of the music (17).

Do not stick to the same tempo throughout a single series of exercises (9).

Do not indulge in the pianistic parody of students' physical imperfections, unless you do so with a gentle smile! (25)

Musical 'Prompts'[21]

Dalcroze later expanded as follows on the types of exercise listed at the start of this chapter:

All these exercises are equipped with commands, whose purpose is to keep mind and body 'under pressure': to prompt pupils, whether into movement or immobility . . .: to set the mind in a state of readiness to select from the ensemble of muscles that most requisite to the action called for . . .: which is to combine and alternate spontaneous rhythms with those ordered by mental process (1945: 159).

I propose to enlarge somewhat on these various commands, as they help illustrate one of the most characteristic resources of improvisation for the Dalcrozian teacher. This type of exercise is in fact nowadays more or less regarded as the paradigm of traditional rhythmic exercises. It is the one generally referred to in rhythmics parlance as the *reaction exercise*, whether auditory, visual, or tactile. Of these, so-called 'auditory reaction' exercises play the relatively greatest role—not surprisingly, in this essentially musical education. What we are concerned with here—still in a traditional sense—is a motor reaction to a sounded signal, which may take the form of a simple *'hup!'* from the teacher's lips, or its equivalent on the piano or some other instrument (a trill, a sudden accent, a repeated note, a short motif), or, more broadly, of what we shall try to define below under the term 'musical prompt' (*'hop' musical*). By means of the prompt—whatever form it may take—we instruct the pupil that he is now to switch

---

[21] *Les 'hop' musicaux.* The interjection equivalent to *hop!* is *hup!*; but 'musical hups' does not work so well in English. (Translator's note)

whatever he is doing from one thing to another in accordance with a predetermined code. Generally speaking, the switch either must be made at a specific point in time (on the beat immediately following the prompt, for example, or after a delay which is either agreed in advance or determined by the signal itself), or else need only be effected as soon as possible after the pupil's perception of it.

Most rhythmics teachers give an important place to this type of exercise in their lessons. Not a few, however, nowadays question both their value and validity, as they do of any exercise which might be interpreted as some sort of constraint imposed from without—often apparently of an arbitrary nature and thus suggesting something akin to drilling or 'conditioning'. Those in favour of the 'prompt' rebut this view: 'By the very fact of calling for a change of direction at any moment, the prompt shows clearly that Eurhythmics is the antithesis of conditioning, since its very function is to prevent pupils from becoming fixed in any particular series of automatic movements!' We may begin to clarify this by describing and analysing some specific examples:

I. TWO EXAMPLES OF SWITCHES MADE ON THE BEAT FOLLOWING THE SIGNAL

First example: This may be described as a 'Stop–Go' exercise (*un exercice dit 'd'incitation et d'inhibition'*). It is often used in demonstration lessons because it enables the audience to participate, from their seats, by clapping in time to the pupils' walking-pace.

The piano sets a pace in crotchets. The pupils walk around in time to it so long as they are not prevented by a musical 'stop' signal, e.g. a rhythmic fragment such as ♫♪ | ♩ . This tells them to freeze on the spot until it reappears, thereby signalling 'Off you go again!' It is rather like a set of traffic lights, but without the colour! The point, then, is to stop or go on the crotchet immediately following the triplet, it alone being charged with the function of making us react, regardless of what goes on between the signals. Note that the teacher may stop playing without actually giving the 'stop' signal, or resume playing without giving the 'go' signal, thereby testing pupils' capacity to resist their natural impulses.

True, the signal does come unexpectedly from the hands of the improviser (though no more than a car may come unexpectedly from around the corner when we are getting ready to cross the road!). Arbitrarily? Well of course, though it is selected not purely at random, but from among those rhythms whose dynamics are suitable for eliciting an immediate response. (Fortunately for us, the appearance of the car is often heralded by the sound of its engine!) Does it 'condition' a reflex? Far from it: what the piano plays in between the unexpected stop–start signals forces the pupil to fight against the reflexes he has already taken on board (sound = move, silence = be still). He must therefore hold in reserve for another occasion reactions not in use in the present situation, in order to deal more economically with the immediate priority.

Second example: The music is in two pulses. The pupils each play with a ball, with one hand bouncing it on the ground on the first pulse and catching it on the second. When the piano gives a more pronounced emphasis to the first pulse (such as by doubling or accentuating the bass line), pupils must catch the ball with their other hand on the pulse immediately following, and continue in this way until another emphasis instructs them to change hands again.

An arbitrary signal? Yes—but not once it is seen as the start of a musical process by which pupils are insensibly led to play this ball-game to the tune of a song such as that in Example 3.5.

Ex. 3.5

$$\downarrow \uparrow = \text{right hand}$$
$$\downarrow \uparrow = \text{left hand}$$

Performed with a conventional accompaniment, the song's overall structure is immediately apparent, with its three phrases of which the last is longest. We should also note, in the present case, that the tune itself actually belies this appearance by the identical repetition of the opening motif at the start of the third phrase. Now experience shows that a single repetition is often enough to inculcate a habit or initiate an automatic response from its next appearance, unless steps are taken to guard against it. For, having in the preceding exercise focused the children's attention on the point at which one phrase leads into another, and having particularly made them conscious of their tendency to do things without thinking (by, for example, emitting signals at regular intervals and then suddenly introducing one sooner or later than expected), we have now enabled them to work out the correct succession of phrases in this song for themselves after falling just once into the tune's little trap. Its correct perception will be further reinforced by the rhyme scheme, which can then take over the signalling role of the piano and allow the tune to be played without any accompaniment at all. The possibility of inventing new rhyming couplets is another way of ensuring that the end of each phrase is properly perceived, while their translation into spatial terms, by gesture and movement, will physically set their respective (or relative) durations in directly visual terms.

It will be objected that the song itself could have been used to initiate the exercise, and the rhyme to be the principal means of defining its phrases. Well, and why not? It will hardly have escaped attention that our exercise was doubly beneficial: it offered us a technique sufficiently generalized for application to any song or piece of music conforming to the same pattern of a binary rhythm and a phrase structure with its climax on the final downbeat, irrespective of how many phrases there are, how long they last, or in what order they appear. It even enabled us to embark upon several different pieces in the course of a single lesson—which would have been rather difficult in any alternative approach. Then again, we avoided the risk of creating too strong an association between rhyme and phrasing, which are by no means always in accord with each other. (One thinks of such a song as '*Le bon roi Dagobert*', where phrase length is governed by the meaning of the text rather than by the nominal rhyme-scheme.[22])

In addition, this exercise (like the first, though different in kind) enabled the pupil to improve his capacity for rapid reaction to *unexpected* sound stimuli, a capacity he could find useful for many purposes, not just musical ones.

2. TWO EXAMPLES OF SWITCHES MADE AS SOON AS POSSIBLE AFTER THE SIGNAL IS HEARD

In the two exercises described below an attempt is made to establish or verify the existence of a stable relationship between the bass and treble notes of the piano and of the concepts *low* and *high* in general. I have

[22] There are some notable examples in hymns, where the sense of the words requires a prolonging of the musical phrase over the metrical scheme.

deliberately chosen two very classical exercises, and present them here in their simplest format so that their respective underlying features may be more easily picked out and compared.

> *First example*: The children walk around to the accompaniment of music in the piano's middle range. The striking of a lower note instructs them all to stamp on the floor (or to hit it with a pair of batons, or perhaps to 'pick a flower', etc.), that of a higher note to strike both batons together, to 'catch a fly', etc.
> *Second example*: Whenever the piano is playing in the bass register the pupils walk around (or move around in any manner suggested to them by the music); when it is playing in the treble they are to clap their hands or beat a tambourine in time to it (or do anything else with the upper part of the body, or the arms or hands, as appropriate to the dynamics of the music).

Let us consider the relative advantages and disadvantages of these two exercises. One of the advantages of the first is that the 'prompt' may be given several times in succession in the same register, whereas in the second exercise it is the *change* of register that acts as a signal, and the actions corresponding to the concepts *high* and *low* therefore necessarily alternate. Hence the first exercise encourages (in theory, at least) an apperception of bass/treble, low/high relationships in absolute terms rather than by recognising one as a function of the other. A complementary risk, however, is that that the newly created association remains narrowly linked to this particular situation and in the long run has little or no bearing on concepts of high and low. (One sort of stimulus induces one reaction, another induces some other reaction; but the two are not set in undisputed opposition, and the properties of 'high' and 'low' are not necessarily related to the actual sounds as such.) This risk can be minimized, however, by carefully introducing as wide a variation as possible in the notes acting as stimulus, so that they may be perceived as occupying some portion of the sound-space situated either 'here' or 'there' in relation to (or above or below) the medium of the piano. In other words, the lowest sounds of the upper register (and the highest in the lower) must be given for the students to hear, as well as those at the extremes of either range.

Another distinctive feature of this exercise is the imperative nature of the signals, which has a risky habit of eliciting all sorts of mis-responses because they are so immediate and made without benefit of thinking-time. If a correct response is preferred to an immediate one, care may be taken to reduce the emphatic nature of the signal so that attention may be redirected onto the quality of the sound itself, though it will then be necessary to sharpen it little by little so as to produce an increasingly prompt response.

By drawing pupils' attention to a very precise signal, this exercise may further serve as the basis for exercises in counting or rhythmic imitation. Here the pupil is called upon to reproduce, not a single note, but a regular 'salvo' of notes which may be longer or shorter, more or less bunched or spaced out, and played in either the treble or bass range of the piano.

The advantage of the second exercise is that it requires pupils to listen more carefully than in the first. Whereas in the previous exercise they could remain deaf to anything that did not constitute a signal, in this one the 'prompt' is not endowed with the same physical quality, subsisting rather in the perception of a difference in range. In a well-run exercise, it is in fact the pupil who, noticing that *something is different*, prompts himself, i.e. instructs himself to make an activity switch. If, now, the piano makes a clef-change coincide with the start of a new section, for example, or heralds such a change by sounding a perfect cadence in the previous clef, it forces the pupil to concentrate not so much on *what* the change is as on *when* it occurs. Now, since this exercise never calls for more than two types of action, the pupil no longer has to think about what his action represents: it is enough to hear that it is time to make a switch. A definite aim is therefore bypassed—as will be confirmed when an inattentive pupil misses one of the changes and thereafter reverses the order of his actions without appearing in the least perturbed about it! On the other hand, and if the improviser knows how to set about it, the cadences or section-changes that he is bound to incorporate in his music may act as 'diversionary prompts' which, in requiring the pupil to resist them, force him to refocus his attention on pitch alone.

Both these exercises obviously aim at 'conditioning', just as it is obvious that any form of education consists largely in 'conditioning'—in implanting those automatic responses without which no subsequent training is possible. But let's be clear about this: the sort of conditioning aimed at here is that which succeeds in relating perceived bass or treble sounds to their position in sound-space, and not that which might establish a fixed relationship between, for example, bass notes and the act of walking, or treble notes and the act of beating. And any risk of this sort of conditioning is nipped in the bud by constantly varying the commands. For example—confining ourselves solely to modes of progression: bass = walk normally, treble = go on tiptoe; bass = wriggle along on the stomach, treble = walk on all fours; bass = walk on all fours, treble = walk normally; bass = walk with head bowed, treble = looking up at the sky, etc. The same can be applied to postures or other forms of movement. At the same time, care will be taken to ensure that the required conditioning is not just carried out by the sound of the piano but also effected by the use of other instruments or the human voice, nor restricted to body-space but as easily transferred to environmental space: objects, walls, the blackboard, sheets of paper, etc.

These examples, especially the last, all go to show how easy it is, unless great care is taken, to fall into rigidly schematic modes of thinking which give rise to a feeble caricature of Eurhythmics and result in the adoption of positions quite the opposite of what was originally intended. In fact, the rhythmician's technical expertise can never be a substitute for sensitivity, nor can it replace a deep understanding of the methods at his disposal and the effects they can produce.

Dalcroze discussed musical 'prompts' in an article under that title (1930a), at a period when the 'shouted or whispered prompt' (p. 14) was probably more widespread than it is today. He reminded rhythmics teachers that the latter could often be replaced by 'a more musical kind of command', which would have the advantage of 'involving the pupil in the music he is called upon to interpret' (p. 14). He capped it (pp. 15–19) with a list containing quite a number of prompts that came to his mind, classifying them by areas of application and always embodying them in a specific exercise. As this is one of the rare articles containing exercises devised by Dalcroze himself, I give below (mainly for rhythmics practitioners) some longish extracts, which will call for explanatory comments.

Exercises Governed by 'Musical Prompts'
(Dalcroze 1930a: 15–19)

DYNAMICS, TIMING, FLEXIBILITY

1. At each chord played on the piano, spread the arms and upper body. If the chord is held *and continues to resonate*, keep arms outstretched; as soon as it stops, drop them.

2. Pupils walk around (or move about) so long as a chord continues to sound. As soon as it stops, they stop. [Note: The same prompt (such as here the continued resonance of a chord) may, according to context, initiate two different or opposite reactions (here, keeping still or continuing to move).]

3. Pupils walk in two files. The piano teacher plays a two-part melody, the upper line staccato, the other legato, or vice versa. One file follows the upper voice, the other the lower, and both change their mode of walking when the teacher changes the two lines over.

4. The pianist plays a legato in quavers. Whenever he 'points' four quavers, pupils walk in staccato fashion to the four which follow . . .

5. Pupils walk [in accordance with a given tempo]. A sudden *ff* introduces a change of pace. Ditto after a sudden pp.

6. A crescendo or diminuendo held over four (or six) quavers calls for the next crotchet to be followed by a gesture, a kick, a jump, a step backwards, . . . a bending of the knee, or a reprise of the theme.

7. Two, three or four successive *accentuations* enjoin, respectively, a pace in two, three, or four beats to the bar.

8. Pupils walk to music in crotchets. A duplet, triplet, or quadruplet played at the piano calls for, respectively, two, three, or four shorter steps to be made immediately afterwards.

9. At the conclusion of a series of crotchets, a quadruplet inaugurates a measure of four beats to a bar, a sextuplet [six in the time of four] one of six beats to the bar, etc.

[. . .]

11. A series of legato rhythms calls for an interpretation based on continued movement, a staccato for modifying the interpretation.

Let us stop here. An attentive reader will have noticed that these 'musical prompts' are not all equivalent either as to role or as to degree of arbitrariness, and that they need classifying in different categories:

Some are very closely related to the actions they solicit, and could, if need be, do without any explanation in advance. Music and movement work in concert together, the latter being shaped by the former, which impresses its own changes upon it (cf. particularly Exercises 1, 3, 11).

Some are designed to solicit a reaction which follows naturally from the prompt (cf. coming to a stop in Exercise 2, and the type of movement in Exercise 6).

Others provide musical patterns calling for an immediate imitative reaction (cf. 4, 8).

Yet others bear a purely conventional relation to the required action. They occur either in the form of a little puzzle for the brain to work on (cf. Exercises 7, 9, where the signal is a sound-signal representing a number that might have been expressed verbally), or in the form of a 'cry of alarm' (cf. Exercise 5, where it is equivalent to some such word as '*Hup*! or '*Go*!').

Some, finally, solicit what might be called a *mixed* response, in that they endeavour to translate the untranslatable without claiming to produce a faithful representation, whilst nevertheless relating to at least some aspects of it, the rest being established by convention. (Thus, in Exercise 2, the fact of walking while—and only so long as— a chord continues to echo is a convention provisionally defined for the purpose of letting the pupil show that he can hear that something is going on). We shall have occasion to look at many more examples below.

Dalcroze lumped all these piano signals together under the heading 'musical prompts' (*les 'hop' musicaux*, literally 'musical *hups*!') in order to distinguish them from the 'shouts . . ., numbers . . ., or beats on a bass drum [formerly used for training] gymnasts or dancers of the old school' (p. 14). Obviously, however, not all these 'prompts' have the same musical value. Personally, I should prefer to restrict the term to those itemized under the first three categories listed above, as well as those in the last category (albeit with a more abstract connotation). The others then might better be described as *conventional or arbitrary sound signals*. They would also include spoken prompts and various oral or verbal injunctions, and need not be regarded as worthless: they have the merit of being able to provoke an immediate response in whatever terms may have been decided in advance, and the advantage (especially when delivered vocally) of rising above the musical proceedings without impeding their flow. Dalcroze said of them that they are 'of some usefulness at the commencement of studies when the child is constantly having to fight against his natural resistance, lapses of concentration, and motor reactions already deeply ingrained' (1930*a*: 14). They will certainly be welcomed on other occasions, as methods of control, or in course of motor games where the pupil can 'take a rest from listening'. But it is a question of using them with discernment, when there can be no doubt about their appropriateness, and of not being induced by convenience or laziness into substituting them for genuinely 'musical' signals, requiring the teacher to engage his sensitivity, his imagination, his musical knowledge, and—let's face it—a bit of technical know-how!

Here is another list of examples devised by Dalcroze himself, and this time I recommend the interested reader to attempt his or her own analysis as to the type of prompt each one brings into play as we go along. Are we talking about 'musical' prompts (including those calling for a 'mixed' response), or about '*conventional or arbitrary sound signals*'?

MELODY AND HARMONY

1. A rising series of four consecutive notes in a scale gets the pupil to walk forwards; a descending series, to walk backwards.
[. . .]
3. After several repetitions of any interval, the pupils start beating time to it as a conductor would, the number of beats in a bar being equal to the number of degrees in the interval; or else they run to the same grouping of quavers.
4. Whole tones are accompanied by forward walking, semitones by walking on the spot (or taking very tiny steps).
5. An appoggiatura from beneath calls for an upward-rising gesture, one from above for a gesture [in a downwards direction].
6. Chords sounded in the middle range of the piano instruct the pupil to walk in crotchets; in the treble range, to run in quavers; in the bass range, to stamp, etc. . . . [it being understood that passing from one range to another while playing involves no change in tempo].
7. Major chords call for the arms to be raised, minor chords for a bending of the upper body and the knees . . .
8. A tune with two melodic lines calls for the pupils to walk in two columns; with three or four lines, to walk in three or four columns.
9. A modulation changes the direction in which pupils are walking or which they are facing.
10. A modulating chord delivered brusquely instructs the pupil to jump or change direction.
14. The ending of a melodic phrase signals a need for a change in direction, whether of walking or of gesture, or for a change of musuclar tension.
17. The teacher, playing something classical in two voices, intro-

duces a discord: the pupil resolves it physically by taking a step backwards, etc.

19. Pupils walk around at a given speed or to a given rhythm while the teacher repeats a chord at the piano. As soon as he alters the chord in any way, they change their speed or rhythm.

20. The same, except that they now react to a change of position or an inversion of the chord.

There will be a tendency to classify these exercises differently according to one's degree of familiarity with musical matters and to what extent they relate to our living, personal experience of them. What follows is the way I would classify them myself, while granting that the reader may entertain differing views.

I would unhesitatingly classify as authentic 'musical prompt' exercises those numbered 5, 7, 9, 10, and 14, and as those calling for a 'mixed' response numbers 1, 3, 4, 8, and 17. As to exercises 6, 19, and 20, they amount to 'sound signals' having no direct relationship with the actions called for.

Let us look at the next areas examined by Dalcroze. I will give my own responses to them as we go along.

RHYTHM AND METRE

1. Changes in walking or leaping, in gesture or accentuation, are prompted by modifications to the rhythm or measure. [*Musical prompt.*]

2. Following a silence lasting *one* beat, the pupil does a single jump; following a *two-beat* silence, two hops; etc. [*Mixed response.*]

4. When the teacher is playing in minims, the pupil performs in a given rhythm, while a dotted minim (or a semibreve) calls for a different rhythm. [*Mixed response, provided, of course, that the rhythm being expressed has the same length as the given time-value.*]

5. A rising anacrusis calls for forward walking, a descending one for walking backwards. [*Mixed response.*]

[. . .]

7. Pupils walk in time to crotchets while the teacher is playing crotchets in unison. When a distinctive figure (a triplet, skip, etc.) is heard in the *treble*, pupils walk forwards, whereas they walk backwards if that figure is played in the bass. [*Mixed response.*]

Here it will be noticed that as soon as one dispenses with simple imitation or the direct influence of the music—in other words, as soon as some faculty of analysis is called for—conventions are now perforce brought into play (and verbal or written responses are included in a variety of possibilities) to show that something has been properly grasped. The grasp one has of it permits a certain degree of self-distancing from a literal interpretation of the given material (i.e. the rhythmic element itself).

TIMBRES AND VISUAL SIGNALS

The next area examined by Dalcroze in the article cited is that of *timbre*. I will not expand on this, as the exercises described here are simply transpositions, to the same end, of such means as using different ranges of the piano or different sorts of accent or figure, e.g. switching between piano and voice or piano and percussion, or between voices singing or various instruments playing, etc. Nearly all these exercises have as their aim that of distinguishing between one *tinbre* and another, either by following the rhythms or rubatos enunciated by them, or by making some sort of arbitrarily selected reaction. I will, however, cite two in particular which strike me as going a little further, or which, with hindsight, may at least be seen as opening the horizons which were to be explored at a later date.

> A baton struck once on a tambourine calls for a hop, on a cymbal for a pirouette, a triangle for a stretch, a kettledrum for kneeling, the rim of a tambourine for a jump, etc. (Exercise 3, 1930*a*: 18)

At first sight these look like purely arbitrary signals, but closer examination shows that they try to draw certain parallels between the actions called for and the *timbre* or relative degree of shrillness of each particular instrument. At issue, therefore, at least in underlying intention, is an authentically 'musical prompt'. With the passage of time, as it happens, more and more attention has been brought to bear on *timbre*, and this type of exercise is nowadays typical of those in which it is left to the pupil to decide on a suitable action to make by absorbing into himself the sensation evoked by one *timbre* or another. In other words, greater importance is nowadays attached to the *physical quality* of sound, and consideration paid to current experiments tending to show that the sound of such and such an instrument reverberates particularly in such and such a part of the body. At least, one hopes it is!

It is precisely for its relevance to the physical nature of sound that I cite this second exercise:

Two percussion instruments (e.g. tambourine and triangle) struck simultaneously call for one bodily response from the pupil, two different instruments call for a different response. Also: the same, with three voices. (Exercise 5, 1930a: 18)

Or with more than three voices, of course. For just as an interval ought to be recognizable by its 'colour', and not just by counting the degrees between its top and bottom notes, and just as a major or minor chord should be recognizable, whether or not in root position, by the general impression it gives, rather than by reference to academic calculations, so should we be able to train ourselves to make holistic perceptions of compound sounds and clusters of *timbres*, and to identify them uniquely in relation to others of more or less similar constitution. Our modern appreciation of music makes this work seem at least as important as that of analysing a total impression with a view to identifying its various components. And in the above exercise the pupil must be capable of nothing less than a holistic perception if he is to react instantaneously to a compound of three voices.

We cannot pass on without mentioning one of the main advantages of percussion instruments for auditory reaction exercises. Unlike the piano, they are easily transportable, and for this reason are convenient for any number of exercises involving the *localization of sound or timbres*, exercises which will often be done with eyes closed. For example: turning to face the direction from which the sound was heard to come; going to the place it emanated from; following a held or rhythmically repeated sound around without being distracted by other sounds or accompanying rhythms not intended for our attention; determining which of two or more sounds emitted simultaneously reaches us from the right, from the left, from in front or behind, and reacting accordingly; etc.

The final area examined by Dalcroze seems to wander off the intended subject of his article. (People in those days were not as formal as they are now, and Dalcroze less so than many—a point, incidentally, which doesn't always make it easy for his readers!) The topic concerned is that of *visual sensations and analyses*. Yet it will be noted that the signals used in the following exercises are in some ways the visual equivalent of auditory commands. For instance:

At an agreed visual signal given by a single person the pupils are required to walk in a particular rhythm (Exercise 1, 1930a: 18).

[We have here the equivalent of a conventional sound signal.]
Four or five people move in a circle while copying the curved and
straight lines dictated by a lone walker, or by someone *drawing*
those lines on the blackboard (Exercise 3, p. 18). [Here we have the
equivalent of a 'musical prompt'.]
Switching the light off for a moment, or making some other change
to it, calls for a given pose to be struck (Exercise 4, p. 19).
Alternating light and darkness dictates equivalent alternations in
tempo or rhythm (Exercise 5, p. 19).
Four or five different rhythms correspond to four or five pieces of
paper or material of different colours; the pupil is required to
concatenate these rhythms in the order shown by the succession of
colours being presented (Exercise 8, p. 19).

These three exercises all represent purely arbitrary signals, but they
show that Dalcroze did not confine the visual field to that of the
moving body!

The advantage of these exercises is that they give the initiative to the
pupils rather than to the teacher (as, indeed, do those of the preceding
group). One may well ask what their musical value is. It all depends,
of course, on how each exercise is handled; but it seems to me to reside
at two levels.

These exercises can perfectly well be done without any external
musical support (as can many others, even those involving sound
signals). They thereby enable pupils to demonstrate that they have
internalized their grasp of the tempo, that they have absorbed into
their muscles and their inner ear the dynamics of a rhythm or the
curve of a melodic phrase. Have we not already noted that one of
Eurhythmics' aims is to 'turn the whole body into . . . a single "inner
ear" '? Well, we have to give it every opportunity to allow itself to act
as such in its own right. Exercises of this sort will provide us with
many such opportunities.

It is equally possible to keep up a continued musical support in
these exercises. In this event the teacher, at the piano, will have to do
as much work as the bulk of his pupils who are following instructions
given by one of their own number, and he will make use of his
improvised music to follow what is happening and turn it into a
musical description. It is perfectly possible for a musically talented
improviser to adapt his playing off the cuff, and without falling into
incoherence, to the curves and accents of his musical argument

following imperatives dictated to him from without. (It is, when you come down to it, one of his stunts! And Eurhythmics will have prepared him for it—see above.) But while doing this, he will also be able, more subtly, to seek occasionally to influence the soloist who is giving the orders. The latter, if his hearing is well enough developed, will be able to take advantage of the musical inflexions he hears and of the fact that they enable him to judge (rather as a good skier can take advantage of each curve in the terrain while continuing to look ahead of himself) the right moment for a suitable change of instruction. Doing the exercise then becomes a work of collaboration, of a complicity in which music plays the leading role.

By contrast, this last area of exercise brings out the extent to which all the auditory reaction exercises considered in the preceding pages bear the marks of a teaching method centred on the teacher's fundamental role of intervention in the rhythmics lesson. He it is who, through monopoly of the piano, manifestly exercises the power. And the thin dividing line between using power and abusing it is very quickly crossed! As, moreover, is that between not wishing to abuse it and not being willing to use it! It is a fact that so-called 'active' methods, whether in general education or musical education in particular (Eurhythmics claiming a foot in both camps), aim to get the pupil to take charge of himself, so far as he is able, and to proceed—within his own rhythm and as directed by his own energy—towards the discovery of that which will prove most useful or valuable to him in life. The teacher, in this context, becomes a facilitator, a consultant, occasionally even a director, but relinquishes his former role as a dispenser of knowledge. In the nature of things, this position demands a considerable amount of preparatory work on his part, much of it carried out 'in the dark'. It is both a preparation for teaching, which will enable him to put his pupils in possession of the right material for exciting their curiosity for, and interest in, the various fields they are expected to enter upon, and a personal preparation, which will enable the teacher to grasp what is going on in the class, in order to bring out its educational aspect.

This sort of approach generally goes hand in hand with the abandonment of all visible trappings of power. The teacher's desk, for example, no longer stands on a dais but comes down to the level of those of the pupils. Now the rhythmics teacher's piano itself counts as one of these trappings, and there are some such teachers who believe that the very fact of being seated at the piano smacks of the abuse of power. But what if this symbolic object happens at the same time to be the best possible means of expression and communication for its user? What if it happens to be the best possible and a virtually inexhaustible source of 'educational material'? Will the history lecturer, who has learnt to handle words with rigour and elegance, have to abandon these properties for nothing but monosyllables and silence when he switches to an indirect method of teaching history? Of course, he will speak less and will permit himself to be interrupted; of course, he will have to develop within himself those qualities of listening to somebody else which he may previously have lacked. But even if he plays straight with his pupils and manages to give the appearance of having forgotten everything so that he can rediscover it with them (and that can hardly fail to offer new perspectives on his subject of which he was previously unaware), the medium of expression and communication already developed within him can hardly be lost, and it would be a mistake to divest himself of something that enables him to clarify situations or illustrate them with a pretty story, to summarize the growth of a movement, to focus attention on a telling point . . . Surely such abilities still lie within his province?

Exactly the same goes for the rhythmics teacher. Here I may be accused of trailing a red herring. At issue here, I will be told, is not the use of piano improvisation so much as the teacher's *manipulation* of his pupils, which comes into effect when, for instance, he gives them 'prompt'-type exercises. But this still threatens to come into effect whether he uses the piano or not.

The Educational Value of Eurhythmics

There can be no doubt that Eurhythmics, in its original form, could not have come into being today without appearing suspect (as indeed it appeared in 1910, but for opposite reasons!): it gives too big a part to the teacher, and its teaching methods are open to a charge of being essentially interventionist. In fact, even in those (increasingly frequent) cases where the whole lesson bases its structure on ideas emanating from the pupils, where they are given the greatest freedom to decide upon their physical movements, where a large proportion of the lesson's music-making is entrusted to them, and where the teacher is more often to be found in their midst than at his piano, the latter requires at least two things of them: to listen and move about, to move about and listen. And no matter how he sets about it, the moment invariably comes at which he is actively working on the *conscious* establishment of links between these two types of activity. That he should dispense with this ambition might well be thought an attractive and desirable thing; but it would no longer be Eurhythmics.

Needless to say, there always have been teachers (in every field) whose chief delight is to see pupils falling over themselves to obey every little command, and who turn such blind obedience into a matter of personal prestige. ('I'm the boss around here, and I'll do as I please!') Yet I think I can safely claim that the rhythmics teacher who gets his pupils to respond to musical 'prompts' has a far more modest view of his role—for from the very moment that he sits down at the piano for this type of exercise he somehow comes to see himself as just another part of the teaching material. In other words, he is in this instance no more than a means of changing some of the variable situations to which the pupil must be able to *adapt himself*.

Assimilation and Accommodation

Piaget, you may recall, drew attention to the twin processes of *assimilation* and *accommodation* by which all living creatures exercise their capacity for adaptation (advanced forms of which are represented, in human beings, by psycho-motor development and the acquisition of knowledge). We may pause here and examine these ideas, as they will give us a better grasp of the functional aspect of Eurhythmics.

When the individual is confronted with a novel datum capable of being integrated into his universe, he seeks to absorb it by a process of *assimilation*. In other words, he compares it with various data already in his possession, checks to see whether or not it can be dealt with in the same way, and then, so long as it is not absolutely alien to his personal experience, he incorporates it into his repertoire of information and actions.

Someone finding a curious object and wondering what on earth its purpose is, will seek to compare its shape, its substance, its components, and the various actions to which it lends itslef, with his recollection of other objects of comparable size and similar usability. Thus he seeks to assimilate it into what he knows in order to make any sense of it.

If you ask a music student to understand the form of a piece he is made to listen to, his ability to proffer a response will depend on the extent to which he is capable of relating it to his accumulated musical experience.

If all children with a reasonable amount of rhythmics experience immediately start skipping around as soon as they hear the piano playing a rhythm such as Example 3.6, it is because they will have assimilated it to all previous situations in which the same rhythm has led them to perform the same action.

Ex. 3.6

If the same pupils, on hearing the rhythm in Example 3.7, are capable of discovering for themselves that they can interpret it by means of, say, a skip followed by a step, it is because they have assimilated this rhythm to the rhythm of a skip, encountered an obstacle to its simple continuance, and resolved the problem by assimilating this 'obstacle' to the action of a single walking step or to a halt.

Ex. 3.7

When one of our colleagues, wishing her pupils to appreciate the difference between a tone and a semitone, got them to listen to the little song in Example 3.8 without saying anything about it, a little girl cried 'Oh—it sounds just as if it's gone into the dark!'.[23] In her process of assimilation, the perception of sound-change became linked to that of light-change somewhere in the mysterious reaches of her imagination.

Ex. 3.8 ('*See the little river, flowing-owing-oh*')

Pe - ti - te   ri - viè - re   fait lou-lou, lou - lou,

pe - ti - te   ri - viè - re   fait lou-lou, lou - lou.

'See the little river, flowing-owing-oh'

[23] I owe this charming anecdote to the late Hélène Finsler.

But if some new datum can be incorporated into our experience to the extent that it lends itself to assimilation, it can enrich that experience only in so far as it offers at least some small point of distinctive difference, or affords some degree of resistance to our preconceived schemata or habituated actions. These must be capable of undergoing modification if they are to adapt themselves to the particular characteristics of the novel datum. Such *accommodation* of thought or deed—or both—has the effect of expanding or diversifying our ways of dealing with the external world.

You have just bought a new-fangled type of corkscrew. A process of assimilation to what you have already learnt about corkscrews will tell you what its function is and hence what you will use it for. But to succeed in using it you will have to accommodate your movements and actions to the shape, size, and mechanics of this particular corkscrew.

You are reading a text in Gothic script. You will find it easier to follow if you succeed in getting accustomed to the oddities of the writing. But it may then be that the meaning of the text—written in Old English, perhaps—still escapes you, in which case you will have to accommodate your own thought-processes to the turns of phrase of that language, even if it means rejecting some of the words because they remain highly resistant to assimilation.

If a music student is asked to beat 3/4 time to a given tune or rhythm while reading from a score, and his gestures seem mechanical in execution and not entirely in step with the music they are supposed to be reinforcing, there is a failure of accommodation at issue. But it may be that such failure stems from inadequate reciprocal assimilation between the first beat of the written bar and that of the accompanying gesture; or perhaps, at a deeper level, from a failure to assimilate the (gestural) first beat of the bar to the general sensation of a strong beat.

If the rhythmics students referred to above manage not only to walk in time to the rhythm being played to them but also, at the same time, to introduce such nuances into it as may be suggested by the piano, they will be demonstrating that they have sufficient mastery over their execution to be able to accommodate themselves to variations of physical energy—to which previous exercises will have enabled them to assimilate variations in nuance perceived through the ear.

From these examples it will be seen, from whatever level we may look at it, that assimilation and accommodation are constantly shuttling back and forth between each other and can never really be separated out. Should either one of them be lacking to any significant degree, there we will find individuals unadapted, unadaptable, and incapable of autonomy.

It follows, then, that it is not enough to be able to put one foot in front of the other (i.e. to have assimilated the mechanics of walking) in order to claim an ability to walk. You must also be able to cope with the incidental features of the terrain: know exactly when to step a little higher so as not to trip, how to wade through stretches of water or bypass them if you don't want to get wet, how to free your foot if it gets stuck in the silt, how to keep your balance if the ground gets slippery or suddenly slopes down . . . You must keep a look-out for possible obstacles so as not to bump into them and know exactly when to stop when confronted with a precipice. A notable part of many rhythmics exercises consists precisely in confronting pupils with a 'featured terrain' (both literally and figuratively). This is, indeed, one of their principal *raisons d'être*, as you will see by referring back to the beginning of this chapter.

In other words, the way in which Eurhythmics helps the pupil to develop 'a swift and economical communications system between all the agents of thought and movement' (see above) consists for the most part in *multiplying opportunities for accommodating his actions* (thoughts and movements) to his immediate surroundings. To this extent, Eurhythmics is primarily a training method. The chief aim of its exercises is not so much to facilitate acquisitions as to enable those already in existence to be drawn out and enriched by the very fact of being obliged to accommodate themselves to countless circumstances— circumstances far more numerous, more systematic, and more finely controllable than could possibly have been encountered outside the lesson in a similar period of time.

But we have also seen that such accommodation is inseparable from assimilation, which gives meaning to things by making connections between them, and so enables the student to integrate new experiences and new data into his repertoire. Eurhythmics makes these connections *manifest and conscious*, whereas in everyday life (or in traditional ways of teaching music or movement) they are more often left implicit or unconscious. In addition, the assimilation so favoured by Eurhythmics is of a type which intentionally relates all space–time–energy perceptions (even the most complex), and all conceptual development (even the most sophisticated), *to their sensory-motor source*—to the deepest level penetrated by the roots of all feeling and all knowledge (cf. above, Ch. 1).

It seems to me that this tendency to lay stress simultaneously on the explicit *assimilation* of external data to our longest-lived and most fundamental depths, and on the *accommodation*[24] of thought and sensory experience to situations deliberately engineered to stimulate them in a thousand and one ways, may be held, in the light of present-day knowledge, to guarantee the educational value of Eurhythmics. It follows that the first concern of the rhythmician who wishes to make this value his own should be to strike a balance between these two poles of experience.

[24] Translator's italics.

4

THE GRAMMAR OF EURHYTHMICS

I count as worthless any item of knowledge that is not preceded by a feeling.
André Gide, *Les Nourritures Terrestres*

Anyone who likes working to cut and dried formulae should bear in mind that a slight alteration to the French word *grammaire*, 'grammar', produces the word *grimoire*—'a book of magicians' spells', as well as 'an illegible scrawl' or 'piece of mumbo-jumbo'. Definitions of 'grammar' offered by the *Petit Robert* dictionary certainly do not appear to class it as one of life's pleasures: 'a set of rules to be followed in order to speak or write a language correctly', and, by analogy, 'set of rules associated with an art form'. In addition: 'the systematic study of the component parts of a language'; 'the study of forms and functions'. And, by extension: 'book, manual, or treatise on grammar'. We shall see how much of all that is worth bearing in mind for the present chapter. What I most enjoy about these definitions—the thing that all of them say without actually saying so—is the fact that grammar is *not* synonymous with the use of language itself.[1] Grammar may be learnt from books, but learning a language can only really be done by living in the country where it is spoken. My choice of title, then, was primarily made to remind the reader that Eurhythmics lies beyond the boundaries of any possible kind of book.

In addition, it happens that I have in my possession a manuscript notebook dating from 1933 in which a student of that time records more than sixty-five exercises, divided between eighteen lessons, from a course which Dalcroze was then giving to prospective professional rhythmicians under the title *Grammaire de la Rythmique*. He expounded on what he meant by that in an article published in 1926,

---

[1] '*la grammaire n'est PAS le langage*', with a change from *langue* used in the preceding passage. The distinction between *la langue* and *le langage* (and *la parole*) does not seem sufficiently at issue here to call for circumlocutionary English equivalents. (Translator's note)

acknowledging that the title was borrowed from the London School of Rhythmics—English-speakers are so often quicker than French-speakers to hit the terminological nail right on the head!

There is nothing bookish about the course itself, however, which simply contains a large number of exercises 'designed to secure strength and flexibility in the muscles, independence of the limbs, a harmonious balance of movements and their promptness of execution . . ., in every possible degree of energy and speed' (1926a: 5). No reference is made to music theory, even though 'a whole series of rhythmic and metric exercises' come first in the proceedings, and even though movements are for the most part 'intimately linked with, perhaps even *woven into*, a musical fabric which simultaneously inspires them and brings them to life' (ibid.). Nor is any attempt made to bring about a theory of movement, even though what is on offer is 'a system of physical techniques available for the use of rhythmicians' (ibid.).

But 'grammar' indeed it is, in the sense that all these exercises will eventually turn each pupil's body into a sort of 'manual', a source of reference in which he will ever after be able to look up, not always the name, but certainly the *motor image* of the parts of speech by which he will be addressed by music, or of any other item in the conjugations of space and time.

Dalcroze thought that Eurhythmics would gain the attention of future teachers possessed of a sound knowledge and mastery of their muscular and nervous potentials.

To have control over one's body, in all its interactions with the mind and the emotions, is to break down such resistance as would otherwise paralyse the free development of our imaginative and creative faculties. (1922a: 10)

But in this respect he did not entirely place his confidence in the methods of physical education then currently in favour. In particular, he accused them of being based essentially on metrical regimes and of paying insufficient attention to nuance and shading in the task of bringing flexibility to various muscles: as far as they are concerned, he observed, there are hardly more than one or two possible ways of running and only one possible walking speed; there are only violent breathing exercises and energetic movements. Whatever value they may have had in their own right, he nevertheless could not but find such methods insufficient for the development of the physical characteristics indispensable to rhythmicians and prospective musicians.

Furthermore, having adopted as his own the principle that 'all muscular sensations enrich the brain with motor images' (1920: 6), an assertion which he was able to prove well-founded on a number of occasions, he feared that physical education of the traditional type very strongly impressed upon its pupils' consciousness only a limited number of such feelings and images, which would then turn into automatic reactions hard to fight against. He did not want his own pupils to find themselves in the same situation as those of whom he noted (1922a: 5):

> Thus, as soon as they try to introduce artistry into their motor activities, they must first learn how to abandon particular techniques which are too firmly rooted in their muscular memories and which inhibit their imagination from freely varying the nuances of muscular energy or duration.

As far as he was concerned, the value of motor images resided, by contrast, in their great number, in their variety, and especially in the ability of pupils to pass rapidly from one to another.

Unable to find in existing methods any that correspond to what he sought, Dalcroze found himself obliged to undertake the exercise of his own imagination, availing himself for this purpose of the assistance of specialists in movement, notably Lily Braun, a well-known expressive movement specialist of the time. In so doing, he made no undertaking to restrict himself to entirely original exercises:

> A certain number of them are in current usage, for the art of developing supple and co-ordinated muscles is a long-established one. But the way in which I am trying to develop and put them together into a rhythmic whole breathes new life into them. And because they are closely bound up with music, these new exercises in physical technique constitute a solid preparation for Eurhythmics in the true sense of the word (1926a: 5).

Nowadays, these 'grammatical' exercises generally form an integral part of rhythmics lessons, or at least form part of the instruction course in physical techniques from which prospective professional rhythmicians benefit. The latter branch has considerably expanded and diversified since Dalcroze was alive, following in this respect the evolution of modern dance and physical expression (which themselves have felt the influence of Dalcroze in various roundabout ways, but that's another story). At present it is often difficult—or it is perhaps less needful?—to distinguish between those exercises designed to impart mastery of physical and expressive possibilities with a view to the *artistic* deployment of physical movement, and those which, devised specifically for rhythmicians, have no other purpose than to put them *in command of their bodies*, thus giving thm access, for their personal use as musicians or teachers, to an instrument suitable for all occasions. It is fortunate that these are not mutually exclusive, and that Dalcrozians who specialize in teaching physical technique are at the same time artists with a sense of staging and choreography. (It was initially in his capacity as an artist that Dalcroze gave his 'grammar course'!) But it is important for Dalcrozians to be persuaded of the difference in *nature*—and not only in degree—between the two aims existing side by side in their teaching. By getting their pupils to grasp it too, they simultaneously enable them to reinforce their understanding of themselves as rhythmicians, while opening up perspectives to those among them whose particular aptitudes will tend to direct them towards physical expression and dance. Speaking personally, I am grateful to Monica Jaquet, a former pupil of both Jaques-Dalcroze and Lily Braun and therefore a *grammairienne* as well as an artist in movement, for clarifying this distinction for me when I was a student. But it is equally important for Dalcrozian musicians to keep in touch with a branch which has been evolving continuously in recent decades, and which often calls upon music for services of a novel genre (or 'style'), which cannot be simply traced from older models without running the risk of breaking off the harmonious relations between music and the movement inspiring it.

The Grammar of Movement

What then were these exercises considered so essential to the training of a rhythmician? Their subjects in general, of which, for reasons to be explained later, I give below a deliberately selective résumé, (cf. Dalcroze 1926*a*: 6–9), are probably most unlikely to contain any surprises for practitioners in movement.

1. *Exercises for the development of muscular elasticity*—in other words, of one's ability to make the body return to the point from which a movement began by means of a supple and automatic reaction, or to impart a voluntary change of direction to it.
2. *Exercises in muscular contraction and relaxation* in various positions, each being secured either progressively or suddenly, and in one or more limbs or in the entire body.

3. *Breathing exercises*: techniques of breathing, and the study of the effects they have on the body, or which the body may have on them.

4. *Study of points of departure and completion of the gesture*, enabling the acquisition of a sense of origin of muscular movements and of their *moments* of completion.

5. *Study of impulses and reactions*, voluntary or involuntary, chiefly in order to determine the influence of these releases of energy on the incitation of secondary movements.

6. *Study of gestures alone and in sequence*, with differing spatial orientations, by bringing different articulations into play, by submitting limbs to stretching and bending, by practising, alone or with others, movements which are continuous and interrupted, towards or away from the centre, and in straight, curved, or broken lines.

7. *Study of different positions of the body*, by learning how to occupy personal space, keeping one's balance, experiencing the sense of a line, shape, or direction suggested by a position or series of positions, giving diverse directions to different parts of the body.

8. *Study of walking and of its 'embellishments'*: of its points of departure, length of step, changes in centre of gravity, different ways of stopping, of reorientating oneself, of negotiating obstacles, of going up or down ramps or steps. Study of leaping with or without preparation, of skipping, running, jumping.

9. *Study of points of contact and support and their associated resistances*, real or imagined. Contact of hand or feet against objects which are stable and unmoving, or moving and unstable; resistance to pulling or pushing; throwing of ball in the air or against the wall; study of positions of the body in these varying situations.

10. *Exercises in the use of space*, of individual and group design, the making of geometric shapes with the use of elevations as well as on flat surfaces.

11. *Exercises in the expression of actions or feelings*, whether real or imagined, by analysing their reciprocal influences on one another and the modifications thereby engendered in the use of body space or of the general surroundings.

Already a wealth of ideas! Yet they hardly include more than those held (or hitherto held) in common by the majority of educational methods for artistic movement. So far, I have deliberately omitted from such exercises those features which give them particular value from a Dalcrozian point of view (this does not, nowadays, mean *only* from

a Dalcrozian viewpoint, as I hasten to add for the benefit of those who
have since managed to arrive at similar considerations by perhaps
different routes!), and which contrast Eurhythmics with methods
referred to by Dalcroze as follows (1926a: 3):

New rhythmic methods . . . cultivate spiritedness for its own sake, without
any concern for metrics. Whatever value they may have for 'physical culture',
we have but scant confidence in their educational and aesthetic virtues. It
really does not suffice for the purpose of putting man in possession of his
personal rhythm, curing him of muscular 'arhythm', educating his nervous
system, prompting and multiplying within him external rhythmic manifestations which more often than not give only the appearance of living forms. It is,
in any case, also necessary to prompt continual exchanges between . . . the two
poles of his being, between his internal nervous system and the nervous
energies of his brain. Education of the rhythmic sense must go hand in hand
with that of the sense of duration . . . It is, indeed, only by establishing
the closest relationships between instinctive and voluntary movements that
Eurhythmics can succeed in constituting a general means of education for the
individual.

By 'instinctive movements' must be understood, in particular, the
exercise of spontaneous rhythms, as manifested, for example, in
swinging, walking, running, jumping, breathing, speaking, etc.,
whereas 'voluntary movements' correspond to what Dalcroze referred
to as 'rhythms created by one's sensitivity or reasoned intentions'
(1921a: 3)—in other words, such as are elicited by exercising control
over one's actions, by deliberately introducing a break, a transformation,
or a change in its course; 'a prolonged cessation or a momentary
interruption, the repetition of a movement, its execution in accordance
with a given time, the abandonment of one activity for another; 'a
change in the speed or intensity of the way in which an action is
accomplished; the alternation or succession of actions contrasting
with one another in respect of time variables, etc.—and a total
awareness of these varied relationships.

Rhythm and Metre

The exercises outlined in the list above will therefore only become
rhythmic exercises to the extent that they incorporate those features,
pointed out by Dalcroze, relating to the institution of relationships
between instinctive and voluntary movements—in particular, between

the spontaneity of rhythm and the discipline of metrics. Dalcroze, as we have seen, was as suspicious of methods based on 'essentially metrical' instruction as he was of those based on rhythm alone, 'without regard to metrics'. He explained on many occasions exactly what he understood by the difference, which he regarded as fundamental, between rhythm and metre, and on the necessity of taking both equally into account:

Metre relates to reflection, and rhythm to intuition. It is important to ensure that the application of metric regularity to the continuous movements of which rhythm is constituted in no way compromises the nature and quality of those movements. (1919c: 164)

To have physical exercises carried out to strict timing undoubtedly constitutes an excellent education in the sense of precision, order, and discipline; but strict timing is not the same as *rhythm*. The latter is always the product of a spontaneous effusion, and, when combined with metre, introduces diversity into unity, whereas the role of metre is to impart unity to diversity. Rhythm is individualistic, metre authoritarian. (1942: 114)

One must know how to impose order on fantasy and fantasy on order by turning metre and rhythm into a pair of intimate helpmeets—of accomplices, even. (1942: 108)

Yet if he did not go so far as to name his method 'Rhythmics and Metrics', it is because rhythm, for him, embraced metre and surpassed it:

Rhythm denotes at one and the same time both order and measure in movement and the personal style in which such movement is executed. (1915b: 89)

Having analysed rhythm into its primordial components—*dynamics*, (i.e. nuances of energy and weight) and *agogics* (i.e., the appreciation of nuances of duration)—and pointed out that these elements are linked by the *flexibility* governing their relationships in space and time, he adds that the latter 'is assisted in its task by metrics, [which] establishes order in all motor manifestations' (1942: 37).

For Dalcroze, the discovery that 'nature in her ceaseless movement vibrates both in and out of metre at one and the same time' (1915a: 75) would become something of a motto. So let us now return to the list of areas quoted above and examine them, as Dalcroze did in their original version (1926a: 6–9), from the twin viewpoints of their rhythmic and metrical resources, but taking some of their aspects a little further forward. The author's own commentaries often make use of musical terminology, and the exercises he himself created on their basis are first and foremost those of a practising musician. Thus the various subjects concerned will, whenever it seems necessary, give rise to a commentary designed to bring out the sense of the musical notions involved, or to underline the connection between a category of physical exercises and the musical faculties of hearing or performing which such exercises are capable of benefiting. Finally, to enable the reader to gain a more book-related image of the 'Grammar of Eurhythmics', each area will be illustrated with one or two examples borrowed either from Dalcroze himself or from other Dalcrozians, with the proviso that such examples be regarded as just a few of many possible applications. It might also be useful to emphasize here that although the order in which these different points are considered is not entirely arbitrary, there is nothing obligatory about it; and even less, in practice, will any exercise be found to restrict itself entirely to any one area.

Muscular Flexibility

Let us start by recalling, with Dalcroze, that there does exist 'a sixth sense, which is the 'muscular sense' and governs the numerous shades of strength and speed in bodily movements' (1919b: 140). Exercises in flexibility (see above, Exercise 1) enable the pupil to experience for himself that the rhythms of the body vary spontaneously in length and strength depending on the weight and size of the limbs involved. The pupil can play about with successions of unequal strengths and durations, and feel 'awaking within [himself] a mysterious kind of music, which is the direct product of [his] own sensations' (1919b: 141). He may seek to combine them, or to pursue them in increasing or decreasing order. He will then try to perform all these movements to a single tempo, whether faster or slower; and this will allow him to discover which parts of his body most easily adapt themselves to a given tempo (more economically, that is, rather than by means of a sudden exertion or a drawn-out pause), and what limits of speed or slowness a movement is unable to attain without the greatest difficulty.

That musical instrument *par excellence*, the entire human body, has a greater ability than any other to interpret sound in all degrees of length, the lighter parts of the body moving at speed and the heavier ones in relative slowness. (1919b: 143)

Then the pupil will learn to oppose the action of two parts of the body activated simultaneously, to feel a tension remaining in the one while the other returns to its starting position. He will thereby train himself in the independent functioning of various parts of the body.

One of the best ways of ensuring independence in any single movement seems to us to be by prompting an awareness of it while simultaneously engaging other parts of the body and contrasting movements from which it must remain clear of any reflexive influence. (1945: 112)

This independence will in consequence enable him to co-ordinate movements of different natures, to incorporate them within the same metrical framework (one movement, for example, being carried out at twice the speed of the other) without thereby losing any of their natural dynamism.

If we think of . . . the conductor, who with one hand indicates shadings of energy and with the other those of grace and gentleness, and who at the same time prompts the execution of rhythms in different time schemes, we shall form a clear image of the alliance between polyrhythmics and polydynamics. It is indispensable for the rhythmician to possess complete independence of the parts of the body. (1907: 43)

In the manuscript notebook already referred to I discovered one of Dalcroze's exercises calling on controlled muscular flexibility and aiming to co-ordinate two contradictory movements while preserving their indpendence from each other. Since this exercise, as written, has proved simple enough for me to test it on personal acquaintances who are not specialists in rhythm, I am confident that readers who may wish to try it out for themselves will have no difficulty in grasping its essentials. Whether they will succeed in actually carrying it out with equal facility is another matter! (Not, however, that there is any need to hound it to death. I repeat, the sample exercises given here do not form a continuous progression but only serve to illustrate a few points of detail. No one need feel obliged to try 'learning' exercises that require some previous experience which they may not have. When any invitation is issued to 'try out' a given exercise, the sole aim of the experiment is to facilitate an understanding of principles involved which the text alone may not be capable of evoking.)

The two movements are as follows: first, a symmetric movement of the arms, which consists in stretching out horizontally, as far as possible, an imaginary piece of elastic being held at either end (a real piece of elastic will improve matters no end), then allowing the elastic to contract entirely at its own speed so as to bring the arms back to their initial position. The second is a calm, natural respiratory movement, in which neither the inhalation must be forced (so that it is neither noisy nor very deep), nor yet each exhalation, the period of which is extended by a brief pause. To each of these two movements must be assigned one and the same total period of execution, which will be determined by the time needed for each act of breathing, but divided into two unequal portions. In the case of each movement, this division will approximately follow the rhythm it most naturally exhibits when carried out in isolation. Thus in the movement of the arms, the expansion will take much longer than the contraction, whereas, in the breathing movement, the inhalation is less deep and hence will take less time than the exhalation, to which is added a moment of rest. The result will therefore be, for the arm movement, a longer followed by a shorter time, and for the breathing movement a shorter followed by a longer.

If, in establishing the exact proportion of long to short time-divisions, the longer time is set to twice the length of the shorter, then the result will appear in musical notation as ♩ ♪ for the arm movement and ♪ ♩ for the breathing. Superposing the two rhythms reveals that the switch from tension to relaxation (from inhalation to exhalation) occurs at a different point in each of the two movements (Fig. 4.1). Try it, if you like. What do you feel? If your two movements do not enjoy total independence, each is going to exert a disturbing effect on the other. You may, for example, observe that just at the point where breathing in gives place to breathing out, the stretching movement of your arms flags a little (or is even completely interrupted). At the point when the arms should be furthest apart and exerting maximum tension you may perhaps experience some loss of muscular control because your breathing, being at its lowest level,

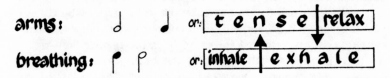

Fig. 4.1

then no longer sustains it. Or again, if the stretching of your arms is carried out too easily, you will notice that your breathing has automatically taken up the same rhythm, and is now being performed to bars of ♩ ♩ . It is in this light that Dalcroze's earlier remark (1919c: 164) must be interpreted: 'It is important to ensure that the application of metric regularity to the continuous movements of which rhythm is constituted in no way compromises the nature and quality of those movements.' Now musical performers (like the conductor and the dancer) are permanently confronted with the necessity of 'exerting metrical control over their movements'. What must they do to be able to 'avoid compromising the quality [of those movements]' when they are having to carry out several at once?

In order to acquire the dissociative capacity required for this type of exercise it is necessary to focus the attention on just the point where it is indispensable. It is indeed often impossible to pay equal attention to two opposing actions executed simultaneously. One of them will have to be, so to speak, effected 'without thinking'. When this occurs, it is a sign that kinaesthetic memory has taken over from conscious attention: in other words, one of the actions has become *automated*, usually the easier of the two, the more natural and more frequently performed. But this involves a power of concentration sufficiently flexible to be able then to momentarily quit the more difficult action on which it is trained, in order to check that the automatized movement is still operating correctly and has not undergone a disruptive effect from the other. This ability to focus the attention now on one activity, now on the other, is the condition which will eventually enable the two to distance themselves from each other sufficiently to enable them to be examined in respect of their reciprocal relationships. Co-operation between them will, in this way, not be secured at the expense of each one's own individuality.

A classic example which will help us illustrate this latter proposition is the well-known instance of 'three against two' so often encountered in musical literature. In this situation a basically ternary rhythm (as illustrated, in terms of movement, by the waltz step, or by certain types of swings) is performed simultaneously with an essentially binary rhythm (experienced for example as the regular 'left–right' alternation of normal walking, or by use of clapping or the voice accentuated two by two). Two groups of three are thereby carried out in the same time as three groups of two (Ex. 4.1). If you imagine these

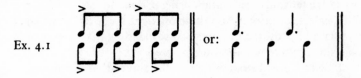

Ex. 4.1

two figures being as it were 'steam-rollered' together onto a single plan of beats, the resultant series of values will here be of the form: ♩ ♫ ♩

Now such a rhythm is nothing other than the product of a little calculation, the result of which actually distances us from the initial musical reality. By contrast, the possibility of rendering one of these movements automatic while devoting oneself to fitting the other into the given time, followed by that of transferring one's attention from one to the other in order to assess their quality, undoubtedly requires dissociative ability of a high order; at the same time it is the source of a certain aesthetic pleasure—that which results from creating a relationship between two movements each of which possesses its own rhythm and character, and which in combination remain distinct.

The foregoing remarks are not restricted to the field of muscular elasticity. It will be noted that most of the subjects dealt with below are capable of eliciting both the dissociation and the co-ordination of movements. It will therefore be readily appreciated that automating exercises designed to secure the independence of gesture will figure prominently in Dalcrozian physical education. These will not set themselves up in opposition to the Dalcrozian aim of *battling against unwanted automatic responses*. Dalcroze (1942: 148) makes explicit exception of 'certain automatic activities of a secondary order which enable primary actions to be performed without resistance. And similarly for those of primary order which may be made subject to the will and whose enactment allows the spirit freedom to imagine complementary acts.

Muscular Tension and Release

In exercises of this kind, the relationship between physical exercises—in all their shades of energy—and musical impressions is clearly apparent from the outset: what is experienced in the case of progressive tension (or relaxation) of a limb is a sort of bodily crescendo (or decrescendo), whereas a sudden tension or relaxation bring to mind the storzando or piano subito aspects of music. And these relations are reversed when energy is replaced by mass: a heaviness corresponding to the sense of *ff* will be obtained by a total relaxation, whereas a *pp* will demand that a heavy limb be restrained from falling by the application of tension. We should note, in passing, that the degree of importance attached to one or other of these ways of obtaining examples of forte or piano in music (energy or mass) form the basis of varying points of view in the application of instrumental techniques (especially pianistic ones).

The effect of dynamics in music is to vary shades of strength and gentleness, the heaviness or lightness of sounds, whether effected without transition, i.e. by sudden oppositions, or progressively, i.e. by crescendo and decrescendo. The instrumentalist charged with the interpretation of shadings in musical dynamics must possess the mechanism necessary to produce sound in its varying degrees of strength, to augment and diminish them according to the composer's intention. If the instrument selected for musical interpretation be the human body in its entirety, it follows that this body must have developed a perfect understanding of all its muscular possibilities, and be capable of deliberately bringing them into effect. (Dalcroze 1919*b*: 142)

But as to the possibility of tensing one part of the body while simultaneously untensing another—of bringing about, in the wink of an eye, the total relaxation of a limb or the entire musculature—of predicting the exact moment of maximum tension—of evaluating the time required for a gradual tensing or for a given number of sudden tensions: this possibility is as requisite to the skier as to the singer, to the motorist as to the pianist, to the thief as to the dancer, to the actor as to the musician! To make rapid self-adjustments to treacherous slopes of snow, to slow down through the gears while maintaining a forward momentum, to finger one's way through the combination of a safe while resisting the impulse to flight, to give the impression of slamming a heavy oaken door without making the cardboard flats fall down—these are not exactly problems you can leave to be solved when you come to them! Nor are we only talking about specialized activities. The thief and the skier will go home by car, and the out-of-work actor may have to initiate himself into the art of lock-picking. Dalcroze was against specialization of any kind. Not in the 'global' sense of the term so widely extolled today, which so often means just skating on the surface of things. It might be fairer to say that he favoured specializing in *everything*. He had in any case a profoundly interdisciplinary mind, and I think I can safely say that anyone who claimed to be incapable of doing anything other than what they were doing at the time would have been regarded by him as the most pitiable of objects! He did not merely deplore the idea that an instrumental musician, in bringing together all the physical and mental aptitudes essential to his art, is unaware of how to use them in their entirety: he would have found it infinitely regrettable that the musician could only make use of them on one particular occasion! (See, on this point, Dalcroze 1942: 130). When one of my friends was staying in America and expressed surprise that the children of an Indian tribe learnt the art of buffalo-hunting at a very early age, one of the elders retorted: 'Where you come from, you have snow and mountains; here, we have prairies and buffalo; it is no harder to learn buffalo-hunting than skiing. What does the difference amount to? No more than our respective landscapes' *height above sea-level!*[2] The reply would have delighted Dalcroze, who was always in favour of studying in depth a small number of areas lying at the base of the most varied activities, so that no one, at the appropriate time, should be prevented from making a completely free choice of options or inclinations by the question of their 'respective landscape'. For he also observed (1921*a*: 2) that:

current educational methods lead to the awakening and practice of only a narrow range of the natural rhythms necessary to everyday life, in terms of our current life-style. And as soon as we find ourselves transplanted outside our conditions of existence and motor activities, we discover ourselves to be deprived of the use of certain natural rhythms, which are no longer manifested in any spontaneous way because they are no longer directly necessary to our mode of existence . . .

Exercises in muscular tension and release, closely related to those of respiration, form part of those several areas in which Eurhythmics seeks to instigate a sense of economy of movement and its potential for diversification. As such, this field of study has also given rise to quite advanced experiments, finding their most accomplished form— at least, as far as our western countries are concerned—in Gerda Alexander's *Eutonie*.[3] 'Eutonics' is more than a method of relaxation or untensing. Its methodology resides, as its name suggests, in the

[2] Gilbert Voyat, in conversation with Antoine Livio, Radio Suisse Romande, 28 Oct. 1979.
[3] Gerda Alexander's *Eutonie* must not be confused with the Alexander Technique of Matthias Alexander (1869–1947), whose ideas and method have awakened increasing interest among instrumental musicians throughout the west. (Translator's note)

quest for that 'perfect tone' (*juste tonus*) whereby all our everyday movements and activities may be carried out with a minimum of effort, and hence fatigue, by virtue of the fact that no undesirable resistance or unnecessary force is allowed to interrupt their flow or to overburden them with superfluous energy. It is because 'the study of muscular release (*décontraction*) lies at the base of all [Eurhythmic] exercises' (Dalcroze 1914: 62)—because '*awareness of rhythm* . . . is formed with the help of repeated experiences of musuclar tension and relaxation, in every degree of energy and speed' (1907: 37)—because, finally, Perfect Tone is 'a state in which every movement is carried out with minimum energy and maximum efficiency' (Brieghel-Müller 1979: 7)—that the principles developed by Gerda Alexander are today an obligatory part (in Geneva, at any rate) of the professional studies of the Dalcrozian practitioner.

At the start of the previous section we saw how close the links are between the dynamics of the body and those of music. And we are not talking of a one-way relationship. Not only is an accurate perception of one's state of bodily tension necessary to musical performance, but also, in return, the dynamic and concentrating power of music constitutes an invaluable aid for a given movement's proper realization. Music, with its power of immediate suggestion, is often able to induce an understanding of things to which neither words nor deeds are capable of imparting signification—as witness the exercise below, which I have taken from Claire-Lise Lombard-Dutoit. She is a Dalcrozian who devoted herself early on to psycho-motor therapy, having become aware that 'music does not borrow its modes of expression from spoken language, and for that reason intimately engages us in different ways from those we follow in everyday life'[4] (Dutoit-Carlier 1965: 409), and having attached a fundamental significance to that observation. By means of music, she has been able in countless situations not only to establish lines of communication previously thought impossible, but also to guide children into a true appreciation of their bodily dynamics and of those concepts by which it may be described. The following example is particularly relevant to our present area of interest:

---

[4] 'La musique n'emprunte pas au langage ses modes d'expression et par là-même offre une collaboration intime par des voies différentes de celles dont nous usons dans la vie quotidienne'

The children are sitting individually on chairs at a good distance from one another. They have made a list of the thousand and one ways of remaining seated, kneeling, perching, crouching, lying, each in turn adopting a newly discovered posture: straddled, flat on stomach, legs behind seat-backs, etc. Intending to turn this exercise into a pretext for relaxing in freely chosen positions, the therapist makes a suggestion: 'Get yourselves each seated as comfortably as possible, however you like. Now you really have got to feel quite comfortable! When you hear the piano, it will be telling you: 'Time to find another comfortable position.' There's no need to hurry; the music will be looking for another comfortable position too. We will all try to get there at the same time, and then we will rest a while in the new position we have found'.

She then plays at the piano, very sostenuto, the phrase given in Example 4.2. Quite quickly, the time allowed for turning around—calculated to encourage a real change of position without letting it come to an end too soon—is recognized by all the children, and the silence following the pedal point is taken as the signal announcing the next turn. A regular succession is instituted little by little, by holding the pedal point on the long note.

Ex. 4.2

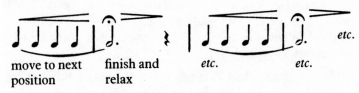

move to next position   finish and relax   *etc.*   *etc.*

But now the teacher reaches the point she has been working towards: just when they are on this long note, and everyone is supposed to be sitting comfortably, she spots an elbow sticking out here, and a knee over there; she sees a foot, a whole leg, hovering without support . . .

'Are you sitting comfortably?'
'Ye-es . . .'
'Try being really relaxed.'
'Like this?' (But nothing has changed.)
'Just now, I played this bit of music: (Ex. 4.3). But looking at you makes me think I played: (Ex. 4.4);' (here, the long note is replaced by a chord, or a cluster of notes, which, unlike previously, does not

Ex. 4.3   Ex. 4.4

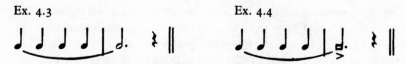

sound like the natural ending of the phrase, but breaks it off in a quite discordant fashion).

(Laughter; and the offending limb gives a little wriggle.)

'I'll play you again the bit of music that says "Find a comfortable position".' (She does so; and the stuck-out knee goes in, the stuck-up hand goes down.)

I have often had occasion to notice how fast the light dawns in such cases, where the word 'relax' would be quite without effect. Which is not to say that such comprehension has been acquired now and for all time to come—only that the door henceforward remains open for more systematic exercises in muscular tension and release because the child has consciously grasped the difference between these two states. The children greatly enjoy the rest of this exercise:

'Now we don't know whether the next position is going to be a comfortable one or not, and whether we are going to be tense or at ease. That will be decided by the music, and only at the last moment! Whichever it is, we'll pretend that we *want* to settle into our new position; perhaps we really will be able to take a rest in it; perhaps there will be something in the music to stop us. It will just have to come as a surprise.'

The contrast thus established between the two types of first-hand experience, and the mutual reinforcement between muscular and auditory sensations, have soon led the child to a clear awareness of the two states of tension and release of tension. Soon, he will be able to declare 'tense!' or 'relaxed!' himself, and then match his own declaration without recourse to music. True; it is as yet no more than a barely differentiated global perception, and he will have to do other exercises before he can learn to introduce shades of intensity into a state of tension, or to relax just one limb on its own. And music, there again, will often have to play the part of helper or revealer.

Here I digress slightly—before entirely finishing with this exercise—to mention one of its possible applications to musical education, namely the development of a sense of harmony. Depending on the extent to which tension or relaxation is or is not felt to receive emphasis in the playing of the final chord in Example 4.3, one will learn to distinguish this chord from those involving a different degree of tension. Thus in a diatonic tonal system the pupil may be made to appreciate (and to express in bodily terms) the tension evoked by a dominant chord as opposed to the relaxation communicated by a chord of the tonic; or, more subtly, the difference in tension between an inverted chord and one in root position, between a chord containing and one not containing extraneous notes, etc. In a tonal or atonal system it is even possible to evoke a distinction between a chord which is out of keeping with the prevailing style and another which respects it, or a group of sounds which reinforce one another and a group of sounds which weaken one another's effect. The possibility of expressing in bodily terms the impression received by auditory means, of taking into account variations in tone (i.e. muscle tone) inspired by harmonic stimuli which it will soon be possible to classify by name, will allow the pupil to integrate harmonic training into the depths of his musical experience.

We saw above how music may often advantageously replace language in its capacity to elicit bodily consciousness. But this assumes that such music emanates from—or relates to choices made by—an individual fully conscious of its range of powers. To transmit purposefully to someone else, through the music one creates or interprets, the impression of a relaxation, a tension, a movement, the rhythmician must first have experienced, understood, and mastered them himself. It is his own movements, his own feelings, internalized and then reconstituted in the instrument by which he expresses them, that enable him to turn music into the richest of all his resources.

Respiration

I will not dwell so long on breathing exercises: this area, a rather controversial one today, is seen in several different lights by various different schools, and it would hardly be possible to embark safely on exercises in breathing techniques without requiring the supervision of someone appropriately qualified. To the interested reader, however, I can recommend Gunna Brieghel-Müller's book *Eutonie et Relaxation* (1979: 108–19), which presents a whole series of graded and safely followable exercises based on the principle of natural respiration and taking individual differences into account.

It was primarily as a musician that Dalcroze interested himself in the subject of breathing, bearing in mind that there is not a single aspect of musical activity that could properly be left out of account. There is not only the point that respiration may be the very essence of musical production (as in singing and the playing of wind instruments), but its mastery necessarily underlies all instrumental performance. A pianist friend of mine once pointed out to me, in particular, how much easier it is to time correctly a note or a chord articulated at either extreme of the keyboard (requiring the hand to make a wide and rapid leap) by matching it to a moment of inhalation, which naturally favours 'opening out' movements, rather than to one of exhalation, which militates against them.[5]

In rhythmics, the breathing exercise is closely linked to that of motor anacrusis, the evident or disguised preparation necessary to any act of movement (see below). Breathing is as necessary to the understanding of musical phrasing as to its execution, especially, for instance, in the case of sung music or the connective relationships between prosody and melody.

The technique of respiration does not consist merely in overcoming breathlessness . . . It assures the preparation, cessation, and continuation of gestures, the shading of sensations, sentiments, and heartfelt emotions, the phrasing and scansion of successive actions. (Dalcroze 1939: 14)

A number of exercises may therefore usefully be carried out to enable pupils to experience the facilitating and strengthening power of breathing in just when they are at the point of executing a movement. The value will be brought out of relationships between the length of the normal act of breathing and the tempo of a piece of music—or the pace of a progression made by walking, running, jumping, etc. Pupils will be reminded, following Ansermet (1965: 159), that 'binary and ternary cadences are the two primary data of our respiratory cadence', the former relating to regular and sustained activity, the latter being extended into a moment of rest or sleep, both of them being of the rising–falling pattern: ♩ | ♩ (binary) and ♩ | ♩ (ternary). Attention will further be drawn to the possible effects of inhalation and exhalation on various attitudes or postures, whose quality of tone and hence expressive value are thereby considerably modified. Yet other exercises will be directed at controlling the timing of an exhalation with a view to

[5] Gérard Desmeules, private communication, 1979.

drawing a sung phrase out to its full term while imparting the desired shading to it, at re-engaging one's breath at a precise moment, at disengaging one's vocal and respiratory apparatus from the over-strong influence of other bodily movements that happen to be going on at the same time (walking, running, etc.), at economically adapting it to various gestural requirements—for which respiration constitutes the most important and most natural points of departure as well as an indispensable support.

Gestural Points of Departure and Arrival

If there is one area of movement on whose importance Dalcroze never ceased to insist it is this:

[The rhythmician's bodily technique] absolutely must have as its object the study of the *points of departure* of movement and their relations with *points of arrival* in all possible degrees of timing and energy and in every spatial dimension (Dalcroze 1924: 4).

Thus the individual feels three sensations: that of setting a gesture in motion, that of following it through, and that of terminating it. [Now] these sensations undergo a total change of character according to whether the limb that moves is set in motion from one or another of its various parts, or again depending on the choice of which limb makes the first move when an overall activity is started up. Thus a given arm movement may take its starting-point from the upper arm, the elbow, the hand, or the finger. If this arm is held tightly against the body, it will involve the body in its movement; in other cases, the upper part of the body may be set in motion by a turning movement of the hips, or of the legs. The body may then, in turn, bring the arms into operation [etc.]. (1945: 216–17)

But the starting-point of a gesture may also be a shift in equilibrium of the body as a whole, or, as we have seen above, a breathing movement. And the direction it takes may be determined by a wish to fall in with its weight or, alternatively, to get away from it (cf. Dalcroze 1922a: 6–7). Or again, it may be imposed from without by a predetermined point of arrival, which acts as the goal of the movement. Amongst many exercises of this sort may be counted one that Valéry Roth calls—for the benefit of children, or at least the child-like!—the 'Flowers-and-Leaves' exercise:

A tambourine held in the hand counts as the 'flower'. A beat from the piano calls for it to be set in a fixed position: high up, for example, or as far out as possible; behind the back, or at knee-height; anywhere will do, you have a free choice; but, once in position, the flower stays where it is (which means the arm that holds it becomes a 'stem', of course!). Immediately afterwards, the teacher calls out a part of the body: elbow, shoulder, chin, knee, etc., and the pupil attempts, in a movement spreading outwards from the named part of the body, to bring it towards the 'flower' (an action Roth describes as 'putting a leaf on it'), then remains motionless for a few seconds in the position imposed as a consequence of the gesture. It may happen that the gap between the 'flower' and the 'leaf' is impossible to close. No matter: the important thing is for the movement to be extended in the right direction for as far as is possible, and for the tambourine to remain within the prolongation of the gesture.

This exercise is carried out in accordance with given dynamics and tempo, which will then be varied to enable different degrees of speed and intensity to be experienced, and to afford it a greater or lesser period of preparation, execution, and subsequent immobility.

In a variant of this exercise, the pupil holds the tambourine not on his own behalf but on that of a comrade, who simultaneously does the same for him. This version has the advantage of requiring the pupil to direct his movements towards a goal which he will often not have thought of for himself, and demands that he divide his attention between the obligation to travel as far as possible towards the goal he is seeking to reach, and that of holding quite still the target being presented to his partner's movement. This exercise is consequently suitable for sharpening up the pupil's body-consciousness, thereby demonstrating to him that

any release of energy creates a current [whose nature] depends on its point of departure; and [that] both its shape and its point of arrival are determined by all the modifications inexorably caused by incidental resistances, as well as by lapses of balance and the requirements of time (Dalcroze 1926a: 4)

Incitation of Movement and Nervous Releases of Energy

Inseparable from the preceding area is that of those impulses and releases (see above) which control every initiation of movement, or serve as a preparation for the action, or guide the gesture towards its climax. Drawing a parallel from the realm of music, in which these different types of impulse play a primordial role, Dalcroze gave these the title *motor anacruses* (1945: 217) and invested them with a degree of importance comparable, in the realm of movement, with that given them in respect of music by his master, the theoretician Mathis Lussy, who had long been drawn toward the study of the different types of anacrusis evident in musical literature.

This term, deriving from the Greek *ana*, 'rising towards', and *krouo*, 'to strike' (cf. Lussy 1884: 7) is one of the key words of the rhythmician's vocabulary, which is why we use it here. It amounts, in other words, to a 'rising' of greater or lesser length, which comes to rest on the downbeat. This latter, the *crusis*, corresponds to the main supporting point of a rhythm or musical phrase, and is generally followed in the shorter or longer term by a *metacrusis* (from *meta*, prefix denoting participation, succession, change). This latter endows the phrase, or that part of it under consideration, with a point of relaxation, or resolution, or of rest, and appears as the consequence of what has gone before.

By way of illustration, we might take the random example (though will it mean much to urban dwellers?) of the woodcutter's action, in which the raising of the weighty axe constitutes the anacrusis of its being driven into the timber, while the ensuing pause or rebound is the metacrusis of the action before the axe is raised again.

Events of the form anacrusis–crusis–metacrusis are legion, and, depending on the scale applied, will cover such varying lengths of time as, say, the batting of an eyelid, a lifetime, or a historical era. The need to forge a link between the present and the past on one hand, the future on the other, by reference to the concepts of preparation and consequence, is undoubtedly inherent in human nature, and there is hardly a sphere of activity in which events are not spontaneously analysed in such terms as these.

In music, there are many forms in which anacrusis can occur. It may consist in the simple rising of a note, as in Example 4.5.[6] Note, too, in this example, how, if you follow the meaning of the text, the whole of the first bar, and not just its introductory leap, acts as an anacrusis to the word 'fellow', and that the musical value sustaining the first syllable of that word—the longest in the phrase—forms in

---

[6] The author here analyses the song 'Marlbrough s'en va-t-en guerre', but as the same tune is equally well known throughout the English-speaking world as that of 'For he's a jolly good fellow' I hope its translation will be deemed acceptable here. (Translator's note)

Ex. 4.5   'For he's a jolly good fellow . . .'

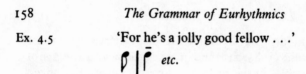

Ex. 4.6

For   he's   a   jol - ly good   fel - low,   for   he's   a   *etc.*

fact the principal crusis, while its final, weaker, syllable is its brief metacrusis (Ex. 4.6).

This sort of thing often occurs in good songs, where the words ride happily along across the barlines and immediately bring out the relative weight of the strong beats. See, for example, the same rhythmic model in Example 4.7, or again the interesting 'J'ai descendu dans mon jardin', where the opening is repeated without affording time for a metacrusis (Ex. 4.8). In all these cases, and many others, the fact of respecting the anacrusic character of the text in the phrase as sung endows the song with a truly musical movement well in keeping with what is being expressed.

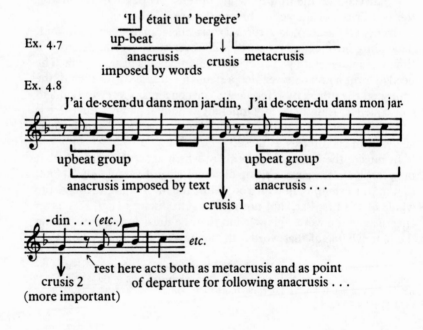

'Il │ était un' bergère'

Ex. 4.7   up-beat   │ ↓ └─────
                 anacrusis   crusis   metacrusis
                 imposed by words

Ex. 4.8

J'ai de·scen·du dans mon jar-din, J'ai de·scen·du dans mon jar·

upbeat group   upbeat group

anacrusis imposed by text ↓   anacrusis . . .

crusis 1

-din . . . (etc.)

etc.

crusis 2   ↖ rest here acts both as metacrusis and as point
(more important)   of departure for following anacrusis . . .

In instrumental music it is almost equally common for anacrusis not to be restricted to the first rise. For example, in the opening of Beethoven's well-known *Für Elise* there can be no disputing that the whole of the first eight notes form an anacrusis, giving the impression of something hanging in suspense, losing its balance, and then falling down (Ex. 4.9). Or again, staying with the same composer, let us examine the first phrase of the third movement of the Sonata, Op. 14 No. 2 (Ex. 4.10). The impression of anacrusis produced by the rising scale carries it up into the repetition of the rhythmic fragment ♫ ♪, in which, moreover, the metrical accent is displaced at each occurrence, a factor which assists the opening of the phrase in freeing itself from heaviness. Quite different in this respect is the impression produced by the same rhythmic fragment in the first movement of the third Brandenburg Concerto (Ex. 4.11). Here, the anacrusis seems to get mixed up with the rise, and the reprise of the motif at a fourth below provides something like a metacrusic response to its first statement. We should note, however, that these responses follow upon one another in descending thirds in the sound-space of the music, and that

Ex. 4.9

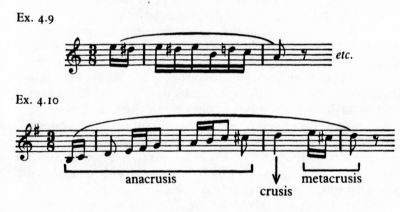

Ex. 4.10

Ex. 4.11

their linear progression leads us in anacrusic fashion down to the D of the second bar, a passing anchor-point, quitted as soon as it is reached and involving us in a new anacrusis that takes over from the one before. Whence the impression, common enough in the music of Bach, of being carried along, holding our breath, by a movement which keeps on delaying its climax.

We won't expand further on examples of anacrusis drawn from the literature of music: practically every one of them is a 'special case', and the impression produced by each anacrusis not only relates to sound-space and the melodic or rhythmic characteristics of the work but also depends equally on its harmonic foundations, tonal functions, tempo, and metrical features. 'In addition, quite often, depending on how one looks at it, it is, as we have seen, the whole phrase (and not just its opening notes), or section, even a whole movement, which will be perceived as an anacrusis leading to a climax, which may be' so far delayed as to reside—why not?—in the very last chord of the piece (whose immediately ensuing silence will, of course, prove to be the indispensable metacrusis!).

But whether or not a work begins with an upward movement, the performer himself always begins the piece with an anacrusic gesture as a prerequisite of every note played. The pianist lifts his hands, the flautist draws his breath, the fiddler wields his bow, the conductor raises his baton . . . It is the first visible gesture of musical performance (and will have been preceded by an invisible anacrusis enabling the musician to launch into *tempo giusto* and to charge himself up with the requisite degree of energy). The concert-goer will benefit from this preparation on his own account, normally devoting the whole of his attention to it, since it enables him to participate in the whole performance. Have you ever noticed how off-putting is the unhappy absence of any such visible anacrusis when you come to play a record? No matter how well prepared we are, its first note always seems to take us by surprise. We can only get 'into' it when the first sounds have reached our ears. If we want to use our hands to beat in the first note of the work, we cannot do so except by way of reaction to its appearance. Now, however prompt a reaction may be, it always demands a delay in respect of whatever acts as its impetus. A truly musical gesture, however, whether designed to produce a sound or, as in dancing, to respond to it, has to be *anticipated*—more or less, according to the degree of sustained effort it demands—in such a way as to occur precisely at the desired moment and with the desired force.

We describe as *anacrusic* the action which does not hide its preparation, so that its visible preparation has an air of being part of the action itself . . . And we describe as *crusic* any action whose preparation is concealed, so that the result of this preparation seems to be the very start of the action itself. (Dalcroze 1919*b*: 146)

Thus every intentional movement presupposes a preparation, whether or not a visible one. It was this minimal (but fundamental) demand of every kind of musical interpretation that Dalcroze accused the classical dancers of his time of not properly understanding. Which is why he got into the habit, in the essays he wrote directly for dancers, as well as on every occasion that he referred to bodily movement, of making his opinion clearly known on this topic and in persuading his readers of its importance in their training as musicians, or as rhythmicians, or as dancers who require a sensitivity to music:

A rhythm is always the result of an impulse that originates in the nervous system . . ., in the mind, or in the affective state of the being. And the movement created by the impulse takes shape depending on the way it collaborates with time. (Dalcroze 1926*a*: 3–4)

Every movement enacted in a given time requires a completely different preparation from one enacted in a longer or a shorter time. (1931*a*: 4)

Every line traversed by a limb in a given space and time becomes shorter and longer according to the degree of muscular energy that activates the movement. (1945: 164–5)

The body's own anacruses will therefore be studied under the twin headings of agogics and dynamics: some exercises will lay stress on the concentration given to the *moments of arrival in time* of a completed gesture, and will make clear to what extent these depend on the conjugation of the duration, direction, and energy of the anacrusic phase of the movement. Other exercises will have as their aim that of bringing out the *points of arrival in space* of movements activated by stronger or weaker impulses originating in different parts of the body. Yet others, finally, will seek to relate these two preceding types of exercises to each other.

By way of example I will quote two exercises aimed first of all at determining the gesture's *moment of arrival*, as devised by two students in one of my courses.[7]

---

[7] Françoise Clerc and Véronique Mattana, 1981.

One student performs a body movement of her own choosing, having the form (*visible*) *anacrusis–crusis–metacrusis*, and repeats it several times. At the piano, a fellow student observes and then plays a special chord or sound cluster to underline the exact moment at which the movement reaches its strongest point. This presupposes that she experiences the preceding phrase internally and thus physically prepares herself to make the sound she produces coincide with the observed bodily stress, and to accompany this with just the right degree of weight. Having thus herself experienced the dynamism and duration of the bodily anacrusis, she will then go on to translate it into pianistic terms, either by creating a chord-progression leading up to the stress climax of body movement, or— what is more difficult—by stopping just before it is reached (the ensuing silence thus adopting the value of stress and climax of the musical phrase). Then, having sought to relate to this bodily progression towards climax, and subsequently to isolate the meta-crusis terminating the sequence, she will finish by extemporizing a musical piece echoing and reflecting this manifestation of the three components of the original movement (i.e. anacrusis–crusis–meta-crusis).

Instead of the piano, use may equally well be made of one or several voices; or again, an attempt may be made to orchestrate the movement by means of various instruments selected and combined in accordance with the musical dynamic.

In the second exercise, the work is done by a group of people, and the object of the exercise is for everyone by common accord to sense the moment when an anacrusis ends without its duration being determined in advance. This takes place without words or any musical support. The members of the group stay close to one another and, in silence, make every effort to sense both in them-selves and on the part of their comrades the preparatory movement of respiration, then the displacement of their centre of gravity, which will bring about the unbalancing required to make them all simultaneously take the first step of a run over to the other side of the room.

In the course of this exercise the students are led to discover that knowledge of what they are preparing themselves *for* is not un-important: the energy invested in the preparatory anacrusis of the first step of a run is not the same as that required for a slow walk, for instance, or for a brisk march. It therefore has some influence on the length of the anacrusis. This observation is even more important when several people are trying to do the same thing simultaneously. (As a corollary: the orchestral conductor often need do no more than raise his baton before everyone knows what to expect by way of tempo and dynamics from the piece they are about to hear!)

At the same time, the students are bound to notice that, even if perfect simultaneity is achieved at the starting-point, the group will have found it difficult to maintain cohesion throughout the whole of the run. This observation affords us an opportunity to refer to a movement's *finishing-point*. Now, in this exercise, the finishing-point is the opposite end of the room and not the taking of the first step. This must necessarily be taken into account *from the beginning* of the group movement: the impulse induced in common consists not only in getting ready to run, but also in making oneself conscious of the fact that one has to run *up to* something or to a given place. In effecting this group movement, it will be understood that its true *crusis* lies not in the starting-point but in the finishing-point of the run. The running itself therefore acts as part of the anacrusis of the group rhythm, and the movement which preceded it (inhalation followed by displacement of centre of gravity) in a way constitutes the metric 'rise' or impulse.

In practice, as soon as the exercise was seen in this new light, the group maintained its cohesiveness for the whole period of movement. Why? Because the ability to regard the latter as a whole, from the first second of its initiation right up to its point of completion (impulse, spot-on departure, running, braking, stopping) ensured that the particular movements set in motion to reach this end were endowed with the *continuous energy* indispensable to their progression through space and their distribution in time.

The Study of Gestures and Gesture Sequences

In Dalcroze's view, continuity in the sequencing together of movements is the most important thing for music performers and dancers to possess if they are to rise above the level of clumsy interpretation.

It is necessary to establish liaisons between bodily movements and to build 'bridges' between their starting- and finishing-points if one wishes to endow them with aesthetic significance and enable them to articulate emotions and sentiments with suppleness and flexibility. (1945: 214–15)

To have the quality of rhythm is not merely to be in possession of a given quantity of motor, mental, or physical rhythms . . . It is to be able to know how to pass easily and flexibly from one action to the next, from one thought to another. (1945: 254)

Thus those exercises allotted to the study of gestures and gesture sequences, which we have already described, will be largely devoted to *continuous movements*, movements 'analogous to those of bow on string, or to the thread of sound through wind instruments' (1945: 215).

Our first job will be to distinguish these movements, whether auditory or physical, from 'stopped' or jerky movements. The distinction between legato and staccato in musical performance is in any case one of the earliest acquired by young students of rhythm, as readily testified to by their own performances. There are many exercises enabling these two types of movement to be set in contrast to each other, either by reacting to gestural or musical stimuli of the same nature, or by seeking to effect a contrast between two successive movements of different types: for example, a smooth and gentle movement carried out by one pupil in the direction of his neighbour elicits from the latter a short, sharp response, and vice versa. Taking advantage of the expression of feelings will often facilitate a better understanding of the link one is seeking to establish between two movements of which one appears to be a continuation or consequence of the other: a push of varying degrees of hardness may produce a fall, a loss of balance, or a slight withdrawal; a restrained threat may give rise to sudden fear; an aggressive or spiteful gesture may be met with supreme aloofness, etc.

We will practice freezing a movement in its tracks, then taking it up again at the point where it was left off; we will also try out certain activities very slowly. Such ways of interrupting or altering movement are nowadays well known to television viewers, and the parallels that can be drawn with certain television techniques, notably in sport and nature programmes, may be used to support the imaginations of pupils of all ages; except, that is, of the youngest of all, for whom the very idea of deliberately sustained movement is still new by virtue of the demand it makes on the controlled expenditure and husbanding of energy. This applies particularly to slowed-down movement, which is 'the product of muscular resistance' (Dalcroze 1945: 127), and additionally requires the ability to represent every single phase of a movement.

I quickly spotted that their instinctive gestures were livelier and more expressive than those taught to them. (1945: 27) It is not in the child's nature to harmonize his movements. He knows neither how to string them together nor how to set them in opposition, except when necessity, the impulse to self-defence, or actions dictated by specific contingencies call forth useful reactions from his mind and body. (1942: 54)

With older children and adults, however, sustained movement may be worked at for its own sake, in the context of harmonizing movements to allow for an uninterrupted passage from one impulse to the next.

In exercises of this type 'the question of tempo plays an important part':

At too fast a pace, a series of impulses ends up in a general dissipation of strength; at too slow a pace, impulses break the movement up. Various shades of *tempo moderato* must therefore be measured out very carefully in such a way as to sustain the influence of the initial impulse, as well as to enable continuity of movement to be maintained by virtue of secondary impulses of the same nature. (1945: 218)

This may be illustrated by the following exercise, which I often get my students to carry out, and which I have taken from C.-L. Lombard-Dutoit: the exercise is known as 'Skein of Wool'.

Two people work together. One of them holds her hands out in front of her in the position normally adopted (formerly adopted?) for holding out a skein of wool ready for winding into a ball—i.e. parallel to each other and with inward-facing palms. The other person, using only one hand, then traces a figure of eight around and between her partner's outstretched hands, passing continuously from one hand to the other (see Figure 4.2). At the same time, the person 'holding the skein' acts as if it were elastic, alternately stretching out the space between her hands and bringing them closer together again, in a movement which is no less continuous but nevertheless much slower than that of her partner. She may, at the same time, impose an overall rotary movement on them, so that both hands narrow their individual angles to the perpendicular (but with palms still parallel and facing one another).

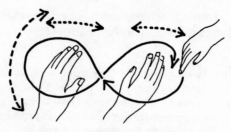

Fig. 4.2

This slow movement should not come to a halt, nor be interrupted, nor be marred by any hesitation at changes of direction; furthermore, it should be maintained at uniform speed. Therein lies the hardest part of the exercise, even if it does lie on the less spectacular side of things. The person tracing the figure of eight will, for her part, have to modify the curve of her gesture to match the ceaselessly changing dimensions and directions of movement. Sometimes she will barely be able to slip her hand between those of her partner; sometimes her whole body will become involved in the movement— she may, for instance, have to stand on tiptoe or bend right down to the ground in order to describe her figure of eight. The hard part for this pupil comes just when the music being played by the teacher as accompaniment to the exercise imposes upon her the regularity of its own beat. The first beat of the bar has to coincide with the crossing-over of the figure of eight. In other words, the pupil will have to vary the speed of her tracing in direct proportion to the length of the trajectory to be followed, without at the same time failing to hold her movements together in an uninterrupted flow. (Is this not, indeed, what the pianist does when he runs arpeggios, scales, or virtuoso lines together in contrary motion, all in quavers, for example, in such a way that the varying amplitude of his movements should not interfere with the smoothness of articulation?) Yet there is less difficulty for the pupil tracing the figure of eight than there would be if she had to rely entirely upon her internal sense of timing: some form of suitable musical support is generally of great help in acquiring the technique of sustained movement, for it carries the movement forwards by enabling the ear to anticipate its moment of arrival, and constantly renews the sense of energy by breathing new impulses into the gesture. (In respect of instrumentalists, each of whose gestures aimed at producing sound slightly precedes the sound itself, it is that much easier to understand how an ear capable of anticipating the musical argument and of grasping it as a unity is essential to the spatio-temporal continuity of their playing.)

The execution of continuous movements is easier to obtain on the part of the arms that on that of the legs, or in walking. The former, as a rule, are more agile than the latter. That is why, in the artistry of movement, it is so often the arms which are entrusted with the task of bringing out the legato and continuous movements of music—sometimes at risk of misuse, for all too prominent arms may mask the expressiveness of the rest of the body (or even, in certain cases, may relieve it of that responsibility). Now continuous movement should be able to 'spread itself throughout the whole organism', so that

each rhythm created by a succession of muscular contractions and relaxations evokes another rhythm in neighbouring groups of muscles and so is propagated in every part of the body. (Dalcroze 1945: 216)

As to walking, an ideal image of its possible smoothness is afforded by the artistry of ice-skating, and the impression of continuity which it ought to be able to give on terra firma calls for working up a technique along lines epitomised by Valéry Roth's evocative (and oft-repeated) injunction: 'Best weights forward! You walk with your body and push with your feet!' The command is equally valid for running and for the slow march, and for any form of stepped movement which seeks to produce a linear effect (one notable physical consequence is that the forward-moving line of shoulders remains parallel to the ground rather than going up and down).

Continuous walking is not bound to comprise steps of equal duration. What counts is that the weight of the body should move forwards smoothly regardless of tempo. (Dalcroze 1942: 146)

What will change according to the speed in question is the temporal relationship between the displacement of the body's centre of gravity and the movement of the leg, and the amount of energy necessary either to hold them back or to propel them forwards in respect of each other. This will be particularly noticeable when, for example, we take on in succession the two complementary roles put forward in the exercise below, which amounts to a transposition, into the scale of forward movement, of the exercise described above (the 'Skein').

Instead of holding two hands out, we have two people standing up facing each other, moving about slowly without taking their eyes off each other, approaching or receding from each other (walking forwards or backwards), or describing a circular motion (moving sideways), in as continuous a way as possible and without losing the feeling of being physically linked to each other. And instead of one hand describing a figure of eight, we have instead a whole person tracing out the same shape in between these two 'moving pillars', at a relatively rapid pace (a run or a 'raised walk'—i.e. fast walking in which the weight is borne only by the front part of the foot, giving the impression of slithering). Then, when it comes to matching the timing of the progression to a regular beat, this assumes a fixed number of steps regardless of the size of the 'eight', and it will be possible to experience a variety of step sizes all executed in the same tempo. Alternatively, only the metre is fixed, and the lone walker has to make up a suitable rhythm as he goes along which will lead him to finish up in the right place at the right time. The reader will appreciate that it is not easy to perform with one's feet what the pianist has already spent a fair amount of time practising doing with his fingers! It will therefore be advisable to set parameters to this exercise (number of steps, maximum amount of space to be covered, pace) which do not exceed the bounds of human capability!

Every effort must be made, however, to ensure that pupils undergo the full experience of continuous movement in all parts of the body before they are made to make conscious use of them to one particular end or another. In this context, the easiest way of eliciting continuous movement on their part is by causing it to result from some external constraint, real or imaginary, rather than by appealing to internal sensations. With children, for example, we might try the 'Radar' exercise, which involves letting oneself be moved some distance away—without walking, however—by means of holding hands with a face-to-face comrade. The hands being moved in a straight line, vertically or horizontally, it will be necessary to hold one's eyes (and hence, also, one's face) to their axis of elongation. Then there is the 'Chewing-Gum' exercise, which I have seen practised in one of Ruth Gianadda's classes (third year primary)—an exercise in which from a ball supposedly of chewing-gum lying on the ground the children draw imaginary threads, short or long, in all directions, taking care to ensure that they do not 'break'. Then the chewing-gum is changed to elastic. First we draw it out ourselves (slowly, because of its natural resistance), then we let ourselves be drawn back by it (faster, because we offer no resistance) and so are brought back to its starting-point. I have recollections of a little girl who, in the course of a very long 'stretch', spontaneously produced a stake or post (or tree?) from her imagination, which enabled her bend her 'elastic chewing-gum' around it. This detour she faithfully followed on the way back, which she did all in one go, thereby demonstrating that she had internalized her representation of the continuous movement.

With adolescents or adults we might prefer the 'Toilet-Roll' exercise, which I learnt from Esther Messmer and used with great success in one of my classes. Use is made here of an actual object, namely, a roll of toilet paper with a total length of some 25 to 30 metres—very soft paper, too, which the slightest jerky pull is liable to tear!

The students start by dispersing themselves around the room and standing motionless. One of them holds the toilet-roll. He carries it over to someone else, who in turn takes it along to a third person, and so on, while the first person keeps hold of the end of the paper in his hand. The object is to get the paper to unwind with no break in continuity as the roll is passed from one student to another, each keeping hold of his bit of it while passing the roll on to the next. The following constraints apply: (1) the exercise must be carried out in silence; (2) the paper must not be allowed to tear (this would bring the exercise to an end); (3) every student, having once begun to walk, must keep on moving till the end of the exercise; (4) the paper must not at any point touch the ground, nor even lightly brush against it; (5) no one, having once taken hold of the paper, must let go of it. It is possible, with such a length of paper, that someone may be given the roll on several occasions. The paper may often cross over or tie up with itself, but each student is individually responsible for the whole. Success in this exercise consequently depends on the capacity of every individual to mesh his own movement in with the continuous movements of his immediate neighbours. A bump, a jerk, would be sufficient to break the whole thing off. Further, in view of the fragility of the material used, most of the movements will tend to be of slight intensity—and for continuous movements to be carried out piano demands a heightened concentration. The requirement of silence will contribute to the quality of attention paid. But it is a difficult exercise, and one would be well advised to start equipped with several rolls of paper in reserve!

In the internal representation of continuous movements and their smooth succession, 'Eutonics' (*l'Eutonie*)—which we have already referred to—has a considerable role to play. I recall, amongst others, this very agreeable exercise which Gunna Brieghel-Müller used to do with her beginners:

This exercise involves passing from a lying-down to a standing position without having any resistances to overcome, but on the contrary following the easiest route. If anything interferes with this (a feeling of tension, a move requiring effort), it must be relinquished· you must revert to the preceding phase and seek another way forwards. You may perhaps spend a long time lying down and working out the most comfortable way of turning on your side, then the most effortless way of setting your knee to the floor. You may perhaps spend a long time finding the best way of raising your back, or how to accomplish that final achievement of finding yourself on both feet as if there had been nothing to it . . . Those who have done this exercise several times, and retain in their 'musuclar memory' a recollection of the most effortless route to its accomplishment, will often be seen getting to their feet with such speed and smoothness as appear to border on the miraculous!

'To get from A to B by the best possible routes—that, basically, is what it means to act rhythmically', wrote Dalcroze (1945: 224). This sentence may help us realize why the concept of continuity is not to be confused with that of legato in instrumental playing or movements of the body, but occurs equally when these movements are followed by stops or brusque movements which either contrast with or follow on from them, and that it subsists in all their relations. A host of combinations and exercises, both individually and collectively, could well be inserted at this point—as, indeed, could almost any rhythmics exercise, to the extent that it can be analysed in such terms. I therefore leave the reader to the task of imagining for himself, enjoining him to bear in mind that if

every human body can become free, not only by virtue of those actions which it will and can accomplish, but also by those which it can prevent itself from impeding (Dalcroze 1945: 273), it is also true that the alternations or conjunctions of movements and 'stops' (silences, rests) which characterize music as well as the human body contribute to their free exercise to the extent that they match the continuity inherent in everything that lives.

Study of Positions and Attitudes of the Body

How admirable a spectacle is presented by the hand of the violinist, the movements of his body, the creases or serenity of his forehead, that visible alternation of immaterial lightness and applied weightiness in his movements . . . All of which, alas, is absent from recordings.

So Dalcroze expressed the matter (1945: 277); and countless are the instances on which he demonstrated—sometimes in earnest, sometimes in bantering terms (cf. 1945: 35 ff)—how sensitive he was to the external activities of the body. His penetrating powers of observation led him to see them sometimes as reflections of internal moods or feelings or states of mind, sometimes as vain forms dictated by convention, a fount of pointless gestures.

For him, any education which consists mainly in encouraging the imitation of models develops nothing but the imitation of forms. He deems it preferable, by contrast, to seek for oneself the form with which to endow one's actions; only then will systematic exercises teach one how to vary these forms 'in a reasoned, plastic, and expressive manner' (1945: 152). This second phase of the programme is, however, as necessary as the first: an educational method preparing one for art as well as life ought to enrich and develop physical means of expression in proportion to the greater number of impressions and sensations one may be led into translating. Seen in this light, the study of stationary positions or attitudes, alone and in series, is the indispensable complement to that of movements.

Dictionaries define the (French) word *attitude* along two main lines, the first in its true sense as 'the manner in which the body is held', the second, more broadly, as 'a bearing corresponding to a particular psychological disposition'. In everyday life these two understandings are often conflated, and it is in this (conflated) sense that static 'attitudes' will be studied—at least to start with, before we study their components separately, or seek to define the way in which they bear reciprocally upon each another.[8] Now what is it that imbues an attitude with its overall significance, if not the movement of which it is the end or the beginning, or of which it takes one fleeting moment and freezes it in time?

Attitudes are periods of time when all motion is stilled. Whenever, in the uninterrupted flow of movements that constitute what might be called the embodiment of the melody in movement (*mélodie plastique*), there occurs a punctuation mark or phrasing instruction—a pause corresponding to a comma, semi-colon, or a full stop in spoken discourse—that movement becomes momentarily static and is perceived as an attitude . . . The true perception of movement is not of a visual order, it is of a muscular order . . . The body, incited by spontaneous sentiments and irresistible emotions, vibrates, launches itself into movement, then freezes itself in attitudes. These latter are the direct product of the movements which separate them . . . (Dalcroze 1919*b*: 140)

When we look at the statue of the Discobolus, we are left with the impression that the man is not just holding the discus but is actively preparing to throw it. A slight acquaintance with this sport might suffice to enable us to predict more or less where the discus would land if the statue were suddenly to come to life, and first-hand experience of it would tell us equally well how the discobolus arrived at his given position and what other actions must have preceded the one depicted. Or again: imagine the attitude of the prisoner in his cell—a future in which space is closed down to nothing and time drawn out to the lengths of eternity: then see how much more vivid our picture becomes when we imagine his former life as a free man, an adventurer, a hunted fugitive, or indeed as an already life-long prisoner.

In other words, what endows an isolated attitude with its forceful or expressive quality is the way in which its present immobility meaningfully relates its past to its future, the space traversed to that to be traversed, the memory to the intention.

All this may be illustrated by means of an exercise in movement. This one is due to Nelly Schintz, who for a long time taught rhythmics and other branches of music to professional students at Bienne. It

---

[8] The English word 'attitude' is subject to the same remarks as the French, but I suspect that its secondary meaning (psychological bearing) more strongly outweighs the primary (physical pose) in English than it does in French. For this reason it is sometimes better translated as 'pose' or 'posture'. Where retained, however, it is important that the English reader interpret it in its primary, physical sense. (Translator's note)

runs as follows in its final version (which presupposes a number of preliminary exercises).

The teacher improvises at the piano in any style of his choice. (It may be a waltz movement, for example, or a highly syncopated rhythm; or a movement slow and smooth, or brisk, lively, virtuoso figures . . .) Instead of improvising, he may prefer to play a series of composed pieces of markedly different character. The students dance or move about in accordance with the character of the music, all the while looking at one another with a view to arriving at a mutual gestural understanding which will match the overall style of the music. If, for example, they find the music expressive of jumping, they will endeavour, without speaking, to reach agreement on a style of jumping; similarly, by mutual concessions, they will agree on what to do with their arms while moving about, etc. At a certain moment the teacher gives a signal at which the pupils, who have previously been numbered, one by one in turn freeze in the attitude of movement which the music led them to adopt, as if they were standing ready to continue it. 'One by one' can mean various things: a randomly timed sequence at the choice of each successive student, or equally timed intervals (for which they will have had to grasp the metrics of the piece while they were moving round); but, whatever the practice, the sequence must convey a coherent collective performance in balance with the piece. Each one halts by reference to those who have already halted, chooses his position in the group and his orientation, and so seeks to contribute to the balance of the ensemble. When the last pupil has reached a halt, the onlookers are confronted with one collective attitude which is the product of a series of individual attitudes. If the exercise is successful, it will give the impression of a photograph taken in the course of a dance, a dance consisting of gyrations in space and time; and the viewer of such a photograph, even if he has not previously heard the piece of music played, will have no difficulty in picking it out from amongst others, relying entirely upon impressions derived from this tableau vivant.

In the context of improvisation or rhythmics lessons I often like to show my rather more advanced students a picture (which may be a photograph) depicting a person in motion, and ask them to interpret the pace and character of that motion at the piano. I might then show them a picture of someone in stationary pose (seated or prone, for example) and ask them to imagine—so as to express verbally, musically, or with the body—what has gone before and how that person has consequently come to adopt that posture; then in the same way to imagine their immediate future, the gestures they may perform, and so on. Through exercises of this type, amongst others, the students gradually come to realise that

to know in which way to come to a halt, to know how and why to come to a halt and for how long to remain motionless, is to establish balance in our actions as well as in our ideas. (Dalcroze 1945: 27)

All the same, to be able to adopt a pose—and, especially, to be able to reproduce or re-adopt it as required—implies that it must be envisaged as the result, the starting-point, or the freezing of a movement, and, equally, with full consciousness of the space currently being occupied (without forgetting the unseen 'space behind'!) as well as of the sensations produced by the relative positions of limbs, head, and trunk. The exercises in relaxation and body-consciousness put forward by Eutonics will be of great help in this respect, as will rhythmics exercises of the type described as 'The Sculptor', which can even be undertaken with children.

In this exercise we must learn to allow ourselves to be positioned by someone else, who will take our limbs one by one and impose on them a particular form (position, angle, orientation), which we must then maintain with controlled muscle tone until the 'sculptor' has finished his piece of work. The exercise can be done to musical accompaniment, and hence, even, in time to a given rhythm.

His work completed, the sculptor is free to give it a title. (Later, when the relationships between the expressive significance and the physical means of expression are more clearly understood, it will be possible to get the 'sculptor' to produce a piece on a given theme.)

In the continuation of the exercise, the other pupils may be asked to imitate the pose of the 'sculpture', thereby testing their *powers of observation*. The pupil being 'sculpted' may be asked to adopt his neutral starting-position and then to resurrect himself again as the statue, which will give some idea of his degree of *body-consciousness*. On this occasion the 'sculptor' may make corrections verbally, which will test both his and his 'subject's' *knowledge of body-space*. Finally the sculptor may be asked himself to adopt, without looking at his model, the attitude he has imposed on his 'creation', thereby putting to the test his *powers of representation* and of internal re-construction.

'The memory of a movement creates a sensation analogous to that of the movement itself. The same goes for attitudes', Dalcroze pointed out in 1945 (p. 136). And he gave the example of one of his pupils, good at drawing, who, to render bodily actions and attitudes, always needed a visible model until—thanks to his experience or rhythmics—he was able to adopt the memory of his own muscular sensations as a self-sufficient model.

In doing exercises of the type we have just been describing, one gradually becomes convinced of the need to trust one's own sensations in order to render with certainty the impression of a line, whether straight or curved, of a slant, a right angle. Looking around (at a teacher, a comrade, a mirror) is necessary in the early stages in order to ascertain when the effect has been achieved. One is then enabled to achieve it alone by forming a conscious relationship between the effect required and the sensation corresponding to it. One may then under-take to render abstract shapes with the whole of the body (a ball, cube, a square, etc.), or even concrete forms of non-human origin. Sub-dividing space into different planes—radiating, as it were, from the body seen as centre of a sphere or a wheel—may sometimes be of considerable help in the identification of postural sensations, in facilitating the representation of bodily sections in all their various possible orientations. All these exercises will be studied in close association with those involving balance and the localization of one's centre of gravity, as well as with those relating to the study of the body's design. Their technical nature, calling for the competence of specialist teachers, may seem to take us far away from the reality of music and rhythmics. This can well occur if steps are not carefully taken to keep these areas in close contact with one another.

We will come to appreciate that the lines of the body, the way they are organized, the balance between them, their linking in a series, their contrasts—all these relate to the *plastic* quality of art, a quality which is also proper to musical rhythm, and which, taken in its broadest sense, 'applies to everything—whether thought or object—which achieves a flexible form that does not change its contours but, on the contrary, makes them more significant' (1945: 104).

In particular, we will come to realize on one hand that a physical attitude may (just like a musical chord) be suggestive in isolation, but it is only the linking and the establishment of relations in space and time between at least two attitudes (or chords) which can bring any light to bear on each one's aesthetic significance (in which respect cf. Dalcroze 1945: 109).

On the other hand, it would be a pity to reserve all the benefit of physical aptitudes favoured by so many different exercises solely to the end of artistic expression. The ability to adopt and re-adopt an attitude, to pass from one to another, ought primarily to be of benefit to oneself in the normal pursuit of everyday life. What is the point of studying the laws of equilibrium and learning how to embody sensations if not to cut down on redundant movement, to economize on expenditures of energy, to remain comfortable in all situations calling for sustained comportment? Now you will often see students sitting at the piano, playing a stringed instrument, singing in a standing or seated posture, walking or running to the rhythms of a given exercise—students who evince practically no grasp of that body-consciousness to which special lessons are devoted for them, even though they do not seem to lack it when embarking specifically upon the artistry of movement. This is because it takes time and perspective (if not an inborn natural facility) to enable certain accomplishments to be transferred to situations other than those which gave rise to them—a fact which is not restricted to the area of exercises in movement. Hence, in the period before a given action can be initiated spontaneously, the teacher's job is to strengthen links that are not yet sufficient for the task. Instrumental or rhythmics teachers will on each occasion call upon abilities which they know have been (or are being) developed in another area, while Dalcrozian teachers of body movement will seek to broaden the field of application covered by their exercises by means of concrete examples and numerous and frequent references to all important situations capable of benefiting from what they have to offer.

Walking, and the 'Grace-notes' of Walking

Exercises involving walking in its various forms have always played a major role in Eurhythmics—so much so that its detractors often reduce it to a succession of steps and beats. 'Eurhythmics? Oh yes!— tap-tap-tap! bang-bang!' one of my colleagues[9] was told by someone

---

[9]   Ruth Gianadda.

who thought they knew all about it! Yet it is not only its detractors—unfortunately—who encourage this caricature of a description, for there are some rhythmicians themselves who seem to have forgotten that somewhere between your feet and your hands there lies a thing called a body, which joins them together and actually has some right to a little attention of its own! Rightly persuaded of the importance of walking in rhythmic education, this certain knowledge suffices them entirely, contrary to what Dalcroze pointed out right at the beginning of Eurhythmics (1907: 39):

> The study of walking is only a starting-point, for the child's feet and legs are not the only parts of the body set in motion by consciously operative muscles. [Indeed,] the consciousness of rhythm requires the working together of all [such] muscles, and it is therefore the body as a whole that education ought to set in motion in order to create the rhythmic consciousness.

The study of walking is nonetheless a 'starting-point', we read. To what end, and for whose benefit?

Locomotion—the process of getting from A to B—is undoubtedly one of the richest sources of natural rhythms. No matter what means we adopt to get from one place to another under our own steam, we repeat the same movement a number of times, since one alone would not be enough to cover the whole distance. Whether we choose to crawl, slide, go on all fours, to bound, walk, or step over things, we usually push, pull, thrust, fall back, or go forwards several times in succession. In other words, we proceed rhythmically. From the moment the child is able to stand alone, walking and its derivatives (running, jumping, sliding, striding) rapidly become the preferred means of locomotion, as opposed to prone or quadrupedal methods. Walking, in particular, practically becomes an automatic activity, though remaining potentially under the control of our conscious will. Now the rhythmic sensations which it produces through the repetition of a spontaneous rhythm (that of raising the leg and setting the foot down) are clearly less intense than those experienced in the previous modes of locomotion, or indeed in on-the-spot movements, whether smooth (swaying, bowing backwards and forwards) or brusque (jumping with feet together, etc.). These, then, are to be preferred as a means of initiating the child into *total rhythmic sensation*.

But what Dalcroze alludes to here is the *feeling for rhythm*, which he defined, we may recall (see above, Ch. 3) as 'a proper sense of the relationships existing between movements in time and movements in space'. We should also remember that it was not for another twenty years or so that Dalcroze began to interest himself in the pre-school age. In the child aged above six, to whom he is referring here, those rhythms 'brought into being by sensitivity or reasoned act of will' can immediately operate in conjunction with instinctive rhythms. In this respect, not only does walking yield nothing to other forms of locomotion, it is superior to them on more than one count. Like them, it may conform to instructions alternately breaking it off and setting it going again; and at an earlier time than they—because differentiated at an earlier age—it lends itself to variations of a spatial, temporal, and dynamic order. Large and small strides, running and slow walking, galloping and skipping, all enable it to generate new spontaneous rhythms. And if at this stage it should not, any more than at any other, be exercised at the expense of activities equally conducive to the acquisition of the sense of rhythm, it will sometimes be preferred for the countless variations to which it can give rise.

What, on the other hand, makes walking the true point of departure for *rhythmic awareness* is the fact that it is possible to walk with sufficient evenness of pace to make of it a sort of natural 'metronome'.

Evenly paced walking provides us with a perfect model for the measurement and division of time into equal parts. (Dalcroze 1907: 39)

In this capacity, walking combines the metrical properties of respiration (a natural model of measured rhythm) and of the heartbeat (a natural model of the division of time into equal parts). Furthermore, it has the advantage over them in being more readily open to conscious control, if only by virtue of the fact that it is an external motor manifestation, and that while measuring time it is also measuring space in a way that is easy to perceive. Finally, more than either of them, it is susceptible to modifications of energy and timing without threatening any danger to the individual. Now, as we saw at the beginning of this chapter, the introduction of measurement into rhythm successfully brings order to motor manifestations. Walking, as much through its necessary alternation of left and right as through its way of subdividing space and time into units of equal length, constitutes an incomparable natural model in this respect. That is why, before seeking to introduce such order into movements (bodily or musical) as a product of thought or reasoning, one will seek to endow the pupil with a valid model which is independent of them by, above all, strengthening and developing his aptitude for evenly paced walking (cf. Ch. 5).

Having viewed walking as a point of departure, let us now examine the depth of possibilities offered by it in this capacity, and see how the quest for mastery over it may sometimes constitute a valid end in itself.

'In the sequencing of bodily movements, walking plays a most important part', observed Dalcroze (1945: 198), undoubtedly implying that such movements are carried out in a standing position. In this activity the legs and feet act as a support for the centre of gravity in forward motion (as also in the act of walking itself). Once the moving individual starts going forward, the ease and proper sequencing of his movements are a function of the ease of his walking. I refer the reader to what was said above about continuous walking, and will here give an example of this ease by recalling a memory which has left a lasting impression on me. Some years ago, I watched a musical event devised by Danièle Baudraz of Nyon, a performance entitled 'The Poet and the Silver Coins'. The adolescent who played the poet—himself, in the event, something of a dreamer, a little vague, subject to hesitations and bursts of wonderment—combined in a quite remarkable way an indecisive bearing with supple and ethereal movements. His creation gave so natural an appearance as to seem almost improvised. If, however, one looked carefully at his feet, it became evident that he was not walking at random, but that each of his steps coincided with a musical accent, each of his pauses with a musical silence, each paced rhythm with a musical rhythm. But everything was so well performed as to pass unnoticed; in the same way, in listening to music one does not pick out from the flow of the work the succession of individual notes of which it is composed, except for the purpose of deliberate analysis. If the requirement to translate musical rhythms into movements of the feet had been seen by this pupil as a more or less painstaking exercise its whole effect would have been destroyed (this is what gives rise to all inept performances, musical or otherwise). Now the desired effect was not that the audience should note the actor's rhythmic precision, nor yet his faithfulness to the musical text, but rather that they should understand, from what they could see and hear, the character of the poet and the drama unfolding within him. The relationship between the music and the movement could not but be subordinate to the quest for this effect; and if the music undoubtedly inspired the style and character of his movements within the poet, only a sufficient technical mastery would enable it, for its part, to appear to emanate directly from his actions and feelings. I believe the

same applies to all forms of (re-)creation—from musical performance
to the visual work of art—so justifying Paul Klee's dictum that 'Art
does not reproduce the visible: it *makes* visible'.[10]

To the rhythmician, 'walking' is an instrument; and, like any
instrument, it serves as well for beginners as for virtuosi. An instrument
which starts off as a way of achieving, through action, the perception,
the understanding, and ultimately the knowledge of music, it gradually
becomes in parallel, and to increasingly greater effect, a means of
reproducing and re-creating it, or—who knows?—of composing it.
And like any form of instrumental training, that of walking is obliged
from the outset to take into account motor aptitudes already in
existence. But these are spread more widely than one might think: is it
not observable that 'depending on one's state of mind, walking may
turn out to be jerky, syncopated, measured, and accented, or calm
and continuous' (Dalcroze 1942: 141), for example? As many spontaneous motor dispositions exist as one can think of—even if they
have hitherto only been practised unconsciously—and as many can be
put to good use: on one hand to be exercised for their own sake, on the
other to be submitted to a process of technical refinement, with a good
chance of leading to what Edith Naef refers to as 'intelligent feet'.
This expression demonstrates that, while the pianist's fingers do not
become part of the piano, the rhythmician's instrument—namely,
walking—is in fact an integral part of the instrumentalist.

Take, as an example dear to rhythmicians (!), those bodily executed
rhythms known as the 'skip' and the 'gallop'. What is a skip? Surely,
just that little start which suddenly bursts upon a child who is happily
dawdling along with his head in the clouds. This little jump of
excitement, which breaks up the monotony of his walking, the child
will repeat just for fun, always on the same foot to start with, then
from time to time on the other. Perhaps it is only in the rhythmics
lesson that he will succeed in joining as many of them together as
possible, yet perhaps he will have discovered this piece of folly for
himself long before. Rhythmics will in any case teach him how to
distinguish aurally between skips and other body rhythms, consciously
to alternate them and combine them at will with walking and running
steps, and to shade their dynamics to meet varying requirements.
It will also teach him how to improve the independence of his
movements: for example, to skip while at the same time keeping an

[10] Cf. Klee, 'Credo du créateur', in Klee 1980: 33.

object in balance on the flat of a tambourine held in the hands, or on the back of one hand.

And what do we mean by 'gallop'? Isn't it basically that impulse which pushes the bounding child along, mixing running and jumping in a sort of paroxysm of motor performance? Linking these together is quite natural from the outset, as they do not thereby interfere with left–right alternation of running or walking in the way that skips do: they merely modify the rhythm, and the initial push is always taken on the same foot. But what if you now deliberately alternate series of skips and gallops? It will probably be found that setting them in opposition to each other, albeit causing some problems in the 'bridge passages', will help banish any possible confusions that may still exist.

At a later date the exercise of these two physical rhythms will be subjected to the process of technical perfection, especially as regards precision in timing. While the child's spontaneous skip operates in ternary time (Ex. 4.12*a*), he will learn to fit it into binary time (4.12*b*), to vary in any given time the relative proportion of long to short notes (*c*), or again, with increasing refinement of muscular sense, to string them together in binary and ternary rhythms (*d*). The same demands of precision will be brought to the rhythm of the gallop, with control also being learnt over the height and length of the jump as well as over its duration. One will also learn how to pass unconsciously from measured to irregular walking, and thence to the gallop, in a crescendo accelerando in course of which it will be necessary to feel for the moment when it becomes impossible to stave off jumping any longer. In the training of musicians a distinction will be drawn between the naturally anacrusic gallop (Ex. 4.12*e*) and the crusic[11] gallop (*f*), which will give scope for making new demands on motor ability. Finally, every combination of different types of skips and gallops will be strung together in different rhythmic patterns, so demonstrating the adaptability of the energetically moving body and of a type of walking whose natural gait is being constantly contradicted. Here is one example, obviously due to Edith Naef, the unrivalled 'arch-thinker' of generations of rhythmicians in respect of everything to do with 'musical grammar'. This succession caused me a great deal of head-scratching as a student, to such an extent that I now still know it off by heart. (Ex. 4.13. Here, I replace the ends of the long notes with a pause, so as better to pick out the points at which the

---

[11] These terms are defined in Part II, Ch. 4.

Ex. 4.12 (*a*)
(*b*) (*c*) (*d*) (*e*)
(*f*)

right   left   right   left

ga - lop!   ga - lop, ga-lop!

Ex. 4.13

ACTION: jump & jump & gal-lop! jump & jump & gal-lop!

FEET: r.   r. l.   l. r. l.   r.   r. l.   l. r. l.

jump & gal-lop!   jump & gal-lop!   gal-lop! gal-lop! jump and ..

r.   r. l. r.   l.   l. r. l.   r. l.   r. l.   r.   r.

performer's feet have left the floor.) Note that when the rhythm is taken up again it starts off on the other foot! It was our teacher's constant concern to assure the establishment of equilibrium in all motor manifestations, and she always kept this in mind in the construction of her rhythmic sequences. The reader will hardly believe it, but the wild delight that grips the student who eventually succeeds in mastering such a sequence is not far removed from that of youngsters who beg for 'more skipping!' and have their desire fulfilled!

But all that is just grammar, and grammar is neither music nor dance of itself. And if the magic of piano improvisation inspiring all our exercises may sometimes make us forget that fact, the best way of remembering it is to put the student in contact with musical works which these exercises make most accessible, with a view to helping him grasp the ungraspable.

Points of Support and Resistance

Rhythm is the outcome of a battle between a resistance and the effort made to avoid losing balance, a compromise between two opposing forces. (Dalcroze 1945: 250)

This definition, paraphrasing Schleich,[12] was made use of again in Dalcroze's penultimate work, thereby demonstrating that it had become his own; certainly there is no discipline other than Eurhythmics in which he could more firmly have proved it to be well founded.

We have seen hitherto how Eurhythmics, having first indulged them, progressively interferes with the free exercise of natural movements, of walking and other spontaneous rhythms. It does so by making use of various kinds of commands (temporal, dynamic, spatial). These commands have the effect of making resistances rise up beneath its pupils' very feet, both literally and figuratively. And the aim of the game is to bring about a situation in which such resistances fail to impede the flow of movement, either by skirting round them or by absorbing them into itself.

I should now like to return to music and seek to establish a parallel which strikes me as relevant in this context. The attempt has often been made to define exactly how, in our western civilization, a piece of music may be considered a work of art. Considerations of form, of stylistic unity and expressive variety, of internal coherence, though useful up to a point, are not sufficient to take into account the qualitative differences between, for example, a movement of a Beethoven symphony and a piece of light music, between the genuine jazz experience and any of its pale imitations, between what the American musicologist L. B. Meyer calls 'developed' and 'primitive' music.

---

[12] Dalcroze was emphasizing this definition from 1910 (see Dalcroze 1920: 8): 'Rhythm, according to Carl Ludwig Schleich's excellent definition, is a sort of compromise between force and resistance. The nature of resistances determines the form taken by spontaneous vital manifestations . . . See also Ch. 1 n. 5.

Meyer, author of *Music, the Arts and Ideas* (1967: esp. pp. 22–41), believes it is possible to identify this criterion as the extent to which a piece of music is able to *resist* its natural inclinations, to impose momentary inhibitions on the flow of its inclinations, to avoid flying straight to the target it has fixed for itself from the outset, but rather to devise means of overcoming the obstacles on the way. Whether the goal is a short-term (such as the end of a phrase), or long-term aim (the end of a movement, or of the whole work), the presence in the work of resistances to be overcome in reaching that goal helps render the content increasingly significant and rich in 'information'. The listener, constantly measuring what he actually hears from what he expects to hear, consciously follows the musical argument through, whereas an uneventful progression would have made no claim on his attention. The nature of the obstacles that modify the path it is expected to follow is, furthermore, capable of arousing his interest in the actual structure of the piece, enabling him to ascertain in what its style and originality consist. (The same goes, of course, for the musical performer, who builds his interpretive discourse on the material to be organized.)

The very terminology of tonal music takes this phenomenon into account when it applies the word 'cadence' (literally a 'falling') to the natural tendency of a musical phrase towards repose—the cadence being described as 'perfect' if nothing intervenes to alter this progression, but as 'interrupted', i.e. temporarily halted or 'avoided', if it is deflected away from its original aim. Needless to say, such deflections are not restricted to the harmonic aspect of tonal music but are to be encountered at all levels of musical construction—rhythm, melody, phrasing, harmony, timbres, form, as well as in its own particular modes of expression and articulation.

Meyer uses the same criterion to oppose 'developed' music to 'primitive' music (in which for this purpose he includes modern western 'pop')—a music characterized by its propensity to follow the most obvious path without ever, so to speak, deviating from its goal.[13] Repetitive in the extreme, and practically devoid of 'information', it makes little or no demand on the musical awareness of either listener or executant, but limits itself to producing or maintaining a physical effect. In the final analysis it consists of nothing but responses.

'I do not include', the author says (Meyer 1967: 32), 'under the term "primitive" the highly sophisticated music which so-called

[13] As the saying goes (source unknown to me): 'The course of a great piece of music is inevitable without being obvious'. (Translator's note)

primitives often play.' On the other hand, a particular distinction will be drawn between some types of western music described as 'facile'—a pejorative term for compositions which principally employ conventional clichés and borrow certain modes of expression from more sophisticated music[14]—as opposed to 'authentic' genres of primitive music, which generate themselves[15] without plagiarizing anyone. The fact remains, though, that both classes have in common the virtually total absence of those resistances observable in the more sophisticated musical works. Meyer believes the explanation for this phenomenon lies in a difference not of *mentality* but of *maturity*, the latter definable as a propensity to put off immediate gratification in favour of the gratification to come. 'Developed' music, then, at least as it has developed in our own culture, may be seen as demonstrating the possibility of delaying the satisfaction of our needs and of turning the anticipation itself, as well as the building up of resistances which prolong or intensify it, into a source of aesthetic satisfaction.[16]

'Today's composers push conflict to its limits . . . but they exaggerate it only to give themselves the pleasure of resolving it', wrote the musicologist Combarieu in 1916 (p. 271). Those of our own 'today' sometimes seem to go so far as to centre the idea of musical satisfaction in its positive irresolution. But if the listener does not find this to his liking, is this not often because, being ill-prepared for it, he does not know what to expect, and therefore cannot employ his capacity for tolerating frustration? However, once he has recognized a path—albeit well disguised or even contradicted—through the new music he is listening to, surely he will enjoy it to the extent that he can contrast his recollection of other pieces of music, and his other expectations, with the resistance it offers him by virtue of its strangeness? As to determining whether or not it counts as 'developed' music (in Meyer's sense of the word), it is for those who have most thoroughly studied its modes of expression and distinctive voice to redefine in other terms that which is resistance and that which is 'natural tendency'. Now,

[14] Dalcroze extended these and certain other characteristics to all works of art 'inferior to their task' (1945: 96). Elsewhere, however, he remarks (1942: 211): 'Do we not err in accusing a particular artist of being merely 'attractive' (*charmeur*) if we fail to point out the benefit of the attraction?'

[15] Cf. 'And then they nursed it | Rehearsed it | And gave out the news | That the South Land | Gave birth to the Blues . . .'

[16] Or of aestheticizing a pleasure not normally regarded as aesthetic, cf. the 12th-cent. phenomenon of courtly love (*amors fins*), which is rooted in a comparable sphere of new-found maturity. In this connection, a reading of William Golding's *The Inheritors* may be found enlightening. (Translator's note)

since the sound, time, and movement which form these two into a single musical structure are the raw materials of all music in all periods, and as the material is always subjected to the same laws of force and resistance, there is no reason to doubt that the criteria of resistance determining a piece of music's degree of 'development' is as valid for contemporary works as for others.

'Primitive' music, on the other hand, may be regarded—from its constant reversion to the tonic, the insistent repetition of its rhythms, the inevitability of its melodic lines, its extreme harmonic poverty— as asserting the need for immediate satisfaction through the intolerance of uncertainty. As dance music or background music,[17] it performs an immediate and timeless function, which is to assure (to express, to arouse) the individual's well-being or to assuage his discomfort.

An examination of the spontaneous music-making of the very young, such as may be effected in children's classes, or seen embodied in nursery rhyme collections, will corroborate the existence of a link between immaturity and the lack of resistance in musical flow. The note you expect is nearly always the note you get, the pause occurs exactly at the point foreseen, notes and values generally follow one another without surprise, to such an extent as to suggest that two identical tunes must surely have seen the light of day in two different places without any influence of either on the other. Knowing as we do, furthermore, that the interval of the falling third is (at least in our culture) the one that children grasp most easily, and that the pentatonic scale is that in which they sing most naturally (cf. Favre-Bulle and Garo 1976: p. vii), we realize even more forcefully why the musical possibilities are so limited in this field. We better understand the virtual absence of chromatics, and the family likenesses that these tunes share with one another: there must be any number of children who have 'invented' a tune beginning like Example 4.14*a* or *b*. These spontaneous tunes more or less flow along of their own accord,

Ex. 4.14 (*a*) (*b*)

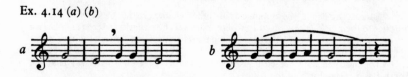

---

[17] Or, in English, 'musical wallpaper', for the aural pollution of 'background music' increasingly inflicted on shoppers, restaurant-goers, and even unsuspecting telephone callers. (Translator's note)

without any conscious intervention, and their movement takes its shape from the model of such elementary activities as swaying, stamping, and going round in circles.

Flawed performances of existing music also point to a link between the lack of musical consciousness and the absence of resistance. To remain with singing, take for example that well-known French tune 'Au clair de la lune'. The length of pause imposed by the dictates of symmetry on the point between the end of the first phrase and its repetition is by no means strictly obligatory to the actual performance; and, indeed, we regularly observe that children singing this song tend to minimize it. Thus they will blithely shorten the third bar of Example 4.15a to that of 4.15b, or they may perhaps follow the minim with a quaver rest enabling them to draw breath again.

Ex. 4.15 (a) (b)

Let's look at another example of a French song: 'Ne pleure pas, Jeannette' obviously originated in a marching-song (Ex. 4.16a). This is popularly deformed into something like Example 4.16b. In the absence of meaningful words, the capacity for resistance required for

Ex. 4.16 (a) (b)

the correct performance of the eighth bar, after the impulse provided by those preceding, finds itself deprived of the physical support originally provided by the marching. Singers who are sitting down are quite unperturbed by the upsetting of the four-square measure caused by their propensity to forge ahead on their own. At least, they remain unperturbed (just as those children do when singing 'Au clair de la lune') only unless they have had sufficient musical education to have acquired the taste or the need for keeping control of time in music, whether out of respect for the original text, by the desire for balance, or for the pleasure of performance and creation.

I found it enlightening for my purposes to hold to a theory appealing to concrete and measurable factors (the presence or absence of 'resistances' in music) with a view to explaining how music, which at a primitive level is so closely attached to the body, to the here-and-now, has been able to develop into an art of thought and time.

What goes for musical consciousness applies equally well to other achievements of the human mind. We know, in particular, that the representation of space can only be developed to the extent that the child can imagine the possibility of making detours in order to get from one place to another; and that his consciousness of time can only be brought about when a number of experiences involving the speed, the slowness, and the cessation of activity have enabled him to relate 'before' to 'after'. Similarly, his access to musical thought presupposes the ability to adopt consciously one path rather than another and to establish temporal relationships between the various points-in-time of musical argument. In music, as in other fields, a sudden insight cannot occur until certain external imperatives are in place to set up some resistance against natural tendencies. Seeking to encourage such insights, Eurhythmics, whose 'aim is the harmonization of all the faculties of the individual', turns the progressive introduction of resistances in the exercise of natural rhythms—physical and musical—into one of the most important of its educational principles. It will be found to subsist in all topics of study, as will already have been noticed in the preceding pages or from a reading of Chapter 3. At the same time, resistances constitute a topic of study in themselves. Bodily resistances and musical resistances—both at a variety of levels—must be identifiable and recognizable as such.

In this connection it will first be necessary to get the pupils to sense consciously the difference between a pathway free of resistances and the same pathway containing them. Here too, as practically always in

Eurhythmics, this understanding will preferably be effected through the establishment of correspondences between musical and physical performance. A nice illustration of this is provided by a variant of the party game 'Musical Chairs'. Here, it is designed to encourage the grasping of harmonic resistance as set up in opposition to the completion of a perfect cadence.

This game, as everybody knows, involves one chair less than the number of players. The chairs may be placed at random around the room, or in rows, or in a circle. The players circulate around the chairs as long as the music keeps going. When it stops, they all sit down, and the player who fails to find an empty chair drops out. Another chair is then removed, and the game continues. Traditionally, the music may be stopped at any point; it takes the players by surprise, and those who are quickest on the uptake turn out to be the winners.

In our variation, the (improvising) pianist starts the game by coinciding his breaks with the ending of musical phrases which finish on a chord of the tonic. In this way he reinforces the sense of there being a support-point, which the pupils learn very quickly to anticipate. Next, he cuts across this sense by replacing the final chord of a perfect cadence with a chord of the sixth degree (interrupted cadence) or modulating chord (evaded cadence), and continuing to play. The pupils who, relying on their sense of anticipation, sat down too soon, realize that their expectation has not been fulfilled. In this way their attention is directed to the necessity of sometimes resisting their natural impulses. Finally, to check that they are truly inhibited from reacting by a *harmonic* sensation (for the tendency to sit down might simply be repressed, only to be resuscitated by the silence of the musical interruption), the improviser stops playing as soon as he reaches the chord, whether it be an inconclusive chord or that of the tonic, although it is still only the latter which authorizes players to sit down. Anyone who sits down in error must then change places with one of the previously eliminated players.

This correspondence between the seated position and the sense of harmonic conclusion, as well as between an inhibition of the impulse to sit down and a particular harmonic feature which sets up a resistance to the expected course of the music, can then be exercised without the 'elimination' threat which for children constitutes the chief attraction of the game and their motivation for playing it. For example, the chairs are randomly arranged around the room and pupils pass from one to another in accordance with musical phrases of equal length, which either come to a halt (sit down) or remain unfulfilled (keep moving). The latter action may be reserved to the interrupted cadence, while an evaded cadence may instruct them—for instance—to go round behind a chair while holding on to the backrest (or again, a modulating chord of the dominant seventh calls for them to climb on the chair, etc.). The opportunity will not be lost to follow up this type of exercise by listening to pieces of music illustrating these particular harmonic features, so that they may be recognized in any context which attaches aesthetic significance to the resistances.

But it is musical resistances of the *rhythmic* type whose correspondences will be most clearly evidenced in physical exercises. Now before they can be instigated at will or deliberately eliminated, before they can be perceived as such and analysed in these terms, bodily resistances must first have been experienced as resulting from physical and material constraints imposed on the body by concrete objects outside itself, or imposed by it upon those self-same objects. Both active and passive resistances are well illustrated by exercises of the type wherein 'one pupil pulls along another who allows himself to be so pulled'. This type of exercise facilitates experience of every nuance from total passivity which imposes exhausting efforts on the part of the pulling player (as indeed may a positive refusal to be pulled along, which may result from the strength of the puller being confronted with an even greater force), to a degree of relaxation which gives place to the slightest pull, thus at the same time abolishing all feeling of tension between the puller and the pulled. The teacher will endeavour to encourage both sides equally to measure out their energy expenditure in such a way as to maintain an optimum degree of tension—in other words, that which enables the maintenance of a steady progress in spite of the resistances seeking to oppose one another, or in such a way as to favour now the puller, now the pulled, without thereby bringing the tension between the two to an end.

With young children, the game of Horse and Coachman may well be used:

Both players put themselves inside the same hoop, which counts for one of them as a harness, for the other as the backrest of a seat, and for both of them as a carriage whose motive power is provided by their legs. (Later, the same effect can be produced by passing a length of cord around the shoulders of one, the other holding both ends of it.) The hold applied to them by the surrounding hoop, at first with and then without the help of their hands, obliges them (not unpleasurably) to go forwards at all costs, the requisite degree of tension being achieved with the help of the natural 'balance of forces' in the whole arrangement.

With more advanced pupils, use will be made of a length of cord of which each holds one end in his hand—or, better still, a length of strong elastic, which will show up every slight shade of tension produced. Alternatively, a stick of deceptive rigidity may be employed. Eventually, such intermediaries will be dispensed with: players will pull one another along by the hands or elbows, or stand back to back and push themselves along with their shoulders. They will then try to act upon one another at a distance and still maintain a feeling of pull and resistance.

In connection with the last of these, a game which will help them pass from the concrete situation to a representation of it sustained solely by internal sensations is that in which, without actually touching anyone, each tries to get an opponent off balance by engaging in an imaginary push-and-pull with him, and offering as great a resistance as possible. (In this case the pupils stand face to face on a narrow bench, or fixedly on two adjacent points. The loser may or may not be decided in advance.)

All two-player resistance exercises are also carried out in accordance with precise timing instructions or musical commands, with phrases of equal or unequal length, responses to accents, crescendos or accelerandos all contributing to an increase in the tension or speed of the movement, and so on.

Faithful conformity to this same device for creating traction and resistance produces an accurate feeling for and execution of *syncopation* —that embodiment *par excellence* of musical rhythm which is best appreciated when it occurs as a 'hiccup' in the musical progress and points towards its resolution (rather than as an underlying regularity, as is so often the case, especially in jazz). Thus two people will walk along together to the same measure, following the natural course of the music. One of the two will then be prompted—whether by the other, by some internal impulse, or by the occurrence of a heard signal—to lurch forwards and so get pushed ahead of the musical tempo. For several steps, the 'downbeats' of his walking will be brought forwards (in 'advance syncopation') and, by pulling at his partner, he will try—in vain—to bring him up to his own level. Then he will allow himself to be brought back by the imperturbability of his comrade, thereby resolving the tension that has just been created (Ex. 4.17).

Ex. 4.17

Alternatively, the syncopation may be carried out by delay, one of the two walkers suddenly refusing to follow their common pace for a while, until after a few steps he allows himself to be pulled up by his partner and so rejoin the original movement (Ex. 4.18).

Ex. 4.18

The teacher will, both through the piano improvisation used in the exercise and by means of examples abounding in musical literature, demonstrate the difference in tension created between two voices according to whether the upper line gets ahead of the harmonic accompaniment or lets itself be drawn to it (Ex. 4.19).

This too will be the time to experience differences in tension between the parts of one's own body: a ball may be thrown up and down at first in time with the walking rhythm and then in syncopated opposition to it; one arm may copy the gesture of another but do so a beat or two later, or may perform a particular movement slowly while the other does the same thing two or three times as fast; the upper part of the body may be held steady or move smoothly so as to contrast with

Ex. 4.19

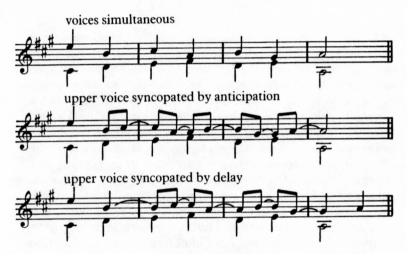

the lower limbs, which are engaged in furious activity (try, for instance, running while carrying a glass of water in one hand!). These exercises will rub shoulders with related work in continuous movement, slow motion, dissociation, and muscular elasticity. The mastery of bodily resistances, added to that of functions described previously, will open the door to polyrhythmic musical performances and everything to do with the plastic quality of music—to the extent, of course, that all the preceding exercises are actually carried out to music! Furthermore, the work done in resistances will reinforce a conscious distinction between metre and rhythm by teaching pupils 'not to confuse rhythm, which animates the body, with metre, which merely regulates it' (Dalcroze 1945: 21), and to feel with Dalcroze (1945: 256) that

rhythm loses its force if it is not ordered and repeated; metre grows monotonous if it is not enlivened by occasional accentuations. Order must be enlivened, and life must be ordered; that is what makes it necessary to study the relations between Metre and Rhythm, between regular and indispensable automatisms and the emotions which interrupt and modify them.

Making Use of Space

For the elementary pupil, surrounding space starts off as no more than a necessary support for his motor exercises. Yet almost immediately—that is, from the first time he moves about—this space acquires the status of an environment with which he must come to grips: on one hand, the walls of the room as well as its particular topographical features (its nooks and crannies, any columns, steps, or fixed pieces of furniture) force the pupil to restrict his moving about to within certain limits, besides imposing changes of direction and other contingent modifications relating to space, time, or energy (stopping, slowing down, etc.). On the other, the ever-present moving obstacles represented by other pupils in his class very soon force him to take active and flexible account of the mobile space surrounding him. Halts, divergences, and curves in his line of movement, his passage between fixed points and avoidance of obstacles, etc., give rise from the outset to numerous exercises explicitly designed to make the surrounding space his own, so that he feels comfortable in it and can move around easily amongst its other occupants (cf. Ch. 5).

We will here assume that such basics have been acquired, so as to examine certain properties of space which are at the same time musical properties, and by which Eurhythmics seeks to turn the varying dimensions of music into a 'visible reality'. In rhythmic exercises centred on the use of surrounding space we can broadly distinguish two possible emphases:

1. The space to be considered is that which links individual pupils (or groups of individuals) to one another when they are moving around. In this case, room space is a collective space, and is closely involved with the way in which a collective occupies it.
2. Space is a blank page on which are drawn and measured the paths and circuits enabling passage from one point to another. In this case each pupil (or group of pupils) embarks for himself upon evaluations of distance, energy, or time.

In the visible translation of musical works, as conceived by Dalcroze through the medium of what he called *la plastique animée* (or *plastique vivante*—'living plasticity'), and which he thought of as the body's equivalent of *solfège* (cf. 1919*b*: 133–4), these two ways of looking at space merge into one another, for each of them is equally necessary to the faithful reconstruction of the musical movement; here, however, we shall see to which aspects of music each one relates more particularly, and how they can be separately made use of from the viewpoint of 'musicianship studies' or the grammar of music.

Collective space—If we imagine a fairly numerous group of individuals gathered together in a room, and then bring our mind to bear upon one individual in isolation in the same space, we find ourselves led, by analogy with the experience of music, to the notion of 'sound-space' (*volume sonore*). In fact, exercises designed to encourage the auditory differentiation of varying degrees of sound-space will often make use of group-to-individual contrasts, or of whole- to sub-groups, or again to such procedures as the following:

When they hear music consisting of widely spread or ornamented chords, the pupils move about at will, making as much claim on space as possible, and seeking in all their peregrinations to make use of every available space; when its notes cluster together almost to the point of unison, the pupils form themselves into a single line and move about as such, becoming 'a single voice'.

Sensations of *sound intensity*, often related to the preceding topic, may also—when required to be experienced through group movements—usefully be derived from the number and spread of participants, even more than from degrees of energy effected by each individual in isolation. In this connection Dalcroze makes a notable point concerning crescendo:

It is in this way that a group of men can produce an impression of crescendo by expansion (the men stepping apart from one another), and also by contraction (the men getting close to one another and giving the impression of a contracting muscle). And vice versa. (1919*b*: 145)

Nonetheless, the subjective connotations associated with these two ways of translating a crescendo into spatial terms are not necessarily fixed. Think, for example, of the inexorable threat represented by a circle which closes in on an individual so that he feels hemmed in on all sides, or (still in the same sense) the heartfelt determination which drives two teams of players to bear down upon a ball thrown down between them. Similarly, a crescendo by expansion can give the impression of a slow blossoming or a rising panic, etc. Subjective these impressions may be, but they do relate—in sometimes unfathomable ways—to matters of speed, tempo, and energy in the movement as a whole.

In this connection, here is an exercise in preparing to occupy space, which is due, if I am not mistaken, to Claire-Lise Dutoit. In this case it involves making a collective adaptation to a constantly shrinking space.

At the start, the whole room belongs to everybody, and everyone moves about with the conscious aim of leaving no place unoccupied. At the sound of a signal, one half of the room vanishes, as if by magic, from the universe of the participants, who have just enough time to get into the other half (if they aren't already there) before an imaginary but impenetrable wall prevents them from escaping. Everyone then starts moving about in this half-room, making use, as before, of every available space. At a second signal, their collective space is again deliberately cut in half, this time in the other orientation (see Figure 4.3), and so on, until all those taking part find themselves confined in one corner of the room, tightly packed together but continuing, nonetheless, to move around without colliding, and seeking out all the unused spaces. The order in which these halving cuts are made will have been decided in advance, in accordance, for example, with the scheme shown in Figure 4.3.

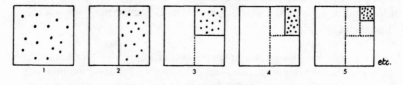

Fig. 4.3

In fact, the exercises will have to be repeated a number of times before all the available space can be accurately evaluated. (We must not forget that the pupils are constantly moving about and no real line ever actually appears on the ground.) The same exercise will be done in reverse, with pupils passing from a small space to one twice the size, then four times as large, and so on.

An examination of the series of sketches in Figure 4.3 may lead us to be struck by either of two features: if we think of the relations of the individuals to one another (as 'points') we become aware of the increase in density; if we think of the whole space, we are more struck by its gradual diminution. This explains why the progression may, with the same result, be illustrated musically by successively over-lapping layers of sound volume in either crescendo or decrescendo, even though individual movements retain the same intensity from the first to the last phase of the exercise. (Actually, this does not usually happen in practice, as variations in loudness almost invariably affect the intensity of individual movements.) We shall be able to verify the reality of this phenomenon by musically illustrating, with alternating crescendo and decrescendo, the same film sequence—or a succession of shots—showing the exercise being previously conducted without music.

The next stage of the exercise therefore consists in replacing the arbitrary signal which instructs pupils to cut space in two with a modification (diminution or augmentation) of the sound level. Because the progression must be capable of being carried out in at least four or five layers, the pupils will have to be aurally sensitive to relatively fine shades of change. The progression from fortissimo to forte, then to mezzoforte, to piano and finally pianissimo (or vice versa) may at first be made more noticeable by correspondingly reducing (or increasing) the sound-space; but the pupils will soon notice that a different relation between space and sound levels is equally valid, and that a large number of variations are possible if potential modifications of tempo, speed, or weight are also taken into account. It will be possible to illustrate some of these combinations by means of suggestions or instructions of an expressive nature. For example, on the theme 'from liberty to confinement' (!), the former can be translated, in a large area, by a light and fluid movement, or, on the other hand, by a sudden excess of energy; a crescendo which calls for space to be cut down might give voice to anguish and despair, or a decrescendo be accompanied by a sense of progressive stupefaction and resignation. Alternatively, 'flight from danger' will cause the fugitives to group together (or disperse) by imparting to them an increasing state of panic, or consolation, or reassurance. On many occasions it will be observed that proceeding first in one direction and then in the other as far as use of space is concerned, it is possible to experience (and to communicate such experience to the onlooker) series of sensations of the same type—and not only impressions of contrasting character. At the same time, this will bring out the extent to which impressions produced by gradations in the sound level in a piece of music are themselves linked to subjective factors and result from the combination and subtle control of various dimensions whose respective relationships are not always easy to determine.

Learning to occupy collective space also means getting acquainted with the *formal characteristics* of music and movement. For example, the pupil will learn to maintain an unvarying distance between himself and anyone else. Exercises in parallel movement between two or more pupils (which find their musical counterpart in the parallel progression of voices or musical chords), whether side by side, face to face, one after the other, etc., and walking forwards, backwards, sideways, etc., will help pupils divide their attention between their own sense of motor activity and the neighbouring presence of their moving comrades, which they ought to be able to feel as their 'doubles'. Little by little, they should develop the capcity for instant mutual adaptation and for the instinct of corrective motion to re-establish their optimal separation distance when it has been momentarily disturbed. This capacity requires the ability to consider oneself as one part of a whole, and to succeed in distancing oneself mentally from this whole in order to achieve a representation of its overall effect. We shall have occasion to see (in Ch. 5) that such distancing cannot be demanded of very young children. It will, however, prove an excellent objective for a number of exercises to practise with older children and adults, so long as they already enjoy satisfactory mastery of their individual capacities for progressive movement and orientation in space.

In the same range of ideas, the collective construction—and sequencing—of geometric figures with either straight or curved lines, as well as other group configurations, will contribute towards the pupils' development of an aptitude for formal construction and to 'training their minds to envisage ensembles in a given space' (Dalcroze 1919*b*: 145). They will then be in a position to find their predetermined place in a group arrangement wherever they may come from and within the limits of the time allowed. The possibility of rapidly memorizing one's place and role in a group arrangement becomes even more important in the case of a moving form, into which each individual must be able to fit while sharing in the general movement without holding it up. Repetitive musical forms will be of particular value in supporting this type of exercise. Rondo form, for instance, is based on the periodic reprise of a refrain which the ear recognizes as being the same (and which is expected to be recognized as soon as it appears again). A rhythmic exercise based on this theme may consist in getting the pupils to ad lib 'body improvisations' (individually or in groups) during the episodes of the rondo piece, and requiring them to be in an exact spot at the right time for each reprise of the theme, so as to execute it together and in a predetermined manner as a thing in itself.

Space as measured and as measurement—The preceding example brings us back to the subject of collaboration between space and time, on whose relationships most exercises in rhythm are based.

Now we know that spatial evaluation starts off, in the child, as something purely qualitative: a particular place is either nearer or further away; you go for either a little walk or a big walk. 'New York is miles and miles away! It's even further away than Lausanne!' said a little boy I know who lives in Geneva. It is not until much later that the child can fall back on objective measurements enabling it to compare one with another and subsequently talk in terms of length, distance, surface, etc., by reference to a fixed unit of measurement. The same goes for time, too: a 'moment' feels longer or shorter, a moving object is seen as fast or slow, a person thought of as young or old, all by virtue of subjective criteria (some of which will last for life) before such phenomena can take their proper place in a system of quantifiable relations.

In everyday speech we will sometimes describe somewhere fairly near as being 'Just a few steps away'. Imprecise as such description is, it is, in every sense of the word, much more informative than a precise specification in yards, in that it implicitly conveys in the same breath some indication of the time and effort involved in getting to the spot required. Similarly, when in olden days a more distant location was reckoned as 'three days' walk away'—or when we nowadays speak of a town being 'a couple of days by car'—such information was (and is) clearly more useful than a precise distance in kilometres, which completely ignores incidental features of the area to be traversed, or the quality and hilliness of the roads.

As to time, we all know how much easier it is to assess a given period by what we can do in it than by reference to a specific measurement in hours and in minutes. When a 6-year-old asks 'When will Daddy get home?', he will find (even if he can tell the time) that an answer like 'At six o'clock' or 'In an hour and a half' tells him nothing really meaningful about the wait involved. A better one is 'When you have finished your tea and done your homework you can start playing, and Daddy should be back by then'. When the same child is being taken for a long walk and says 'When can we have a rest?', the reply 'When we get to that tree over there' leads him to see the time separating him from the desired goal in terms of the effort he must put into getting there. As far as distance is concerned, the child concentrates solely on the arrival point (the tree). Whether he regards it as nearer or further away depends on how tired he is, and not on such things as how many twists and turns there are in the path that gets him there. If, in following it, he finds the distance longer or shorter than he thought, this merely leads him to correct his previous estimate of what that distance was.

In fact, it might be said—'historically' speaking—that it is by reference to the activity that fills a period of time that one arrives at a sense of its duration. And it is by a sense of the period required for the forward movement that one forms an intuitive notion of the distance that has been or is to be travelled.

Consequently, from an educational viewpoint, it will be useful to begin exercises in spatial evaluation by making reference to a framework of time before trying to concentrate on space in its own right, or using it, for its part, as a way of measuring time. Now, in Eurhythmics, the time aspect of a movement may be brought out (in some sense 'objectivized') by means of music. Music may in this way help render distinct two notions (space and time) which otherwise tend to remain inextricably bound together when involved in movement, which acts for both of them primarily—and for a long time uniquely—as the means of measuring them.

Here, by way of example, are two exercises which attempt to measure space intuitively in terms of time. I saw the first of them used by Ruth Gianadda in a class of fifteen pupils in the third year of primary school.

Each child stands next to a ball lying on the ground. (Soon, pupils will have to move around between the balls without touching them; the choice of such a potentially unstable object emphasizes that importance attaches to *where* they walk rather than to the mere fact of walking.) The first instruction goes as follows: 'We're going on a walk, and there will be music to go with it. When the music stops, the walk comes to an end and we go back to our places, next to our own ball.' The rhythmician then improvises a longish, sixteen-bar tune at the piano, in form AABB', with its four phrases of equal length following on from one another without interruption. Throughout the exercise she will adhere to the same melodic form and the same overall length, but with the melody itself being constantly improvised and therefore never reproducing itself again exactly.

At the end of the first attempt most of the pupils finish up at some distance from their ball, and it is only the ensuing silence which prompts them to return to base.

Second instruction: 'This time try and reach the end of your walk at the same time as I reach the end of the tune. Try to feel how long the music takes. You can guess when it's coming to an end, and that's the moment when you should be well on your way back to your ball.

This time, some four or five pupils will manage to make their return coincide with the end of the tune. Others, as yet unable to anticipate sufficiently well, suddenly run back to their spot just when they hear the last note of the piece (or, strictly speaking, one or two seconds before). Some, on the other hand, will not have plucked up enough courage to move more than a few steps away from the ball, being obsessed by the idea of having to get back in time—for which reason they will get there too early, the only thing of significance to them being the place of arrival. For these last two groups, the teacher will—rightly—back-pedal somewhat in order to concentrate on duration alone.

'This time there is no need to go back to your ball. You can if you like; but what really counts is to listen to the music and to stop at the same time *it* stops. The important thing is not so much *where* you stop as exactly *when* you stop'.

Thus relieved of spatial constraint, every child, without exception, this time succeeds in stopping at the desired moment. This demonstrates very well that anticipating the moment of arrival is learnt much earlier than its associated place of arrival.

Then the rhythmician will draw the children's attention to the way in which the establishment of a suitable path can be helped by getting the length of the tune correctly fixed in their heads: 'You've seen how everyone knows exactly when they have to stop because, at a certain moment, something in the music tells you that the end of the piece is coming, then something says that now is the moment to stop. Now the same thing happens when we are taking our walk. When we set off, we know that we're at the beginning, and that we can wander some distance away from the ball. Then something in the music tells us that it's about time we started making our way back, and finally that we had better get there right away if we don't want to arrive too late. And because we are very nearly there, we don't have to run'. With some trial and error, most of the pupils succeed in completing the exercise. Some will time their return from the beginning of the third phrase; others will wait for it to be repeated, as it still allows them enough time to get back. They will all seem to have grasped what it is all about, without at any time ever having felt it necessary (either for themselves or for the teacher) to do anything like counting the steps or the number of phrases. They need do no more than plot a pathway in advance, or decide beforehand on a series of intermediate stations. For this reason the exercise will, in my view, have been of real value to them as much from a musical viewpoint as from that of structuring space, even if their actual performances may still occasionally leave something to be desired.

The second exercise is that of Bowling the Hoop, which children greatly enjoy (especially those I see in motor therapy classes).

Having learnt how to bowl a hoop around and catch it without letting it fall, the child then learns to hold the moment back at which he has to grab it. He may, for instance, wait until the order is given by a signal rather than plunge headlong into seizing it (which he will be predisposed towards by the excitement of the game and the fear of letting it fall). In this way he will gradually succeed in judging the exact moment when it becomes necessary to catch the hoop because it is slowing down dangerously. Once this mastery has been acquired, the rolling hoop can be used as a way of measuring space with time. Having given the hoop its initial impetus, the child now goes some way off from it, trying to follow as long a pathway as the hoop allows him time for. At first, it is quite a job to allow one's eyes to let go of the hoop. At every moment the child experiences the need to check that the hoop is still going round, as if it only needed a moment's visual inattention to it for it to run the risk of falling (even though the child has already observed for himself that it can keep going a long time). To help convince him that the hoop does not need to be watched to go on turning, the teacher will make use of music. 'I am going to play the piano along with the movement of the hoop, like this (sustained trill). When you hear the music start to slow down, that will tell you that the hoop is also slowing down, and that now's the time to go back and catch it.' Thanks to this ability to exercise aural control, the child walks boldly away from the hoop. Generally, the first time the music suggests that it is time to return, he runs back at top speed. When he realizes there is no need to hurry, he will be capable of internalizing the approximate time available for his walk, and it will then be possible to get him to fix his attention on the distance involved. 'You will now try and go for as long a walk as you did before, but this time without the music, and trying to remember how long the hoop can go on turning.' Helped by further experience, the child will gradually succeed in estimating the length of his route as a function of variations in time depending on the strength of the initial impulse given to the hoop.

These two exercises may be numbered amongst those exemplifying the use of rhythmics *by means of* music (as opposed to *for the purposes* of music). But in the long run they also serve the latter function, by enabling a start to be made on metrics proper without running the risk of getting it muddled up with either music, in which it is one of several elements, or rhythm, to which it acts as a supporting framework.

The introduction of units of measurement allowing quantitative comparisons to be made is of relatively late appearance in the child, both as to measurements of time and those of space. Further, both the metric and the 'chronometric' systems have little and only a very minor part to play in the areas of music and bodily movement. In music, time will be spoken of by reference to minutes and seconds only in very specific circumstances, such as a need to know how long a given piece is when drawing up a programme or planning a run-through, or in involving the use of a metronome as an aid to characterizing a tempo. Such notions do not occur in music itself, except for certain contemporary works in which pauses or bursts of sound may be subject to split-second timing. (This presumably becomes vital in works in the course of which all reference to any stable or common tempo is abandoned, and whose written scores do not allow musicians to latch on to the sort of measured bars which in traditional scores acted as a kind of 'chronometer'; or again when the performance of the work involves the use of a pre-recording which includes blank tracks of a particular length laid by for musical interventions on the part of the live performers.) But music like this, in which composers play about with real clock-time, may still be considered relatively exceptional in the repertoire of existing musical works, for which the unit of measurement in time is not the second but the beat.

Similarly, in the realm of bodily movement, metres and centimetres will hardly be spoken of, unless to establish the dimensions of a stage or to decide on particular toe-marks, or occasionally to suggest a rough distance between two performers: 'Don't get any closer than a metre apart'; 'remain a couple of centimetres apart'. But in fact you are far more likely to hear 'There ought to be an arm's length between you', or 'Stand as close as possible without actually touching'; for measurements of that sort, besides being sufficiently accurate for their purpose, are permanently verifiable. In this case the unit of measurement is not the metre but the *step*.

Both cadence and step are, it is true, variable units; yet, once established by means of a repeated movement charged with a given amount of energy, they remain sufficiently stable and precise to be, if required, measurable in terms of seconds or centimetres (though this is rarely necessary, as we have seen), and, as such, capable of giving rise to proportional measurements. Thus a twelve-step move is twice as long as an equally paced six-step move, and three times as long as one of four steps; a sequence of twelve notes played with a given cadence will last as long as one of twenty-four notes played twice as fast; and so on. But above all—and this is what we are driving at—the fact that the cadence and the step share a common origin in the energy with which a movement is charged means that both may be used to measure space and time by means of each other. (Cf. 'pace', in English.)

In the first of the two examples quoted above we saw how the possibility of judging the length in time of a given tune could be used as a way of judging the length of a physical movement. We made use, remember, of a tune shaped AABB' and consisting of four phrases of four bars each. It is quite obvious that this very squareness, a regular metrical superstructure here rendered even more apparent by the repetition of phrases in pairs, must have assisted the successful execution of the exercise (even without its being explicitly pointed out). It enabled, in fact, a feeling for the space–time relationship of the whole tune to be transferred to a narrower range of units of movement; hence the number of steps to each phrase had a good chance of being faithfully reproduced even though no suggestion had been made as to the possibility of counting them. (This maintenance of squareness did not exist, however, in the Turning Hoop exercise, where the child had to rely on his internal timing of the movement as a whole.)

The 'squaring-up'—structuring in fours, or groups of four—of bars or groups of bars follows a metrical logic deriving from binary movement (as illustrated by walking and other movements parallel to the bodily axis). It is so to speak omnipresent in classical and modern western music, as well as (and not without reason) in dance music and jazz. This 'four-square' sense will quite often be found in people with the barest minimum of musical experience. (Though is it possible to go through life nowadays without hearing any music? And isn't that very music which we do not choose to hear—so generously dispensed as it is in places of public resort—often the most implacably 'four-square' music that ever was?) One might almost go so far as to ask whether squareness has not become virtually one of our cultural archetypes! Yet symmetry in music—that is to say its architectural equilibrium—is not limited to squareness in the strict sense of the word, and there are probably just as many examples of works in which this property is countered as there are works in which it is present. Furthermore they are often both exemplified in the same work, and we appreciate counter-squareness all the more when it satisfyingly disturbs the predicted flow of regularly paced music while yet enabling us to cross-refer to its regularity. For example, a three-bar phrase may be heard as the repetition of an original four-bar phrase truncated or condensed; or the insertion of a bar of three-time into a repeated series of 2/4 bars may impart a sense of 'stretching' to the tune, etc. Dalcroze himself, in his instrumental and vocal compositions, made great play (often systematically) of such modifications to squareness as would lead to a shift in the musical equilibrium. To be able to appreciate such transgressions, interruptions, and reorganizations of the rhythmic and metrical material to the full, it is even more necessary to possess in oneself an instinctive feeling for everything covered by the concepts of balance and imbalance in music.

One of the rhythm exercises designed to ensure that the sense of squareness is present in the pupil's audio-motor memory consists in playing him, as he walks along, a four-square piece of music which he does not already know and asking him to stop when it reaches the end and to clap his hands exactly in time with the final note. One then embarks upon the piece, warning the pupil that the music will cut out somewhere along the way and that he will have to pursue his walk by singing the rest of the piece to himself (or by following another tune, if his memory proves unreliable) right up to its presumed end, at which point, as before, he has to stop and clap the final note. The piano stops playing shortly after reaching the second half of the piece. (Towards the end of the exercise it will be possible, after about the third time, to stop the music before the end of the first half.)

Some pupils, even among those displaying a satisfactory sense of 'squareness' when doing exercises of this sort, often have difficulty in keeping it up when trying to get along on their own, especially when they have to sing to themselves a hitherto unknown tune. It is one thing to cut it short (or even lengthen it) by a certain number of notes; but often, albeit conscious of having gone wrong somewhere, they are quite unable to determine what effect they have actually produced on the length of the tune. Was it too long, or too short? They do not know. On such occasions it is often helpful to resort to space as a measuring device, as for example in the following form (the basic idea of which I borrow from Dominique Porte):

Toe-marks are established on the floor at equidistant intervals (actually in the form of a square), between which the pupil must be able 'comfortably' to take a number of steps equivalent to the number of prompts determined by the cadence of the melodic phrase. The teacher starts by getting the pupil to experience this equivalence by accompanying his progress from one point to another with melodic phrases of equal length, it being understood that at the start of each new phrase he changes direction and heads for the following point. The teacher then plays him (or sings him) only every other phrase. In the intervening gap he sings the bit of tune he has just heard while continuing to walk. He thereby benefits from the possibility of exerting firsthand control over his singing, which generally has the (not very surprising?) effect of reducing from the outset the number of mistakes he makes, not only those of timing but also those deriving from lapses of melodic memory. Depending on the aim of the exercise, or the topic being worked on, the repetition of a heard melody may be replaced by getting the pupil to improvise phrases forming a natural continuation to those played to him. He may also be required to clap hands, while walking, to the rhythm of the tune he has just been listening to (or to one of his own invention but equal in length). Again, the pupil may be required to imagine a free bodily rhythm (jumping, running, pulling up, slow stepping, etc.) which fills up the time taken to get from one point to another and leads him to the next point in the time required to enable him to continue his interrupted walk just as the next phrase starts.

When, by means of bodily movements and progressions, one tries to translate the temporal and dynamic flow of the music, passage from one point to the next may not always take place at the most comfortable speed, contrary to what I suggested in the above example. To catch up with a group some way off in a brief space of time: to advance imperceptibly along a straight line in a timespan that seems infinite: to return to a starting-point in a period half as long as it took to get there in the first place—*now* we're talking business! Now it's a matter of applying just the right degree of energy to every single movement, of properly sequencing them without the slightest error of judgement, even while relations between time and space are changing from one moment to the next.

Here is an exercise in 'grammar' which I think is bound to favour this sort of control. I owe the basic idea to Edith Naef, and I will try to bring out a few of its possibilities.

A large rectangle is marked out in the room with the aid of nine tambourines (or, better still, nine cardboard squares so that they may be stepped on, or nine hoops). These represent the corners, the median points of each side, and the centre of the rectangle, as in Figure 4.4. The distance between two neighbouring objects will be a, b, or c.

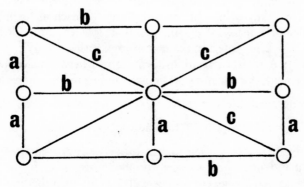

Fig. 4.4

Stage 1: Fix on a number of steps; say seven. The pupils then must get from one point to its neighbour in seven steps in any direction they like, that is to say by following a segment *a*, *b*, or *c*. Thus they are free to choose their pathways, and on each occasion are forced to adapt the length of their stride to the chosen segment. The exercise is carried out to a given tempo; thereafter it can be done to a slower tempo, at running speed, etc. (Alternatively, the exercise can be done again later starting off with a different number of steps.) At this stage, attention is focused on varying the expenditure of energy in proportion to variations in space, with the duration of movements remaining constant, as well as the number of steps.

Stage 2: Different speeds are now assigned to different lengths. For example, it may be agreed that the speed at which steps are taken should relate directly to the length of the segements: segment *c* is run, *b* is walked at normal speed, *a* done at a slow pace. (But the exact opposite is also a possibility, and different assignments may be agreed on another occasion.) The number of steps between two points remains constant. At this stage, speed of decision-making plays an important part. Every change in direction is accompanied by an appropriate change of tempo, and an immediate decision must be taken as to which change of direction is coming up. A good sense of direction is an invaluable aid in this respect. Reference to Figure 4.4 will show that all segments *a* are actually depicted as verticals, *b* as horizontals, *c* as diagonals (corresponding to length, width, and diagonals in the real space of the room). This phase of the exercise is done without external musical accompaniment, it being left to the pupils to pace their three different speeds for themselves, they being obliged to ensure that each of them is as regular and consistent as possible. At first, it will be found helpful to call for a brief pause at the end of each series of steps.

Stage 3: A metrical relationship is agreed between the speeds of movement; for example a single/double proportion between increasing speeds (i.e. $a = \bf{\downarrow}$, $b = \bf{\downarrow}$, $c = \bf{\downarrow}$), or else a single/triple ($a = \bf{\downarrow}$, $b = \bf{\downarrow}$, $c = \bf{\downarrow}$ in $\bf{\downarrow\downarrow}$). Then decide on a number of steps which relates to the chosen metre. In fact, at every moment the different cadences must be reciprocally controllable. In the first example quoted above, eight steps will do it (or any other multiple of four); in the second, nine will be convenient, as well as any other multiple of three. Twelve steps will be found suitable for several different relative proportions; for example $a = \text{♩.}$, $b = \text{♩.}$, $c = \text{♪}$; or $a = \text{♩.}$, $b = \text{♩}$, $c = \text{♪}$, etc. On the other hand, it does require a room of more than comfortable dimensions! Here, a musical accompaniment will facilitate the perception of pathways as constituting an overall symmetrical figure. If the number of steps is judiciously selected, the different points of the rectangle become meeting points, sometimes rallying points. When the exercise is capable of being carried out with precision by the whole group of pupils, the onlooker will experience a visual impression similar to that of a kaleidoscope, in which independently moving and differently coloured pieces of glass slide around to form momentary patterns by the magic of symmetry.

It is possible to think up multiple variations on this exercise: entries in canon, replacement of regular paces by rhythmic walks, variations in the weightiness of movement, group creations producing mirror-image symmetry, and so on.

Dalcroze was so convinced of the primordial role of the muscular sense in the evaluation of space that he went on with success to devise many rhythmic exercises specifically for the blind (see 1942: 85–103). He thereby removed the advantage enjoyed by sighted pupils through exercises to be done without the aid of sight, thus enabling them to concentrate on other modes of perception. In fact,

after a little while, [the pupil] becomes accustomed to dispensing with visual reference points, and subsequently feels that his faculties of orientation depend on new muscular perceptions, dictated by a specialized sense as rich as that of sight in its easy and natural manifestations . . . And it is in much the same way that the pianist never really becomes master of keyboard space until he can play with his eyes closed, and dispense with ocular control (1942: 90).

In rhythmic exercises belonging to this category one ought to be able—for instance—to run over a distance with both eyes shut, accompanied by music suitably underlining the tempo, and then return to one's starting-point in silence at the same speed, or twice as quickly and taking twice as many steps. One will seek to orientate oneself by reference to timbres of sound, locating their point of origin and estimating how far away they are in number of steps. One will try to discern the proximity of other individuals—then the gaps between individuals standing in a line—by relying on an emanation of their skin temperature, or on the echo of one's own footsteps. Or one may even do the following exercise, with which I close this section (cf. Dalcroze 1942: 101, exercise 10):

> All the pupils but one are arranged in a circle and sufficiently spaced apart to enable a person to pass between them without touching. Each holds a tambourine or other small percussion instrument. The odd one out then starts going round the circle, passing alternately in front of and behind each member of it, thereby tracing a sinusoidal path. He does this with his eyes closed, guided by sounds made by the striking of nearby instruments as he circumambulates, so that he hears them coming from his right at one moment and his left the next. A difficult exercise, for which others will have been employed to pave the way . . .

Exercises done without the aid of sight, when added to the others, show that a good use of space is the product of complex data. No single type of exercise suffices to bring them all into play; but the spatial exercises all complement one another to the end of a greater sensitivity on the part of the pupil to everything which helps his body develop into a flexible and intelligent instrument.

Actions and Feelings

Any form of artistic expression one can think of brings us ultimately to the notion of movement on the individual's part: to his internal movements on the one hand—to the sentiment of intention which shapes the form his external production takes; on the other, to the action by which he makes his sentiments or intentions manifest. All this leaves traces of a more or less lasting nature. It is in the form of material traces that the painter, the writer, and the composer submit their completed works to the good offices of the public, while the musician, the actor, and the dancer communicate their actual movements; and the traces left by these are subjected to the presence and the memory of auditory or visual experiences. The relatively recent ability to preserve such traces by means of film or sound recordings does nothing to impugn the fact that action is the very stuff of the work of art, to which it serves as both the medium and the message.

An action is there to be performed, just as a sentiment is there to be experienced. It is no easy matter to step back and consider either one objectively from the viewpoint of the other. Yet just this must be done by all who wish to bring them together in a given form of expression. For example, we speak a language without paying particular attention to its technical resources or its incidental connotations; but such attention is of the essence in writing verse or setting words to music, or in teaching one's native language to a foreigner. Similarly, we habitually move around without bringing into question such things as the regular pacing of our steps, or how it will be effected when our centre of gravity is displaced. But bodily consciousness may become imperative when movement has to be submitted to precise spatio-temporal constraints. Such constraints are very powerful in musical performance and in choreography; but they are also to be found, with varying degrees of strictness, in other forms of motor or athletic performances.

In another connection, it requires no great perspicacity to observe how often an individual's internal condition is reflected in his external behaviour, even in situations as contrasted as walking and talking. It is particularly noticeable that lack of coherence in a train of thought gives rise to meaningless gestures, that self-confidence inspires the gait no less than the voice, or that a drop in energy—whether through fatigue or discouragement—slows up pace or output, etc. Here too a conscious grasp is as necessary to one who wishes to resist the untimely influence of an inward state as to one who wishes to take advantage of it to artistic ends. This is convincingly demonstrated by means of the example below, in which both intentions obtain at the same time, albeit at different levels.

In one of his best-known sketches, the comedian Bernard Haller does a pianist interpreting Beethoven's sonata, Op. 27 No. 2 ('Moonlight'). A pre-recorded voice played over the performance of the musical piece enables the audience to hear the thoughts that pass through the pianist's head as he is engaged in playing. He allows his mind to wander as his hands play this well-worn piece more or less of their own accord. At a particular moment, the pianist's boredom leads him to think back nostalgically to his holidays, the sea, the sand . . . and his pianistic performance moulds itself to his reverie, passing from Beethoven to the song immortalized by Trenet: 'La mer qu'on voit danser'. The performer attains to rare comic effect here by simulating a lapse of attention which is reflected in his performance, which nevertheless remains entirely within the limits of the plausible. In this particular example, in fact, the transformation of one musical passage into another one equally well known takes advantage of the characteristics they have in common to suggest some sort of family relationship between them, thus adding to the public's enjoyment.

This sort of wire-crossing, used here for comic effect, often occurs involuntarily; hence it is as important for the actor as for the dancer or musician to be able to guard against it consciously, with the aid of sufficient technical competence and power of concentration.

As to mastery over one's powers of expression, Stanislavski, at the beginning of the twentieth century, rose up against the gestural stereotypes which were current in the theatre for the purely conventional portrayal of emotions (tearing one's hair for despair, hitting oneself on the left of the chest to express moral dejection or remorse, etc.). In doing this he made the actor conscious of the fact that theatrical performance is based first and foremost on personal expression, and relates to the past history of the actor as well as to his particular characteristics of physique and movement. The actor should not seek to identify himself with the character he is embodying, but should, rather, take that person's place by becoming so to speak his corporeal double. It is through him that life is breathed into the words and gestures attributed to the character to whom he lends his body, and who exists only by virtue of the actor's own existence (cf. Stanislavski 1976).

The same thing applies to musical interpretation, where the personality, the 'musical nature' of the artist, is quite essential to the communication of the work being re-created. It is a well-known fact that works are not necessarily more convincing when performed by their own composers: to give birth to something in the realm of art is not the same thing as to give it life. In a letter to a young pianist, Dinu Lipatti pointed out:

we must not forget that a text, to have true life of its own, must receive our *own* life; just like a building, we must add to the concrete framework of our devotion to the text everything a house needs to be considered finished— that's to say, the beating of our hearts, the spontaneity, liberty, and diversity of feelings (Lipatti 1970).

The autonomy of the artist in relation to the action of the creator has become, in western civilization, a prerogative of all the arts. Eurhythmics, which Dalcroze described as not an art but 'a preparation for art' (1924: 2), set out precisely to follow and reinforce this autonomy by enabling the individual to establish conscious links between his own sensations, movement, and sentiments.

The important thing for all who see the moving body as the direct interpreter of human emotions is not to disdain any method of augmenting and perfecting his physical means of expression. (Dalcroze 1942: 125)

Dalcroze insisted that, in an individual's experience of rhythm, the expression of the 'musical feeling'[18] should be controlled by *conscious muscular feeling*. Indeed, the expression of a feeling, an intention, or an inward state will have some bearing on the individual's muscle tone, and hence upon the energy and speed of his movement as well as on the way in which he occupies space. Concentration on the muscular sensations experienced on such occasions produces the ability to reproduce them immediately, having first recorded them in one's motor memory and then being able to pick them out again from amongst the others when the need is felt to recreate inside oneself the sentiment that corresponds to them.

Sensations are transformed into sentiments: in other words, external actions induce internal activity. The recollection of a movement creates a sensation analogous to that of the movement itself. (Dalcroze 1945: 135–6)

Seen from this viewpoint, music assumes two roles in Dalcrozian education. In the first place it acts, chiefly in the form of the teacher's piano improvisations, as an underlying support of time and energy enabling the maintenance and control of the stability of experienced sensations. In the second, it affords, by reference to various works, an area of application offering many opportunities to put the technique acquired to the test by adapting it to new expressive or formal demands.

The question as to whether music bears significance within itself has used up so much ink as to lie beyond further discussion here. According to the composer Aaron Copland (1977: 13), such a question

---

[18] We may also recall that, for Dalcroze, the adjective 'musical' sometimes passed beyond the framework of music in sound and, in the Greek sense of the term, would refer to the harmonious conjunction of movements 'of the soul' (emotions), of the spoken word, and of the body.

ought never to have been posed, for it can only lead to vague and woolly responses liable to upset literary minds; whereas the musician finds imprecision less of an embarrassment than a fertilising medium for his creative imagination. He writes (p. 7):

The more I live the life of music, the more I am convinced that it is the freely imaginative mind that is at the core of all vital music making and music listening.

One may or may not subscribe to Stravinsky's view when he writes, in *Chroniques de ma vie* (cited in Maneveau 1976: 111):

Expressing things has never been an inherent property of music . . . If, as is usually the case, music seems to express something, it is only an illusion, not a reality.

What is not illusion, at any rate, is the fact that music *impresses* itself on the sensitivity of the listener, that it physically gets through to the level of elementary emotions. As Copland puts it (1977: 13–14):

On that level, whatever the music may be, we experience basic reactions such as tension and release, density and transparency, a smooth or angry surface, the music's swellings and subsidings, its pushing forward or hanging back, its length, its speed, its thunders and whisperings—and a thousand other psychologically based reflections of our physical life of movement and gesture, and our inner, subconscious mental life.

Through the channel of sensations, impressions, and feelings there are created images and associations of ideas which tend to ascribe a meaning to the musical argument:

But as a musician [adds Copland (1977: 7)], what fascinates me is the thought that by its very nature music invites imaginative treatment, and that the facts of music, so called, are only meaningful insofar as the imagination is given free play.

If expression is not—in Stravinsky's terms—an inherent property of music, it is at least a fact in the individual who performs the musical act (or, in general terms, any artistic act). It is so because it entrusts to movement, to the body moved by will to give form to an inward feeling, the task of drawing it out of oneself, and ultimately turning it into an aesthetic object by the power of the imagination and the mind working in conjunction. Hence artistic impression and expression both pass through the body as well as through the channels of imagination. In rhythmic exercises, therefore, every effort will be made to treat these two eminently personal and individual areas conjointly, so that they can exercise their influence on one another and develop their potential to the full.

Amongst the types of exercise suggested by Dalcroze (1926a: 9, and see above, No 11), let us pause first at *analysis of different actions and of their relation to feelings.* We notice for example, he says, that fear (or an imagined sense of fear) operates a sense of shrinking, joy a sense of expansion; that will favours muscle contraction, desire a reaching out, etc.

By way of example, here is an exercise I have made use of when taking Eurhythmics students.

Phase 1: Correspondence is established between certain body movements and certain metrical values (or groups of values), for example:

quavers ♪ = head movements; crotchets ♩ = walk forwards; triplets ♪♪♪ = walk backwards; quadruplets ♬♬ = half-turns; minims ♩ = arm movements.

Each movement is practised by itself for a moment. The piano tells them when to switch, and, by means of variations in dynamics and sound-space, suggests various qualities of movement in respect of its strength, weight, fullness, etc.

Phase 2: The note-values quoted above may be combined ad lib to produce a sequence such as Example 4.20. This sequence is written up on the blackboard and defines a particular series of the movements exercised above. What we now have to do is string these values together by means of the movements corresponding to them in such a way as to imbue this sequence with *musical sense*, of which it is completely devoid in its capacity as a mere line of metrical notes. Students quickly discover that it is not enough simply to string the movements together with precision and in the right order, but rather that their succession, if it is to be perceived as a whole, must be

Ex. 4.20

supported by an inward sentiment, by a determination to explain how the appearance of each movement relates to each moment of the sequence.

Phase 3: The students are then asked to envisage this series of gestures as the external manifestation of an inward state: a feeling of fear or assurance, of impatience, curiosity, dissimulation, arrogance, etc. Each starts thinking up a situation that would breathe life into this metrical model. And it soon becomes noticeable that the feeling thus evoked governs, by the strength and breadth of the movements it gives rise to, the tempo of the rhythmic sequence, the length of its episodes and phrasing, the smooth or jerky passage from one time-value to the next, the evolving or unchanging character of the way energy is released, etc. Each student is then invited to make a vocal improvisation on his particular rhythmic creation, then to do likewise at the piano or some other melodic instrument.

Phase 4: The next thing is to transform the above metrical notation into one of rhythm, with the aid of appropriate dynamics and markings (indications of tempo, of expressiveness; accents, breathings, phrasing, shading). This is done by means of *internal singing* and *recalled sensations* undergone during the preceding phases of the exercise. This notation may be the effort of the student who created the rhythm, or carried out by a comrade under the 'dictation' of the movement he is watching. In doing so, he will bear in mind that 'an accurate perception of movement is not of a visual [but] of a muscular order' (Dalcroze 1919*b*: 140).

Or again, attention will be drawn, at the same time as to its rhythm, to the tune which it naturally gives rise to in the 'inner ear' while it is being performed. These two examples (Ex. 4.21*a* and *b*) illustrate, firstly, a 'quality of circumspection', secondly a 'sense of fullness'.

Throughout this type of exercise the students are led to discover that a musical rhythm—just like a tune or a suite of movements forming a whole—comprises more than the sum of its parts. They will also realize that artistic expression is not necessarily the product of total freedom, but may be well served by constraints, even severe and arbitrary ones.

Two other areas of exercise outlined by Dalcroze are the *seeking out of gestural rhythms corresponding to affective rhythms* and the *stylization of spontaneous gestures* (1926*a*: 9).

Ex. 4.21 (*a*) (*b*)

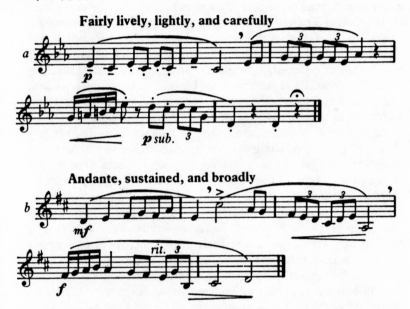

Every expressive movement comes down to a particular combination of elements of time, energy, and space, which, if it were artificially simulated with a view to fairly detailed analysis, should be able to produce a similar impression to that of the equivalent natural movement executed spontaneously. Now experience shows that a good deal less than that will often suffice to obtain the desired effect. One or two significant features (though the whole problem consists in knowing which ones to choose) are enough to evoke a situation or an object to the life (or even more faithfully than the life, if these features are deliberately exaggerated). Mimics, puppeteers, caricaturists, and other creators of animations or sound effects continuously demonstrate that 'it is by economizing on means of expression that one assures them of their most powerful possibilities' (Dalcroze 1945: 256). In doing this they land a cushy job, so to speak, for they can permanently count on the viewer's or listener's propensity to attach meaning to any observed situation, in so far as he can relate it, one way or another, to his own experience.

This urge to meaning, it would appear, is so deeply rooted in human nature as to operate equally strongly when even inanimate objects display series of movements: they are just as readily perceived as organized, even expressive. By way of proof I offer the experiment by Heider and Simmel[19] in which geometric figures (circles or triangles of various sizes) are set in motion by means of animated film. The ways in which they are made to come together, fall apart, or move in parallel are interpreted, anthropomorphically, in terms of meeting, shunning, fleeing, and pursuing ('the big one's going to catch the little one', 'the little one's hiding while the big one passes by', etc.) by viewers who have been asked to describe what they see.[20]

But inward movements, emotions and feelings, too—and not only their external manifestations—are equally liable to be read into objects which by definition do not actually possess them. (Herein may be found the origin of toys, dolls, and other inert objects which are more or less faithful representations of living beings, as well as the many simulation games to which they lend themselves.) I particularly remember being the bemused victim of a similar illusion created by the following visual device. On a screen appears the enlarged photograph of a man reading a letter. His face is expressionless; he is absorbed in his reading. Meanwhile, a voice off reads the letter out so that the audience can hear it. The voice is supposed to be that of the writer. After the first reading, another text is read out by a different voice, and the same thing happens several times again. The audience hears, in turn, a love letter, a rather racy letter, a begging letter, a threatening letter, and so on. The illusion consists in this: that the face of the man in the photo does not remain neutral. It may be seen taking on, as one letter gives way to another, an expression of tenderness, of amusement, of sadness, of concern. You see him breathe, smile; you see his hands tremble, his shoulders hunch. Nevertheless, it remains one and the same photograph throughout!

In much the same way, music often has the power (as may be observed in certain films and operas) of making us see the same landscape, the same background, in a gay or lugubrious light, or threatening or boring as the case may be. This subjective intervention on the part of the spectator or listener, his tendency to attribute to the world of things the power of experiencing or expressing emotions analogous to those within himself, afford a better understanding of

[19] Heider and Simmel 1944: 57, 243–59 (Christiane Gillièron, private communication).

[20] We may note again, in the realm of entertainment, how magnificently the Mummenschanz troupe exploited the art of inspiring life and meaning into moving objects of indefinite identity.

what Stravinsky (above) was getting at by the word *illusion*. But it also serves to invite everyone involved in the communicative arts to try to pierce the secret of this wonderful alchemy which we call the power of suggestion.

Playing with time: The same gesture takes on a different signification according to its particular expression, its direction, its unrest, or its brilliance . . . There are egotistical gestures and altruistic ones, gestures direct, oblique, or zig-zagging, gestures that localize, others that punctuate or accentuate, that imply, or that underline what words may express—disordered gestures, dry and measured gestures, unctuous gestures . . . We must not forget that every gesture may change in meaning according to whether it is accompanied by movements of the eyes or eyebrows, of the forehead, nose, and mouth, as well as by the way the head bows or turns . . . As to the all-expressive shoulder, it might be called the barometer of the emotions. (Dalcroze 1945: 36–7)

Imagine an extremely simple situation, consisting of three spatially oriented movements made by two characters, A and B.

A is sitting on a chair; B stands on his right, slightly back. Both are facing the same way and looking straight ahead. Three movements are open to them:

(a) B inclines his head (and gaze) towards A;
(b) B rests his hand on A's shoulder;
(c) A turns his head towards B.

(At the end of the sequence, A and B will be in physical contact and looking at one another.)

Given these spatial data, let us play around with time, and do some counting:

1. The three movements, a, b, and c, may be carried out in any order, and either *successively* or *simultaneously*. We may count as simultaneous two (or three) movements which start at the same time, and as successive those which begin when the previous one has finished. We therefore get six possible sequences made up of three successive movements: a + b + c, a + c + b, b + a + c, b + c + a, c + a + b, c + b + a; and seven sequences comprising at least two simultaneous movements: ab + c, c + ab, ac + b, b + ac, bc + a, a + bc, abc.

2. If we now allow each movement to be carried out either *fast* or *slowly*, each of the sequences enumerated above may appear in any of the following eight modes (where f = fast, s = slow): fff, ffs, fsf, sff,

fss, sfs, ssf, sss. This increases the number of combinations from thirteen to a hundred and four.

3. Let's imagine an additional possibility: that of two moves in a sequence following on either *immediately*, or after a *waiting time* which we will represent by ( ). Each of the three-move sequences now undergoes a quadrupling of its possible appearances, for example a + b + c, a ( ) + b + c, a + b ( ) + c, a ( ) + b ( ) + c, while the number of two-move sequences is doubled—for instance, a + bc or a ( ) + bc. The addition of this new mode brings the total of possible combinations to two hundred and ninety-six! Yet, basically, we are dealing with only three moves. What would happen if we allowed A the additional move of turning his head in the opposite direction, or if the whole thing began with B entering the room? And then, we have only played with time. No thought has been given to the roundness or stiffness of their gestures, or to the expressions on their faces. If we had to take those into systematic account as well, we should soon find ourselves in astronomic numbers. But let's take advantage of the fact that we do not live in an entirely automated world by allowing them the spontaneity of actors, while we now try to get some idea, by means of two random examples, of the multiplicity of possible arrangements.

Situation 1: $c_f($ $) + b_s + a_f$

Description: A turns his head quickly in the direction of B, who is looking straight ahead; after a moment, B, still without looking at A, moves his hand slowly towards A's shoulder, and, as soon as he touches it, he for his part turns his face quickly towards A, and their eyes meet.

Interpretation: We might imagine that A is asking a question with his eyes, and that B is in the throes of inner turmoil. Sensing A's look fixed upon him, he eventually decides to make a reassuring gesture—or one requesting help (the smile or way of looking in the third phase of the movement would assist in this respect). We might also imagine that A expresses in his gaze a degree of impatience, and, by the briskness of his movement, a desire to attract B's attention, the latter being absorbed in something he can see before him. His somewhat indifferent gesture is now going to reduce A's patience even further, and a quick look at A confirms that this is indeed the case.

Situation 2: $b_f + a_s c_s$

Description/interpretation: B puts his hand on A's shoulder rapidly (violently, furtively, imperiously), then both in one movement turn their heads slowly (cautiously, stiffly, fearfully) towards each other and exchange looks (disturbed, enchanted, vindictive, terror-struck, etc.).

This type of exercise can be followed through by means of improvisation, the two protagonists being allowed to react according to their reading of the situation, bearing the constraints in mind and without agreeing in advance on an amount of time reserved to each movement. But the movements may be stylized as well, by adapting themselves to a framework of time imposed from without. For example, the piano may be playing ♫♫ , or ♩ ♩ ♩ or ♩ ♩ , and the two actors thereafter run through one of the possible scene variations in time to the playing of one or the other rhythm. Or, again, each of the moves may be associated with a particular instrument or keyboard register, so that what is imposed from without is the whole sequence.

On different occasions, in this case, the instructor will be careful to let one group of students act as spectators to the other, so as to encourage an exchange of views as to the impressions received and the presence or absence of expressive intention.

Many examples will be found in music of such playing about with time. They may be sought out especially in serial music, in Messaien's rhythms, in the open-ended forms of aleatory music or in electro-acoustical composition (in which respect see Maneveau 1977: 39–40, 218–22). But there is nothing wrong with looking for them in the music of the past, which harbours a goodly number. An instance I am particularly fond of occurs in Brahms's Intermezzo No. 2, in Op. 119. The upper voice of the opening theme comprises the sequence of notes shown in Example 4.22*a*. The first phrase of the theme appears as in 4.22*b*, both restrained and agitato at the same time. It undergoes an initial treatment (being transposed into *A* minor and passing from binary to ternary time), which gives the feeling of simultaneously tightening up and mellowing (4.22*c*). Then a third version (in *F* minor) has the phrase panting for breath with jerky, off-beat playing (4.22*d*). There follows a fourth evocation, which puts us in mind of

Ex. 4.22 (*a*) (*b*) (*c*) (*d*) (*e*) (*f*)

(bars 1 ff.)

(bars 13 ff.)

(bars 18 ff.)

(bars 29 ff.)

(bars 36 ff.)

the first, albeit simplified, but takes us into an imporant crescendo (4.22*e*). But the fifth really breaks away from what has gone before: going into the major, changing in tempo, rearranging its supporting points, splitting the measure in two, it ushers in the second section of the piece (4.22*f*).

If the 'tone-row' constituting the melodic substratum of these different versions is envisaged as a pathway through surrounding space, or as a continuous group movement, what modifications may this pathway or movement not be subjected to if at each turn it models itself on these different rhythms? What effect will it produce on the performers? On the spectators? I have in fact experimented along these lines with groups of students, with the aim of getting them to evaluate the relative roles played by change and permanence and to describe the visual, auditory, and motor impressions associated with them.

The primary function of music [wrote Dalcroze (1922*a*: 9)] is above all to excite in the human soul the need for imagination and representation. Why renounce this power? . . . Music is born, within us, of the imperative need to escape from ourselves . . . Why not make use of the support it offers as soon as we feel the need to express ourselves by means of a human mechanism as unknown by the majority of beings as the very origins of their thoughts and actions?

By way of concluding this approach to a grammar of Eurhythmics, let's take up one or two 'recommendations' which Dalcroze addressed to instructors in his method (1926*b*: 11, 14):

Without the close and inextricable collaboration of the nervous and muscular systems, Eurhythmics in music does not differentiate itself from the usual methods [of music education]. For this reason I must again insist on the fact that it is not enough for the teacher to present exercises in rhythm in a musical fashion. It is of the utmost importance for him to get the pupil to be able to convert them into bodily experiences . . . If, on the other hand, our educational method were to be deprived of its essential basis in Music, it would amount to a form of physical training indistinguishable from so many others. Thus it is right, for the future of these ideas, that our teachers undergo all the experiences necessary to enable them to cultivate with the same devotion the sister branches of our twofold education. Whether or not they attain to complete mastery is not the important point: what really counts is that they should not sacrifice one branch to the other, but assiduously seek to draw nourishment from their common fount of life.

PART III

5

EURHYTHMICS AND CHILDREN

Eurhythmics in Schools

What is the role of Eurhythmics in state schools? But first—what part does Eurhythmics play in schooling generally? A look at the programme of schools in Switzerland incorporating rhythmics in their curricula brings out two facts in particular:

1. The overall period devoted to these studies rarely exceeds two or three consecutive years.

2. These few years cover different age-groups depending on the schools, regions, or cantons concerned.[1]

WHY A LIMITED PERIOD?

We may well ask on what grounds the period devoted to rhythmics is so limited in different schools. The answers to this question will vary according to case: administrative prejudice, failure on teachers' part, lack of resources, etc. Dalcroze had no shortage of arguments with which to back up his advocacy of long-term rhythmics study, which he saw in the light of continuity and co-ordination with other branches of the educational programme:

It is important that education bring both intellectual and physical development to the fore, and it seems to me that Eurhythmics should exert a beneficient influence in this respect. (1915b: 95)

There are, in short, very few who doubt that if all artistic progress is impelled by a general evolution of the mind, the regeneration of musical education can only be made possible through a regenerated education in general. (1919c: 162)

It is my conviction that education into and by means of rhythm is capable of arousing the artistic sense in all who submit themselves to it. And that is why

[1] Details omitted from English-language edition. (Translator's note)

I will fight to the end for its introduction into schools and for making educationalists appreciate the important and decisive role that art ought to play in a people's education. (1915b: 94)

But this project required for its realization a collective adherence to Dalcroze's ideas on the part of teachers and educational authorities. Eurhythmics, in its founder's eyes, would become a fundamental branch of teaching. It was virtually only in the private sector that Dalcroze could hope to see so radical a transformation of existing structures take place with any degree of rapidity. The most successful fulfilment that ever occurred in his lifetime was unquestionably that at Moira House, Eastbourne (England). For several decades from 1910 onwards, Gertrude Ingham (from a family including the very earliest Dalcrozians) kept this girls' school alive, she being its headmistress, under the rubric 'Dalcrozian Eurhythmics'. Not only did all her pupils, aged from 7 to 16, have two or three hours of rhythmics per week, but also even the staff itself had regular lessons in it. Rhythmics not only enjoyed the status of principal subject, but also lent its underlying educational principles to all other branches of study. And that not only to geography, history, and astronomy, but also to literature and elocution, to mathematics, chemistry, and even Latin: exercises were all planned in keeping with the spirit of Dalcrozian procedures.

Except in a few special cases, it was not a question of translating 'Dalcrozian method' exercises into the various branches of study, or of 'doing everything to music', in the words of the usual facile indictment [reported Jo Baeriswyl, who specialized in the application of Dalcrozian principles to the school curriculum].

It was a question of, on one hand, applying to each educational exercise the faculties of order, precision, dissociation, memorizing, and spontaneity acquired or developed through the practice of rhythmic gymnastics, and, on the other, of bringing out physiological technique in every intellectual exercise required of the pupil and getting her to acquire [it . . .] through the [rhythmic] medium. (Baeriswyl 1926: 221, and cf. 1922: 14–18)

If it produced immediate results in the realm of musical education and instrumental training, where they were most expected, they very soon manifested themselves in others: 'We had looked for some of these results, but we found many more than we expected', as Ingham was to report after fifteen years' experience (Ingham 1926: 163). In every branch of study the pupils had been led to build up great reserves of personal participation, speed of comprehension, and capacity for concentration. The majority of pupils had an outgoing personality, expressed themselves with confidence, and displayed the powers of an inventive mind (Ingham 1926: 163–4). This positive experiment, though far removed from us in time, struck me as well worth drawing to the attention of those who believe, with Dalcroze, that 'we must teach our children above all to become conscious of their personality, to develop their aptitudes, to free the rhythm of their daily lives from all forms of resistance' (1919*a*: 7). It also shows that one condition of its success was the collaboration obtaining amongst the staff, a collaboration which was perhaps of greater significance in its own right than the privileged situation in which they found themselves.

Introduced officially into the state schooling of Switzerland from 1928—in Geneva to start with, thanks to the results obtained by Jo Baeriswyl—Eurhythmics entered school by the back door, so to speak. With a single class here, a grade there, it gradually made headway in Switzerland as well as other countries through the efforts of ardent supporters, but always little by little, according to the needs or resources of the moment. The revolution in the established educational system which its overall adoption would have entailed was then unthinkable, and we are forced to admit that from this viewpoint the situation has remained much the same to the present day. Though widespread in French-speaking Switzerland, and known of elsewhere, albeit in restricted circles, Eurhythmics is nevertheless generally looked upon in schools as having shot its bolt, and in many cases is undoubtedly underemployed. However welcome its introduction into state schools might now be, it could not be simply annexed to existing structures without being cut off from its vital dimensions as a universal system of education into art and into life. And that despite the confidence with which Dalcroze exclaimed (1916*a*: 7–8):

[Our method] is not immune from that law of human nature which activates an instinctive resistance to any new endeavour breaking with tradition. Yet neither will it remain immune—and herein lies our consolation and our hope—from the law of *adaptation* to which everyone has to submit. It is they who will adapt themselves to our ideas, not we who must adapt our ideas to present-day mentality. Our aim is to bring about the evolution of that mentality.

Was he right? Schooling is notorious for the way it lags behind life, but in this respect avant-garde methods are limited in their powers, and their fate is often to be overtaken in their turn without having ever been taken up. They await rebirth in other forms or under other names, or, when the time is ripe, will neatly adapt themselves 'to present-day mentality' with a view to assimilating its jargon, its techniques and forms of expression. 'It isn't true that "that which has been, will be",' Dalcroze was to say at a later date (1935*b*: 15–16):

No social activity, no artistic activity, can remain fixed in the same forms . . . Evolution as a whole demands mental flexibility of those who wish to follow it.

DIVERSITY AND MULTIVALENCY

What Eurhythmics has lost in continuity through its introduction into schools it has regained by the diversity of its applications. On looking at the whole body of educational institutions where it is taught, we find Eurhythmics playing multivalent roles. Here it features in the activities of nursery schools, there it will be found at middle or secondary level, elsewhere it will be found in one or another branch of primary education. It is significant that educational organizations which include Eurhythmics in their programmes are not always of a like mind as to the point in the cycle of studies when its introduction is most opportune. Even in those instances where a school decides to allow greater scope to the teaching of Eurhythmics, it does so within a scheme of priority which inevitably differs from that adopted elsewhere.

In effect, this means that Eurhythmics does not find itself embraced in its entirety in any areas where it is put to use, nor any more inside schools than outside them. There are numerous aspects of it which do succeed in attracting interest: some schools retain it as a valued and integral part of musical education, others for the artistic opportunities it affords in the realm of movement and display, others again for its capacity to forge links between action and reflection, for the exercise and refinement of the motricity it favours, for the real-life perspective it offers on notions of space and time, for the relaxation it procures in the context of the whole school day, for the help it brings to children in difficulty. It is, perhaps, only the rhythmician who takes all this into account at once, and in each and every one of his lessons. Unless, that is, he is so overcome by routine or isolated in his particular workplace as to be unable to draw comparisons, and little by little succumbs to a fragmented vision of the whole. This may take the form of reductionism, over-systematization, syncretism, and all such temptations as accompany a loss of perspective or the lack of opportunity for give and take. It also threatens to give a distorted image of Eurhythmics (which would be a lesser evil), and, more dangerously, of bypassing its essential significance: namely, that if Eurhythmics is suitable for all grades of schooling, this is not only because it is capable of responding to any particular need, but primarily because in every one of its exercises it brings to the fore, *at one and the same time*, the three essential components of the human child: its physical instrument, the body; its capacity to think and to reflect; and its power of imagination, to which is linked the development of the aesthetic sense. In this combination of demands must be seen the key to all those particular achievements which Eurhythmics helps attain, and it is in music, from which it gladly accounts itself inseparable, that must be seen the means *par excellence* by which the simultaneity of this combination is rendered possible.

Infant-school Age

In modern schools, much care is taken, and with success, to cultivate the senses of touch, of hearing, and of smell in very young children: but cultivation of the nervous and muscular sense does not—in my judgement—occupy more than a minimal place in the timetable. (Dalcroze 1932c: 22–3; repeated in 1942: 55)

His first year at school brings about a great change in the young child's life, namely, his entry into the peer group. Up till now he has occupied (and will continue to occupy in parallel) a position of privilege in the nucleus of the family. The first thing school does is to make him share this primary role with a considerable number of other children. This obligation will be more or less strongly felt, depending on the pedagogical principles on which that school is run, but it will always be there. In return, it will give him the opportunity of embarking on the acquisition of modes of conduct and of basic ideas essential to his subsequent development at school.

THE IMPORTANCE OF INITIAL SOCIAL DEVELOPMENT

It is easy to underestimate the bearing which this initial social training has, as such, on the process of conceptualization. If in this respect we rely solely upon the techniques and resources generally known as 'educational games', we will deprive ourselves of a practically inexhaustible source of exercises of fundamental importance.

By way of example, I should like to describe here an exercise I witnessed in a rhythmics demonstration by Liliane Fevre-Bulle at Nyon. I must add that the way in which it was performed struck me as surprisingly beautiful:

> On stage is a fairly long, low wall, quite plain and unadorned. In the background, the rhythmics instructress softly plays two notes on a flute, sounding like a cuckoo. In response to this call, a child emerges from his hiding-place behind the wall and rests his elbows on it. Another cuckoo call causes a second child to arise to the left of the first; and so it goes on, each call adding to the line a new face peeping out from between two elbows. Thus each child has in his or her own turn been introduced to the audience. Each one has made an appearance, has become identifiable—a blond head here, then a curly-haired one, a serious-looking face, an innocent one, a little Chinese, a bit of a joker, one little girl a bit too previous, one with her nose in the air, a boy who nearly misses his cue, one with chubby cheeks . . . about fifteen of them, aged about four or five. Whatever order they come in, they make a ravishing picture.
>
> But a wall has got to be 'for' something—for clambering on, walking along, jumping off and getting on again. They do all these, following various instructions from the piano. They walk along it in single file, they weave in and out of one another without putting a foot down on either side, they jump over it one after the other without falling . . . They will finish by adopting any position of their choice: kneeling down, on all fours, sitting cross-legged, lying face down or on their sides, each, essentially, following his or her own idea. They remain motionless. Here, too, the picture is well worth looking at: fifteen different but natural postures, fifteen children on a wall, as much at home as swallows on a telegraph wire!

The spectator is overwhelmed. He knows full well that what he has just seen is so simple, yet such simplicity, combined with the spontaneity of the performance and the inspired way in which the exercise has been carried out, has succeeded in arousing in him the full force of a genuine aesthetic experience.

Quite simple? Yes, just as $1 + 1 + 1 + 1 + 1 + 1 + 1$ is quite simple when you know how to add up (but you have to be on the ball and not miss one of the terms out!). For the child just entering school, such instructions as 'One after the other', and 'Each in turn' are very trying novelties. The cries of 'Me, me, me!' heard whenever the smallest thing is being given out or the slightest response invited denotes, in children of this age, not so much the desire to be 'first served' as to be the *only* one attended to. The very fact that things take place in order at all—let alone the actual order in which they take place—is not yet seen by them as having any degree of necessity about it. Nevertheless, without the opportunity of establishing and mastering such an idea of order, the child will have extreme difficulty in ever acquiring, for example, the ability to read and write, or (to skip a few stages) the faculty of following the argument of a text or the statement of a problem, or of following through a chain of reasoning. Not to mention that such everyday lists as the succession of months or the days of the week—even assuming the child knows them by heart—would fail to relate to any temporal reality enabling us to decide which month we are in: whether it will be February next month, or whether Monday is nearer to Thursday than to Sunday!

In the first part of the exercise described above, the children showed that they had learnt two things:

1. They had learnt to await their turn for making an appearance. One of them knew he was going to be first and that he had to wait for the first sound of the flute. The others knew that they were not going to be first. They were all primed up with patience.

2. They had learnt the real-life meaning of the concept of precedent. The first one knew that no one would precede him. The others knew they had to get up immediately after the person next to them.

What enables us to assert that they have learnt to wait their turn is that not one of them got up in someone else's place or at the same time as anyone else. And if I remarked that one little girl was slightly previous, putting in an appearance before her particular flute-call had finished sounding, it is only to point out here that patience is one of those things which are acquired with time, that at this age it comes out as the fruit of a touching effort, which nevertheless may still find itself subject to 'contagious' thinking. ('My neighbour's up, so I get up as well!')

What enables us to assert in the second place that they have acquired a real-life concept of precedent is not just the fact that they made their appearance one after the other and in the right order, but that they were able to do so in response to a musical signal. The spectator would have found the result the same, visually speaking, if the rhythmician had called the children by their first names; in which case, however, she would have been doing their work for them! The use of a sounded signal that makes an appeal, and sounds the same in each case, meant that at any moment every single child could have thought 'That one's for me!'. Because there was a previously agreed sequence, however, they were able to check their impulse to respond to the flute's invitation. All the same, they were not expected to stop paying attention to it, for when their moment came they had to respond immediately. Their ability to divide their attention between what was happening behind the wall and what was calling to them from across the wall shows just how much they understood the situation. I referred to one little boy who nearly missed his cue: perhaps he had not fully grasped the exact idea of precedence, and someone by him with a bit more nous had given him a prod. Perhaps he had merely allowed his attention to be distracted, or had stopped listening, or stopped watching his neighbour. No; it was not all that simple an exercise, looked at from behind the wall!

To accept that he often has to wait his turn is not the only concession the child has to make to his new social life. He must also learn how to live in the space he has to share with others. He must learn how to regulate his motor behaviour. He must agree to modulate the loudness of his voice. In short, he must display, for the general well-being of the community and for his own eventual functioning, a little of that *savoir-vivre*, that grasp of life which at school is known as 'socialization'. Many astonishing or frustrating things will happen, and there will be many instances of disobedience or more or less thinly disguised rebellion, if this socialization is directed solely by the whim of the teacher. 'I don't know why we have to keep on sitting down when we're at school', wailed the little girl (aged 4) of one of my friends. She seemed to be implying: 'as if proper work can't be done standing up, walking around, or being dragged along the floor!' Dalcroze felt constrained to remark (1942: 56): 'At 4, the child is animated by a more intense curiosity and urge to movement than at the age of 8, or 14.' From the viewpoint of Eurhythmics, all behaviour tending to group integration and the instigation of collective discipline can be acquired, and should so be, not sitting at a table but in conditions which allow children the free play of their own movements. We saw above that the cornerstone of Eurhythmics consists in simultaneously engaging the three basic components of childhood: its body (motricity and perception), its ability to think, and its power of expression and imagination. In the young child these three components are perpetually present. As yet they are too little differentiated not to interfere with one another at any given moment. The 4-year-old who is busy running or jumping is almost invariably also busy shouting, or at least being busy loudly. When you ask him to think of a part of his body, or a particular object, he can't help touching or looking at it. To him, singing a song 'in your head' means singing the words to himself very quietly. He finds it the devil's own job to watch a ball rolling along without pitching himself after it. Tell him a sad story, and he practically weeps; and he really is afraid of the big, bad wolf! To move in silence, to shout without moving, to look without touching, to keep both eyes shut without the help of both hands, to think without speaking—these actions are still entirely alien to him. Whatever you ask him to do either involves every part of his being, or it doesn't engage his attention at all.

This lack of differentiation is generally perceived as a weakness, a fault to be corrected. The child's development is said not to have been 'completed', almost as if it had turned out badly. And he is funnelled into compartments designed to aggravate this differentiation, rather as a prosthesis is slipped on to an amputee! Eurhythmics, however, holds that a global approach meets a need on the part of the child. The latter has got to use all his potentials for action *at the same time* in order to make sense of the world, until such time as one experience and one insight are enough to let him select those actions which are most useful, and to organize the different facets of his behaviour with economy. It is at the level of organizing such economy that Eurhythmics operates, and to this end it places enormous value on the youngster's relatively undifferentiated nature, of which it is very careful not to favour any one aspect at the expense of all the others.

IMITATION AND CONTRASTS

In current pedagogic practice care is taken to avoid the term *imitation*, which brings to mind the 'Do as I do!' (or, worse: 'Do as everybody else does!') approach of traditional education. Quite rightly, no one now accepts that the child only has to reproduce models (copy, learn by heart, blindly apply a rule) in order to realize their underlying meaning. Yet the fact remains that imitation is one of the child's most important cognitive functions. For him it is first and foremost a spontaneous and necessary activity. Piaget sees in the development of the imitative faculty an illustration *par excellence* of the process whereby thought gets to grips with external reality. The child finds in his capacity for imitation an irreplaceable way of broadening his experience of the world. He uses it in the family circle just as he uses it at school, and whether or not his models are deliberately imposed on him by others. It is the school's job to multiply the young child's opportunities for exercising his imitative faculty; no less, however, than to encourage the conscious perception of what starts out as no more than an unconscious practice. It is indeed only by his ability to make conscious demands on his attention (and hence, where necessary, of refusing to take this line) that the child will be able to make effective use of it in his future education, and eventually succeed in shaping it into something personal and original. Eurhythmics has a useful role to play from both these points of view, and we shall see how in this context music fulfils the function of what might be called a 'consciousness-raising accelerator'.

The child does not wait until school-going age before exercising this function, which is so essential for his future development. The feelings he enjoys, the activities he delights in, the people he admires, start off for him as the models for more or less successful experiments in imitation. But it must be recognized that in this respect school considerably broadens his field of choice, since here he finds a wealth of models cast in the same mould as himself—his classroom peers, a number of other selves with whom he can identify one by one according to circumstances. Teachers well know how hard it sometimes is to get their young charges to produce a piece of work with the slightest air of originality about it. A choice of material, of colour, of a subject for drawing, is hardly suggested by one of the children before being taken up by half a dozen others. It is a matter of sticking together spontaneously; the child is not aware that he is imitating. He doesn't copy: he makes an idea his own. He can be forced into changing it, but not convinced into it by being exhorted to value the originality implicit in a different choice. He sticks to what he is doing as if he were its 'onlie begetter', ready, nevertheless, to cry 'Copy-cat!' in a different tone of voice when he casts his eye over the drawing of the neighbour from whom he borrowed his idea in the first place.

This tendency for everyone to do what everyone else is doing, this propensity of the imagination to stick with the current situation, recurs in numerous circumstances. Take, for example, well-known exercises designed to improve the gestural imaginations of older children or adults, such as those miming games which involve taking some everyday object and at each turn using it in such a way as to bring out various and incongruous significances. What happens when this is tried with 4- or 5-year-olds?

> Here the object is a drumstick, which the children are required one after the other to make use of 'as if it weren't a drumstick but something else . . ., then something else again'. The first one gets an idea and says 'It's a spoon'. Matching deed to word, he declares with gusto 'I'm eating a bowl of custard!' The next one copies the same action and pulls the same faces. 'But you're doing the same as Oliver did!', I protest. He: 'No, miss—I'm eating meat!' I slip in some words to the effect 'Yes, but can you really say it's something different from a spoon?' No good!—same action, same expressions, and the announcement 'Now I'm eating vegetables, with a fork!' And so on. It has become a question of thinking up the most delicious food. They will enjoy everyone else's performances as much as their own, and could continue in this vein for quite some time to come.
>
> At the second attempt, the drumstick has become a trumpet. For this purpose I had to declare 'This time the drumstick isn't a spoon, and it isn't a fork; in fact, it isn't anything for eating with.' So the trumpet is promptly followed by a cohort of wind instruments, with flutes, pipes, and various types of whistle conforming to exactly the same device of holding the stick in the hand and bringing one end of it up to the mouth. (In which connection, note the family likeness of the concepts 'spoon' and 'trumpet'!)

The least that can be said about this exercise is that it has not exactly done a lot for the children's gestural imaginations! With older pupils, the object usually undergoes any number of metamorphoses; it is imaginative transformations such as these which shape the representative actions. Here, by contrast, the action serves as a pretext for several variations bearing on its imaginary or symbolic content (food, wind instruments), but the things evoked have no bearing on the action itself. The only time it is possible to get something different out of them is when the child's attention is drawn to the movement he is making and he is encouraged to change it. It's not a question of imagining the stick as something else so much as bringing the previous action to an end in order to *turn it into* something else. At this age, you see, the object is defined as a function of the action that brings it into play. Thus a child will say 'It's for hitting', whether talking of the stick he hits things with or the tambourine he is learning to hit. 'It's for eating', he declares, whether talking of the food he consumes or the spoon by which he conveys it to his mouth.

Only by dint of experimenting with the various actions to which an object lends itself can the child succeed in building up and broadening his definition of the object. Thanks to his ability to keep track of all its different facets, he will then be able to subject it to imaginative changes of form—or use it to different ends—by relating it, in thought and action, to other objects with which he has had comparable experiences. The door will thereby be opened to ingenuity. Until then, indications of this new capacity remain, in the child, unrealized and limited in number.

To enable the child to broaden his horizons by means of real-life experimentation is the essence of an active pedagogy. In Eurhythmics, the number of exercises whose framework can be summed up as 'pretending to *do* something else'—or 'pretending to *do* it *differently*' —is countless: exercises in which use is made of objects, certainly, but also, and primarily, exercises in which the most important object is the whole body, on which transformations and metamorphoses are carried out, and which at the same time is gradually revealing its multiplicity of potential, the source and fount of a multiplicity of sensations.

Every one of the child's acts is intimately linked to the sensation evoked by that act [observed Dalcroze (1935*a*: 3)]. Every imaginative act is the consequence of a sensation transformed into an image. The thought process by which a chain of images is ordered . . . itself originates in a sensation. It is therefore proper, in educating the child, to put him in the position of experiencing as many sensations as possible.

Hence the game called 'Lots of ways of walking', in which each child is allowed to walk across the room in his own way, provided that he adopts a style or gait which no one has yet made use of. More and more varied inventions can be drawn out by imposing progressive constraints: 'Only feet and hands are allowed to touch the ground'; 'You can touch the ground with any part of your body except your feet'; 'You must remain upright'; 'However you like, but without making a sound'; etc. The teacher will be guided in each new instruction by noting what has just preceded it,[2] and the whole group can then try to recreate the most amusing performances.

Hence, too, the game called 'Statues', in which each child has to 'freeze' in a distinctive attitude. (This brings us back to the exercise I described at the beginning of the chapter, in which fifteen children settled themselves on a wall in a variety of postures.) In one of the innumerable versions of this game, the teacher becomes a photographer going for a walk in a 'garden statuary' and 'photographing' all those which do not resemble others already seen before. This provides an opportunity for the master to be accompanied by a 'guide' who takes him from one statue to the next, and to whom he can put questions as to the kind of variations observed. In one extension of this exercise, the statues are of a provocative turn of mind and keep changing when he isn't looking at them. This may be done so well that the photographer cannot recognize any of the statues he has already admired. While he is loading his camera, the statues reproduce their original attitudes, and the frustrated photographer, on seeing them again, exclaims 'I must have been dreaming!' Such alternation of two contrasting postures gets the child to feel, *in action*, the opposing relationship which defines each one by reference to the other.

Then there is the 'See-saw game', where the action is now specified. The child's aim is to establish a sense of swinging by imposing on his body the toing and froing associated with it, and this regardless of the posture he happens to be adopting. Here too he will be striving for a position unlike any other, but at the same time he will be demonstrating that, in this unique position, he can succeed in doing as the others do. Then he will be invited to adopt several different positions of his choice in succession, 'to see if he can still succeed in keeping his balance'. In this instance his attention will be drawn to the similarity of action despite the variation in attitude.

And so on. In effect, to play at *not* doing the same thing is first and foremost to detach oneself from the tendency to imitate by contagion; it is also, consequently, to open the door to the exercise of voluntary imitation, whose field of application will broaden out in such a way as to keep pace with the development of the child's powers of observation and his individual experiences.

----

[2] Announcing instructions like this makes demands on a capacity for abstraction as yet undeveloped in children of this age. It follows that nothing is gained by announcing them oneself. At primary school level, on the contrary, it will be right to cede the initiative gradually to the pupils.

But we ought to note, on the other hand, that reality at this age might better be translated by referring to such exercises as 'playing at *not* doing the same thing'! For the young child, indeed, action itself is always positive, and any negation bears upon the content of the action. That portion which is denied has a tangible reality, thanks to which the first comparisons can be consciously made and the first contrasts consciously defined. In the same range of ideas, we know that before being able to define the relationship of opposition by means of two antonyms—big and small, high and low, loud and soft—the child must start by denying one of the two terms: big/not big, heavy/not heavy, etc. In the same way he will say: much/not much, after/not after, on top/not on top, etc. Neither space nor time, nor quantities, qualities, nor any other aspects of his life escape this way of dividing the world into two parts, the one a denial of the other. As for *not doing something*, for the action denied, he still sees it as a sort of action—it's 'doing a non-thing'. This is why stopping oneself from doing something, ceasing from motion to order, or, at a signal, displacing one activity for another, demands on the part of the very young child the mustering of all his reserves of will.

> J'ai deux pieds
> Qui marchent
> Si je veux, je peux m'arrêter:
> je n'avance plus,
> Quand je suis là, je ne suis pas là-bas;
> il faut que j'y aille . . .
> oui, mais alors là-bas, je n'y suis plus.
> Je suis un.
> Si je rencontre quelqu'un,
> ça fait un plus un
> . . .
> J'ai deux bras,
> avec au bout des étoiles,
> à cinq branches chacune,
> qui bougent . . .
> Je puis les voir,
> avec deux yeux,
> les suivre,
> aller plus loin qu'elles:
> les enfants,
> au fond du jardin,
> ils jouent, ils rient, je les entends.

J'entends!

Si je vous écoute bien, je vous entends respirer!

. . .

Mais respirez, alors!

. . .

Bénédict Gampert, 'Miracle'

(Gampert 1971)

I have two feet | That walk | If I want to, I can stop: | I go no further forwards. | When I'm here, I can't be there; | I'd better go there . . . | Yes, but when I'm there, I can't be here. | I am just one. | If I meet someone, | that makes one and one | . . . | I have two arms, | each ending in a star | with five rays coming out of each | that move . . . | I can see them | with two eyes, | follow them, | go further on ahead: | the children, | at the bottom of the garden, | are playing, are laughing, I hear them. | I can hear! | If I listen to you carefully, I can hear you breathe! | . . . | Well, go on then—breathe! . . .

MUSIC AS REINFORCEMENT AND REVELATOR

In establishing the relationships of contrast and opposition (a process in which each negated term gradually acquires its own name and identity), as well as in the conscious exercise of the imitative faculty, Eurhythmics finds in music a helpmeet of the first degree. Music, in fact, offers all who know how to avail themselves of it a wide range of methods suitable for accompanying or arousing actions on the part of the child, for strengthening them or for modifying their progress.

In translating activity into the plane of music by means of piano improvisation, the rhythmics teacher draws the child's attention to that action on two levels at once:

1. On the kinaesthetic plane, music reinforces the sense of movement by virtue of its dynamic qualities. The power it spontaneously exerts on the nervous and motor sensations enables it to play the role of incitement to action, of a regulator or modifier of bodily movement. From this point of view music provides an invaluable aid when it comes to relaxing a movement which has not come about spontaneously, extending or revitalizing an insufficiently sustained action, putting an immediate stop to an automatic gesture, and so on. The effects arising from sound and musical rhythm are generally produced before anything of a conscious nature has intervened, and may be observed in many situations where words or models would have been powerless to achieve anything.

2. On the representational plane, music gives movement a 'sound image' which endows it with some objective reality. Because the music which the pupil hears and perceives directly nevertheless emanates from somewhere outside himself, it plays for him the part of a 'developer', or consciousness-raising agent. It is on the child's first distancing of himself from his activity, combined with the practical understanding he has gained of his action by means of his movements, that all his future comprehensions will be based.

In practice, musical improvisation at times imitates the pupil's spontaneous movements, at times invokes them, and again at times seeks to suggest new ones to him. At first, music does little more than imitate the child by reflecting back to him the image of his movements and his mental states. But very soon he learns to recognize them (if not to name them) when he hears them reinvoked. It takes only a few lessons for him to be up to playing his part in the following impromptu story, or any other of a similar kind:

The rhythmics teacher[3] tells the story of the 'Game of cats and mice'. The children have already selected their roles. They play them out, off the cuff, to the telling of the story, in which musical improvisation is used to underline each distinctive action as it occurs: 'The mice are running about without making a sound, so as not to wake the cats (a fast, light, prudent fluttering of fingers over the keyboard) . . . But now they have forgotten where they are and start running and jumping more and more wildly (crescendo) . . . The cats wake up and stretch (slow, sustained arpeggios) . . . They spot the mice and hurl themselves after them (it goes without saying that the wild delight with which the mice are chased is matched in intensity only by the silence in which the sleeping cats were formerly embedded!)' Then the story starts again, but with a minimum of words. This time they will come when each piece of musical evocation has already started instead of in advance of it. By the second or third time round they can be dispensed with completely, and the time devoted to the performance of each action can be prolonged or curtailed depending on whether the teacher is aiming to test the children's capacity for *attention* or alternatively their speed of *reaction*. And in the next lesson the children will

---

[3] Liliane Favre-Bulle, lesson given on 6 Nov. 79.

recognize the different sections of the story even if they are evoked musically in a different order.

On another occasion the children themselves will make up the story to be played out, basing it on a theme they have chosen for themselves. Or again, the piano may be used to pose little riddles to which the answers must be acted out. But there again, it is the child who sets the mood, so to speak. By virtue of his size, his level of motor development, and his individual muscle tone, his movements are exercised within limits which will broaden out with the years, but which it is vital that he should not be made to transgress too early if it is intended to establish a close correspondence between his motor and aural sensations.

TEMPO AND QUALITATIVE COMPARISONS

As I cannot here give a practical demonstration, let me take the easiest example to describe in words: that of *tempo*. The tempo of the young child's movement ranges between two extremes which are much closer together than those of the adult or older child. The shortness of his legs means that his 'slow walk' is by no means as slow as ours. He would, furthermore, have to enjoy a sense of balance and mastery over his body which he has not yet acquired in order to sense a continuity of movement in slow walking. Hence to make him walk to an even slower tempo than he can naturally cope with would be to deprive him at the same time of any sensation of slow walking. In like manner, the tempo of his running, though much higher than that of normal adult running speed, is nevertheless limited by virtue of the universality of his motor activity, while the older pupil has access to dissociative abilities enabling him to attain to a faster tempo with little training. Here too, the importance of matching movement and auditory sensation forces the rhythmician to adapt his musical playing to the child's natural tempi.

The same will go for areas other than that of tempo. Range of voice, rhythmic performance, ability to organize spatial phenomena, not to mention the duration of performances or of reaction times, the number of instructions capable of registering, the capacity for auditory and visual discrimination, and so on, accept limits which absolutely must be respected in establishing the basics of 'an education through and into music'. Furthermore, this observation applies equally well to older children and adults. Their limits will be set at different levels and—where due only to lack of training—sooner or later exceeded; but the principle remains the same. In every case the establishment of a close link between body expression and sensation on one hand, and the music which supports and brings them out on the other, will be attained by starting with what the pupil *is actually doing*, reverting to what he *has already done*, and going on to explore the field of what he *is capable of doing*. This educational principle of Dalcroze Eurhythmics is further taken to hold good for all forms of education. What's more, it appears to correspond to a very real need on the part of the learner. Piaget, notably, drew attention to the spontaneous appearance of the same process in the baby whose imitative faculty is beginning to develop: when he starts reproducing a pattern of activity, the first requirement is that this pattern reflect precisely the activity he happens to be engaged in; he then repeats it, and the presence of the pattern sustains the activity, extending its repetition period. Then the baby goes on to imitate a different activity from the one he is engaged in, provided that it is one he is used to, that lies within his repertoire. Only then will he be able to imitate a new activity, always on condition, however, that he does so without delay and that the pattern presented to him does not depart too far from his spontaneous activities. Eventually he gets to distance himself sufficiently from the pattern to be able, having now internalized it, to reproduce a given activity after the event, even though the pattern is no longer present and several hours or several days have since elapsed.

In the Dalcrozian scheme of things, it is not until the child has sufficient experience to be able to feel music as the dimension of sound which both extends and recalls his activity, that music in its turn will be able to guide him down hitherto unexplored avenues and eventually be seen by him as a distinct domain in its own right—one from which he will be able to differentiate himself and with which he will be able to enjoy deliberate relations: to follow a rhythm or tempo suddenly presented without warning, to adapt the line of his walk to a sequence of phrases, to draw a distinction, in dialogue, between the expressive quality of his own movements and that, somewhat different, of the music, and so on. That will be the time to draw upon the wealth of resources contained in the repertoire of all music of all musical periods. But, until then, the aim being pursued by the child will require the rhythmician to have the ability to create his own music.

On the other hand, the child may be led to experience, *within the limits of his natural tempo*, 'every shade of energy and duration' (1926a: 2).

Dalcroze rightly maintained that such experience should be as varied as possible, so that the child should acquire as many 'motor images' as possible, which should enable him gradually to recognize as his own the many motor sensations and evocations which reach him through the medium of music. It would therefore be a great pity to limit this initial experience to the consolidation of the three basic spontaneous tempi of running, walking, and slow motion. It is, indeed, a simple matter, with the aid of appropriately paced music, to get the child to move 'just a little bit faster' or 'just a little bit slower', hence to vary his tempo slightly as well as to get him to act on these instructions for himself, 'with no other control than that of "the muscular sense"' (1924: 4). He will be enabled to do so by the instinctive comparisons he has learnt to make between the various sensations he has experienced. But it is in the *expressive quality of movement* that such modifications of tempo will come into their own. As often as possible, the purely motor exercise of running or walking will be associated with expressive intent, from which the desired variations will naturally flow—not only those of speed, but also of weight, of tone, of centre of gravity: a slow pace resulting from fatigue is not the same as one inspired by caution. How you run when the devil is breathing down your neck is quite different from how you run when you're just pretending to be a horse!

Similarly, modifying the quality or loudness of a sound will do much more—and much more effectively than words ever could—to calm down an excessively turbulent pace, to revitalize one that is flagging, and so on. These considerations, it follows naturally, will apply to all body exercises involving rhythm and tempo, and not only in the sphere of walking. Great care must be taken here. The rhythmician owes it to himself to be vigilant in this respect: laziness and habit, combined with a natural tendency to limit the variety of one's spontaneous keyboard output, sometimes threaten to reduce the child's tempi to three metronome markings! Sometimes, too, he may deliberately take advantage of this tendency to establish a premature metrical relationship between three particular tempi, to which he invariably and unerringly resorts. (Running speed is fixed at twice that of walking, and the slow walk at half that speed again.) He thereby lays the ground for the acquisition of those strictly mathematical time-values encountered in the literature of music. For reasons explained above, it is to be feared that this procedure will produce the opposite effect from that intended: once a child has learnt (especially if at a very early age) that 'quavers run and crotchets walk', and, furthermore, experienced such half-truths at an unvarying metronome marking of (say) 96 to the crotchet, he is in danger of subsequently being unable to shake off these ideas and received impressions, for this would require him to unlearn something which has become too deeply ingrained. But in Eurhythmics there should be nothing to unlearn, and if this type of conditioning may appear profitable at first sight (it can, indeed, lead to performances giving the impression that children have mastered the notion of proportionality, when in fact they have done nothing of the sort) its adoption will soon lead to disillusionment as to its effectiveness in practice. And this even despite an intention to go for greater relativity in due course.

Quite the opposite applies if the teacher can bring himself to aim at relativity from the outset. If, however, a child of this age is completely dead to the concepts of 'twice as' or 'three times as' (and even at the instinctive level he is still incapable of grasping the quantifiability of a relationship between different tempi), it is still nevertheless possible to educate him into making *qualitative comparisons*.

Furthermore, this budding capacity is perhaps that which in every department (time, space, number, quantities, etc.) most distinguishes him from the younger child, for whom all data assume an absolute and inherent value, and the older one, who by now can co-ordinate such data and incorporate them into measuring systems. What Eurhythmics has set itself out to exploit, remember, is the whole realm of *possibility*. And that of qualitative comparisons is indeed a vast domain, but one for which it finds itself singularly well equipped to explore. I will go so far as to state my conviction that this is a field in which no other pedagogical experiment can be so favourably compared. Because Eurhythmics 'is based on muscular sensation and its relations with feeling and imagination' (Dalcroze 1924: 4), it goes right to the heart of all qualitative impressions. And because it sets out to vary these impressions with the objectifying aid of music in 'every shade of energy and duration and in every spatial plane' (ibid.), it favours comparisons between them in the most varied frames of reference.

Thus, to revert to the example of tempo, imagine that the child is led to experience and hear by name such a relation as (say) 'a little faster', associated with varying degrees of absolute speed; to feel, in particular, that when he 'walks slowly' and then 'a little faster', this same 'faster' is nevertheless still 'quite slow', whereas when he is running 'a little faster' he is actually running 'very fast indeed'; to do the same thing several times, on each occasion activating every part of his body in pursuit of various games and exercises; and that his ear is now attuned to the shift of a *tempo primo* into one 'a little faster', and himself able to illustrate it by following an appropriate instruction (for example: walk or run to a given tempo, and repair to a particular spot whenever you hear the music suddenly go 'a little faster'). The systematic, universal, and diversified experience which he has thereby gained assuredly holds an advantage over that which he would otherwise have had if everything had been left to chance and his attention not been focused on the point at issue. If this is true, we are justified in thinking that such an experience affords him a unique preparation for the other acquisitions he is to make later (such as—to stay within the realm of music—grasping the relative character of musical notation corresponding to both proportional and non-proportional time values). Such assurance does not mean that he will be able to make these acquisitions at an earlier age than other children will, involving, as they do, the use of structures which as yet he lacks, but rather that, when the time is ripe, these acquisitions will be better made, because they will be founded on a more solid base. And if each and every department to which they relate has been approached with the same conscientious degree of practical understanding, then great expectations will be in order, for these acquisitions will be made not only effectively but also rapidly and with great ease!

When we ask a child who is sent to us for psycho-motor therapy if he knows why he is there, he usually says it is because 'he doesn't know how to do' one thing or other. We promptly suggest to him that he is there first and foremost to 'try and find out all the things he *can* do'; that there certainly will be things he doesn't yet know whether he can do or not, but there are such things and we're going to work them out together. And that, in effect, is exactly what happens. Starting with his first spontaneous acts of self-expression, sometimes very poor, sometimes very uncoordinated, and activities so extremely well known to him as to inspire confidence, this child soon attains to expressive activities which he might think of (or those who know him might have thought of) as unexecutable performances. By means of discreet encouragement mostly imparted in non-verbal ways—notably through the medium of music or sounds—his first activity extends in all directions, then begins to diversify and achieve order, and eventually can be used to further activities of a more complex nature.

This particular example has been chosen to illustrate the idea that the child's spontaneous expressions are not to be confused with the limits imposed on him by his size, age, or level of development. What the child succeeds in expressing spontaneously, left to his own devices, generally lies far below his whole range of potential. And not only the child, if it comes to that; for, as Dalcroze noted, 'conventional education seeks to evoke the range and practice of only a limited number of the natural rhythms necessary for everyday living, to the extent that it is defined by our present-day habits' (1921*a*: 2). In this regard, the two opposed regimes of which one concentrates on the selection, reinforcement, and automatization of a small number of spontaneous rhythms, and the other on letting the child experiment freely, without regulations or constraints, are jointly and equally productive of poverty when it comes to the achievements attainable through them. The truly *educational* value of Eurhythmics, on the other hand, lies in the fact that, starting out with the possibilities of spontaneous expression, it actively seeks 'to establish relationships between instinctive bodily rhythms and rhythms created by the senses or rational thought' (ibid. p. 3), in other words, as obtained by deliberately introducing a break or change in the unfolding of the action: whether prolonged immobility or a momentary interruption, the repetition of a movement, the abandonment of one activity for another; a modification in the strength or speed with which an action is performed; alternation or succession of contrasting actions; and so on.

Eurhythmics has often been accused of confining itself to the creation and reinforcement of a series of conditioned reflexes. It is undeniable that certain of the methods it uses are of the type which could be quite effectively employed to this end; hence it is important not to minimise the risks run by those who use them without due flexibility. But to the eyes of those who reveal Eurhythmics in all its original dimensions and intentions it appears rather as the practical realization of a vast *deconditioning* project.

THE RESOURCES OF THE PIANO AND THE SINGING VOICE

The fact that Eurhythmics entrusts the rhythmician with the task of translating, illustrating, and then evoking spontaneous movement by bringing it into the plane of sound, distances it a priori from methods based on the systematic use of selectively pre-recorded music, whether with the intention of allying it to movement, or of creating atmosphere, or even of obtaining a specific psychosomatic effect. Useful background on some of these experiments may be gathered from a reading of, in particular, *Le Pouvoir des Sons*, a collection of interviews published in 1978 (Dumaurier 1978). Far from questioning 'the power of sound'— which it also puts to use!—any more than the positive results obtained through the diffusion of recorded music, Dalcroze Eurhythmics merely adopts a different position by virtue of its conception of the role of music as the principal agent of development. It may happen that recordings are used as a source of illustration or as a supporting medium for choreographic realizations: nevertheless, it takes a clearly opposite stance from those who, under the name and rubric of 'rhythmics', but constrained by their own limitations, always use recordings in their lessons *instead of, and in place of, their own musical improvisation.* There are also those who claim to be rhythmics teachers, and who, under the pretext of respecting the child's natural rhythms, delay as long as possible the point at which they introduce music (recorded or otherwise) into their lessons—almost turning it into a sort of ultimate reward, the crowning of a series of bodily exercises by the addition of an aesthetic or unifying dimension. Such methods are quite in-compatible with the basic postulate of Eurhythmics, namely, that music should be considered as a *constituent part of* psycho-motor education, and be used in that capacity.

A balance must be struck between tradition and reason in assessing the Dalcroze rhythmician's well-known attachment to his preferred instrument: the piano. Without going into detail at this point, let us merely affirm our conviction that the only real ground we might find for criticizing the rhythmician's attachment to the piano would be that of taking the word *attach* too literally: the rhythmician apparently screwed into his seat from start to finish of the lesson is undoubtedly doing music as much of a disservice as one who never goes near the instrument! And if the latter is depriving himself of extraordinarily effective resources, the former's abuse of them largely deprives them of their very effectiveness.

Let us take note of Dalcroze, who was able to observe (1921*a*: 5)

that rhythms clapped out by the teacher's hands or tapped out with a stick on the floor can be reproduced by children with precision, energy, and intel-ligence, but they do nothing to encourage the children to complete them or to give them any personal shading, whereas, as soon as they are played on the piano, they infuse joy and spirit into their little bodies as well as into their young minds, and promptly stimulate their inventive powers;

but added almost immediately:

Clearly, one must not make the children undergo a whole lesson being stimulated and inspired by the sort of music which deprives them of their free control and removes the challenge from what they are required to do. It is therefore right to ensure that music does not play a constant part in the lesson or be involved in every single exercise.

He concludes, however:

This does not reduce the master's obligation to be ready to resort to this superior form of stimulation as soon as he sees fit . . . It is up to him to regulate the use of musical methods, and to make use in his teaching only of a simple type of music appropriate to [the] age and character [of his pupils.]

This clearly implies that in his view rhythmics teaching should be carried out by 'masters possessed of the musical instinct' . . . (ibid.). When Dalcroze asserts the superiority of rhythms played at the piano over those merely clapped with the hands, he obviously means that such rhythms should be *played well*. In other words the rhythmician's pianistic touch, the rhythmical precision of his playing, his choice of resonances and melodic lines should themselves be charged with the dynamic or imaginative qualities which he is aiming to communicate to his pupils' movements. When these conditions are fulfilled, the advantage held by the piano over other instruments would appear incontestable, since it is only here that the greatest range of musical dimensions are virtually all to be found.[4] Does this mean it embraces them all? Surely not. In particular, it is not in itself capable of giving any idea of the wealth of timbres available in sound, and it is equally clear that the intervals it presents to the ear are fixed once and for all time, so that the passage from one sound to another at the piano gives

---

[4] This has not been entirely true since the invention of the synthesizer, which offers a virtually infinite number of possibilities. We can but hope that its more widespread use will enable rhythmicians to explore profitably the enormous range of perspectives it opens up, particularly in respect of relating sound and movement. At this moment (1989), the Dalcroze Institute of Geneva is undertaking a total building renovation which makes possible the creation of a fully equipped electro-acoustic studio. It will be understood, though, that from a Dalcrozian point of view the synthesizer cannot be expected to substitute entirely for instruments which, like the piano, involve the performer in a motor participation, an involvement of the body which has the effect of making music emanate from him.

only an approximation of the precision and continuity obtainable on, say, a bowed instrument.

What it does mean is that the piano must be used with discernment and with due regard to its capabilities. Its privileged position in no way releases the rhythmician from having recourse to other instruments. This obvious fact applies with even greater force in the case of young children. Teaching rhythmics to little children in fact often requires the teacher to take his place amongst them and join in the exercises with them, at least to start with. For this reason he needs to be able to make use of conveniently portable instruments—not least his own voice.

If the voice does not allow of all the effects obtainable with the piano, it is, by contrast, more intimately linked than any other instrument to the physical senses and the movement of the whole person. We have seen how, in the very young child, voice and motricity work in concert before they can begin to be dissociated from one another. Hence, exercises involving listening to and using the voice will be employed from the start in conjunction with motor work. And, as we also saw, it is important to the child right from the start that he be presented with models *of the same type* as his spontaneous activities. As far as his voice is concerned, it is therefore essential that he be able to refer to vocal models. To reproduce vocally a sound or tune played at the piano puts him to an effort of interpretation which at a later date will strengthen the satisfactory development of his auditory capacities, but one which should not be imposed on him from the outset.

It follows that the rhythmician should have as great a mastery over the use of his voice as over his piano improvisation. He must be able to employ it with flexibility, expressiveness, and accuracy. His qualities as an improviser will be revealed in his ability, when the situation demands, to find off-the-cuff words to the tunes he sings, appropriate to the task of supporting a movement, conveying a corrective instruction, suggesting an action without either interrupting or disturbing the flow of music. He will also be able to make his voice blend with the use of judiciously selected percussion instruments. Their use in alternation or conjunction with that of the voice will very often be able to substitute effectively for the piano. 'There are so many people', Dalcroze often complained (e.g. 1935*a*: 16), 'who confuse music with the piano!'—'Music, here, is the body itself!' says, and impresses upon her pupils, the dancer and Dalcrozian, Valéry Roth. Perhaps we may follow their thoughts right through by maintaining in our turn that any rhythmician worthy of the name should be able to generate music with every one of his gestures and through every instrument he touches—even the piano!

But let us revert to giving the piano its due by mentioning an area of exploration in which it remains unrivalled, an area that has been shown to be of primordial importance at primary school level: that of contrasts, and especially in their extreme form of *contraries*. Not that the piano is the only instrument capable of bringing this out; but the very great number of possible oppositions offered by the keyboard makes it a particularly economical instrument, without which the equivalent could only be obtained by getting a small orchestra together, complete with players.

The piano, combining as it does some of the characteristics of percussion with those of melodic instruments, additionally displays properties which neither of these can match alone, the first being a range of over seven octaves, which enables it to make variations in pitch between very wide extremes, the second the richness and variety of sound weight and overtones obtainable from it.

It was no accident that Dalcroze was to prefer the piano to other instruments. (It may well be asked whether it was not because he actually was a pianist that he came to invent Eurhythmics!) He needed a percussion instrument to stimulate the most instinctive bodily rhythms and to be able to reproduce them in all their shades of weight. He needed a melodic instrument to underline the plastic qualities of the body in movement, to accompany it on its peregrinations, and to imbue it with a sense of continuity in time. He needed a harmonic and polyphonic instrument to bring out the whole complexity and distinctiveness of a being in relation to its surrounding space. Finally, he needed a unique and multivalent instrumentalist, capable of establishing—of himself representing—the link between these various powers as well as of making on-the-spot choices between their respective roles in the multifarious combinations to which they lend themselves.

THE RELATIONSHIPS OF OPPOSITION

In the realm of contrasts, the piano enables, in particular, the relations of opposition to be translated into terms expressed by the child himself, i.e. undifferentiated ones. For him, indeed, the 'positive' dimensions of energy, space, and duration are not distinct from one another, and the same goes for their 'negative' dimensions. Thus the (for us) distinct concepts of 'strong', 'big' ('much'/'many'), and 'fast' are all one to the child, as too are 'gently', '(a) little', and 'slowly'. He need only be asked to change one of these dimensions for the other two to undergo an automatic reversal. If, for example, his attention is drawn to the sound made as an invitation to fall silent, his tempo immediately slows down and his gestures diminish; if asked to increase his speed, the noise he makes increases in proportion to the space filled by his acts and movements. He will readily describe fast music as 'strong' and slow as 'soft'.[5] (Though don't we all do the same, on occasion? And doesn't our tendency to persist in this confusion perhaps hark back to the primacy of our sense of energy before all others—to that time in our lives when the only way of forming some idea of space and time consisted in the amount of effort we put into our own actions?)

Before being presented with these dimensions in isolation, the child will therefore be given the opportunity of hearing them all and comparing one with another. Soon, however, it will become possible to vary them in isolation at the piano, and to convey the sensation of such changes to the child without his actually becoming aware of it— as happens, for example, in the game of 'Cats and mice' described above.

Later, his attention may be deliberately drawn to the nature of such differences. A particularly effective way of reaching this point is to start by reinforcing the sense of change in tempo or dynamics with a concomitant change of register. The difference in the nature of the sound is grasped immediately by the child, and passing from one register to another performs the function of a call to attract the attention of his ear. We must take care, however, not to make such changes in register too systematic: a habit is rapidly acquired, and sounds are very prompt in their appeal. If changes always take place in the same direction—such as accompanying the running child with all the high notes—we will stop focusing his attention on the dimension we are seeking to bring out (e.g. tempo or intensity) and afford him only the opportunity of acting on a reflex. The only 'reflex' which such

[5] *Il dira volontiers que cela va 'fort' quand cela va 'vite', 'doucement' quand cela va 'lentement'.* This seems to refer as much to the activity as to the music and I have paraphrased slightly to take account of what English-speaking children might say in equivalent circumstances. Note, too, the author's earlier comment that we tend, often mistakenly, to think of musical 'slow' movements as synonymous with 'quiet' ones. (Translator's note)

changes of register should be able to instigate at this stage is that of attracting the attention. It is possible to convey an impression of lively running with low notes as well as high; similarly, violent action, a continuous or sudden movement, a series of jumps, a turbulent gathering, a harmonious swaying, and so on, will find their equivalent in sound equally well in the lower or middle or upper reaches of the keyboard. On the other hand, the choice of a particular register may bring out the *expressive quality* of an action and imbue it with its affective or emotional value. Example: once, as part of a lesson with children involving piano improvisation, I got the pupils to listen to a series of perfect fifths played very quietly on the lower half of the keyboard. 'Oh—it frightens me!' cried one little girl, shivering all over. Hence such a choice as this is never neutral; which is all the more reason for not schematizing the associations suggested by it.

Following his first experiment of sensations of contrast, the child, if asked what has happened, will reply along such lines as: 'It started off fast, but now it isn't very fast', or 'Now we're running about quietly; no one's making a noise'. But the point at which the child actually reveals that he has become aware of such oppositions, and is capable of considering each one without reference to the others, occurs when he is able to attach meaning to some *middling term* lying half-way between the two opposite extremes. When he gets to the point of describing a tempo moderato as 'Not really fast, just a little bit fast', or a mezzo forte as 'A bit quiet', or 'Not very loud', and of being able to distinguish three levels in the speed of his actions, that's the time to start referring to things by name. In particular, this is the moment to embark upon the specific subject of the three registers, with a view to his future education into music. The fact is, even if he has so far been able to sense the qualitative difference between the low and high registers of the piano, any attempt to get him to conceptualize the opposition between them can only have been a hit-or-miss affair. It is indeed a well-known fact that the terms 'high' and 'low' as applied to registers is subject to an almost systematic confusion in most children's minds, a confusion easily explained by the child's propensity to allow his various impressions to be reinforced by means of one another. A low note, being rich in overtones, will be perceived as larger and more spacious than a high note, which will be thought of as 'little' and therefore 'low'. This impression tends to be reinforced in other contexts by the way in which adults speak of 'height' and 'depth' in relation to the concepts 'loud' and 'soft' ('Speak *up*'—'*Lower* your voice'). Furthermore, the lower timbre suggests his father's voice, and is therefore 'bigger' than his own high-pitched voice. Hence there is nothing surprising about the fact that the child's associations of 'high' and 'low' are the opposite of adult[6] usage.[7] There are teachers who try to avoid this stumbling-block and clear the way by speaking of 'light' and 'dark' sounds.[8] In any event, whatever the term selected, its value is revealed as soon as the introduction of the 'middling term' intervenes to create a necessary relation between two extremes ('higher than', 'lower than'). At that point the child is capable of, even desirous of, giving a name to that relationship. He can be encouraged to think of one for himself, so long as it does not interfere with any used in other musical dimensions. But the French words *aigu* and *grave*, as sanctioned by usage, can also be suggested to him, or even—why not?—*haut* and *bas* (though these are not really needed until the time comes to start reading and writing music).[9]

But it is actually (by contrast, oddly enough, with what happens in other areas) through the real-life experience of 'ascent' and 'descent', as opposed to the use of these words as labels, that the latter terms acquire their true meaning: the 'lightening' power, on movement, of a rising sequence of notes is self-evident (as is the 'weighting down' power of a descending sequence), and probably precedes any conscious apprehension. The child will quite often be able to feel (and demonstrate, and even know) that 'It's going up' before being able to describe a note as 'high'. An example of this may be found in the following exercise, devised by Esther Messmer-Hirt for a group of youngsters who had not yet been put in touch with the concepts under discussion.

The room is hung with lengths of wool, each having one end attached to the wall and the other to the floor, or to an opposite wall but at a different height. The children are positioned each next to one of these slanting lines and play at 'cable-cars'. One hand rests on the line to represent the car itself, and each child in turn slides it down to the bottom of the line and back up again. Each one does so

[6] Original reads 'the opposite of usage'. Translator has added 'adult' for clarity.

[7] Their usage is justified—much later—in another way, by the subjective sensation of the weight (or mass) of sounds and the fact that their source of emission is situated within the body.

[8] Cf. Esther Messmer-Hirt, interview recorded 10 Oct. 1979.

[9] English-speakers will no doubt find their own equivalences, though perhaps none more confusing than the fact that French *haut*, *bas*, mean 'high', 'low' in one context and 'loud', 'soft' in another. (Translator's note)

to his own rhythm, no unison being called for. The children are invited to vocalize their manoeuvres [i.e. make suitable accompanying noises]. The teacher will find that all these individual vocalizations spontaneously follow the direction of movement: the voice getting higher as the hand slides up and lower as it comes down. She then goes to the piano and in her own turn, on her own account, begins to play pianistic runs alternately rising and descending. As the music gradually imposes its own momentum upon them, nearly all the children will finish by adapting their movement to the intended pace, without any word of instruction having been spoken.[10]

Eventually, by a process of pausing at each note culminating an ascent or descent, getting the children to hear and sing it, and gradually doing away with the intervening sounds, the concept of a 'high' and a 'low' note will be impressed upon them, and they will learn to relate any given sound to any other in such terms.

The contradiction between what happens in the domains of 'height' of sounds and those of energy or tempo is only an apparent one: fast and slow, loud and soft, are concepts which characterize movements, and are, as such, significant in themselves. High and low, on the other hand, characterize [spatial] positions. Hence it is natural (and in accord with Dalcrozian insights) that such positions achieve significance for children only to the extent that they result from movement.

SPACE AND 'OTHERS'

In the minds of all who do so, the practice of rhythmics is inseparable from the existence of a space (a room or hall) set aside for this purpose. The way in which it is used requires that such space be comfortably large, but not excessively so, as free as possible from things like desks and columns which are likely to get in the way of circulating children, and equipped with a piano. It is clear that difficulties in getting all these conditions together is one of the causes of a school's rejecting the introduction of rhythmics into its curriculum (cf., for instance, Verteuil 1976: 109). An admittedly lesser reason, but one which should also be taken into consideration, is that even though rhythmics can accommodate itself to many different kinds of space when circumstances so require, it is important to feel that the space is not, so to speak, entirely disinterested. For it is not just a case of finding rhythmics pupils a place in which they can move around comfortably;

[10] Cf. Esther Messmer-Hirt, interview recorded 10 Oct. 1979.

rather, it is especially important to secure for them an environment with which they can closely 'work together'. In other words, if the rhythmics room is indeed the place where they can ideally feel their bodies moving around without constraint, the space it offers (whether larger or smaller, or more or less 'structured') ought to be able to be felt as an integral part of the exercises. Localization and orientation in space, the process of organizing and structuring it, the judgement of distances and measurement of pathways, all form an integral part of rhythmics. For its chief role—surely?—is to seize the temporal and energetic manifestations of music, the various modalities of the world of sound—to translate them into terms of the surrounding space, and thereby make them visible. In return, and in the scale of the moving body, it leads to the establishment of relationships between those diverse elements of space, time, and energy which will be found to underlie all the activities of the child.

SPATIAL STRUCTURING

We shall have occasion to revert to this topic in the following section, which deals with the age at which such relationships can begin to be established. At the age which interests us here, the child has a quite distinctive way of structuring the space surrounding him. As yet he does not bring its various dimensions into relationship with one another, but rather envisages this space as a series of spots he can go to and occupy, these spots being absolute and having no particular connection with one another. He understands, for example, and has no problem in carrying out, such instructions as 'next to the piano', 'by the door', 'on the bench', 'against the wall without a window', and so on. It is therefore desirable to be able to personalize his circulation of space by reference to certain fixed points, not too far apart but easily distinguishable from one another, which can be put to use in the pursuit of various exercises, such as, for example, the establishment of a pathway from one point to another, or between various successive points. In this respect we may cite the following exercise, whose successful performance presupposes an already fairly high level of acquisition, and which will therefore have been preceded by a number of exercises of a more elementary nature:

> This exercise consists in getting the group to follow, after some delay, the route traced out by one of the children between different points in the room. A noticeable halt is observed at each point of

arrival. To start with, one child detaches himself from the group and goes to any point he chooses. (He may do so by running or walking, or by any other method of locomotion agreed in advance, but he must go there directly: what counts is the actual point of arrival.) Once there, he can call the others over, saying for example 'Come over here by the door! Now *I'm* going somewhere else! And as the group makes for the spot he has just left, he gets himself to a new position and repeats his call: 'Over here by the wall! Now *I'm* going somewhere else!'; and so on. It is rather as if a canon in movement were being performed by a soloist and a group.

By naming the point he has reached, the first child helps the others focus their attention on the goal of their movement, even though their initial inclination is to follow him immediately to the next arrival point. Hence it will clearly be necessary to appoint to this role a fairly independent child, one accustomed to taking the initiative; for there will be a great temptation for him to await the arrival of the group before setting off again, or, in course of moving elsewhere, to keep his eyes fixed on the others to ensure that they are doing their bit right at risk of himself forgetting where he has decided to head for; or again, purely and simply to keep going backwards and forwards between the same arrival points by virtue of returning to the point the group has just left instead of choosing somewhere new. An ability to escape these various forms of contagion presupposes the attainment of some capacity for conceptual differentiation, whereby the child can cope with the simultaneity of two actions entirely independent of each other. It follows that the success of this exercise cannot be taken for granted. It also makes demands on the child's capacity for waiting without moving, and for alternating this with periods of intense activity. The intervention of music can contribute effectively to mastery over the waiting period, for it will fall to the piano to give the signal for departure after a period of silence, and to suggest the speed of movement. And the teacher will vary the length of the silences depending on the speed with which the children set their sights on each new goal.

When children appear to have come to grips with this exercise, it can be done without words, though it will undoubtedly be necessary to remind them of the rules from time to time. Eventually, it will be possible to control individual levels of acquisition by having the exercise performed in pairs, with one child following the other's peregrinations.

This exercise easily lends itself to a number of variants according to the teacher's current aim. For example, different actions might be called for on reaching the arrival points, instead of naming the place reached: jumping up and down with feet together, knocking on the door and suchlike, the various actions being left to the leader's imagination. And these may be usefully employed in pursuit of a recapitulation during which the children try to recall not only what they did at each particular place (which isn't very difficult), but also what they did *first*, then second, after that, and so on. If such a temporal sequence can be established, it will be possible to see the pathway as a whole, as will be confirmed when the child can eventually go through all the sections of the route in order without having to pause at each point. (An even better, but delayed, confirmation—it generally takes several years to reach it—will lie in the child's ability to follow the whole procedure in reverse, from the final to the initial station.) The establishment of such a spatio-temporal sequence obviously presupposes not too great a number of stages—four or five would seem a reasonable number at this level! It will also be appreciated to what extent music, accompanying the child in all his movements and thereby imparting life and duration to the path itself, can help turn this pathway into a structured whole in terms of space and time.

SPATIAL ORIENTATION

Making use of fixed points in the surrounding space will be of equal help when it comes to exercises in bodily orientation: turning to face the window, facing the far wall, turning one's back to a row of chairs, raising the arm on the side nearer the cupboard, and so on. With the very young, the establishment of such relations at a distance requires training. They will at first be seen hurtling towards the place suggested, as if seeing it were inseparable from touching it. The fact is that turning one's back to the wall is, for them, primarily a case of touching the wall with one's back! The first need, then, is for preparatory exercises bringing out the idea of increasing distance and proximity, as well as exercises centring on suitable actions lacking external reference points (turning round in one direction or the other) and on actions at a distance (pointing with the finger, looking at without going towards, throwing a ball in a purposive direction).

In the context of these first orientation exercises it is quite possible to do without any form of music at all. But there is no reason why music should not be used with proper understanding, and for this purpose the rhythmician will find many ways of enriching, influencing, or complementing an exercise which itself may be too schematic. For example, he may use music to bring out the relatively different ways of performing orientation movements: turning round can be done briskly or held back, and fear or apprehension, curiosity or indifference may be stimulated by it. Such sudden changes and expressive movements will come into their own when activities of more artistic intent are embarked upon, such as dancing in rounds or miming songs. He may also use music in such a way as to demand increased attention on the child's part. It may, for example, determine the exact moment at which a movement is to be started, or the pace at which movements should follow upon one another; or it may be used to indicate a point of reference by which to take up a position by means of a conventional signal of a momentary and more or less arbitrary nature, serving to free the child little by little from his subservience to immediate data.

The concern of the rhythmician to pay constant attention to the musical dimension of the exercises he is carrying through, his propensity to decide on suitable points for the introduction of music —and, on such occasions, to what end and in what form—at a given point in the activity, are, we believe, the principal characteristics of the true Dalcrozian, and authorize the attribution of this adjective to all the exercises in his repertoire, even those which are not necessarily (as many are not) the prerogative of rhythmics lessons.

USE OF SPACE AND ADAPTATION TO VARYING ENVIRONMENTS

But spatial and orientation exercises are by no means limited to those involving fixed reference points. With the aid of portable and easily manipulable equipment (wooden bricks, sticks, hoops, cord, benches, and various objects and supports) modifications will be made to the physiognomy of the room in its three spatial dimensions. This may be done for the purpose of introducing variety into motricity exercises or of giving direction to movements or progressions; in any case it will involve the children in adapting themselves to a greater or lesser degree to the structure of this novel space. Whether learning to position themselves (or bounce a ball) inside or outside the rim of a hoop, or to pass on all fours beneath a cord stretched between two of their comrades (or jump over it), or to wend their way through (or step over) a wide range of assorted obstacles on the ground without stumbling into them, or make their way around the room without touching the floor by selecting a route amongst a number of bricks scattered about, or to move forwards by jumping from one side to the other of a piece of cord stretched out on the ground, the children will have many opportunities to measure themselves against an environment which pits its own resistances and laws against them whilst at the same time affording them numerous openings for new types of activity. And all these exercises will, from the viewpoint of musical education, act as pretexts for an equal number of correspondences to be made between physical space and the space of sounds. The height of notes, the flow of tunes, phrasings, silences, accents, and so on, will thus be vividly illustrated. They will in turn contribute, as an immediately evocative sensory reinforcement, to the disposition of spatial structures.

At the same time, the 'material' *par excellence* through which the child will gradually succeed in gaining mastery over his surrounding space is furnished by the presence of his comrades, themselves also in movement and each equally possessed of a personal space. He will have to learn to take them into account, as well as to distance himself from them.

When dealing with twenty youngsters sitting more or less quietly at their desks in the primary school class, or gathered in little groups in the various zones designed for pre-school activities, it may just about be possible to entertain illusions about their natural ability to occupy a space collectively. Some of these will be lost as soon as any attempt is made, for example, to get them to arrange themselves in two lines for the purpose of an outing. But they are all sure to collapse the moment they are invited to dispose themselves in freely chosen positions within an empty room! Agglutination and immobility, collisions and mounting agitation are the immediate products of such unstructured freedom, which they have absolutely no idea what to do with. How to move around without bumping into others, or to direct one's steps in such a way as to trace as variable a route as possible, are not the least of the acquisitions they must learn to make. 'Try going somewhere where there isn't anyone else' is in this regard the suggestion perhaps most likely to produce the best results, in conjunction with 'Follow a twisting, turning pathway that makes you go through every single bit of the room'.

This exercise demands an adaptive effort on the beginner's part at

any age, and especially with 4- to 6-year-olds, who are still centred on
their own particular viewpoint and are consequently powerless to
foresee the exact spot and moment at which a neighbouring pathway
will intersect with theirs. Their increasing skill at avoiding others will
therefore prove to be the fruit of well-controlled reactions rather than
of accurate predictions as to points of intersection. For this reason,
amongst others, it will be impossible to insist too strongly on the
benefits to children of this age of ensuring that the rhythmics class is
kept *small*. Bearing in mind how varied may be the total area available,
no one will want to have to deal with more than ten to twelve children
in the same lesson: two half-lessons with half the class each are, if
otherwise unavoidable, certainly preferable to a single lesson with the
whole group, especially to start with! When it is remembered that, to
succeed in moving around amongst others without bumping into
them, the 5-year-old is in a position to rely only on the promptness of
his own reactions, it may be understood why running and rapid
movement, in which he takes such delight, become virtually impossible
for him when he is swamped by too large a number of comrades to
avoid. As Dalcroze pointed out in another connection (1942: 66): 'The
child who adores speed is condemned to perpetual sloth!' It may be
objected that there are ways of overcoming the inconvenience involved
—such as getting separate groups of children to take it in turns to run
about, or ensuring that the movement as a whole takes place in a
broadly circular manner. But these are last resorts, as soon becomes
apparent, and often pose as many problems for teachers as frustrations
for children!

Take the example of moving in circles. This offers undoubted
advantages when dealing with older children (especially from the
viewpoint of the teacher, who is thereby better placed to keep an eye
on each and every pupil), but at pre-school level it amounts to
attempting the impossible. And all efforts to bring it about soon prove
profitless: that nice round circle achieved with great difficulty by
getting everyone to hold hands—or to stand in front of one of a
number of tambourines arranged on the ground in a circle—that
lovely circle, as soon as any attempt is made to get it to turn, collapses
with the slightest puff of air! Whether it breaks through one child's
lapse of attention, or falls out of shape through a corporate failure of
movement control, the children show themselves quite incapable of
spontaneously getting it together again. The exercise is interrupted,
and everything has to start again from scratch. It's one thing to be able

to hold hands with your right and left neighbours; and one thing again to position yourself in relation to something already positioned in advance: but in accordance with the propensity of the child of that age to consider everything from his own point of view, he will simply never be able to see his role (much less that of anyone else) as a single element relating to the overall shape. Let one segment of the circle start moving to the right, and the children positioned diametrically opposite will promptly mirror them by setting off to the left. Let the circle collapse at a bad moment, or shrink or stretch itself out of shape, and any chance of referring back to the ideal shape just as promptly flies out of the window. Let one of the children inadvertently diverge from the circular path, and those behind will likewise follow in his footsteps, for their horizon is limited to the neighbour immediately in front of them, and they do no more than pass from one point to the next. In these circumstances it will be understood that even if there are sometimes practical reasons for trying to establish such a circle (notably in exercises carried out in fixed floor positions, or games involving changing places, for example), there are more important things in life than struggling to get children to move in a harmonious circle, the uncertain success of which is unlikely to repay the efforts it will have cost.

Note, however, that what may sometimes be attained without any special effort is a shape which, if not perfectly circular, at least resembles the rounded rectangle of a closed buckle, and that is when children are asked to walk in single file. What in fact happens is that the head of the line, instead of keeping up his own initiative, lets himself be magnetized by its tail when his pathway happens to come a little too near it, and then begins to follow the child at the end. In this respect he faithfully obeys his natural tendency to go from spot to spot when moving forwards. When this happens, furthermore, it is only the outside observer who notices that the line has turned itself into a buckle: as far as the children are concerned, they are hardly aware of anything but their immediate neighbours! Thus exercises devised to strengthen the individual leader's sense of initiative, as opposed to the docility of those who follow, have their place here. They also help to introduce flexibility into the child's viewpoint by thrusting him into both roles alternately. Similarly with exercises designed to distinguish the head of the line from its tail, or exercises in which the first become last by doing a half-turn on the spot (which, for the children who are not at either extremity, consists in thinking 'I was behind him before;

now I'm behind her'); or exercises in which, at a given signal, the head of the line goes to take up position at the other end and so become its tail. (The opposite exercise, in which the tail goes and takes the place of the head, will not work until later, as it is not easy to keep track of what is happening outside one's field of vision, and becoming conscious of the empty space behind one's back is something that calls for an exercise of its own.) All the same, this type of exercise, being fairly restrictive and allowing the child little freedom of movement, should not form too important a part of the lesson. This is underlined by Piaget in his introduction to the book by Laurendeau and Pinard, *Les Premières Notions spatiales de l'enfant*:

with action playing an essential and central role in knowledge, the child must first exploit this role before being able to place his own action in the context of those displaying other characteristics or capable of being envisaged from other points of view (Laurendeau and Pinard 1968: 7)

In this regard, there is an obvious advantage in attaching pride of place to individual exercises. For example, and to revert to the idea of the circle discussed above, I should like to mention an exercise I saw employed by Dorothea Huber at Geneva in the summer of 1979 (at an International Dalcroze Eurhythmics Congress designed for children). The children were slightly older than those we are concerned with here, but the exercise lends itself to either age-range:

> The teacher asks the children to 'draw' circles with different parts of the body—with knees or hips or heels; with the shoulder, the elbow, the chin; with one finger, the toes, the head, the whole body, or whatever. Nice round circles, as large as possible or very small indeed, dashed off boldly or lightly sketched in, faster or slower as the case may be. It's up to everyone to come up with some part of the body that hasn't already been thought of.

Not only do the children explore with pleasure the sensation of circular movement in every part of the body, but when they achieve it they are really a delight to watch. 'That which is done well is beautiful', Claire-Lise Dutoit would often say of motor exercises; and she lost no opportunity in getting her pupils to appreciate it, even the very young. In little children, natural movement goes hand in hand with well-being and physical harmony (later, it will take much effort to arrive at such concordance), and no opportunity should be lost of letting them exercise in this way to the full, nor of drawing the child's attention to the pleasure which he not only experiences himself but also, at the time, brings to those who are watching. Dalcroze often emphasized, in addition to the support Eurhythmics can bring to bear on the individual's general functioning, the role the body can play in its capacity as an 'instrument of the arts' (1931*a*: 5). He declared himself convinced that

the child who has reached the point of being conscious of feeling straight, curved, or broken lines within his own body will quite naturally respond to them in such works of painting, sculpture, or architecture as he may find himself presented with; for man is so made as to take pleasure in recognising a priori, in works of art, that which strikes him as echoing his own sensations or reflecting his own thoughts.

For, (he continues),

it is undeniable that in every department of mental endeavour ideas live, to a greater or lesser degree, under the sway of direct sensations of which a marked recollection persists . . . or is transformed (1931*b*: 10–11)

Thus it is, for him, that

the rhythm of a work of plastic art cannot be apprehended by the child until he has experienced, in his own muscles and nerves, sensations of a spatial and dynamic nature . . . [Consequently,] by giving the child the benefit of an immeasurably long series of sense experiences of every kind, which it is the duty of our imaginations to create and endlessly vary, he will be led to appreciate the elements of life and beauty without even being aware of it. (1931*b*: 13).

EXERCISES IN PAIRS

Let's now get back down to the actual rhythmics room to bring out a final type of exercise essential to the development of the child's earliest spatio-temporal concepts: and here I speak of those which get them working together in pairs. We saw above, when talking about imitation, how important it is for the child to be able to identify and compare himself with other children of his own age. He may not yet be able to put himself in the position of his neighbour, but the latter will, on the other hand, afford him not a few opportunities of learning something about himself and at the same time becoming conscious of some of his ways of acting in and reacting to his world's surroundings. At the earliest stage, it is through the medium of a partner that the child will be able both gradually to identify his relationships with a shifting environment and at the same time increasingly to see this environment in its social perspective, by progressively attaining to mastery over the relations of alternation, simultaneity, exchange, reciprocity, and the like.

He is already acquainted with many parts of his body, and he will see it as a game to find positions enabling him to put them in one-to-one correspondence with those of his partner: knee to knee, shoulder to shoulder, tummy to tummy, nose to nose; then knee to hip, elbow on foot, shoulder under chin, head against back; and finally reciprocal relations, whereby, for example, each grasps his neighbour's ankles with one hand. Now can you do the same thing standing up, without losing balance? There will be a chance to learn how to give names to symmetrical relations: face to face (and, soon, standing on opposite sides), back to back, side by side—and to asymmetrical ones: one behind the other, one in front of the other, one on top of the other. And one to the *right* of the other? Relationships involving left and right are known to take longer to clarify than the others. In this regard we may cite the authors of the book mentioned above (Laurendeau and Pinard 1968: 204), who point out:

Piaget notes that the ability to identify parts of one's own body as 'left' and 'right' is acquired by the age of 5; but the purely absolute character of this differentiation—bearing in mind that left and right are as yet no more than, so to speak, names applied to one limb or another—is demonstrated by the fact that not until the age of 8 does the child succeed in correctly identifying the left and right parts of a questioner looked at full face, or in infallibly recognizing that such and such an object is in the right or the left hand of the questioner still being seen from the front.

Similarly, he will find it difficult to understand that if his neighbour is on his right, he must be on his neighbour's left. As for the ability to identify an object as lying both to the right of one thing and the left of another,

Piaget's results clearly show that this last type of relativity . . . is not reached before the age of 11 or 12 (depending on on whether or not the objects remain in full view of the subject). (ibid.)

Care must therefore be taken not to insist too systematically on relations of this type, but to concentrate instead on increasing opportunities to practise those presenting fewer problems. These will act as a pretext for the adoption of a variety of poses and postures calling upon bodily consciousness and imagination as well as on the sense of balance. With both children seated, get one to put an arm around his neighbour's back and a leg over his knees; with one of them standing, get one to put his right hand on the seated neighbour's shoulder, his left foot on the other shoulder; and so on.

Doing exercises two by two will also start on the experience of being together or apart, close to or far away from each other; of being able to separate and lose sight of one another, then come together again amongst everybody else; of learning to exercise relationships at a distance, such as by rolling a ball to each other, or by making gestures or striking attitudes from a distance which the other one then has to imitate; even of learning to change partners. To these various activities music will render a not inconsiderable degree of assistance. For example, in the form of variously contrasting sound-instructions it will tell the child that he has to pass immediately from one situation to another, when by nature the child would be more inclined to prolong the situation, centred as he is on the action of the moment.

SPACE AND AUDITORY DISCRIMINATION

The ability to alternate individual activities with activities in pairs is also widely used with a view to musical education, as oppositions between isolated and connected actions find numerous parallels in the world of sound. In this respect, a successful outcome to the exercise will be recognized in the quality of the child's listening, and the musical contribution will be increasingly finely tuned in such a way as to induce in the child a growing power of discrimination. Thus, for example, the ability to distinguish two voices in alternation or in unison will be helped by presenting them first in markedly different registers (low/high) or on two very different instruments (e.g. drum/triangle), then gradually reducing the differences until the minutest interval remains between the two voices.

Following a similar train of thought, and with the aim of illustrating our twin themes of Eurhythmics as a musical method of education and a method of education for music, I will finish with two examples of relating music and space which have certain characteristics in common but with each considered from one or the other of these two points of view.

As education through music: One of my pupils has considerable difficulty in moving harmoniously through space. She is a mentally handicapped 8-year-old exhibiting difficulties in every respect. Amongst other things, she has the peculiarity of always turning round in the same direction, like a fish in a bowl. You might say that, having made one turn, the other side no longer exists for her.

I arranged three rows of hoops with a view to getting her to experience the alternation of a left turn followed by a right turn, and so on. She is supposed to make her way through these three rows so as to follow an S-shaped path (Fig. 5.1). But once she gets as far as the second row, she seems systematically to ignore the third and come back to the first, thus following a permanently circular movement (Fig. 5.2).

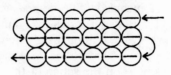

Fig. 5.1

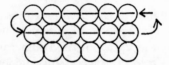

Fig. 5.2

It so happens that this little girl is very fond of singing and knows a great many songs. By associating each row of hoops with a different song, which I get her to listen to before doing the exercise, I find that the third row of hoops suddenly begins to exist for her. Then when she is just about to return to the first row, as is her custom, the reminder of the third song causes her to change her mind—and her direction! Having experienced with her body the sensation of change by reference to a song she knows well, the mere reminder of its first few notes is soon enough to set her going in the right direction. By progressively transforming the three songs, at first retaining only their rhythms, then going so far as to mix them up, I soon get her to the point of dispensing with the musical support. Then I introduce other songs and other forms of musical prompts in order to break the first association made, which only served a temporary purpose. In this way she succeeds in associating, not a given song with a given place, but the perception of a change in music with the sensation of a change in direction which she must bring about herself.

In subsequent lessons new types of course will be laid out on the ground, and eventually they will be suppressed. Once the motor sensation has been brought out, the little girl will henceforth be able to recapture it whenever necessary, with or without the aid of music.

As education into music: Here, too, songs will undergo transformations —not with a view to eventually being dispensed with or replaced by others, but in order to be recognized despite the modification or suppression of some of their dimensions. And space will here be used as a form of control, to enable the children to show that they have identified the song in question.

The area is divided into three or four zones and correspondingly associated with three or four different songs. Such association may be established by means, for example, of objects suggestive of the content of the song, and placed in different positions. In previous lessons everyone will have sung the songs together and played them out several times. In the subsequent listening exercise, each child has to make his way as fast as possible to the place corresponding to the song he thinks he has recognized. The latter, however, is played in a modified version which makes it more or less recognizable, being, for instance, played very fast or very slowly, transposed into a lower or higher register, played in a minor key if it was previously major, hummed without words and given a different character; it may be stripped of its opening bars or of some of its notes, or perhaps elaborated with additional notes, deprived of its tune so as to retain only its rhythm, which may then be rapped out on a percussion instrument, or may even be decked out with a new melodic line; and so on.

In this exercise, by the very act of going to the spot associated (for the time being) with one or other of the songs, the child demonstrates not just to the observer but also to himself that which is of underlying *permanence* in successive transformations.

GAMES AND SONGS

The best, and perhaps the only, opportunity one may have of seeing the child of pre-school age take his rhythmics lesson 'seriously' consists in presenting him with all the exercises (especially those described in this chapter) in the guise of games. But not as any old games: the adult and older child have rather different ideas about the meaning of this term from those of children under 6. In particular, they are attracted by games in which interest focuses on the achievement of a final outcome (contests and other games involving the idea of competition or targets to beat), or which are governed by a set of rules whose very application is a source of enjoyment (games of patience, deduction, combination, and suchlike).

Nothing of this sort exists in the young child, for whom play is, so to speak, his way of living in the world (at least, when he isn't busy sleeping, eating, or—heaven help us!—obeying the obscure dictates of adult reasoning!). In other words, and to recall those of Dalcroze (1942: 60):

In a school game he finds himself forced to concentrate on his master's instructions, to follow the game through until everything is working as it should, which is to say academically; whereas in the game as he conceives it, which springs fresh and trim and sparkling from his own little life, itself so varied, agitated, and reckless, he plays *for the sake of playing*, thinking of nothing but the pleasure of escaping from the rut of everyday existence . . . For it is in his nature to prefer the games *invented by himself* to those imposed upon him. (1942: 59)

But what are these games that he invents? They can be broadly divided into two classes, which, however, often overlap. The first class is of *exercising games*, by means of which the child experiments with the workings of his body and the impact of his actions on other things. This type of game—which, as a baby, he started practising long before gaining access to speech or even to walking—is characterized by the repetition of movements (exercizing for the fun of it), and by the quest for and discovery of ways of effecting ever new performances. These features underlie the notions of *training* and *perfecting* to be found, for example, in the pursuit of sports or in various types of technical training.

The second class is that of *symbolic games*—games of 'let's pretend' —activities opened up to the child by his access to representation and speech, and in which he makes use of his capacities for imitation and imagination. Games of this type are superbly illustrated by poetry and the theatre.

The relationship between exercising and symbolic games will later bring into being—depending on the weight attached to one or other of these types of activity—the ingenuity of the craftsman as well as the creativity of the artist. It will also, when brought to maturity by a power of objectivization as yet lacking in the child of this age, lead to more sophisticated games, or *jeux de règle* ('rule-determined games'). These are exemplified by certain adult games and in the pursuit of competitive sports; but they may also be used in the processes of intellectual or formal creativity, processes no less typical of scientific thought than of that of the artist.

To bring a symbolic dimension to exercising games, and to introduce exercising (and instructions, little by little, as the forerunners of rules) into symbolic activity—herein lies the role of the rhythmician in his lessons for pre-school ages. This role is greatly facilitated by what music has to offer, which can alternately inspire and ordain, as Dalcroze pointed out (1942: 60)

his mind is so open that you can, if you know how to set about it, offer it any other way or ways of playing: you can simply waft ideas across to him. And he will assuredly waft some back to you in turn.

'If you know how to set about it', he carefully observes. For it is not enough to conjure up a pretty picture or a good idea to make an exercise more suggestive or attractive. More important is that such a picture or idea should match something meaningful to the child. 'You hardly ever see any more a group of children who, when invited to move in a line, promptly go "Choo-choo!" and pretend to be a train', notes Liliane Favre-Bulle; 'but it was once a very useful image! . . . Nowadays other noises and images spring to their minds, and we have to keep track of them.' But, she adds, 'It's still the same imagination: they're still all the same kids underneath!'[11] The child must therefore be left, as far as possible, to find his own most satisfying images; or, if he can't think of anything, he may be referred to suggestions that have already been made ('One little boy I know thought it was rather like . . .), or perhaps to one's own childhood memories:

One only has to look behind to recall one's own childish fantasies. I firmly believe that nearly all children from the age of 4 to 6 have the same impressions of life. The same things make them laugh and cry, engage or irritate them. (Dalcroze 1942: 60)

[11] Liliane Favre-Bulle, interview recorded 6 Nov. 1979.

But one will also not hesitate to appeal to the enchantment of words in order to capture the youngsters' interest. They are enraptured by made-up words, or words whose exact meaning escapes them, such as certain archaisms, and would not have them replaced by anything else in the world. Quite obviously, such words do not hinder their understanding of the actions called for; indeed, it is noticeable that they bring an additional charm into play, and that the children not only adopt them but actually use them as titles for a game.

The Chicory Box: How many children today know what a chicory box is? Yet it is by reference to it that one of my little groups of children clamour with all their might and main for the exercise based on this ditty (5.1). My ignorance as to the origin of this song (which I don't think I have ever seen written down) inspired me to treat it freely in the following way:

> It is not your real grandma that you have so irreverently shut up in the *boîte à chicorée*; instead, this place of magic and mystery harbours figures borrowed from the child's bestiary and from the world of dreams and nightmares: a rabbit, a horse, a duck, a lion, a dragon, a fairy, a brigand. One child squats down and whispers his idea into the ears of the others, who conceal him from view by huddling over him. They sing the song, and, on its final notes, pull apart to enable the stated character to emerge. The latter then goes around 'in the skin of his character': jumping if a frog, striding if an ogre, and so on. The piano takes up the appropriate movement, and the other children turn into ogres or frogs and set to work accordingly.

Ex. 5.1

Ma grand-mère est en-fer-mée dans la boîte à chi-co-rée! Quand la boî-te s'ouv-ri-ra, ma grand-mè-re sor-ti-ra!

Many existing songs lend themselves to felicitous transformations and adaptations enabling, as above, the introduction of exercising into symbolic games. The reverse, on the other hand, is less often encountered in the literature: relatively few songs have been written that expressly grow out of and relate specifically to children in movement. Dalcroze, as might be expected, is one of those who did feel sufficiently moved to enrich the childhood repertoire with songs of such a nature. In fact, he wrote dozens and dozens of them,[12] some of which retain a very up-to-date character. One of many examples is the song he called 'Les braves petites jambes'.[13] These 'little legs' are 'so obliging' that they do everything the child tells them to do: 'Forward, march! Left, right! Jolly good! Backward, march! Left, right, left, right! Jolly good! Sideways, march! Some other way, march! And now, forwards, jump! Little legs, my wish is your command!' Better known to the public are songs designed to encourage gestures, such as 'La maisonnette comm'ça'',[14] or in the 'Ronde des petits nains de la montagne', who sweep the floor and rock babies to sleep. Rhythmicians have access to all these songs and many more besides,[15] but they often find themselves put to the task of writing their own songs, sometimes off the cuff, to cater in their exercises for the needs of the moment. It was in answer to this requirement that the tune in Example 5.2 was composed, which I thought up one day for the help of a little girl who liked songs, but found it difficult to stretch out restfully on the floor when doing exercises in body-consciousness.

The little girl soon entered into the spirit of the game as the doll who closes her eyes, and it is due to her very good ear for tunes and the taste she developed both for this little song and for the game it describes that I can remember to this day what started out as nothing more than a 'jobbing' song designed to impart a symbolic dimension to a motor exercise.

If every rhythmician is thrown into this kind of spontaneous composition at some time or other, a good many of them are sufficiently encouraged by the activity to *write* songs for children, with words and harmony included. Those who do so very soon discover for

---

[12] See Dénes, 'Catalogue complet', in Martin, Dénes, and Berchtold 1965: 484 ff.
[13] Dalcroze 1906, No. 5.   [14] Dalcroze 1904, No. 1.
[15] See for instance the twenty-four songs in Action Songs (Dalcroze 1919d), the *Six Chansons animées pour les enfants* (1930b), the *Six Chansons de gestes, Op. 58* (1900b), *Cueillons des chansons* (1927), etc.

Ex. 5.2

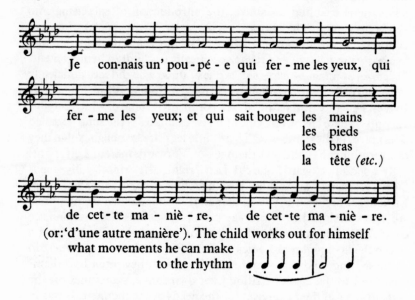

Je   con-nais un' pou-pé - e qui fer - me les yeux, qui

fer - me les   yeux; et qui sait bouger les   mains
les   pieds
les   bras
la   tête *(etc.)*

de cet-te ma - niè - re,   de cet-te ma - niè - re.

(or:'d'une autre manière'). The child works out for himself
what movements he can make
to the rhythm

themselves how well-founded is Dalcroze's caution in this respect
(1942: 30):

> [No one] who gets the idea of writing songs for children should imagine that
> the task is as easy as it might appear—or that it affords an interest of
> secondary value. To ensure that this type of composition maintains the
> quality of art one must strive to condense one's thought into a brief space of
> time, to eliminate any pointless affectation, to be simple without becoming
> facile, to excite youngsters' imaginations with as few images as possible . . . If
> the songster is content to express humdrum thoughts in words that have no
> particular appeal for children, and in tunes which they cannot follow either
> immediately or by efforts afforded by a technique suitable for *adults*, then it
> will quite probably be of no interest to either children or adults.

Given that his training has afforded him experience of the close
links between music and movement, and his professional practice a
knowledge of all the motor and musical capacities of the children for
whom he is writing, the rhythmician who composes songs for children
finds himself theoretically well equipped. But the recommendations
bequeathed him by Dalcroze (1942: 30) will be a reminder, as well as
an aid for the non-rhythmician who embarks on this sort of enterprise,

or even for the browser confronted with the task of hunting through the repertoire for songs adapted to the capabilities of youngsters:

Above all it is right that we should present the young singer with tunes that just ask to be sung, fairly simple harmonies that do not divert him from the melodic line, and rhythms which he has already learnt and become familiar with through his own impulsive speech and gestures. The child generally accompanies his speech with lively gestures which . . . facilitate the flow of words. He does not prolong his syllables and often prefers to repeat them . . . The song-writer will meet this need by obeying the instinct for repetition which characterizes the way children articulate, especially when the child is alone, and singing and talking to himself rather than to others . . . And you will not forget to give the little band of singers frequent occasion to dance at the same time as singing, as do all primitive peoples from Papuans to Redskins to babies in Genevan suburbia![16]

Nevertheless, whether songs and motor exercises are the cause or the effect of one another, it is with an eye to their status as *games*—and hence to the enjoyment implicit in games—that they should be carried out with liveliness and with the best chance of being followed through successfully. Furthermore, this will not prevent the teacher from emphasizing at the end of the lesson how well the children have 'worked', and to make a survey of the various things they have achieved while doing so, by pointing out each one's individual successes and by bearing in mind that at this age 'to succeed' means 'to do one's best' by putting everything one has into the effort.

The areas and examples covered in this chapter on children of pre-school age do not claim—far from it—to have dealt with absolutely everything to do with Eurhythmics in the nursery school. My purpose in pointing out some notable characteristics of this age-group has been first and foremost to show how the teaching sector which Dalcroze took longest to set about exploring may well be that which makes the greatest demands on the rhythmician's professional skill and understanding of the nature of the younger child. It is also that which requires the greatest flexibility, so as not to lose the slightest opportunity of enabling or encouraging children to get all their faculties for action and imagination working together; for is it not on such faculties that their inner well-being and their enjoyment of life is going to depend at every age they pass through?

[16] '*Bébés de Plan-les-Ouates*', the latter glossed as 'a commune in the canton of Geneva'. (Translator's note)

Primary-school Level

In the pre-school or nursery-school period, at an age when the young child is gaining his first experiences of group and school life and still sees work and play as one and the same thing in which to throw himself wholeheartedly, there is an obvious place for the contribution Eurhythmics can make, and it can easily be considered an integral part of everyday life. Such a role is indeed accorded to it by several academic institutions, which hold that rhythmics at this age does not require the services of a specialist teacher but is the business of the nursery-school teacher, and place rhythmics and its teaching on the curriculum of future primary-school heads, or those who will exercise responsibility for the running of nursery schools. This approach would have delighted Dalcroze, who recommended (1910: 23) the practice of giving young children 'a [daily] half-hour lesson in the form of *play*'. For at this age, he added, 'If the teaching is irregular and too spaced out, it achieves nothing.'

But the role of Eurhythmics is less obvious when the child reaches the stage of doing school work in the proper sense of the word, when he is learning to differentiate between 'play' and so-called 'serious' activities, and in the latter category to distinguish between the various disciplines involved. At the age when everything in the child's life is conspiring to encourage him to compartmentalize his experiences, Eurhythmics for its part tries to maintain or to create the potential for close links' between his various spheres of activity.

One cannot overemphasize the benefits offered in this respect by a properly understood collaboration between the schoolteacher and the rhythmician. The fact is that the latter very rarely has access to the class he meets with once a week. Whenever those children are engaged in writing or problem-solving, his own work takes him elsewhere. The teacher himself generally has an opportunity to take part regularly in rhythmics lessons. On his personal commitment and his sensitive understanding will largely depend the benefits which children are able to derive from this weekly lesson, both for themselves as individuals and for their school lives. But it is the rhythmician's job, on the other hand, to keep himself *au fait* with the broad outlines of the curriculum relating to a given age-group, as well as to inform himself as he goes along of what sort of acquisitions are in course of pursuit or form the current focus of interest. Such an attempt is made, for her part (and she is not alone in this), by Ruth Gianadda in Geneva, who on occasion has gone so far as to gather together at the start of the school year the class-teachers of all those with whom she would come into contact, in order to introduce them to Eurhythmics and to inform them of the aims of her work.[17] In some respects she approaches a view expressed as follows in an article by Dominique Porte:

Eurhythmics ought to have a place in the overall school programme! . . . The child evinces all the more interest in the rhythmics lesson when he finds it confirmed in new ways [in the acquisitions he has been able to make] in other lessons! . . . I think one ought also to take all learning activities into account and put all the child's current acquisitions into operation, like a key which correctly works the lock because it respects its internal mechanism. (Porte 1966: 4)

Without successful collaboration between rhythmicians and teachers, rhythmics undoubtedly loses its linking potential. Yet that does not mean it ceases to have any effect—despite the restricted place made for it—as a discipline in its own right working towards the individual's overall personal harmony. Today's rhythmicians often adopt this viewpoint, as witness such thoughts as the following:

It is extraordinary to what extent a child may be marked by something in which he finds complete enjoyment . . . I see what school involves, what its rhythms are, and how many hours they impose on the children from seven upwards! I think Eurhythmics can serve to enable the child to find the means that exist within himself, and to succeed in discovering his own rhythm and personal style.[18]

To improve classroom concentration, or bring success in some aspect of school life or other, is not the *raison d'être* of Eurhythmics so far as I'm concerned. The mobilization and exercise of all the senses strikes me as sufficient justification in its own right, in so far as they are the source of personal enrichment; and this not with the aim of enabling the child to do better at the things we ourselves should expect of him, but with that of enabling him to decide for himself what he is going to do with this new-found sensitivity.[19]

The same disinterested viewpoint was also that of the master when he asserted (1909: 67):

The primary outcome of a well-planned course in rhythmic gymnastics is the ability to see into oneself with clarity, to get to know oneself exactly as one is

---

[17] Ruth Gianadda, interview recorded 31 Oct. 1979.
[18] Monique Bosshard, interview recorded 8 Nov. 1979.
[19] Esther Messmer-Hirt, interview recorded 10 Oct. 1979.

and to take full advantage of all one's faculties. And it seems to me that this outcome should by nature attract the attention of pedagogues and secure for education through and into music—regardless of its particular form or the way it works—an important place in everyday culture.

And, with modesty, he accorded second place to the object in which he personally took the most heartfelt interest:

But in my capacity as an artist, I have to add that the second outcome of such an education should be to press the individual's integrally developed faculties into the service of art, and thus to place at art's disposal that most versatile and self-contained of media, the human body.

In his eyes, this secondary objective would alone have sufficed to justify the introduction of Eurhythmics into the school curriculum:

School prepares children for every profession except a career in art. But by introducing the study of rhythm into its courses it necessarily prepares the child for art appreciation, for rhythm lies at the root of all artistic expression —of sculpture as of music, of architecture as of poetry. Children who have once mastered their own movements and come to appreciate the movements of others will find easy access to the emotions evoked by everything in the arts which brings movement to mind. (1910: 28–9)

It will be objected that we no longer live in 1910 and that school has had plenty of time in which to make significant progress. But has it? In 1979 Jacques Beauvais, a director of the Centre National d'Etudes et de Formation pour l'Adaptation scolaire et l'Education spécialisée (France) declared (Beauvais 1981 33–4):

To note how small a part musical instruction plays in school activities as a whole is to be struck by the evidence . . . [Even so,] the teaching of music is not exceptional by comparison with other disciplines. It suffers from the same inadequacies observable in the realm of the graphic and pictorial disciplines, as in that of bodily disciplines such as physical education, dance, and figurative expression. All such teaching—especially at primary-school level —is peripheral, and thought of as lying outside essential forms of training.[20]

And Beauvais offers two complementary explanations for this state of affairs, the first being 'an implicit devaluing [of the role of these disciplines] in school achievement, whose criteria still attach essentially

---

[20] But for a Swiss counter-example see *Plan d'études pour l'enseignement primaire de la Suisse romande* (1972: 1).

to written language and mathematics'; the second consisting in the continuing '[conception of] art as the manifestation of a gift', and consequently in the '[hiving off of] those evidently not cut out for full participation in it'. As a result, 'the fate reserved for the artistic disciplines betrays a *de facto* dichotomy between the essential and the superfluous, between the useful and the merely nice'. One can almost hear Dalcroze exclaiming, at a distance of more than three-quarters of a century and with a sense of humour that never allowed him to feel discouraged (1900a: 46–7):

A music teacher will never be accounted the equal of a teacher of arithmetic or of handwriting; for music is only something on the side, one of those nice arty things—whereas a course in arithmetic will at least enable you to count your money out correctly to the last penny, and a course in handwriting to write the proper sort of letter for demanding money from a debtor. Public opinion disputes your usefulness, dear teacher: just you think about it!

The future seems to have justified this pessimistic vision, even if motives and terminology have changed in our passage from a bureaucratic era to a technological age! For his part, Beauvais echoes this when he observes:

The so-called basic disciplines, such as French and maths, find themselves pedagogically limited by being shaped towards that which is socially useful. (Beauvais 1981: 35)

Thus it is that, even today, the child still spends the greater part of his time learning things society requires of him, things that will be useful 'when he gets older'. At least, that is what he is often led to believe. And perhaps not least of the arguments in favour of teaching rhythmics at school is to afford him now—quite freely—something which will sustain him in his present circumstances and enable him, at this particular age and for his immediate benefit, to take full advantage of the potential residing within him.

The first thing the child must be taught is the use of all his faculties. Only then should he be instructed in the beliefs and conclusions of others. (Dalcroze 1914: 59) It seems to me that children should be taught, before anything else, to become conscious of their personality, to develop their temperament, to free the rhythm of their individual lives from every resistance. (1919a: 7)

But who, exactly, are these children?

WHICH CHILDREN?

I have observed on many occasions that some of my Children's Songs which used to be sung with great delight by our lads and lasses some thirty years ago no longer appeal to those of today. (Dalcroze 1942: 30)

Nowadays, children see such a lot of things and hear such a lot of things . . . that they have stopped listening to anything, stopped being surprised by anything. And we, basically, must try to attract their interest quite differently from the way in which we ourselves were attracted, as children.[21]

Who, at one time or another, has not heard a pedagogue or educationist give vent to the generally mournful observation 'Children aren't what they used to be!'? As teachers, which of us has not on more than one occasion delivered himself of the same remark, with annoyance, regret, resignation, or—why not?—wonderment? This assertion is no doubt received with greater or lesser sympathy depending on whether or not it supports our own beliefs. But it often comes as a surprise to notice that the age of the complainant is less venerable than one might have been led to believe; and one cannot but harbour a suspicion that this stranger or this colleague is suffering from a short memory: has he already reached the point of idealizing his own childhood? Or (if he is older): were those children he was dealing with in the prime of life really different from the ones who tire him out so quickly today?

Admissible questions, certainly; but let us not make the mistake of regarding them as purely rhetorical, even if we are putting them to someone who has clearly lost control of the situation. For 'lost', indeed, is what he is! Everything seems to suggest in fact that the child 'is no longer what he was', and that the point in time at which he lived is not unrelated to the way in which he develops. If we recall the concept of the accelerating speed of change described by Toffler (see Introduction), we should in fact expect to find ourselves saying 'children aren't what they used to be' on an increasing number of occasions, and, perhaps, preparing ourselves for that eventuality.

Without having to detail all the differences here, it is evident that a refusal to take them into consideration threatens teaching with fossilization. If we berate the child for no longer resembling the child we used to know, if we stubbornly persist in denying that something important has changed, we conspire to turn school into a place bearing

---

[21] Liliane Favre-Bulle, interview recorded 6 Nov. 1979.

no relation to everyday life. In the former case, the unhappy or rancorous teacher blames the children for his own failures: their standards have been 'lowered', their concentration is 'non-existent', they are no longer 'interested in anything'. Faced with this assessment he oscillates between two reactions—*laissez-faire* and coercion. In the latter, the schoolmaster—more strongly sustained, perhaps, by his pedagogic talents and powers of persuasion—happily dispenses the same instruction to successive cohorts, remaining firmly convinced that children are children and that there are certain eternal truths, some essential and others contingent, which ought to be instilled into them so that they may have some chance of making a go of their lives. Neither one nor the other is ever likely to get down to revising the content of his teaching, but remains faithful to a course which at the most may have undergone one or two superficial modifications over the years. Equally, neither one nor the other is ever likely to question the fact (or to regard it as other than negligible) that amongst their 'less able' pupils are to be found those who already see themselves as, say, astronomers or electronics engineers, and who, at barely 11, talk of 'printed circuits', 'black holes', and science fiction with a familiarity that negates all preconceived notions about them. Yet it is they—they and their gentle neighbours, the budding poets—who would offer the world its best chances of survival if only it could be made to listen to them.

Of course there are other children, and more of them, who are quite incapable of finding such compensatory treasures outside the school environment. Little encouraged by their own family circle, they are increasingly left to their own devices without the support of necessary resources as school increasingly fails to offer them outlets directly relevant to the life to which they are being called. Yet it is to this life that they belong. This is the life in which they must sink or swim all the time they are not actually having lessons. This is the life which they must succeed in forging either means of access to or defences from if they are to avert the risk of submitting themselves blindly to it (as part of what has always been referred to as 'the masses'), or of becoming those who give up and dig themselves in—the outsiders, the washed-up, the 'fringes' of a society already too overburdened to be worthy of the name.

Finally, there are a certain number of children (and it would be interesting to see whether the proportion has changed) who find themselves equally at ease at home and school. These are the ones addressed by yesterday's teaching methods, the ones teachers have always been pleased to think of as the future élite, who for generations have perpetuated the status quo of education. Cocooned as far as possible from the aggressions and vulgarities of the outside world, brought up to the ideal of the eternity of cultural values, they remain today the consolation of more than one teacher, who, confounding cause and effect, sees them as the proof of a well-balanced education. When, as adults, they have taken the place of their masters, will they find any reason to cast a critical eye over the system that has succeeded so well for them? Why should they offer more than the most paltry concessions to the unfulfilled, whose deepest feelings are foreign to them? As for those who are able to face the evidence, are they sufficiently well equipped to deal with it?

CHILDHOOD CONSTANTS

My experience as a teacher has been shaped by the comparisons I have been able to make between the temperament and character of children of all countries by a thousand performances of my Children's Songs throughout Europe. I have everywhere seen . . . the same desire for movement, the same joy induced, in every language, by these texts inspired directly by the language of children. (Dalcrose 1942: 39–40)

We have got to find for ourselves the paths they follow, with their pre-occupations, the games they play, the things they take an interest in today . . . and we discover that every one of them is still at heart a poet . . ., that they are still like all kids everywhere![22]

Children are undoubtedly no longer what they were, yet the teacher who maintains that the property of childhood remains the same in spite of external changes, who echoes the sentiment that 'a child is always a child', also has truth on his side.

The coexistence of the three types of children described above, as well as our allusion to the differences they present from preceding generations, are themselves witness to one of the most permanent characteristics of childhood; its amazing plasticity.

When as adults we find ourselves subjected, often against our wills, to the influence of changes which plunge society into a movement that overwhelms it, the child, for his part, swims with the tide and unflinchingly adopts the pace it imposes on him. Should he be deliberately withdrawn from it, as is possible within a family closed in

---

[22] Liliane Favre-Bulle, interview recorded 6 Nov. 1979.

upon itself, he will adapt to the image expected of him. But let a breach once be opened in this fortress, and he will at once slip through it, and on the outside draw that breath of fresh or polluted air with a satisfaction that can easily be imagined! This ability will last, perhaps, up to the point at which, like a long-caged animal, he no longer knows how to take advantage of an open door.

When a child is unwilling or demonstrably unable to adapt his behaviour to the current situation, it is generally a sign that something is wrong. Rigidity, when it comes to replace his customary plasticity, is always a disturbing symptom: paediatricians, therapists, and other specialists in so-called 'maladjusted' children known this well. For when normality reigns this plasticity is so great that it always enables the child to fit exactly into the niche prepared for him. It is a well-known fact that the children of yesteryear took on adult roles when they had barely attained the 'age of reason'—artisans at 7, warriors at 11, king at 14. Today's child, so classified to quite an advanced age, in many ways experiences the consequences of the consideration accorded to him. In particular, he must adapt himself to the vast quantity of information placed at his disposal, of which that part specially reserved to him would alone be enough to keep his head filled for the rest of his life. If it is therefore difficult, unless care is taken, for him to cut himself a pathway through such abundance, or to be other than vacillating in the face of so many possibilities, no surprise need be felt. But we must also bear in mind the responsibility laid upon the educator and society as a whole in respect of children's development, and how necessary it is to put them in possession of faculties of which they can truly avail themselves, not just tomorrow and the day after, but today as well. We mustn't turn our inability to read the future into an excuse for confining ourselves to the past: rather, it offers all the more reason to concentrate, in the present, on what might reasonably be considered as the 'constants' of childhood.

In a novel of 1946 entitled *Le Baton de Miouhou*, that remarkable science fiction writer Theodor Sturgeon tells a strange tale which may be outlined as follows:

An extraterrestrial spacecraft lands on earth, and from it emerges a magnificent being having all the appearance of a very large human being. His bearing and clothing suggest that he belongs to a greatly advanced civilization, as does the curious implement he carries with him: a sort of metallic stick, which he has only to hold horizontally above his head to enable himself to rise a few metres into the air; by which means, for instance, he climbs effortlessly onto the roofs of the surrounding houses. He soon becomes the object of the attention of the most eminent sages, who, in spite of all their efforts, are unable to establish any satisfactory form of communication with him. His speech remains unintelligible to them, and his behaviour enigmatic to each and every one. He seems not to share either our sense of danger or our simple proprieties. Furthermore, he is obviously very attracted to earthmen's motor vehicles, which he never tires of driving. This penchant results in his becoming the victim of a road accident and being carted off to hospital. The medical examination to which he is subjected reveals to the dumbfounded sages that they have been dealing with a very young being, still in the process of growing, whose great size had misled them. In a word, a child! A child of a race of giants, perhaps, but nonetheless a child through and through! And his magic stick? A highly developed toy—he would probably have been hard put to explain what it was made of or how it worked. (Sturgeon 1977)

Why did they not discover the truth about him earlier? What was it that prevented people from seeing the child in this being, who, like their own children, could never keep still, gave vent to inarticulate cries, left the table at quite the wrong moment to go and play with his favourite toy, and evinced an endless fascination for handling steering wheels and the noise of motors? Nothing but appearances. Two of them were enough: his large size, to which they were able to relate; and the fact that he belonged to another civilization, which turned him into a foreigner. A foreigner, and, in the present case, an excusable one: no one was going to denounce as infantile the incomprehensible behaviour of somebody who came from a race which all the evidence suggested were possessed of superior powers. (As a corollary: haven't we sometimes heard it said of an individual belonging to a supposedly primitive race and behaving incomprehensibly that 'He's just a big child!'?)

Don't appearances and prejudices often prevent the child from being seen for what he is, and lead to his being considered one moment 'too old for such babyish things' and the next 'too young to understand'? And doesn't the habit of comparing him with the adult he has yet to become (generally to his disadvantage, occasionally to accord him, from nostalgia, the exclusiveness of a favoured role) tend to make one lose interest in him to a certain extent? And as for school—apart from one or two gratifying exceptions—how much longer will it continue to justify Dalcroze's complaint (1916*a*: 12) that 'The moment the child enters secondary education, the school curriculum seems to try and make the child forget that he exists'?

PARALLELS AND DIVERGENCES

It may come as a surprise to observe that the child who starts on rhythmics at primary-school level presents right from the first lessons some of the characteristics which in the previous chapter we associated with nursery-school children. In particular, that he will be seen to have some difficulty in adapting his behaviour and movements to the wide open spaces of the rhythmics room, that he is hardly able to catch a ball, that he has difficulty in imitating particular movements, that he seems to have no sense of judging distance any more than he has an exact sense of timing, that he doesn't easily concentrate, that his relations with others are essentially egocentric. It may be that he is only 7 and that his difficulties really represent impossibilities: we know that this is a critical age at which children cannot be expected to have reached in every department the level of development necessary to cope with the opening stages of academic instruction, and can imagine the adaptive effort required of them by a course of work often as yet beyond their powers. 'I am always struck by 7-year-olds', observes Esther Messmer. 'Shortly after they enter school I often notice signs of regression, socially as well as at the level of concentration. And, almost immediately, an element of competition takes over from pure interest in doing an exercise. But what I also see is that they are all under pressure, that they have energy to get rid of by way of motor activity. I therefore give them lots of exercises involving movement and imagination, and rather few to do with concentration, to start with.'[23]

But perhaps the child embarking on rhythmics is 8, or 9, or older. To a lack of rhythmics experience is added, in his case, certain reactions related to school conditioning, if only some degree of distrust about any activity radically different from what he has become accustomed to at school. It could equally well be a difficulty in focusing his attention on stimuli other than verbal ones (whether spoken or written), a loss of the habit of responding to requests with the total mobilization of his mental and physical faculties, a nascent self-consciousness which makes him hesitate to compromise himself in front of his teachers by giving way to something which, he believes, adults normally hold to be beneath his age.

[23] Esther Messmer-Hirt, interview recorded 10 Oct. 1979.

The child's emotions are externally manifested in an even stronger and often disordered way if he has not been exposed to the sort of education that leads to self-control. But such an education can only be undertaken at the age when children start to have a sense of order, a sense of reason, a sense of . . . ridicule. On the other hand there are some youngsters whose shyness holds their emotive expressions in check, it being then necessary to fight their inhibitions and to stimulate, by way of exciting games, the externalization of their musical sensations and their own feelings. (Dalcroze 1942: 105)

Some of the exercises which have been used to arouse the aural attention of little children, to get a sense of order across to them, to direct their attention to others, to help them structure their surrounding space, or to test the imaginative deployment of their bodies, may in consequence be advantageously applied to the older child, albeit in a spirit that takes account of his age and his personal powers of comprehension, and with the primary object of getting him to make himself function in this uncustomary mode. Especially, no opportunity will be lost of explaining the whys and wherefores of the exercises and to establish parallels between them and the various areas of his everyday life.

At the start of my teaching career, one little girl made a priceless remark to me, which I have never forgotten: 'Monsieur Jacques, I'd really like to know what this exercise is *for*!' Ever since, I have never failed to explain to my pupils . . . the aim of these pieces of work [that] I make them do, and I may well get them to guess the aim for themselves. (Dalcroze 1948: 168)

I refer the interested reader to the first section of this chapter so that I need only concentrate here on what concerns the potentials of, on average, the 7-year-old. These, furthermore, will be quickly revealed on the occasion of the most elementary exercises (those which can be done with the very young), by the speed with which the initial difficulties are overcome, and by the possibility offered by each exercise of having itself carried much further forward. Take the example of the exercise in which pairs of children roll a ball to each other, an exercise whose successful performance is an end in itself in a class of very young children. It may well be that in the primary-school class, once it has been attempted, quite a number of pupils will be shown up as quite maladroit in this activity, and will miss their goal, or fail to establish that preliminary relation between space and energy by which their movements must be informed. But whereas little ones display a failure of structuring (inability to foresee the path of the ball as the projection of an imaginary straight line, or to take simultaneous account of two dimensions—in this case space and energy—so as to exercise control over one as a function of the other), such structures do exist amongst the older ones, even if a lack of training prevents them from showing it to start with. The proof of this will lie in the fact that only a short period of adjustment is required for success to be achieved—unless failure itself comes to be a source of excitement for the child, who, finding the exercise not to his taste, discovers sabotage to be a good way of relieving his boredom! Hence there is no reason at all to dwell at length upon such an elementary exercise in quest of perfection. If the child is capable of bringing it off, it's a case of making him want to, by providing him with a suitable kind of motivation.

For example, and to take one I saw performed by a fourth-year primary-school class run by Ruth Gianadda, the children can be asked to find out with which parts of the body it is possible not only to block the passage of a ball sent to them but also to send it back without using the hands. Each pupil in turn imposes his own method of doing so on his partner, so you will see, for instance, two children lying flat on their stomachs, facing each other, and each in turn raising himself in such a way as to trap the ball beneath his breastbone. Sending it back calls for a propulsive effort involving a preliminary recursive movement. Two other children have decided to use their knees. In this case throwing it presents no problems, but the object is to find just the right point of impact to set the ball flying straight to its goal. Catching it is not much easier either: a rounded knee and a rounded ball lend themselves to little surface contact, and it soon becomes apparent that success is made at the expense of speed. As the aim of such an exercise is to get the child to judge the effectiveness of whatever mode of activity he has chosen for himself, he will generally be very keen to discover the best method of doing it and will gladly accept comments and suggestions which may lead him on towards success. Thereafter, it will be possible to impart a temporal dimension to this type of exercise by getting them to carry it out to a given tempo or rhythm, etc.

Let's tarry awhile in the realm of ball games, those great exponents of the relationships between space, time, and energy. I have very often observed the following phenomenon, with adults as well as with children of all ages or professional student beginners: In course of doing the exercise whereby each on his own is bouncing a ball on the ground and catching it again, I suggest, once a certain regularity has been established, 'And now, *faster!*' Invariably, nearly every single pupil starts bouncing his ball more *forcefully*, with the immediate result that it now flies up far above his head—thereby delaying the moment when he is in a position to catch it again, and, as a second consequence, slowing down the regularity with which the ball hits the ground. (Or, at least, maintaining its original regularity, but at the expense of considerable effort: the pupils jump and throw their arms up to catch the ball earlier and bounce it back down on the ground as fast as possible, often without properly judging its path and so causing the ball to pass completely out of their control.)

The striking thing is that so few come up with any spontaneous modifications tending to economize on the energy put into it and hence on the space in which the game takes place. At most, when some pupils realize that the inertial point of the ball above them represents a loss of time, they so position themselves as to intercept it the moment it comes within reach; but here, too, they do not husband their energy, and the force imparted to their movements works against the economy and precision of their effort. All, however, when asked to find a way of 'playing without overtaxing yourself'—or, better still, when their attention is drawn to a change in the musical dynamics pointing in the required direction and they are asked to 'follow the music'—soon manage to economize on energy by cutting down on space. Similarly, if they are asked to spend a little time in reflection and then explain exactly what they think is going to happen when they want to speed their ball-play up, they are quite capable of replying, from the age of 8 or 9, 'You have to stop throwing it (= bouncing it) so high!', whereupon they slightly lower or diminish the strength of their actions.

This example well illustrates, I believe, how the unexpected solicitation of hitherto unconscious reactions can put us in the position of young children for whom all possible spheres of activity are still jumbled up in a global response, even though in our minds or in our daily round we keep these spheres distinct and are quite capable of grasping the mutual effects they have on one another. Primary-school age is particularly well-favoured for achieving this sort of consciousness in the many spheres of psycho-motor activity. In this respect the rhythmics lesson affords the pupil a fine opportunity. Consequently:

it is obvious that a full knowledge of all the possible ways of moving possessed by our bodies is necessary to every Eurhythmics teacher. As between the various ways of carrying out a given series of movements he must be able to select that requiring the least degree of effort, and it is by means of repeated sensations, and by comparing and analysing them, that he will succeed in this endeavour. This elementary technique should be possessed by every one of us, just as piano improvisation requires a fingering technique . . . (Dalcroze 1916*a*: 6)

And it is because he will already have experimented with it himself on countless occasions that the rhythmician will in his turn be able to seek to bring out in the pupil 'the simultaneity of unconscious acts and conscious acts, to inaugurate and facilitate exchanges between them, to establish rapid communications between the faculties of will and reaction, of imagination, analysis, realization, and creation' (1942: 70).

What differentiates the primary-school child from that of the preceding age range? If, in most countries, it has long been the custom to start primary school education from the age of about 6 or 7, it is because the child of this age is generally recognized—whether empirically or on more explicit psychological grounds—as evincing the property of 'reason', and being capable of successfully embarking upon the acquisition of such basic skills as reading, writing, and counting. It is indeed to the control and practice of such skills that the greater part of primary education is directed, so that they may be perfectly integrated into the functioning of the individual when, at a more advanced level, he will come to use them as the tools of investigation and expression for the exploration and understanding of various spheres of knowledge.

From a psychological point of view, what exactly is covered by the term 'reason' or 'reasoning' as applied to the child of 7 and upwards? What exactly do his maturity and experience bear in their train, such that he is suddenly perceived as capable of employing strategies and assimilating ideas hitherto incomprehensible to him, of taking on new responsibilities, of persuading himself (or trying to persuade others) by means of logical argument, of evaluating a situation and taking its relative contingencies into account? To this it may be replied, in substance, that the process which from birth assures the child of increasing autonomy and socialization enables him to achieve, between the ages of 7 and 11, a new degree of *decentration* (Piaget's term for the process of moving away from an egocentric focus).

Remember that through activity the baby gradually succeeds in distinguishing himself from the world of things and other living beings, attaining to a 'motor-sensory intelligence' characterized by, amongst others, the ability to recognize objects and act upon them, to get from one place to another by a variety of routes, to retrace his steps; in short, to establish by means of his continuing movements a number of 'performed' relationships between one point (place, person, object) and another (see, in particular, Piaget 1959).

Remember that in the next period (from about one-and-a-half years) the child takes another step forward at the point where he passes from motor-sensory intelligence to that of representation; in other words, the moment when the purely physical and performed experience he has of the outside world is capable of being internalized in thought. He reaches this level helped by the appearance of a new function, the *semiotic* or *symbolic function*, which enables him to distinguish a *signifier* from a *signified* and to relate them to each other. The word 'cat' is not a cat, any more than is the picture of a cat, or a child miaowing and pretending to be a cat; but these different signifiers—the word, the picture, symbolic play—bear witness to the existence of an internal image, of a mental representation corresponding to the object evoked (see, for example, Piaget and Inhelder 1968: 41 ff). Up to the age of 6, symbolic play, pictures, and language will be fully exercised in themselves or in interactions between one another, as so many activities by which the child displays his capacity for thought.

Nevertheless, while from the age of 18 months the child is capable of reversible actions—or at least, of what appear to the outside observer so to be—such as coming in and going out, hiding an object and finding it again, tracing and retracing his steps, and so on, up to the age of 6 or 7 years his intellectual behaviour is restricted by the irreversibility of his representations. In other words, his thoughts are not yet sufficiently mobile, not yet sufficiently independent of his own point of view or his physical actions to enable him to internalize that sense of transferability vital to his ability to translate a given action into the representation of its opposite—a real transformation and the representation of its reverse transformation.

If, for example, he has been able to count correctly two equivalent lines of objects, and one of them is rearranged in a new configuration (more closed up, spaced out, heaped together), he will ignore the conservation of equality and estimate the number of objects as a function of the space occupied, being mentally unable to grasp simultaneously the unity of actions by which one state is transformed into another.

If he makes a comparison between two of those objects, it is only by taking account of one of their dimensions at a time (their height *or* their width, for example), without yet being able to co-ordinate the two by passing mentally from one to the other. Thus two volumes will be thought equivalent if they are of the same height, regardless of the surface area of their bases; or again, if the liquid contents of one glass are poured into another with different dimensions, the quantity will be thought to have changed, through lack of ability to make a proper comparison between the dimensions of the two glasses.

If he does succeed in adopting the point of view of someone opposite and facing him, it is only by a process of putting himself physically in the latter's place and making this point of view his own, but without reference to his former viewpoint and without being able to co-ordinate the two. (We have seen elsewhere how this inability relates to the sense of left–right differentiation.)

If he compares two non-congruent paths, it is by concentrating on either one of their ends—but not both—that he estimates their relative length. For example, one path will be considered longer than another because it finishes 'further away'.

Such examples could be multiplied. Let us merely emphasize that the age of 7 marks only the *beginning* of that decentring of thought which will facilitate those 'mental operations' by which the older child and the adult solve problems of this kind. In fact, the passage from irreversibility to reversibility of thought is carried out in several stages appearing at various times depending upon which aspect of reality it relates to (see Piaget 1972: 9–13, 23–9, 63 ff). For example, the operations underlying certain activities of seriation, of classification, or of one-to-one relationships become possible before those by which space and time are structured, such as the construction of two-dimensional space or the estimation of simultaneity. On the whole, though, it can be said that from the age of 9 the child comes to grips with both. At this age he is capable, in particular, of discovering the principles of multiplication for himself, and feels the need to be able to refer himself to some system of measurement. Nevertheless, it will take him at least another year to grasp the principle of dealing with things in three dimensions, such as the construction and comparison of volumes, the estimation of proportions, or the co-ordination of

three points of view (e.g., given three objects, the ability to imagine
how each one of them is sited in relation to the other two).

Let us bear in mind for our purposes that in the course of primary-
school education the age of nine years (or thereabouts) is a pivotal one.
The 8-year-old can add and subtract; at 9, he can multiply and divide.
Between these two abilities lies not only a difference in nature but also
a difference in the structure of the mental processes they presuppose.
This is to say that though it may be possible, through training, to instil
into the children a receptivity to multiplication, a real understanding
of the basic principle involved remains the product of the natural
evolution of their mental struture. Other observations lend support to
the recognition of this age as constituting a turning-point. It is also at 9
that the child's drawing begins to relate formally to its model, at 9
that reading and writing skills are sufficiently mastered to be fluently
exercised (see Zazzo 1960: 186). As far as writing is concerned, the
same author points out (ibid.): 'Responsibility rests no longer with the
hand but with the eye that guides the hand . . . The child can make
himself independent of motor conditions and exert control over
them'.

Ages 7 to 9

When, at the age of 7, the child begins to be able to lay aside an
immediate interest (play, motor activity) and commit himself to
activities of a more intellectual or technical nature, his overall behaviour
remains largely governed by his potential for effective action. Motor
exercise and expressive activities become manifestly needful to him,
as well as being an indispensable factor in his development. To him
in particular applies that observation of Dalcroze already cited in
Chapter 1, but which I repeat by way of reminder:

the child's curiosity is best expressed—naturally—in those acts he is capable
of carrying out for himself. Nothing appeals to him more than an understanding of the resources at his disposal. The child joyfully engages himself in
all those exercises in which his body can play a part. Let us engage this interest
and use it for our future educational projects.

Thus Eurhythmics lessons will still make extensive use of exercises
centring on the discovery, deployment, and improvement of motor
and imaginative possibilities. I refer the reader to some of the exercises

described in the course of this work[24] and here add three examples which will show what an embarrassment of riches we have to choose from in this area, and that there are thousands of ways of helping the child of this age to experience the pleasure of movement for its own sake by means of sometimes quite strict instructions.

Going through the hoop: This exercise encourages the child to become aware of his body's limitations—especially those to his rear which are less easy to control—and to learn how to shift his centre of gravity in direct relation to changes in bodily posture. It is taken from Claire-Lise Lombard-Dutoit of Geneva.

The teacher (or a pupil) stands a hoop upright on the floor and keeps it in place by lightly pressing on it with a single finger. Each child in turn tries to get through the hoop without making it fall over. (It must, in fact, be so lightly restrained as to collapse at the slightest touch.) Can you do it without touching the ground with your hands? Which part of you goes through first—your head? your leg? your shoulder? What about going through backwards? Instead of making the hoop stand, it may also be suspended from one finger so that it is about ten or twenty centimetres from the floor. Now can you get through it on all fours without knocking it down? Or do it feet first? And so on. The exercise can also be done in pairs, each child learning to hold the hoop in place with the minimum of pressure; or in two groups, with half the class holding hoops and the other half following in single file behind a leader who makes his route up as he goes along. In this case each hoop knocked over sends the perpetrator back to the end of the queue.

The squirrel game: This exercise-cum-game, devised and named by Liliane Favre-Bulle of Nyon, is, she says, one which children keep asking for up to the age of 14. This often happens to games that evoke a pleasing *frisson* of danger and in which everyone is entirely responsible for his own fate. It also affords practice in very light jumping with feet together, as well as in self-control and visual alertness. Why *squirrel*? 'Because (says its inventor) squirrels are little creatures who can very cleverly jump about *without anyone being able to hear them*. On top of that, we have here a race of squirrels who are *dumb*. As they are very rare, I should like to catch one, using this ball which you can see. But as I don't want to hurt him, I will try and catch him by the feet, by sending the ball off with my

[24] Especially those in Chs. 2, 4, and 5.

own foot like this. But beware: my ball may well bounce off the wall and catch you from behind!'[25] Of course, the captured squirrel in turn can become the hunter, which will be a good exercise for him. But there is something about the pitting of adult against child which in games of this sort (as, for instance, in the Wolf game) provides an emotional tension which is one of the chief attractions for young children!

Eight-legged animals: This is an exercise in the imaginative use of the body and in movement co-ordination which I have seen performed by a girls' class under Monique Bosshard of Lausanne. There were ten of them, aged 6 and 7. The exercise is done in pairs. It involves finding a position enabling each of them to make use of her four limbs so that the fantastic creature which they form together can move along on all eight legs. Each animal is quite different: one pair may go in cross formation, another head-to-tail in parallel, another one on top of the other, another with arms and legs entwined, another on their backs or their knees. But they don't all find it equally easy to move along. For example, in cross formation or parallel head-to-tail, you have to decide which one of you is the 'head'. Furthermore, in the former you cannot be entirely convinced that the whole animal is going forwards, when one member of it herself has the feeling of going sideways (Fig. 5.3).

Fig. 5.3

This observation points up another important aspect of the child's development: to ensure the establishment of genuine *co-operation*, the child must succeed in co-ordinating her point of view with that of someone else. In this example, the co-ordination required at an imaginative level is brought into relief by the physical need for each performer to co-ordinate her movements with those of the other.

[25] Liliane Favre-Bulle, interview recorded 6 Nov. 1979.

Now, as we have seen many times, the need to obey a physical sort of imperative is often the best way for the child to achieve an understanding or successful execution hitherto beyond his or her reach. Hence exercises enabling children to make spontaneous discoveries of this order are of considerable pedagogic value. They are often the ones which make calls upon the motor imagination and leave the choice of methods up to the child. But they are even more effective when it is possible to seize the opportunity to give some commentary appropriate to the situation (often, a simple description of what the child has done will be enough) which will draw the child's attention to that aspect of his activity which is most helpful to the exercise in question.

On the other hand it is desirable at this age not to embark on exercises whose success vitally depends on a spirit of co-operation. Up to the age of 9, co-operation can sometimes be the happy consequence of group activity, but cannot well be demanded as a condition of it. Let us rather take advantage of the fact that in some respects the child's way of thinking tends to maintain him in a degree of apartness from his peers, so that he is in a position to seek to develop the curiosity and interest he has in his own particular functioning, to enable his power of concentration to grow, and to give him every opportunity to express his own view of things in various different ways.

From amongst individual rhythmics exercises, then, we shall pick out those that will make the child pass beyond spontaneous and unpremeditated performances. Some will be found requiring sustained attention, others which, in Dalcroze's own words, 'keep the mind and body *under pressure*', and yet others (or perhaps the same ones) that make demands on the power of comparison and of establishing relationships between various data, thereby encouraging the child to seek his own answers to the questions posed. Care will be taken, all the same, not to devote the whole lesson to them, for even when they are presented in the guise of games they still demand a certain effort on the child's part. Yet neither will we forget that one exercise, however difficult, rests on the back of another, and that tiredness more often than not results from monotony.

RHYTHMICS EXERCISES AND INITIATION INTO ART

Apart from their contribution to the child's way of thinking, rhythmics exercises prepare him for the acquisition of basic musical ideas, through the conscious establishment of relations between motor, sensory, and spatio-temporal phenomena. Some such exercises have been described in preceding chapters.[26]

Before describing any more, I wish to pause at those which consist in assuring the sense and maintenance of a *regular tempo*, for they will be found to underlie many exercises serving to develop a consciousness of rhythm and metre, or to attain to the balance and control of psycho-motor activities. We saw above how, up to the age of 6, it is the child who sets the pace in this respect, and that exercises in adapting to a tempo are modelled on those of spontaneous motor activities. With pupils of all ages from 7 up, we will try, once we are *au fait* with the tempi that come most naturally to them, to give them the means and the opportunity for adopting any tempo that may be suggested.

Affording them the means consists in, firstly, making their motor mechanisms flexible enough to ensure that regularity becomes natural to them in every possible degree of rapidity and slowness. To this end, particular attention will be paid to walking and running exercises, since, on one hand, the sensation of regularity within them is communication to the whole body (which is not the case with the movement of individual parts of it) and, on the other, they will be capable, with sufficient training, of exercising with precision regardless of the particular speed selected (which is not the case with overall movements of the whole body). Now it is not unusual to observe, in the case of insufficiently trained pupils, a certain asymmetry of behaviour, a tendency to favour one side of the body at the expense of the other, with the result that every other step they take is cut a little short and lasts a little less long. Thanks, however, to his ability to improvise at the piano, the teacher is in possession of very effective ways of correcting this, as Claire-Lise Lombard-Dutoit was the first to make me aware:

> For one thing, you have walking to ¾ time, which puts the accent now on one foot, now on the other, and thereby neutralizes the motor sensation of the predominant side;
>
> For another, you have walking to ¾ time in which you take care to ensure that the down-beat coincides with the pupil's 'weak' step, so as to strengthen the motor sensation of the deficient side; hence it is here that the teacher, watching his pupils, adapts his piano-playing to those he thinks ought to benefit from this corrective measure.

---

[26] See above, Ch. 1 Exercise 1, Ch. 3, Ch. 4.

These two ways of assuring the regularity and symmetry of the motor sensation can be as effectively used with pupils whose activity is merely irregular (unintentional slowing down, loss of muscle-tone, excessive haste, unequal strides) as with those in whom it is typically asymmetric. But it is essential that such exercises are carried out to the medium of the piano—or at least to some form of complete musical stimulus, i.e. conveying regularity, dynamism, and continuity at the same time, these three qualities being simultaneously required for any repetitive and stable motor sensation, and together defining a *tempo*.

It can be said [writes composer Frank Martin (1977: 86)] . . . that the weighty movement of the whole body, especially that of walking, provides us with rhythmic continuity and emphasizes its basis in the repetition of equal notes. On that is founded the notion of tempo, which is not just a question of speed, as metronome markings might lead us to believe. Tempo is itself a matter of relations between energy, mass, and trajectory, in that the application of great muscular energy to a heavy weight imparts the same speed as that of little energy to a light one, and that a short gesture requires less energy than a long one if it is to last the same amount of time.

Once the pupil has been assured of regularity of movement regardless of the current tempo, he will be able to use it as an instrument of analysis and measurement. Adapting his movements to the cadence of a given piece enables him to grasp its underlying flow. Using the regular cadence of his footsteps to keep time to a song learnt phrase by phrase (i.e. listening to a phrase and then singing it in repetition, without interrupting the walk) enables him to grasp its time-relation-ships instinctively, to learn not to minimize the pauses, to respect the length of silences, without having to count it out carefully and without losing the plastic quality of the melodic line. This is why, in Dalcrozian music lessons (*solfège*), as well as in the case of songs to be learnt in rhythmics lessons, walking exercises will be allied to singing exercises whenever it is desired to encourage pupils to grasp the relationship between the continuity of a tune and its pace, between its unfolding in the dimension of sound and its arrangement in musical time. It is possible to check that this sensation has been firmly established by playing the tune again rubato or in a different tempo. And the exercise will be repeated until there is no doubt that the pupil enjoys a sufficiently stable inward sense of the pace to be able to imagine its movement without having to realize it bodily. He will then become accustomed to singing without moving, or in accordance with gestured

guidelines (which may incorporate rubato, pauses, unexpected interruptions, sudden accelerations or rallentandos) given by the teacher
or another pupil.

Dominique Porte, lecturer in pedagogy at the institute of which he
is the Principal, rightly insists that, in Dalcrozian *solfège*, the role of
rhythmics should be to *facilitate* training in music. Thus in lessons
described as 'Eurhythmic (or Dalcrozian) ear-training' it is not just a
case of putting together two branches of which one is devoted to the
development of psycho-motor abilities and the other to the acquisition
of musical concepts, but rather of combining the two in such a way
that such acquisitions are firmly based on the physical plane as well as
on musical appreciation, the former acting as a support to the latter
whereby musical concepts can be more easily absorbed, and as a
method of externalization enabling the pupil to confirm in a 'material'
way that such concepts have been properly assimilated.

As to rhythmics lessons not involving *solfège*, the preceding remarks
remain equally valid, with a slight difference of emphasis in that
aquisitions of *solfège* are here replaced by those of different substance,
albeit fundamentally of a comparable nature; namely, 'corporal *solfège*',
as it relates to the given phenomena of space and time, of sensitivity to
art, development of powers of concentration and imagination, and so
on. One will therefore be careful, on one hand, not to let the
intellectual side of the exercises absorb all the pupil's energy at the
expense of his motor sensations and physical interpretations, nor, on
the other, to restrict such exercises to expression and bodily technique
in their own right—bearing in mind Eurhythmics was conceived as a
way of facilitating the mutual integration of the individual's motor,
perceptive, intellectual, and imaginative functions, whether or not in
the context of musical education as such.

Regularity of walking gives us a perfect model for the measurement of time
and its division into equal parts . . . But the study of walking is only a starting-
point, for the child's feet and legs are not the only limbs set in motion by
conscious muscles . . . This rhythmic consciousness requires the collaboration
of all conscious muscles, and it is therefore the whole body that education
should set in motion in order to bring the rhythmic sense into being.
(Dalcroze 1907: 39)

It is at the time of entry into primary school that the natural
rhythms of the body can properly be placed at the disposal of
conscious activity (though this will certainly be easier if the child has

had experience of rhythmics from a relatively early age). In return, conscious activity can helpfully be encouraged to distinguish, refine, and perfect these rhythms in ever-increasing proportions.

But exactly what definition or definitions of 'rhythm' are we presupposing here? Rather a lot have been proposed over the course of years. Indeed, to show just how difficult it is to delimit the concept, the well-known pedagogue M. Martenot reports (1981: 151) that his opposite number E. Willems must have listed 'over three hundred definitions of the word *rhythm*'—other than his own—in an appendix to one of his works. (His editor apparently refused to publish the list through pressure of space!) For myself, I will hold to two of them. The first is due to the German musicologist Schleich and has already been cited (see Ch. 1 n. 5), but I repeat it here for its beauty and evocative power: 'Rhythm, that compromise between a force and a resistance'. Dalcroze, and Ansermet after him (1924: 6), were quite carried away by this definition. The second bears not so much on rhythm itself as on the *rhythmic sense*, thereby reminding us that rhythm does not exist in the abstract but is essentially the product of perceptive activity. We owe this to Dalcroze himself: 'The rhythmic sense, by which is meant an accurate appreciation of the relationships between movements in time and movements in space' (1909: 64). And if in the course of our descriptive survey we encounter other definitions of rhythm (sometimes more precise, or more delimited), they will invariably be regarded as subordinate to the two just given, which have the merit of not divorcing rhythm from life. Without the properties of force and resistance, of space and time conjoined which give it the essential quality of *movement*, rhythm (whether musical, corporal, cosmic, or whatever) would remain for Dalcroze and those who profess his principles nothing but an empty word.

As far as musical rhythm in particular is concerned, I take the following from Frank Martin (1977: 86 ff.):

> It is on these three elements: gestures of weight and of lightness, and a feeling for number—that I believe musical rhythm is based.

The feeling for number referred to here has nothing to do with the ability to count up to infinity, but consists, according to the above writer, in 'an extremely limited, and hence all the more powerful, datum of our consciousness', and is limited to two, three, and their first multiples. From this, it would appear, flows every formal device of music: the grouping of notes in a motif, the sense of time-signature, a sense of symmetry, and so on. It will thus be found already at work, in the state of feeling that precedes any conscious apprehension, in such exercises as the two following:

Words in music: This exercise involving listening and reacting is designed to familarize the child with the idea of secondary symbolism. Written language is a conventional way of symbolizing speech, which itself is a conventional way of symbolizing thought. The conventional device of written music, for its part, represents sounds which have been given conventional names. Similarly, this exercise will call on a convention which symbolizes the spoken word—a less arbitrary convention, however, than those above, since it consists in the rhythmic imitation of spoken words.

Ex. 5.3

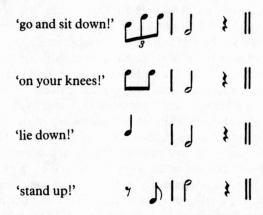

'go and sit down!'

'on your knees!'

'lie down!'

'stand up!'

Four different injunctions may be effected by the piano (Ex. 5.3). These various instructions being first executed without reference to anything else, the child will learn to identify them and then pass rapidly from one posture to another. He will then be encouraged to develop a facility for performing them in sequence, with full control of his balance and a minimum of effort. They will then be included in the course of a musical improvisation, during which the child will move about at various suggested speeds while concentrating his attention on complying with any given instruction as soon as he hears it.

It may be arranged that a musical instruction enjoin silence, thus enabling every child to listen to the rhythmic motif resonating within him- or herself, and, by watching everyone else, to ensure that the posture adopted matches properly the order given. In this event the fact of starting the music up again is an instruction to start walking round again. Alternatively, one may continue playing, so that only the order 'Up you get!' will give them permission to continue walking.

This exercise is typical of those in which instructions may be given by the children themselves, and capable of being turned into a game. For example:

In little groups we venture into a country full of dangers. At the head of each group there is a look-out, armed with a percussion instrument of indefinite pitch (Chinese block, drumsticks, tambourine). He it is who, in accordance with his sense of the imminence of danger or apparent tranquility of the surroundings, taps a rhythm out which will advise his companions how to act appropriately. It is, of course, possible to invent other, verbal, orders requiring symbolization according to their rhythms. As for the look-out, he will be motivated to greater precision by his very desire to be understood and obeyed, a desire which—for all anyone knows—may be more deeply ingrained in human nature, and hence a more prominent stimulant, than that of passing exams!

The tale of the six-legged fly: 'I know a fly which has six legs', announces Valéry Roth in her Paris class in 1979, in the manner of one reporting some freak news item, 'and it uses these legs for running forwards and jumping; then it flies off for a trip lasting six minutes'—this in the manner of one recounting a prodigious fantasy. And matching deed to word, she sits down at the piano and improvises, at a rather rapid pace, a rhythm which may perhaps be most closely represented as in Example 5.4, with a melodic and harmonic structure suggestive of an overture.

Ex. 5.4

'Then the fly lands somewhere else, and once again starts jumping off for another six-minute flight. Now, you are going to imitate the way the fly's feet move when it is getting ready to jump by tapping the tambourine you have in your hands—and, of course, moving the tambourine forwards to show that the fly is moving forwards. Then your hand will turn into the fly and make a wide sweep up into the air, and after 'six minutes' it will come back down again to settle on the tambourine—only this time not in the same place as it was before—before getting ready to fly off again.'

The ten little girls taking part in this (aged from 7½ to 9) soon discovered a movement corresponding to the musical rhythm. Their whole bodies were thrown into the leap, following the direction pointed by the tambourine; then the upper parts of their bodies suddenly found themselves freed of all encumbrance as at the point of 'taking flight' their arms opened out in a broad, sweeping movement. From head to toe, not a muscle was omitted from the engagement. Their bodies were tensed in instability, and every time their arms started the closing-in movement which would enable them to take off again their centre of gravity would be displaced. At each new point of departure a new surge was produced in a new direction—upwards, downwards, obliquely, horizontally as the case might be. It became a matter of finding arrival points which would enable them to make the flight last not for six real minutes but for the length of a dotted minim, without losing their balance prematurely. So far, the number six (six legs, six minutes) has been of purely anecdotal import. None of the children has been bothering to count, nor have they been asked to. But by repeating this rhythm time and time again they impress upon themselves its overall length, the amount of space required for the movement which interprets it, the series of short, repetitive notes, the longer period which follows them, the exact moment when their bodies must be ready to swing into action once again. 'Oh—poor fly!', the teacher continues: 'I'm afraid she has broken a leg! Fortunately, this won't stop her from being able to run.' And she illustrates her point on the piano (Ex. 5.5a). And the pupils, who have spotted the 'gap' in the procession of notes, laughingly imitate the poor fly, who in fact seems not in the least bit perturbed, and flies just as well as she did before. 'Then another day, she broke a different leg' (Ex. 5.5b). And so it goes on. The fly even manages to break two legs at once (5.5c). And finally there comes the question: Which leg(s)? (Caution: in this case it is important to listen, and not to watch the pianist's hands at the keyboard; also, before replying, to reproduce the heard rhythm within oneself.) The number six keeps coming to mind. The girls quickly discovered that it was the third leg which had got broken, for instance, or when it was the second and the fifth. They took turns in getting one another to guess which it would be. It was well understood that a broken leg never actually impeded the fly's progress. In other words, *modifications to the time and dynamics of the rhythmic flow have to be perceived within the framework of a rhythm which retains its overall unity.* From then on, the pupils are quite capable of apprehending rhythms such as Example 5.5*d*, etc., and of reproducing them with ease and in a musical way.

Ex. 5.5 (*a*) (*b*) (*c*) (*d*)

These same pupils would also be capable of advancing to the stage of reading and writing music, or of themselves inventing graphic symbols for the rhythms which they have already succeeded in subjecting to the beginning of analysis, and which they might be said to have 'engraved' already on their repertoire of motor sensations. They will not actually do so in practice, as Valéry Roth's Eurhythmics course happens to be designed as preparation for dancing. On the other hand, they will lose no time in applying their new acquisitions to the movement of dance, in which they already have a degree of practical experience. Take, for example, a sequence established at the end of the preceding exercise (Ex. 5.6). This will be used as the basis for a sequence of running or sliding steps, stretching movements,

Ex. 5.6

jumps, and so on, in such a way as to structure a vital unity paralleling that of the rhythmic structure. The sequence will be repeated at various speeds and strengths, thus enabling the pupils to explore their own boundaries. The teacher will ask the pupils to use what they know already as a basis for new inventions, or to create variations on the rhythms presented to them.

It is quite apparent that Valéry Roth is mainly seeking to communicate to the children the general feeling for a rhythmic sequence, rather than to perfect the literal interpretation of each of its individual moments. The latter will come of its own accord. 'Here, the musical instrument is the body itself', she is fond of repeating, and all her exercises indeed work together to make her pupils' bodies intrinsically more musical. Long before they know the names of basic dance steps, these pupils manifest a deep, real-life awareness of what they are doing, and capacities of adaptation and analysis enabling them to translate into harmonious movements both a variety of rhythmic instructions and their own expressive intentions. Let us not hesitate to paraphrase Dalcroze—it being his belief as well—by substituting 'dancers' and 'dance' for the words 'musicians' and 'music' in his original text (1948: 236): the study of rhythm 'will be useful not just to dancers, but to dance itself'.

Language and the fantasy of the imagination are by no means the only sources of rhythmic inspiration. The most comprehensive repository is undoubtedly that offered by the literature of written music. But any given rhythmic motif encountered in a particular piece often exhibits a totally different aspect when encountered somewhere else! Which is more valuable from the viewpoint of musical training? To take it out of context and present it in its barest, most unadorned form, for example ♫♫♩♩ , so that the child may be taught to recognize its shape, tap it out, perhaps walk to it, then pronounce it, read it, and write it, before he discovers it in tunes 'suitable for age so-and-so', or in *solfège* lessons? Or to get him to hear it dressed up in different ways that sometimes make it unrecognizable, in pieces of serious music that may be beyond him, in an attempt to help him absorb its immanent and fugitive life—perhaps even to get him to like it?

'Now I pull you past': I borrow the basic idea of this exercise from Ruth Gianadda, presenting it for the purpose of illustration in a

slightly different form from that in which I saw it carried out in one of her classes (twenty children of a second-year primary class) in November 1979.

The children stand side by side in pairs (see Figure 5.4), each holding in the right hand one end of a folded length of string or rope about 30 cm. long. Child A stays put and gets his partner to pass in front of him by pulling him round with the string. Child B has to move round as fast as possible, giving way to his partner as the latter pulls him round, and finishes up by standing at his right. In following this little path he must turn round on his own axis in such a way as to face the other. It then becomes his turn to pull his partner round in front of himself.

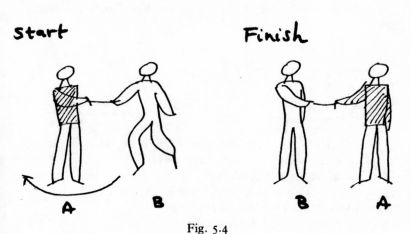

Fig. 5.4

This sequence of actions is not easy and needs to be practised in isolation. What is still particularly difficult at even seven or eight years of age is to alternate the movements accurately. Each child, whether A or B, is in effect both the doer and the done-to. A must stay in position, but he it is who makes B move. B must move round quickly, but at the same time must submit himself to A's pulling. Each of them must immediately change roles. Yet the object of the exercise remains quite clear to both children. Its overall significance is easily understood. Then again, playing at pulling one another along makes for an enjoyable game: and these two conditions are sufficient to bring about a desire to get through it successfully, if not necessarily the actual

ability to do so. Here, too, the teacher can make use of language to
bring out the actions and the rhythmic alternation. And each child
should also be able to say in turn 'Now I pull you past! Now you pull
me past!', or—concentrating on his own activity—'Now I pull you
past! Now I pass you by!' (or even 'Now I pull you past! Now I can go
past!', etc., depending on which phase of the activity the teacher
wishes to draw the child's attention to). While one of them is saying
these phrases, the other is saying them the other way round. All these

'verbal motifs' correspond to the same rhythmic model:

The latter is taken up by the piano in such a way as to bring out the
circularity of the motion, the motifs being grouped two by two as if the
piano were itself repeating the two phrases enunciated by the child at
each turn. It may be said to take over the function of the words
(Ex. 5.7).

Ex. 5.7

From then on the child can base himself on what he hears:
furthermore, he doesn't necessarily match every note of the motif but
allows himself to be carried along by them. 'The important thing',
emphasizes the teacher, 'is to stop at the end of the motif. It doesn't
matter if you're not exactly in the right position.'

Now it is with a quite specific end in view that the teacher has
chosen to work with this rhythmic motif rather than with any other,
and in this particular form:

'Listen to this piece. In it you will recognize what we have just been
doing. But you will find there are other things in it as well . . .' She
plays them the first section (24 bars in A minor) of the Allegretto
alla turca from Mozart's Sonata in A major (K. 331)—an exemplary
piece for its formal clarity, its repetitions, the simplicity and
neatness of its motifs. 'The first phrase starts in the same way as the
work we have been doing' (the teacher plays it), 'but—what
happens then?' The children point out that the third motif 'keeps
on turning round'. They try to find some way of performing this
(for example, the two children turn round together). The move-

ments consequent upon this opening phrase are then passed through, and the teacher gets them to listen to the ending again. Very probably, at least one child will comment that at this point the music 'makes you want to start running'. 'So it does. So we'll trip lightly around, two by two together, without letting go of the string but without tugging it either. We'll try and run quite a long way, but when the music stops we will have arrived.' The children go over this communal exercise several times, following instructions. Then the whole phrase is taken up again, but, to start with, each sequence being followed by a break. Eventually, we will try the whole sequence run smoothly together (Ex. 5.8).

Ex. 5.8

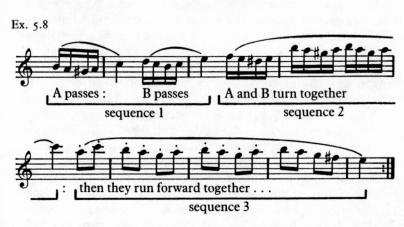

Finally, we listen to the whole piece all over again, drawing the children's attention to the reappearance of that opening phrase: 'Show me when you can hear it!' We talk about Mozart, then do some more listening . . .

In a following lesson we might well (why not?) look for a suitable movement to express the only rhythmic motif in this piece which has not yet made its appearance (Ex. 5.9). It may lend itself to the discovery of new partners, to a bow or curtsey, a volte-face, and so on.

We might also make this two-person exercise the basis of a collective

Ex. 5.9

dance, which further requires us to define a way of using the space collectively and to establish certain technical rules (such as which foot to start on) designed to facilitate the performance and give it an overall harmonic unity. To this we may then add some refinements of an aesthetic nature, or some modification of detail intended to bring out some of the music's distinctive but secondary features. But such a potential culmination greatly depends on the degree of control achieved by the pupils, bearing in mind that the earlier phase of the exercise does not make control a primary goal but need only be regarded as a way of approaching and 'discovering' the music.

Which is of greater value? To invite the child to represent the word 'garden' graphically and then to copy it, spell it, write it, recognize it in his reading, and make use of it in sentences? Or to let him run about on the grass inhaling the scent of flowers whose names are probably a mystery to him? The two, it might be said, are not mutually exclusive. That's all very well—but which does not exclude the other? How many reason 'The former does not exclude the latter', rather than 'If the latter, the former will be entailed in due course'? Why, once we are put in charge of teaching children music, does it become so hard to run across the road and into the garden with them, even though we know perfectly well that the drawing they do of it when they get back will be infinitely richer and more vibrant with life? Why is it that teachers whose very love of music has led them into their profession so often act as if music were something *for later on*? For the end of the year, for instance, when a dance exhibition will be arranged. Or for when the children have got through their harmony course and will hence be more properly equipped for it?

It would in fact appear [as Dalcroze wrote] that the following idea is held: 'Music is an artistic whole, a fortress which must be besieged on every side at once. Those on the inside who honour this palace take pains to praise its magnificence to the skies, to emphasize its splendour and immensity; they harp on the number of wings and attachments that go to make it up, and then express amazement that anyone should fear to inhabit it, though they themselves have depicted it as inhabitable and accessible, only to an élite. It is, however, open to all, provided that they make it worth visiting . . .' (1907: 45)

But what is meant by 'worth visiting'?

To limit music education to the teaching of a few patriotic songs is to seek to give the child 'an impression of the ocean by showing him a drop of water lying at the bottom of a tumbler'. (1915b: 88)

'But we have progressed from there!', it will be said. True enough—
we now have different songs. And we have other—sometimes very
felicitous—ways of doing things. But years ago they were also saying
'We have progressed from there!':

It is beyond all doubt that there is now an almost universal deeply felt desire to
reform music education. And yet the greatest confusion still reigns as to how
this reform should properly be carried out, since the pedagogic modifications
we are seeking are only superficial . . . (1915*b*: 87)

Why this state of affairs? Is there an answer to it? What shall we make
of those given by Dalcroze?

Music education today, as well as school education in general, is motivated by
the desire . . . to fix knowledge in a theoretical way and to regulate life,
[a desire] which is basically metrical in nature . . . Instead of directing musical
studies towards rhythm, they are directed towards metrical values. (1919*c*:
164)

Poor music! And yet the greatest minds of ancient and modern times have
accorded it a place of exceptional importance in education! . . . [Now] if we try
to limit the time devoted to music education to one hour per week throughout
the period of schooling, we must retort: 'Better still, drop music completely
from your syllabus!' (1915*b*: 86, 87)

This dispirited remark appeared some ten years after the publication
of his 'Essai de réforme' (1905; trans. H. F. Rubinstein in *Rhythm,
Music and Education*). In this sometimes trenchant article, to which
I refer the reader, Dalcroze is not arguing so much about the number of
hours devoted to the teaching of music as about the way in which these
hours are filled. He also puts some questions:

After doing four or five years of musical study in primary-school establishments, are at least fifty per cent of the pupils capable of:

1. Beating the time of a tune played rubato by the teacher?

2. Smoothly and accurately sight-reading either the first or the second part of
a popular song *complete with words*?

3. Deciding whether a song which is sung to them . . . has two, three, or four
beats to the bar, and whether it is in a major or a minor key?

I really don't think this is asking an awful lot! Much more is demanded of
pupils to whom a foreign language is being taught when, in examinations,
they are expected to be able to read and even write it without too many
mistakes. Note, too, that I speak only of fifty per cent of the pupils . . . (p. 21)

After six years of study in secondary and upper schools, are pupils capable of:

1. Doing what was asked (above) of primary school pupils?

2. Writing down, with at least fifty per cent accuracy, an easy tune which is sung to them for the first time, and another tune, more difficult this time, which they know by heart but which they have not hitherto seen written down?

3. Recognizing whether a short piece played to them is a gavotte, a minuet, a march, or a mazurka?

4. Improvising a few bars to a given key-signature?

5. Perceiving a modulation?

6. Perceiving and writing down a change of time-signature when listening to music?

7. [. . .] giving two lines of poetry a musical translation?

8. Citing and putting to practical use one technical term relating to phrasing or expression?

9. Naming three famous composers and their most significant works?

10. Giving a brief account of the difference between a *Lied*, a sonata, and a symphony?

Questions 2 . . . and 4 parallel the expectation made of a sixth-year pupil in English or German that he be able to write down a dictated English or German sentence and reply with a few words of German or English to a question put to him in the same language . . . (pp. 21–2)

Yes, this was in 1905, and present-day reformers are even more insistent on 'doing music' in accordance with modern methods; and rightly so, in that they remain conscious of the change in motivation arising from the availability of all the recordings made of all the music in existence (see, in this respect, Maneveau 1977), or are grounded in the recent discoveries of genetic psychology (Bamberger 1978). But it is always important to be clear of aims and the goals we seek to achieve in music learning, and to be able to answer 'Yes' to at least fifty per cent of the questions we put to ourselves.

If I may be allowed to express my deepest thoughts on the subject, let me say how hard it is to have to put such early dates on questions which are just as applicable to the present situation. It is as if nothing at all had happened in the intervening years. Yes, there have been a few brilliant flashes, one or two veins of precious metal which have petered out in the stultifying rock, lots of ideas—but, really . . .? If we accept the value of musical thinking and understanding of musical material that is reflected in his list, incomplete though it is in regard to music education today, and not including certain important contemporary developments, the question still remains as to how this musical thinking can best be achieved at the secondary and tertiary levels in our climate of educational change.

SPONTANEOUS RHYTHMIC NOTATION

When I was staying in England recently, I heard the following inspiring anecdote about Mary McDonald, a Dalcrozian working in Hertfordshire. In a school of music, she had to prepare a group of children for a music theory examination generally considered quite difficult. After several months one or two parents were beginning to agitate: their children weren't using any textbooks, or pencils, or exercise books. They had no homework—just rhythmics, and nothing but rhythmics! Their children were just moving about, dancing, singing, and listening to music. A few months later, the parents began to panic: nothing had changed; those teachers had to be reminded of their duties! But the teacher held out; it was not until a week or two before judgement day that pencils and notebooks made their appearance—and not a child failed the actual examination.[27] As we observed before, 'The two are not mutually exclusive'!

Traditionally, basic music education, instrumental as well as theoretical, lays stress on particular aspects such as counting, playing (or singing or beating) in proper time, knowing the names of the notes, learning to recognize intervals regardless of how they are used in the musical phrase, and so on. But at the same time it is dispiriting to see young beginners playing so stiffly, accentuating each note—doubly so in the case of a downbeat—and one starts yearning for them to play 'more musically', to bring out the phrasing, or even to put some feeling into it. It is only later, when they are more advanced and will be considered to have the means of understanding, that they will be made to attend to rhythmic as opposed to metric grouping, or helped to grasp the functional difference between one note or chord and another depending on its context. On these occasions, they will be asked to determine—whether by listening or by examining the score—in what way such musical elements *go together*. Now in doing this, appeal is made to a form of intuitive understanding which has been present for a long time, and which could have been allowed to show itself much earlier. It's just that the fact of centring all teaching on the formal system of notation—and of believing (or encouraging

[27] Elisabeth Vanderspar, private communication, 1980.

the belief) that those features of music which this system is capable of capturing actually *constitute* the whole of its description—have veiled any manifestations of this intuitive approach without which music cannot possibly exist.

Such, in substance, are the thoughts of Jeanne Bamberger (1978: 32), who concludes:

If children manage to make the coordination [between their capacity for the intuitive apprehension of music and the formal system to which their training has conditioned them] it is almost in spite of schooling not because of it.

Jeanne Bamberger, an American musician and psychologist specializing in cognitive development with particular reference to the acquisition of musical concepts, bases her argument on the analysis of numerous data and observations of adults and children of all ages, from which she has distilled the elements of a typology descriptive of the various different levels encountered. In particular, she has long concerned herself with the matter of graphical representations of rhythm (see Bamberger 1978 and 1980).

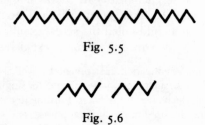

Fig. 5.5

Fig. 5.6

What does Figure 5.5 represent? It's the rhythm of galloping, repeated ad lib, as notated from memory by two children—one aged about 7, the other at least a year older—after first galloping about and then tapping out on a tambourine the rhythm they have just been expressing with their bodies. And Figure 5.6? It's the rhythm of Example 5.10, as notated by some American children in a class of 8- and 9-year-olds, after being given the opportunity of tapping it out several times and learning it by heart in the course of a group performance (cf. Bamberger 1980: 173–4). The first of these two

Ex. 5.10

graphics was done (together with several others which we will come to later) in the very first session of the Eurhythmics Congress for children (Geneva, 1979) in my class of children aged from 7 to 10 (all but one, in fact, were at least 8). None of these children had yet done any rhythmics, and, apart from one or two of them, had absolutely no knowledge of musical notation. I asked them to do a drawing in which the rhythm of galloping could be seen and recognized. As for the second graphic, it illustrates the *primary level* of classification established by Bamberger from those spontaneously produced by twenty-five children aged 8 and 9 who were first played the rhythm and then asked to draw 'whatever you think will help you remember the class piece tomorrow or help someone else to play it who isn't here today' (Bamberger 1980: 173).

The reader may well think these drawings bear little relation to their subjects. If so, it is because he hasn't watched them being drawn! The galloping graphic was done very rhythmically, with a moment's pause after each pair of lines forming the peak. The same goes for the other rhythm: the author informs us (p. 181) that the children who produced this type of drawing 'actually used the pencil to "play" the rhythm on the paper'. This *modus operandi* corresponds to what are known as *action drawings*. The resultant graphics are nothing but the traces left by an activity. They well illustrate the child's difficulty in divorcing his representation from his own movement. The young child cannot really imagine that anyone else looking at his drawing would fail to see everything he put into it at the time.

Does this mean these drawings preserve nothing of the original rhythm? Far from it. The first one shows the continuous and ordered repetition of a cell containing two elements (ʌ or v): but isn't this exactly what a succession of gallops or the tapping out of the rhythm ♪ ♩ is too? The second shows that a single sequence has been reproduced twice, and accurately records the number of elements it comprises. The reader who tries to reproduce this rhythm will at least know that it involves two equal phrases of five elements each. Of course, we are told nothing about the relative length of the notes; but it can hardly be denied that the imitation and repetition of a motif, its continuous movement, the order in which its elements proceed, and its phrasing, are the *fundamental* constituents of musical rhythm—not the least of them!

Getting back to our gallops: Of the two children who produced this type of graphic, the 7-year-old actually started by drawing—a horse! A horse drawing a cart whose driver emitted a ballooned caption reading 'Off you galup!' It was not until I told the child I would like him to draw something which would help somebody else 'see the noise of the gallop' that he came up with the graphic in question. As for the other child, his graphic was done at first attempt. It was finished off with the drawing of a drum surmounted by two sticks (sound on one hand, movement on the other!). When I asked him for a drawing which 'copied the noise', this child produced three on the trot (each one containing seven 'gallops') (Fig. 5.7). Here, too, we are into *action*

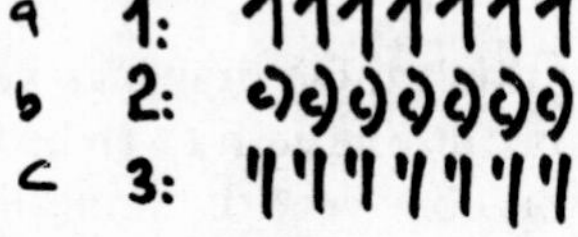

Fig. 5.7 (a) (b) (c)

drawing. All three were executed rhythmically; but in this case, unlike the first drawings we saw, the motifs preserve their rhythmic identity in the eyes of a future 'reader'. Similarly, another child progressed from a cloud of rhythmically drawn dots, where repetition remains the sole record of an initial rhythm (Fig. 5.8) to another *action drawing* in which the rhythm now puts in an appearance and the order of succession begins to be discerned (Fig. 5.9).

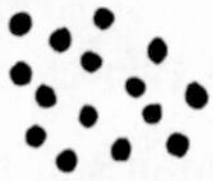

Fig. 5.8

Fig. 5.9

As to one of the pupils who said she knew how to 'write real music', she took me at my word when I said 'show what a galloping sound looks like': she drew a tambourine (indicated by the word 'tambureen' accompanied by an arrow), and on it a hand with three pairs of quavers illustrating the sound produced by hitting it. When I persuaded her that we only wanted to see the noise, she knew at once how to draw a distinction between the short and long notes of a gallop, and accordingly drew—not to the rhythm, but taking her time over it— the drawing reproduced in Figure 5.10.

Fig. 5.10

The fact that this drawing was not executed rhythmically shows that the child had *internalized her representation* of the time-sequence short–long, which she translated into little–big. Note too that each pair of circles delineates a figure sharply separated from the other circles in the drawing: the rhythm is perceived as a whole contained within its own limits, as witnessed by its representation. These characteristics summarize the *secondary level* of the typology established by Bamberger. Remember that the same little girl originally symbolized this rhythm by pairs of quavers, which themselves are also

very distinct and kept within their own boundaries: ♫ ♫ ♫ .

They can just as well be used to describe the galloping rhythm as the drawing in Figure 5.11, with which another child covered the whole page and which is equally typical of the secondary level. As a corollary, learning how to string an unbroken succession of quaver-pairs together, when reading a rhythm, presupposes that we can first manage to do without feeling that they are separate from one another! This little girl had evidently not yet reached that stage, since she used each pair of quavers as a distinct rhythm. On the other hand, she had also done something else: perhaps because her pairs of circles reminded her of moons and suns, or a sky full of planets, she finished her drawing off with three pairs of birds in just the same formation.

Fig. 5.11

Curiously, though, in these addenda the smaller of the two objects was placed to the right of the larger. Was she 'thinking' the rhythm from right to left? Or had she simply forgotten it, having divorced her drawing from the memory of the action?

Several children began by representing the galloping rhythm quite 'literally', in the manner of those mentioned above (especially Figure 5.7c). We might note in passing that this way of doing it—half-way between the stage at which the 'action' graphic leaves no visible record of the relative lengths of the rhythmic elements (Fig. 5.5), and that in which the representation is entirely divorced from the action—does not figure in Bamberger's typology (1978 and 1981). We shall come back to this later.

But most of the children were almost immediately able to get away from the 'action' approach (and thus to attain to the second level), and to translate their first 'on-the-hoof' impression by means of more elaborate graphics taking longer to effect and consequently divorced from the duration of the movement. Figure 5.12 shows some examples

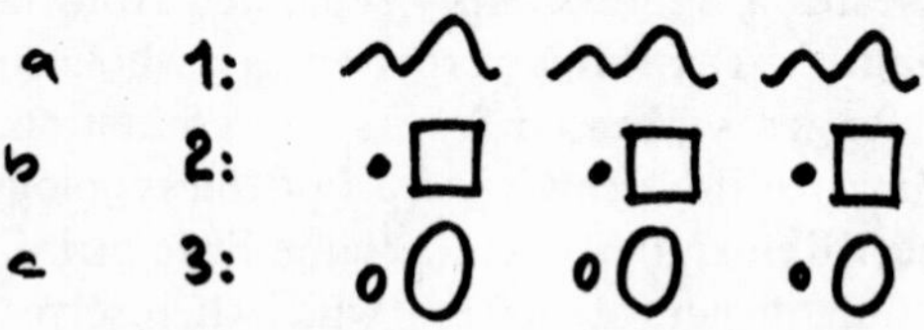

Fig. 5.12 (a) (b) (c)

taken from three different children. In contrast to *action drawings*, Bamberger gives the title *thought actions* to these symbolic descriptions of rhythms by means of patterns in space. In all these drawings, a grouping figure is felt to be prevalent; the rhythm is an inseparable whole even when the two parts of the symbol are not joined together.

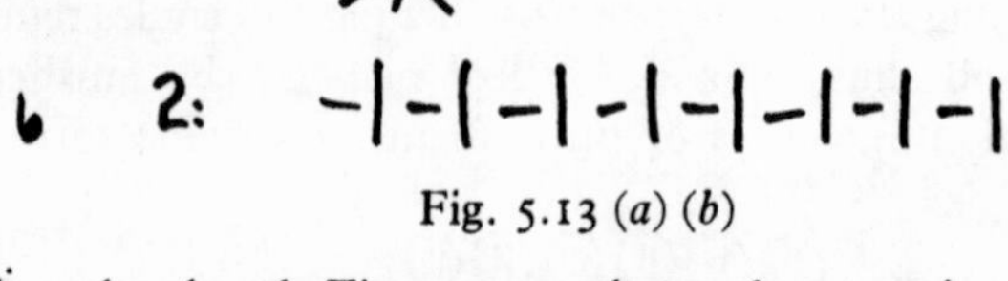

Fig. 5.13 (a) (b)

On the other hand, Figure 5.13 shows the opposite: here are two versions of the galloping rhythm done by the same child. In these you can 'see' the time—but *where* has the rhythm gone? What goes with what? Which of the sun's rays are we supposed to 'read' first? And to which of its neighbours are we supposed to attach the first vertical line? The impression we get is not much clearer than that imparted by a first-level drawing, and hardly more informative. In fact, all that counts in these drawings is the relativity and successiveness of the time-values; grouping is no longer important. We slip away from rhythm and enter the metrical era. This evolution corresponds to the *third level* described by Bamberger, a level centred on the relative evaluation of lengths; and this will be followed by a *fourth level*, at which the child begins to feel the need for a metrical reference unit by which he can more or less 're-invent' the conventional notation of musical symbols. At issue here is a fairly elaborate system so that the multiple combinations of lengths it allows of, as well as their division into equivalent metrical groupings ('bars'), can be mixed together, from a distance and under certain conditions, with that which musicians and other artists understand by *rhythm*.

Let's look at the evidence: the evolution of the child's thought processes—even when they have not been subjected to the 'deforming' effect of a musical education—lead him naturally towards *measurement* rather than musical rhythm. Then what of rhythm? Rhythm is where he starts from! These considerations throw a whole new light on the quotation from Dalcroze about the 'metrical' outlook of education in general: school seems, in some way, to play along with the children! And music at school can only be something of a spoil-sport! Unless, of course, it fits into a—well, a 'metric system'.

What does it mean to pursue an art, if not to preserve or to rediscover in oneself the ability to participate, body and soul, in an activity whose only justification lies in the pleasure it affords, and to put this ability to the service of thought or action furnished by culture, training, education, and experience acquired in the course of years?

The evolution of thought in children shows that this potential for total participation, as well as that for making a vital and faithful outward expression of an internal emotion, are present well before the child manages to develop the conceptual frameworks fitted to take them into account (or eventually fitted, being at first insufficient for the purpose). These are the frameworks, in fact, that traditional education favours; and if the child's natural evolution directs him more and more into the paths of measurement, so that he tends to become a mathematician or a technician, such tendencies will be reinforced by school as well as by society in general. Yet here and there you come across a mathematical musician, a painterly technician ... Perhaps we should see in such happy juxtapositions the triumph of the child who has succeeded in not forgetting himself (or in not letting himself be suffocated) under successive strata of intellectual acquisitions and ulterior educational goals. But of what vital force must he be possessed! Or, at least, how well nurtured he must have been! Not every child has the opportunity, because or in spite of the education he receives, to keep in contact with those modes of thought and action which characterize artistic sensitivity—and which most children do in fact make use of in their early years. On the contrary, it is all too often observable that

that boredom brought about by the aridity of technical procedures and the artistic poverty of educational textbooks imposed on childhood represses the instincts and strangles the imagination. (Dalcroze 1942: 66)

For it would be a delusion to believe that artistic sensitivity will let itself be grafted onto a technically well-turned educational product. Blessed indeed are those few who, having reached the end of their traditional term of education, seem to justify such a belief; for they are the ones whose sensitivity has survived such deprivation or found their nourishment elsewhere. Their very rarity further lends support to the idea that one is dealing with 'musical talent' as if it were a natural gift, and thus, by definition, ineducable. Dalcroze's own opinion on this point was as follows:

Education's job is to meet the child's musicality half-way. The education of the senses is too greatly ignored in our schools, and that is why we are so inartistic as a nation. [Nevertheless,] art is not a domain restricted to an élite (1912a: 50). Whatever the child's natural artistic dispositions, it is beyond doubt that a conscientious study of everything that moves within him and within nature will lead him to a more vital understanding of art. (1915b: 94)

PREPARATORY EXERCISES TOWARDS A NOTATION
OF RHYTHM

In one of the more restricted definitions that Dalcroze accorded to rhythmics, he once wrote that 'its aim is the bodily representation of musical notes', adding that 'such a representation . . . is only the natural externalization of internal attitudes shaped by the same emotions as those which inspire music' (1919b: 132).

In contrast to the action of merely tapping something—which engages only one portion of the body and results in an inevitably brief sound, no matter how rapidly successive taps are made—rhythm as translated into bodily terms through walking, moving about, and engaging the whole body as well as the respiratory system (and as, at the same time, aurally and visually perceived in its entire space–time dimension) may be regarded as an *action drawing* in the medium of the body. There is nothing surprising about the *faithfulness* of the children's graphic representation of rhythm, either when it is done 'in action' or when it becomes a *thought action* (as described above). The latter observation calls for two further series of comments.

In the first place, it is significant that the majority of the 8- to 10-year-olds whom I asked to make a graphic representation of the galloping rhythm were able to do so respecting the short–long alternation, even those experiencing only their first lesson in rhythmics. I don't think that just any simple rhythm would have had as good a chance of being grasped in only the first lesson, and it is less to the simplicity of the rhythm that the children owed their ability to represent it than to the fact that the galloping rhythm in particular had already *existed within them*—had been an integral part of their make-up, of their natural activities and their games—for a long time. The exercises we did in that lesson, leading up to graphic notation, did no more than to draw that sensation out. This comment tends to support the Dalcrozian belief that any rhythmics exercise should be addressed to movements of the whole body, and this over as long a period as necessary to impress the *motor image* upon the organism.

'From the age of 5 or 6', as rhythmician Esther Messmer discovered,[28] 'children have no difficulty in drawing a graphic distinction between long and short notes, if they have had an opportunity to experience them physically, aurally, and visually.' For example, she asks them to slide one hand along a short baton when the piano plays brief, closely spaced chords, then a long one to the sound of slow, sustained chords. In the former case, the child senses the brevity of his movement, and is soon led to repeat it. In the second he must draw his movement out, which brings his whole body into play and requires a modicum of energy and time.

She gets them to compare objects of various lengths by using the body as a measuring device: this thing is as long as a whole body, that

[28] Esther Messmer-Hirt, interview recorded 10 Oct. 1979.

one as long as an arm or a forearm, the other no longer than a finger. She encourages the children to notice that these different parts of the body can be moved at greater or lesser speeds (inversely proportional to their length, in fact).

Or again, she arms the children with a simple flute through which they are required to blow as long as a ball is rolling which she pushes along with her foot and stops after a longer or shorter period (though never so long as to exhaust the respiratory capacities of the blowers).

And when, after three or four lessons involving this sort of exercise, she gets them to notate a simple rhythm played on the piano (such as Example 5.10), giving everyone a free choice of graphic representation, she observes that *all* the children respect the relative values in their spontaneous notations. All, that is, *except those who have missed several of the preparatory lessons*.

In the second place, the fact that Bamberger's typology (see above) makes no place for 'faithful' drawings done *in action* but only for *action drawings* composed of equivalent segments (such as Figure 5.14a or b), is hardly surprising, since the rhythms notated by her guinea-pigs had only been tapped out. Tapping a rhythm out may well be done by means of equally broad gestures, even if the intervals between them are varied. This, too, explains one of the demands made by Dalcroze and his pupils of the tapping-out of rhythms (of which Eurhythmics makes frequent use, especially in dissociative and polyrhythmic exercises): they insist on the necessity of representing variations in length by corresponding variations in the amplitude of the gesture following each tap. The gesture thereby images the sustained note, since it 'inhabits' a time-period in a way perceptible to sight and muscular feeling.

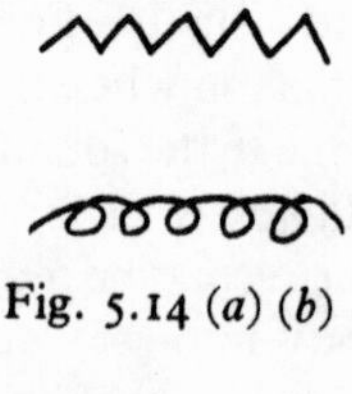

Fig. 5.14 (a) (b)

In this way, the pupil learns to distinguish held notes from those interrupted by silent breaks and requiring interpretation through broken gestures. This distinction may not be essential when it comes to metrical performance, but it certainly is in the field of rhythmics and playing an instrument. And it will become so when it comes to reading music and to interpreting it.

An exercise also borrowed from Esther Messmer, relating to the perception of broken movements and of musical staccato, is 'Tiddly-winks':

The first time round, some of the children start advancing the little coloured counters so named, following the normal practice of flipping them on the edge with a larger one. Each colour corresponds to a percussion instrument held by one of the other children, who are standing still. Each of these strikes his instrument every time a counter of 'his' colour is flipped. The ensuing silence, of variable length, corresponds to the time separating two flips of the counter. Preference should be given to instruments that make sustained sounds (triangles, cymbals, etc.) rather than sharp ones (wooden blocks, etc.), so that it becomes necessary to stifle their resonance as soon as they have been sounded. This has the advantage of equally focusing the young instrumentalist's attention on the silence following the sound he makes. By creating this silence himself, he becomes in some way aware of its material nature, and will consequently find himself better equipped to take it into account in his movements or his graphic representations.

Next time round, the teacher himself becomes the 'big counter', and flips the 'edges' (shoulders) of the smaller 'tiddlywinks' (pupils). A greater or lesser pressure induces a more or less energetic jump with feet together (which must be made instantaneously and followed by total immobility). After that, the proper rules of tiddlywinks are abandoned, so that the pupil may be given, not one tactile stimulus but two or three at a time, with variations, from one time to another, in the lapse of time between flips—three light flips, separated by longish silences; two connected flips, precisely separated by a third one of greater intensity, and so on. The pupil must then so jump as to reproduce the command communicated in a tactile way, while respecting the temporal division so communicated.

The same thing will then be done by making use of sounded commands and musical rhythms; or it may be the children who give one another tactile instructions.

When graphics are embarked upon, these various physical experiences will be illustrated by the child's ability to draw a distinction between sustained and broken-off sounds (regardless of how loud they are), and to make provision for silences, either by establishing a greater or lesser distance (gap) between the signs representing sounds, or by inventing different signs to symbolize the silences themselves.

In the same way, albeit in a different category of ideas, it is easy to get even little children to spot the difference between a tune with two beats to the bar and three notes to a beat, which they will readily associate with a bodily sway, and one with two beats and two notes to a beat, which prompts them to tap out or sketch a marching rhythm. With children of about six, I often found myself engaging in little vocal improvisations of a question-and-answer type. I would sing them the question, to which they promptly adapted a gentle rocking movement or marching on the spot, and they would improvise the response which would bring the song to a close. Their graphics reflected their motor sensations: curved lines for ternary groups, two usually unconnected marks for binary groups; and afterwards they succeeded in notating a succession of notes which they had heard either sung or played at the piano—such as Example 5.11—with the help of *action* graphics of the type in Figure 5.15.

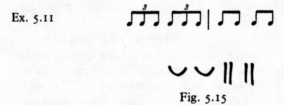

Ex. 5.11

Fig. 5.15

All these examples show that the constituents of musical rhythm may become the object of conscious awareness through the medium of bodily experience and spontaneous graphic expression *before* being dealt with in the framework of a formal system of musical notation. In Eurhythmics, from the start, this belief has been taken as one of the basic principles of music education. Nina Gorter, one of the first rhythmicians to involve Dalcrozian instruction in the musical education of children, pointed out (1919: 3):

It is essential for the child to have listened to and executed a lot of rhythms and sounds before learning how to write them down. The representation of rhythm and sound must precede their written expression, and the sight of written signs should evoke the motor and sound image required for the execution of the music.

In other words, the learning of conventional musical notation (whether writing or reading) must be the *consequence* of initiation into music— not a *condition* of it. The first Dalcrozians did not yet mention spontaneous notation (*action drawings* or *thought actions*) as described in the preceding pages. Body movements would suffice, so to say:

The organs of movement should follow, like mercury in a thermometer, the slightest as well as the greatest impulses [of music]. If they possess this quality, perfection of execution will no longer depend on anything but the perfection of internal feeling (Gorter 1919: 4).

Right at the beginning of the century, the heirs of Romanticism, in their need for musical as well as theatrical renewal, laid emphasis rather on the expression of individual feelings than on the quest for new forms of auditory or visual means of expression. The latter, however, in breaking off from what had gone before, rapidly demonstrated an inclination to react against the humanist and individualist vision, at the same time as being a logical consequence of it. Today, when artistic tendencies of sometimes radically conflicting outlooks coexist in the realm of music, and to pass from one century to another, or one continent to another (musically speaking) is often but the work of a moment, it seems even more desirable that the adoption of a conventional system of musical notation should not be taken to entail the abandonment of more intuitive or more generalized approaches, but rather that these should continue to be exercised together and alongside with it.

For, on one hand, the traditional system of musical notation, if the most widely practised, is no longer the only way of communicating music in writing. With increasing frequency, contemporary scores call for graphic devices which bear little or no apparent relation to the former system, whether they are embodied in the form of figures or symbols intelligible only to the initiated, or more closely approach intuitive forms of notation typical of non-initiates, communicating to the performers more or less approximate indications as to the length, pitch, loudness, or expressiveness of sounds. It therefore seems at the same time both more economical and more in keeping with the real world of today to approach traditional notation as one of many possible systems. Dalcroze would have been the first to embrace this interpretation, having since 1916 been of the opinion that it was necessary to

try to unburden ourselves of all our preconceptions, to *purge* ourselves of ready-made doctrines and automated actions so that we may be able . . . each in our own way . . . irresistibly to express our new feelings—free at last of outmoded forms and antiquated educational methods, and fully conscious of the future in every fibre of our being! (1916a: 11)

On the other hand, while accepting that one should retain the classical notation system, we must remember that the features it brings to the forefront (the length of notes and rests, the exact pitch of every sound, barlines and numerical figures) are powerless to translate musical reality in all its fullness. To take one of the more telling examples: just what do we ask of a trainee singer whom we wish to encourage to interpret a *Lied* or romance more *musically*? We ask him to forget the barlines and bear in mind the overall shape and sense of the text, which determine its anchor-points and suggest its nuances. That, too, is what is asked of the pupil instrumentalist, or the child doing sol-fa: to feel for the sense of the musical argument without stopping at the barlines; but here, in the absence of written words which instruct the singer in the curve of their rhythms, the bars are even harder to ignore if one has got into the habit of schematically associating them with the strong beats of the music. Isn't it a pity that, in order to draw attention to that which is of the greatest musical importance, one must first *unlearn* something which is, in this respect, of secondary importance? But that's the price you have to pay for musical training based on metrics. Marguerite Oehl, one of Dalcroze's first pupils, observed (1920: 5):

[The pupil] should not be expected to look for an exaggerated accentuation in all the rhythms played to him. The important thing is that he should develop his musical ear and recognize the basic time signature from the flow of the tune, by the cadence of phrase, and through the harmony. He must reach the point of differentiating two bars of unequal length solely through the melodic line and harmonization. This, I believe, is the line to take from the outset . . .

If in fact the pupil is taught to consider above all the 'shape' of the music—punctuation, breathings, phrasing, inflexions, support points; repetition of a sequence, superpositions, parallelisms, melodic convergence or divergence, the weight of sound, etc.; things which he is capable not only of grasping through ear and eye, but also of interpreting through his own movements and unpremeditated graphics—then we enable him to avoid reducing music to its metrical skeleton.

It is my opinion that 'learning' a four-bar phrase one bar at a time is not very useful because it is too fragmentary. The pupil must have an eye to the whole as often as possible. This takes a long time and requires patience, but eventually will be achieved. In this way, the musical faculties of children will be as fully developed as possible by getting them to appreciate nuances, and even style at this stage, since music itself is the basis of our instruction. (Oehl 1920: 6)

Everything about phrasing and nuancing is so easy to explain, so natural and attractive, so ready to be immediately grasped and understood even by the child least *au fait* with questions of technique! (Dalcroze 1905: 35)

And let us be able to apply ourselves to such concentration that at first hearing we may be able to perceive precisely the general nature of the rhythm coming across, even if a few of its details are lost on us. (Dalcroze 1916a: 6)

As we see, the type of education which aims to bring out the general features of a musical rhythm or phrase before getting down to its structural detail has been described, from the beginning of Eurhythmics, as a primordial and indispensable method. Herein, from a Dalcrozian viewpoint, lies one's *initiation* into music and musical rhythm.

Ages 9 and Upwards

'It's a good thing', Dalcroze recommended, 'to bring children to art at an age when they have not yet been intellectualized into analysing before observing, and expressing before experiencing.' (1942: 54)

He was well aware, before the discoveries of genetic psychology came to confirm his insights, that the young child already possesses the appropriate faculties for becoming one 'endowed with the artistic outlook'.

Such initiation thus comes very late when undertaken with children who already have several years of schooling behind them (perhaps even of learning music), and who are, moreover, at an age when their own natural development is leading them to envision the world with an increasingly metrical eye. Consequently, with pupils who embark on rhythmics at the age of 9, the Dalcrozian teacher's every effort will be trained on restoring, through the child himself, ways of thinking and behaving which were natural to him several years before, without giving him the impression of regressing. We are talking here of a very difficult and delicate enterprise which, if not sufficiently grounded in a regard for the characteristics of this age, may lead (as sometimes happens) to complete contempt for the rhythmics lesson, which pupils will be heard to describe as 'babyish', as 'kid's stuff', or—worst of all!—'for girls'.

We must in particular not forget that the 9-year-old, especially the male of the species, is not overly fond of stepping into the limelight. The little girl, faithful to the image one likes to have of her, may well be pleased to bring her graceful movements into evidence, but the boy disdains all initiatives pointing in this direction, and takes no interest in his body except in so far as he can relate it to the notion of performance. Does this mean that it will be impossible to get 9-year-old boys to indulge in rhythmic dances or musical games? Far from it, so long as dancing is not confused with the external manifestation of something aesthetic but is regarded as a living game emanating from personal pleasure which offers something for everyone. Many Genevan rhythmicians will, for instance, recall the Russian dances put on by Madeleine Hussy, in which they saw young, black-booted Cossacks outdo themselves in that well-known and difficult dance requiring such strong and supple legs, while the girls' red dresses swirled about them. And the children who, thanks to Florence Séchehaye, played and danced the story of the *Brave Little Tailor*, 'who killed seven with a single blow', will not have forgotten—any more than their audience—that happy moment full of poetry and incident when every one of them took on a role made to measure. Or again, I remember more recently a marvellous rendering of Saint-Saëns's *Carnival of the Animals* arranged by Mireille Weber, who managed to involve all her classes in this enterprise, from the smallest to the biggest. Each class had been assigned one or another section of this work which, as if by magic, contained such musical and expressive characteristics as the children of a given age (or class) were in the best position to grasp and then re-create by means of movements possessing all the requisite spontaneity and precision. Seeing the successive performances of these groups of boys and girls from 5 to 13 all 'playing the game' in such an eminently natural way, one would have thought the music had been written specially for them.

From the age of 9, boys and girls are often sharply conscious of their respective roles. Is this a good thing? Is it a bad thing? Certainly nothing is to be gained by mixing the two up. But if boys do embark reluctantly on (or even overtly reject) exercises which they have some reason to think are 'meant for girls', it is on the other hand important to remember—all the more so in a mixed education—that, in general, exercises which boys can enjoy will also be enjoyed by girls. Amongst the exercises we have described already will be found a large number matching up to this criterion.[29] Generally speaking, it is those which are an end in themselves, and which either enable the child to evaluate his own performances, or confer upon him a certain element of power over his surroundings. All the same, a certain number of these exercises ought perhaps to be modified for possible application to a class of mixed 9-year-olds or above, both as to the form they take and as to the material involved, or to what sort of verbal explanations or illustrations should be associated with them.[30]

All educationalists will agree with me in asserting that in any form of instruction one must start the lesson by arousing in the child some curiosity in the subject to be dealt with, by getting him to grasp the general sense and feel the importance of it, by forging links between the matter under discussion and the child's own everyday life . . . (Dalcroze 1942: 63)

This means that exercises which have some other aim than immediate success—those for example designed to bring about the incorporation of a novel concept or to improve the aural faculties[31]—should be matched by an adequate motivation, that their purpose should be clearly spelt out and that its usefulness should be evident to every pupil. Failing that, one will seek to bring this type of exercise into line with those of the previous category by making them as attractive as possible in their own right. Whatever the case, if it is certain that any enjoyable exercise is not necessarily a rhythmics exercise, it is no less certain that every rhythmics exercise ought to be capable of being done with enjoyment. An exercise inspiring boredom does not deserve to remain in the repertoire. Even so, before rejecting it outright, we ought to ask ourselves why it is so boring. In much the same way, whenever we hear a boring piece of music, it is right to ask oneself: Is it the composer's fault? Or the performer's? Or (more rarely) the public's?

TOWARDS CO-OPERATION

Group work may, perhaps, be undertaken profitably from the age of 9. The child's thought is both flexible enough and autonomous enough to enable him, on one hand, to collaborate with others with

---

[29] See for example those mentioned in Ch. 2, Ch. 3 (Nos. 2, 4), and Ch. 4.
[30] As, for example, in such exercises.
[31] Cf. for example Ch. 2 (No. 1), Ch. 3 (No. 19), and those in Ch. 4.

a view to performances whose success depends on the adequate participation of every individual, and, on the other, to appreciate properly the drawing of relationships between complementary actions each of which may be carried out in relation to the whole while at the same time preserving its individuality.

The success of many rhythmics exercises depends on the possibility of putting two or more different actions into a working relationship with one another, and primarily on that of understanding the principle of such association. Be it in the opposition of two groups in motion, in the complementary gestures of two partners, or in an individual's capacity to perform dissociated movements, it is to the extent that the child can relate each part to the whole, by shuttling mentally between one and the other, that he can benefit from such exercises on his own account, and even contribute to their further development. If they are undertaken too soon, it may be possible to give a prospective audience the impression of a co-ordinated ensemble; but this, being imposed from without, ever remains at the mercy of a group's or a soloist's inability to readjust his action to the overall display should it happen to start coming apart for one reason or another. Let us remember, all the same, that the unifying and co-ordinating power of music is great. I have already spoken of its role as an *accelerator of developing awareness*. Hence it is quite possible that certain exercises expected to succeed with 9-year-olds can equally well be undertaken by younger children, if they have been following rhythmics lessons properly based on music for long enough.

To say that the 9-year-old is ready to co-operate is not to say that he reaches that point in a flash and without any preliminary training. With some exceptions, school will have accustomed him more to individual activities—alongside those of his peers in the context of an overall discipline—than to those based on the active collaboration of two or more partners. It is, rather, out-of-school activities (family games, team sports, scouting, theatre—even rhythmics) that the child has to thank for having sometimes gained a little experience in this respect. Yet we should not expect him to provide evidence, in his first lessons in rhythmics, of a capacity that certainly lies within his reach, but which still requires to be developed in its own right. Many exercises will provide a suitable opportunity for this. Amongst others, we might mention those described as *machine games*, of which there are a great many kinds and variants.

Gearing exercises, for example, are those in which two children (and, later, a group of children) are respectively equipped with a hoop and a stick and have to impart a repetitive movement to the object they are holding—a movement which will be different for each of them, but must be in some way co-ordinated with each other in order to show that they somehow 'go together'.

Each of them may accompany the rhythm of his movement by making an appropriate noise, or perhaps other children may match sound to action by using percussion instruments of their own choice. Subsequently, in place of a held object, they will use the whole of the body to act as a component of the machine.

Then again there is the 'Conveyor-belt game', in which the children are arranged in a line or semi circle and at regular intervals pass from one to another an object which must first be subjected to some special sort of treatment before it can go to the next one in the line.

For example, the first child dips his hand into a stockpile of large wooden blocks and slides them one after the other to the second pupil. The latter places each block on its edge and slides it to the third, who gives it several pretended hammer-blows. The fourth may turn it on its axis, and so on. It is for each one to select a rhythmic action different from all the others and to find some way of respecting the time period devoted to each component activity. The vocal rhythms by which such actions can be transferred to the plane of sound have in this case not only the merit of integrating each action with the overall activity but also of establishing a communal rhythm by their unchanging repetitiveness. To strengthen this sense, it may equally be agreed that the passing of a block to the next pupil be accompanied by a sound made by all of them, or, on the other hand, by a complete silence in which the sliding noise of the blocks can be heard. Then it will be the teacher's turn, at the piano or some other instrument, to provide a rhythm which may be gradually speeded up or slowed down, or to play a piece with a pronounced rhythm particularly suited to this sort of representation. The form taken by this exercise can also be made to fit in with rhythmic motifs imposed from without, or read; or it may consist of rhythmic movements performed in canon, etc.

These exercises call for individually selected actions, and the difficulty lies in integrating them with an overall activity. Other exercises will direct their efforts towards the spontaneous agreement which should exist between the members of a group or a couple, and upon each one's ability to momentarily sacrifice his personal ambition to the common interest. Of this type, for example, are the communal representations of *geometric figures*.

> In as brief a period of time as possible—or for the length of a piece of music—each group of children must, without bumping into one another, adopt an overall configuration such as a straight line, a semicircle, a square, a cross, a letter of the alphabet, or whatever. (Later, it will be the group itself which decides what shape to adopt, in which case 'thinking time' is included in the total amount of time allowed for it.)

Following the same order of ideas, an exercise which always proves a great success is Valéry Roth's 'Pipe game':

> The children are grouped in threes and fours, and each group is given a name or number to distinguish it from the others. All the pupils, each carrying a tambourine, move freely around the room. When a particular group is called out, its various members, separated from one another, suddenly freeze, holding their tambourines in a posture of their own choice. The other pupils then withdraw to the sides of the room, and wait for the signal which tells them to run over to one of the motionless pupils and place their own tambourines in the form of an extension to that of the selected pupil. When several children have done so (the tambourines being close but not touching), they thereby create a sort of 'stove pipe', with tambourines forming some of its sections. Each pupil remains motionless in a freely chosen posture (Fig. 5.16).
>
> Certain complications will subsequently be added: as soon as the figure has taken shape, each pupil must move about without moving the position of the tambourine; as soon as the figure has taken shape, the whole group must bodily carry the pipe somewhere else without letting it break up.

Good mutual understanding will be equally necessary for exercises in *mirror movement*, in which, for example, children arranged in pairs are asked to act in such a way that no one can guess which one of them is a reflection of the other:

> Or this question may be made the subject of a secret agreement between the two children—which in the case of the 'leading' pupil

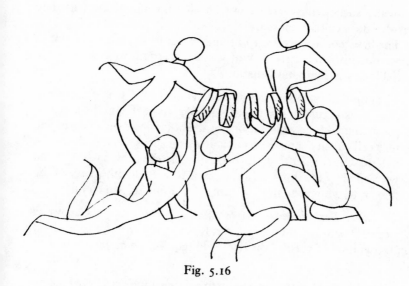

Fig. 5.16

must ensure that its demands are geared to the abilities of his 'reflection'—or again they can be asked to act in such a way that neither of them knows which is 'leading' the other, as if they were both having the same idea at exactly the same time.

Exercises of this sort will at first bring out the tendency of certain children to impose their will on others, while others follow them like sheep or put up a passive resistance. But the possibility of understanding that something of communal interest is involved (speed of performance, maintenance of an overall configuration, successful mystification of others, etc.) motivates them to fight their personal inclinations often rather better than if they were being left to their own devices. All the same, exercises in which success more or less depends on the strength of the weakest link (like the integrity of a chain) will be employed with moderation—especially if the pupils exhibit very unequal abilities in this respect—for fear of proving as nerve-racking to the stronger as to the weaker! Care will especially be taken to alternate such exercises with entirely individual-based ones, or with collective exercises in which success or failure attaches only to the individual. We may mention two such exercises which bring into play the decentring capacity appropriate to this age. They are thus capable of being successfully carried out by all, though the content they involve does call for some training.

The first requires presence of mind, the ability to locate a point in space quickly, and variability of gestural strength to accord with a variable spatio-temporal situation.

The pupils are arranged in a circle and throw a ball to one another in time to as regular a rhythm as possible. As each child is about to throw the ball, he calls out one of the other children's names. He may call out any name *except* that of the one he is about to throw the ball to! The catcher then throws the ball to the person whose name was called by the thrower, at the same time calling the name of the person to whom the next in turn is to throw it; and so on.

The second exercise, taken from Malou Hatt-Arnold of Geneva, is structurally similar, though physically easier to carry out. It is based on recognition of parts of the body and requires no particular type of skill.

The pupils are scattered about the room. One pupil goes up to another and touches a part of the latter's body (such as the hand) with one part of his own (such as the knee). The second then goes up to a third and, using that part of his own body touched by the first (in this case the hand), touches him on a different part (such as the back). This continues in the same way, the rule being that the part of one's own body touched by the previous person is the part with which one will touch the next, and that the points of contact with each of the two others involved should always be different. Each child therefore has to take three different parts of the body into account.

I have mentioned this exercise primarily to underline that it is beyond the reach of younger children, whose mental structures do not yet enable them to detach themselves from a given situation in order to envisage a new one which nevertheless refers back to the first with a view to avoiding one of its components: either they will touch the next pupil with the same part of the body as they themselves were touched with, remembering only that they have to touch; or they correctly touch with the part of their body previously touched but touch the same part of the following pupil; or they do one thing one time and another thing the next, and are not beyond occasionally doing it right, for a variety of reasons which do not derive from a reasoned assessment of the situation. Hence it is not an easy exercise, although each action in itself is easily performed by every child who has learnt to distinguish one part of the body from another. A fair number of rhythmics exercises relate, like this one, to different levels of capacity depending on whether their structure or their content is in question; for there are many which, following Dalcrozian principles, involve simple movements, natural rhythms, or elementary actions which in themselves are within the reach of all. Thus it is important to avoid confusing the structure of an exercise with the physical elements which it puts into operation when one is trying to assess its difficulty.

My second reason for mentioning this exercise is as follows: given that it is undoubtedly fairly easy to perform with 9-year-olds and over, nevertheless at the level of its affective content it does run some risk of causing problems. The child of this age does not take to being touched just *anywhere* on the body, unless he has been gradually prepared for the experience or has always lived in surroundings where physical contact is the norm. Such is rarely the case with our primary-school children. One should therefore not impose physical contact exercises on 9-year-olds—not, at least, without extreme care, or without bearing in mind the degree of mutual understanding that exists among the children, and refraining from any determined attempt to free them from the inhibitions encountered at this age (amongst others!). In this area it will be found preferable to use exercises based on a secondary stage of physical contact—under the cover of performance, for example. Here is one such, recently invented by an 8-year-old boy in my psycho-motor therapy class.

In pairs, the pupils play at duelling with 'swords' (actually hand-held sticks). You may only touch the other person lightly, using the tip of the stick. But the person so touched must immediately bind his 'wound' by using another part of his own body (for example, rest his arm against his upper body if that is where he has been touched, enfold his wrist in the other hand if it is the wrist that has been wounded) and so remain for the rest of the combat. Thus every blow that lands paralyses one's adversary a little more. The duel ends when one of the two is left with no option but to protect himself by lying down on his back. This exercise can be elaborated by imposing a rule prohibiting an aggressor from 'wounding' his opposite number in a place where he has himself been hit. It may also be stylized by matching it to a regular rhythm, or by giving it a collective form as in the exercise described above (in this case it is somewhat easier, as it is always a hand that is holding the sword); the aim will then be to be the last one still standing, or a member of the winning party (in which case the combat may be called on to be carried out in silence, or be punctuated by sounds indicative of party adherence and rallying cries, provided that such sounds may be made only by the 'wounded' at the time they are hit, and so on).

JUDGING THE DISTANCE TO BE COVERED

Exercises in space assessment, such as those requiring one to pass from one point to another in a constant number of steps regardless of distance, are well understood by the children being discussed here, and it is possible to get them to try equalizing the length of their steps in relation to the distance specified. Whereas at a younger age they would have concentrated solely on the point they were aiming to reach (and perhaps on the actual moment of arrival), or would have taken pains to regularize their steps but then left the overall distance out of account, from 9 years of age their ability to measure will enable them to divide a distance into segments of equal length, and to impart a spatio-temporal unity to the overall period of time. Covering a given distance at a given speed in a given number of steps determined by a repeated musical phrase is therefore part of the possible repertoire of children of this age. The child generally shows himself anxious to succeed in this type of activity, provided that it is presented to him with due seriousness; for, at every age, he likes to put his most recent acquisitions to the test, these being, in his eyes, the ones most worthy of respect.

Several of the exercises hitherto described involve the evaluation of space. In particular, the reader may wish to refer to some descriptions given in previous chapters, especially Chapters 2 and 4.

The points between which the children move may be decided and arranged beforehand on the ground. They may, for example, take the form of hoops. There are thousands of ways of passing from one to the other by engaging immediately in the assessment of space. Here are just a few:

Following phrases of equal length matching the number of steps given, with a pausing time within each hoop;

following equal phrases but without the pause (reaching the hoop coincides with the down-beat of the phrase);

following alternating phrases of unequal length, each matching a different number of steps. (For example: alternating a sequence of six steps with a sequence of four, with or without a pause at points of arrival; or a sequence corresponding to the unequal bars or phrases of a piece of music which is being played during this period);

following alternating phrases of unequal duration but containing the same number of steps (for example, eight march steps followed by eight of running);

following equal phrases, but these following one another in canon, each coming in one length behind its predecessor, and with the first pupil to go choosing the path to follow.

Needless to say, steps may be replaced by jumps, hops, rhythmic motifs, and so on.

But the reference-points may themselves be mobile. The simplest case is that in which the children are paired off and the first of each pair, equipped with a tambourine, advances in time to a rhythm played at the piano, adapting the length of his stride to the dynamics of the playing, eventually stopping to present his tambourine to the second. The latter then makes his way round to the first, employing the same number of steps (the piano may repeat the first phrase, or play an answering phrase of the same length, or the child may proceed while recalling the tune in silence or singing it out loud); and he strikes his partner's tambourine when he comes to a halt. The form of this exercise lends itself to many variations. I will mention two, which miss out a couple of stages, but which it is quite possible to get children of nine to eleven to do if they already have several years of rhythmics behind them.

Instead of equally spaced steps, the first one follows a rhythm of his own invention; the second watches him, then joins him in pacing out the same rhythm; eventually, he taps the rhythm out on a tambourine being held out by his partner. If he makes a mistake, the latter repeats his original rhythm instead of inventing another when it comes to the ensuing sequence.

Or an attempt may be made to establish a link between rhythm and metre: the first pupil paces out a number of steps matching the underlying beats of a rhythm which the teacher plays at the piano; the second pupil listens to his musical rhythm, then steps it in time to the first (Ex. 5.12).

Ex. 5.12

Both listen to the piano rhythm once again, then, doing a half-turn on the spot, return to their starting-point together, performing at the same time the action which they had done one after the other a few moments before. The job of the pupil enacting the rhythm is to match the pace of his fellow, who is taking steps of equal length. Finally, they both tap the rhythm out (or interpret it bodily), imparting to it all the nuances heard.

While taking advantage of the new aptitudes developed by the child of 9, it is important, as we saw above, to ensure that they are not exercised at the expense of his musicality. In particular, care will be taken to see that he retains (or acquires) a sense of musical continuity and a feeling for the overall rhythm, especially when doing exercises in spatio-temporal evaluation. Here are two more examples of exercises suited to this aim:

The first requires the children to be few in number. Each pupil starts with a ball at his feet. The piano plays, at a reasonably flowing pace, a series of phrases equal in length, but of a length that has not been determined in advance. At the point of attack of each phrase, the pupils push the balls forward with the tips of their toes; then they travel forwards in time to the piano and if possible at the same speed as the ball, which they have to stop by placing one foot lightly upon it when the phrase has reached its end. After a certain amount of time, the piano changes the length of the phrases, and the children must adapt to it as soon as possible. This is quite a difficult exercise, but one that children generally enjoy. All the same, care will be taken to raise the level of demands made on them little by little, and not to ask too much at once.

The second is practised with great success by several rhythmicians, notably Liliane Favre-Bulle and Ruth Gianadda. From the latter I borrow the particular description she gives of it. (The exercise can be carried out with different materials and different types of jumping, and the following is just one of several possible variants.)

The pupils first practise making their way through a line of hoops, which lie flat on the ground, by jumping with both feet to a regular tempo. The hoops are then spaced slightly apart, and the pupils now insert between every two feet-together jumps (and every two hoops) a jump on one foot, serving as something of a push to the following two-footed jump. Because landing on two feet is noticeably heavier than jumping on one foot, the impression is easily gained, both physically and aurally, of the sequence in Example 5.13a. Later, the requirement could be imposed of ensuring that all jumps are of equal length, if it is desired to obtain a rhythm by alternating the accentuation of notes of equal length (Ex. 5.13b). After that, the hoops are spaced a little further apart, and every two double-footed jumps are now to be separated by two single-footed jumps instead of one (Ex. 5.13c).

Ex. 5.13 (a) (b) (c) (d)

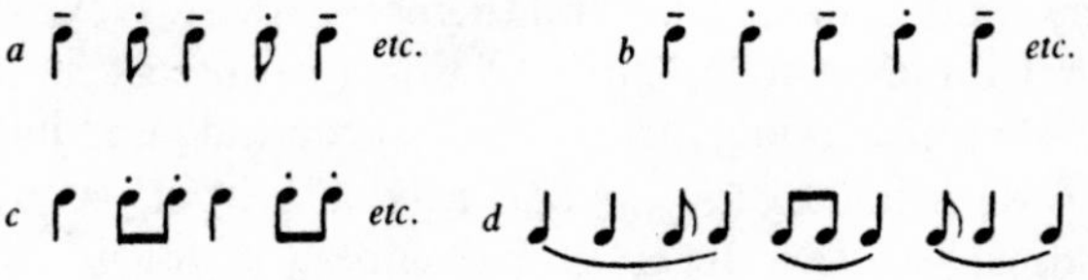

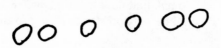

After these preparatory exercises, the hoops are arranged in a particular pattern, as in Figure 5.17, for example:

$$\mathcal{O O} \quad \mathcal{O} \quad \mathcal{O} \quad \mathcal{O O}$$

Fig. 5.17

which communicates the following rhythm in Example 5.13d both to the execution and to the ears. When all the children have had the opportunity of working their way through different hoop patterns, they will be encouraged to preserve the memory of a given rhythm: they may be asked to tap out, at the sight of a particular arrangement of hoops, the rhythm which they have just been jumping out, then to do the same thing with their eyes closed; or to reproduce the jumped rhythm in a space from which the hoops have been removed but as if they were still there; or to listen to the jumping rhythm of a fellow-pupil emanating from behind them and then to reproduce it by clapping hands for each one-footed jump and slapping the ground or their knees for each double-footed jump; and so on. They may also be asked to tap a rhythm out on a percussion instrument while 'reading' a new pattern from left to right (preparatory to rhythm-reading), or to space the hoops out in accordance with a rhythm 'dictated' by the piano at a greater or lesser speed, and which they will have to grasp as a whole (preparatory to rhythmic notation); and so on.

COUNTING AND MEASURING IN MUSIC

When doing exercises of the sort described above, as with all those requiring spatio-temporal co-ordination or precision, it often happens that the 9-year-old resorts to counting of his own accord even if it is not explicitly suggested to him. The rhythmics teacher should certainly be careful not to take unthinking advantage of this propensity in the course of any exercises that may lend themselves to it. Nevertheless, he should not forget that the child of this age, just as he likes to understand what he is doing, actually *enjoys* counting and indulging himself in little calculations. Beyond a certain level, such things are in any case necessary to an understanding of music from the viewpoint of analysis. Especially let us remember, with Frank Martin, that measurement 'is certainly born of our awareness of number' (Martin 1977: 87). The important thing is that music, in the minds of children, should not limit itself to the countable or calculable. Care will therefore be taken not to leave anything to doubt in this area.

Certain motor or audio-motor exercises may involve counting, which then, while acting as a form of motivation for the pupils, also becomes a way of exercising their reactions and expanding their powers of concentration. We shall see some examples of this below. They are not generally musical exercises as such, though they are supported by a musical improvisation which plays some part of their realization. However, for reasons which will become apparent, the psycho-motor skills which undergo improvement as a result of these exercises are those which can then be put to use in musical expression, interpretation, or comprehension.

An exercise in speed of reaction, re-establishment of centre of gravity, and maintenance of an internal tempo (Valéry Roth, Paris)

The pupils run about lightly to music from the piano. On hearing a number called, they will follow their current step with a number of *walking* steps equivalent to the number specified, and clap their hands immediately upon reaching the final step of the walked section. They then continue running. The piano accompanies their walking as well as their running steps, establishing between these a speed relationship of one to two (or one to three). When this relationship seems to have been properly grasped on the motor plane, the piano ceases to accompany the walked section, and only joins up with the pupils again at the moment they clap. Then the pupils themselves freeze on the first step of the walking section, and count to themselves while the piano remains silent up to the time when they clap.

A similar exercise involving an enforced total internalization of the tempo (Lisa Parker, Boston)

The pupils follow the tempo of the piano. On hearing a number called out (it can be quite a high one) they again take a corresponding number of steps, then stop for an equivalent period of time— either counting to themselves, or mentally going over the section of tune they heard during the previous *n* steps—while forcing themselves to stand absolutely stock-still: not a sign of the pulsation must be apparent, whether in the wiggling of a toe, the tapping of a hand, or the tensing of the jaws: it must remain entirely internal. At the end of the internalized sequence, the pupils resume their walking, then the piano imposes a new tempo upon them.

Memorizing a series of gestures (Claire-Lise Lombard-Dutoit, Geneva)

Such a series, whether designed by the teacher or the pupils, will be the more memorable if it forms a progression: for example, seven symmetrical gestures in ascending sequence: (1) hands on knees, (2) hands on tummy, (3) hands behind backs, (4) arms spread out sideways, (5) hands on shoulders, (6) hands on head, (7) arms stretched up. It should be possible to perform the series smoothly and unhesitatingly, and at different tempi from lento to moderato. The series is then performed in reverse order.

In order to check that the sequence has been properly memorized, a complication may be introduced for the purpose of distracting a good part of the attention. For example, the children play with a ball, and perform each movement of the series between bouncing the ball and catching it again. Or they may carry out the sequence in canon, with one arm always one movement ahead of the other; or with one arm following the sequence normally as the other simultaneously does so in reverse.

Similarly, the sequence may be done out of order, to ensure that the correct action is associated with each number called out: two or three numbers are called, and the children perform the appropriate actions several times in succession in a certain tempo or according to the rhythm proposed. Or else the series may again be done in order, and, when a number is called, each child freezes in his or her current attitude, only resuming movement at the moment corresponding to the gesture whose number was called. In the interim, they will have imagined going through the intermediate stages, while the piano continues to play regularly at an uninterrupted tempo.

Relative localization of sounds (Madeleine Duret, Geneva)

This is an exercise involving listening and immediate memorization. It is directly related to the education of the ear, and in it melodic memory will very quickly take the place of counting.

It is hardly necessary to count beyond four in this exercise (in fact, one could well start at three): the piano enunciates a series of four (or three) notes while the children are walking, all with a ball in one hand. For the following four steps, carried out in silence, they must throw their ball in the air on the step corresponding to the highest note of the series played; as in Example 5.14a, for instance. It is not possible to tell which note of the series is the highest until the

Ex. 5.14 (*a*) (*b*) (*c*)

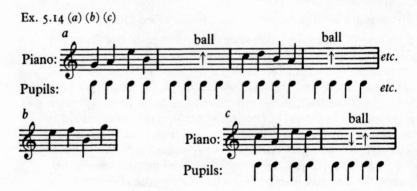

series ends (as, for instance, in Example 5.14*b*). This exercise therefore calls for mental agility sufficient to make an immediate overall assessment of the comparisons given.

The same thing is then done by reference to the lowest note of the series, at which point the children are to bounce their balls down on the floor. Then they are asked to pick out the two extreme sounds (highest and lowest) of a single series, such as Example 5.14*c*.

When this exercise is over and the teacher embarks on the translation into movement (with or without objects, balls, or scarves) of a short piece of music incorporating pronounced melodic peaks and troughs—such as Scarlatti's ravishing Aria in D minor[32]—it will be found that most of the groundwork has already been laid.

I referred above to a large class of exercises which make deliberate use of number awareness, namely *metrical exercises*. Like those above, these need not be planned as musical exercises, but there are many ways in which they may be turned to this end, so as to make the child aware of the auxiliary yet at the same time indispensable role of measurement in music. Frank Martin, who, as we saw above, derived measurement from our sense of number, points out (1977: 87): 'If measurement proceeded from bodily movement alone it would have been linked to music from the very beginning.' Now such is not the case, and the same author elsewhere defends the point of view whereby measurement is born, in music, from the need for a 'communal standard of measurement' (Martin 1927: 3). In accepting the idea that measurement is mainly a consequence of communal need, our principal occasion for drawing children's attention to the metrical aspect of an exercise will be when it emphasizes the need for simultaneity, when it imposes particular requirements of collective order and precision, or when it brings into question the idea of proportionality. We will also remember that many spontaneous natural movements can act as suitable measuring units, and that the sense of regularity they impart can exist perfectly well without conscious counting. We can illustrate this by reference to Combarieu's anecdote (1916: 147) about a Senegalese divers' song. The divers, needing to correlate their efforts in the final, decisive push to retrieve those of their boats which had been disabled and were buried in the silt, had found a very reliable way of overcoming the impossibility of normal communications underwater: they would swim up to the surface and

---

[32] In Scarlatti, *Eighteen Easy Pieces* (Kirkpatrick no. 32).

sing together, and at a certain point in their song they would dive as one man down towards the wreck, continuing to sing internally until they reached another key point in the song, whereupon they all joined in the assault together. Could it be that they didn't know how to count? Perhaps it was just that they had come to realize that music was even better than conscious counting for the purpose of maintaining pace and stability and assuring continuity of action when the need arose for a common measure!

A ball game in common time

I owe the basic principle of this exercise to Ruth Gianadda of Geneva, and present it here in a slightly modified format.

> The children are each equipped with a ball; the teacher asks them to find a way of playing with it in common time, the game being one in which they count regularly up to four several times in succession. The only special condition is that the ball must always touch the ground on the first beat. As to the rest, it is entirely invented. The children are left to work out whatever appeals to them. So far, no communal instruction has been given. They come up with various inventions. Some of the children will bounce the ball fairly hard and catch it on the second beat, others will catch it sooner and throw it in the air on the second beat, yet others let it bounce a second time before catching it, and so on. At this stage, of course, the exercise is done without the piano. Then the teacher draws attention to the first beat: 'I'd like to hear every ball hitting the ground at the same time'. Children rarely succeed in doing this of their own accord unless they have been specially coached. The teacher invited them to make helpful suggestions:
>
> somebody has to say 'Now!';
>
> somebody has to count so everyone can hear;
>
> everybody has to count;
>
> play something on the piano.
>
> We try these various suggestions out. This time some of the children notice that they have to slow their movement down or perhaps speed it up, to bounce their ball with greater force, or less. When unity has been reached through the establishment of a common measure they will do without the external aid and carry on in silence. Then the piano accompanies the pupils, gradually

disguising the four beats to a bar with ornamentations and differing rhythms, and slowly imposing a rubato which now speeds up the general movement and now slows it down again. Then each pupil in turn demonstrates the procedure he is following twice in succession. The piano keeps the same pace going to smooth the passage to the next pupil's demonstration. Eventually, the teacher calls out two or three children with markedly dissimilar ball games and gets them to demonstrate them again one after the other in front of all the others. The teacher then interprets one of them at the piano without saying which: 'Which of the three games does the music make you think of?' The children give their answers, or the one who thinks it is his performs it again. On another occasion the teacher will play a rhythm of his own invention, or a musical excerpt, and *referring back to the exercise above*, will ask the pupils to discover what time it is in, and to invent a ball game which best reflects the character of the music.

During this exercise it would also have been possible to change $\frac{4}{4}$ into $\frac{3}{4}$ or $\frac{2}{4}$ time, by suppressing, for example, the final movement(s) so that the game matches the change of measures. But this activity does not encourage them to stop counting, and it is therefore necessary to have a clear idea of what one is aiming at when doing so. Exercises devised for the recognition of different time signatures are legion and new ones are easily invented. With a view to his long-term musical training it really is important that the child should be able numerically to distinguish three to a bar from four- or five-time; but, with a view to safeguarding his musicality and spontaneity, it is equally important that numerical distinction *should not precede* the aural and corporal sensation of these differences when they are not yet being subjected to analysis. The pupils, therefore, when moving about or on the spot, will have had to be able to adapt themselves as they go to the piano's playing of simple rhythms corresponding to different time signatures (such as Example 5.15),[33] and to become accustomed to taking very

Ex. 5.15

[33] Compare the exercise described above (Ch. 3).

rapid notice of unexpected switches from one to another, before being given their next instruction; for example:

> If the rhythm is in ²/₄, the children walk to that rhythm and group together in pairs; if it is in ³/₄, they form groups of three, etc. Having got together, the groups then tap out the rhythm, or otherwise use the hand to beat it out.

Instead of repetitive rhythms, one may equally well play measured rhythms which do not necessarily repeat (taken, as often as possible, from written works). In this case the pupils, instead of walking to these rhythms, will improvise movements or progressions while seeking to bring out the underlying time signature of the piece. Whatever that may be, in every case in which the attempt is being made to bring metrical awareness into being, care will be taken to preserve the rhythmic identity of the physical or musical exercise in question, no opportunity being lost of finding various ways of bringing out the distinction between rhythm and metre which Dalcroze emphasized: 'Rhythm is individual, measure disciplinarian' (1942: 114).

Establishing the *proportionality of time values* is also a mine of exercises, especially as children of this age are likely to discover it for themselves; hence this is the ideal moment at which to embark upon it systematically, taking care to set it within a musical or expressive context. Alongside this, one will also engage the pupil's interest in the idea of notating bar measures (a subject I will not touch on here): his ability to co-ordinate the various dimensions will make him capable of discovering their real significance—in particular, of understanding the principle of metrical transformations: ⁶/₈ into ³/₄, the grouping of twelve quavers by 2, 3, 4, or 6, and so on.

The child of 9 can discover for himself, if any interest is shown in the matter, that walking twice as fast as someone else and keeping up with him at the same time involves taking two steps to every one of his companion's, but two steps of only half the length. Or that travelling twice as fast as him means arriving before him, and also involves taking two steps to every one of his, but two steps of the same length. Is it possible to take two steps to his every one and yet travel at a lesser speed? Of course it is: you can travel forward taking very tiny steps or even stay where you are, in which case you can walk faster but travel more slowly! Different combinations like this are an excuse for practising aural dissociations in which the object is not only to distinguish which of two voices (or instruments) is twice as fast as the other but also to discover which of them gives the impression of getting further ahead, of making more efficient use of space—that is, to define for each voice that space–time–energy complex which, for Frank Martin, characterizes its tempo. Many suitable examples will be found in musical literature to demonstrate how it is that two voices of which one is moving faster than the other nevertheless give the impression of proceeding together, or, on the other hand, how one of them may appear to be standing still; and so on.

Such aural dissociations are matched by *bodily dissociations*, for true dissociations are not exclusively metrical in nature (and, furthermore, need not be metrical at all); they are, rather, polydynamic (and consequently, more often than not, polyrhythmic). To beat time twice as quickly as one is walking it, or the reverse—or even to pace out a sequence of different notes (e.g. ♩ ♫ ♩) while beating its opposite (♩ ♫ ♩)—need be no more than a metrical combination in which, after a little calculation, each note is punctually fitted into its proper place; on the other hand, if care is taken to accord the right dynamics to each succession of similar or dissimilar note-values—that is, to keep up the feeling of movement by which one note succeeds another and the first note of a rhythm proceeds to the last—then a true dissociation is achieved. This is sometimes difficult to obtain, and requires a great many preparatory exercises aimed at ensuring the independence of each part of the body (an example of which occurs in the first extension to the 'Stove-pipe' exercises above (see also Ch. 5.)[34] But once dissociation has been achieved, we shall have the satisfaction of having united two different activities which go together and yet remain distinct.

To assist the pupils, use may be made at first of expressive ideas or descriptions of concrete situations, or perhaps of objects capable of supporting gestures of differing dynamics (such as with a stick in one hand and a scarf in the other). But as soon (and as often) as possible, music will take over the reins from these images, for to its power of evocation is added its ability to breathe life into movements of the body and to sustain their dynamism—always provided that the children listen to it, learn how to listen to it, and have the desire to hear it.

[34] Cf. also above, Ch. 4.

SOUND-SPACE AND SOLFÈGE[35]

How complicated it seems, when you come to think of it, to embark upon the necessary steps towards learning how to read a musical score! Even to read a simple tune confronts one from the outset with an inescapable demand: that of correlating two dimensions of music within two dimensions of visible space: from left to right, time; and, in the vertical plane, 'sound-space'. Horizontal sections correspond to intervals of time, vertical ones to intervals of pitch.

To succeed in singing (or playing) a tune at first sight therefore presupposes the ability to make sense of a horizontal organization (the succession of sounds in time) in conjunction with a vertical one (the embodiment of moments in sound), and to ensure that both are immediately translated into those auditory and motor equivalents required to activate muscles charged with the creation of sound—whether vocally or through the medium of an instrument—in the proper direction and at the proper moment. We shall not be surprised if our pupils younger than 9—and even older ones—prefer to 'learn it by ear' and are often weak at decipherment. We may, rather, be amazed to find that some of them, sometimes even younger than 9, acquit themselves honourably in this endeavour, and ought to credit this to the almost magical power of musical rhythm—not to mention the teacher who was able to recognize this power!

From a purely spatial point of view, in fact, it is hardly before the age of 9 that children show themselves capable of co-ordinating two dimensions. If we also bear in mind the required co-ordination of two different types of symbolization—that of musical pitch and all it implies (lines and spaces, clefs, the names of notes, intervals, melodic direction, etc.) and that of duration (notes and pauses, bars, proportional groups)—we will unhesitatingly advance by a year or two the point at which the child might be expected to be capable of grasping the principle of musical notation. Add further the time needed for practice in the habit of sight-reading and it will be not much before adolescence that a child is able to follow a tune. Now we know that things turn out quite different in reality, and that by 9 years of age a good number of suitably trained pupils manage to read and sing tunes which they have never heard before—and that there are others, furthermore, children and adults, who can sight-read very

[35] For the explanation of this term, refer to Ch. 2 n. 10.

little, and not very well at that, in spite of a good deal of thorough musical grounding (vocal or instrumental). Many more pages would be needed to seek to clarify the reasons for success or failure in this respect; but, in connection with the former, I have already mentioned the power of musical rhythm, and this I will now explain.

Let us first of all imagine a simplified system of co-ordinates in musical notation, in which one of the two dimensions remains constant (Ex. 5.16a and b).

Ex. 5.16 (a) (b)

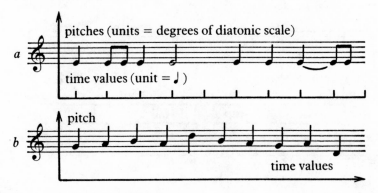

If we ask somebody what he sees in these two figures, the chances are that, if he has 'done any music', he will reply: a rhythm on a single note in the first figure, and a series of notes without any rhythm in the second. And yet, if we remember that Dalcroze defines rhythm as characterized by 'continuity and repetition' (1919c: 163), and that 'its primordial elements', nuances of dynamics and weight, and of duration, 'are combined by the flexibility governing their relations in space and time' (1942: 37), the second figure may be considered a better rhythmic model than the first. Suppose we experiment with it as follows: sing each of these sequences several times over, fairly quickly and without either prolonging the last note or following it with a silence. From the time it is repeated, or even before, the melodic sequence of Example 5.16b is perceived as a symmetric whole by virtue of the relation of tonic to dominant established between the first and fifth notes and between the first and the last. This auditory sensation, which wills the tonic to lead to the dominant, and the latter to demand a return to the tonic, will be familiar to all western ears.

Here, the feeling of symmetry is reinforced by the change of direction
in pitch, the relative weight of the notes in the tonal scale, the
alternation of conjunct and disjunct intervals: everything calls for the
main caesura to fall after the first five notes: then it becomes noticeable
that the right-hand half is more or less a repetition in reverse of the
left, and that in each group of five the notes naturally divide into *three
plus two*. Not that it is impossible or unmusical for other groupings to
be made: one could perfectly well justify a grouping of *two plus three*
(Ex. 5.17*a*), or—why not?—of *four–four–two* (Ex. 5.17*b*). But this

Ex. 5.17 (*a*) (*b*) (*c*) (*d*)

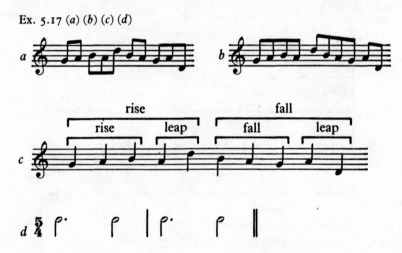

would require a certain 'rhythmic propensity'. In our first version, the
three–two grouping corresponds to the most significant contour of the
melodic sequence (Ex. 5.17*c* or Fig. 5.18). Each starting-point corresponds to a break in the upward or downward progression of notes,
whether sung or played instrumentally; each group is a simple and
unindirectional movement, which, with economy of effort, tends to
follow on or to repeat itself (Fig. 5.19).

Fig. 5.18

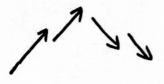

Fig. 5.19

This is why it might be said that such a sequence of sounds of exactly the same length in fact organizes itself into a rhythm, and that its most natural rhythm is the one whose space best lends itself to a natural harmonization of the motor, aural, and visual sensations of the performer (Ex. 5.17d).

Returning to Example 5.16a, that of the written 'rhythm', we notice that only a 'musical propensity' could justify this particular sequence of note-lengths and their division into equal and unequal groupings. In associating dynamic nuances and the muscular sensation of rhythmic continuity with it, or attaching a melodic dimension to its continuity, almost any way of grouping the motifs together could be justified somehow. Even so, we have at least one natural guide: the fact that, in music, long time-values more often than not go hand in hand with greater weight. But shall we pick out the longest notes by making them the first beats in the bar or by accenting them (Ex. 5.18a or b)? Only our rhythmic propensities and internal sense of rhythm will enable us to choose a dynamic (and later a melodic and harmonic) dimension to give this sequence of notes some sort of musical meaning.

In the two examples under consideration (Ex. 5.16) we were concerned with a sequence of note-lengths which were not organized and, by contrast, a sequence of sounded notes which were. Let us now assume the opposite, that is, a sequence of note-lengths with a very

Ex. 5.18 (a) (b)

Ex. 5.19
(a) (b) (c)
(d) (e) (f)

obvious organization (Ex. 5.19a), and a sequence of sounded notes lacking any rhythmic structure, such as Example 5.19b or even 5.19c. There is an evident symmetry in the sequence of note-lengths, but only a feeling of rhythm or melody will enable us to settle on their internal grouping as two or four crotchets, the crusic or anacrusic nature of the start of each motif, and the rhythmic and musical value of the whole (Ex. 5.19d or e). As to the unstructured succession of notes, they are in need of spatial and temporal division (groupings and changes of length will impart relative weight to each one) if it is desired to impart melodic value to them, as in Example 5.19f or g.

All these examples tend to affirm, with Dalcroze, that 'the two primordial elements of rhythm, space and time, cannot be separated from one another' (1919c: 163). In other words, access to musical literature and thought presupposes the possibility of apprehending space and duration in an overall and intuitive way. Now, as we have seen, this possibility begins to develop in the child, through his own activities, long before he is up to the task of co-ordinating two perceived dimensions or categories intellectually. This may possibly suggest that children who have undergone a musical education based *at every level* on the model of their natural movements may be able, earlier than other children (who may indeed never reach that point)— and often earlier than a consideration of their mental structures alone may lead us to admit—to grasp at sight the sense of a tune with due regard to its contours, its metrics, and its rhythm.

Any number of exercises have been devised by Dalcroze and his successors for the teaching of *solfège*. They are primarily based on those principles common to Eurhythmics and music which we have been illustrating here—that is, on the development of ideas which evoke in physical exercise a *visible* response to the questions posed: those concerned with the division and relationships of time intervals, with the accentuation of sounds and their relative intensity, with breathing, metrics, melodic curves, nuances of speed and dynamics— in short, with *musical rhythm*. In the second place, the Dalcrozian exercises are also based on *the ability to recognize immediately and infallibly the difference between a tone and a semitone:*

Not before [the pupil] can unhesitatingly pick out this distinction, whether in singing or in listening, can there be any question of embarking on a further subject of study. (Dalcroze 1905: 30–1)

Once this aptitude has been secured, several original approaches are available to guide the pupil into recognizing intervals, clef changes, the appreciation of modulations and harmonic construction. Let us mention the two principal ones:

1. *The study of polychords* (dichords, trichords, tetrachords, etc.), which teaches how to group rising or falling series of tones and semitones in twos, threes, or more; how to transpose them—within or regardless of any tonality—to identify the interval between their extreme notes, to name this interval and find different ways of filling it by means of tones, semitones, augmented seconds, and so on.

We may quote, as regards concepts of this order, an exercise relating to the composition of the interval of the third, which I saw carried out by Lisa Parker. In this listening exercise, the pupils sing trichords played by the piano at different pitches. At the same time, they clap their hands at the first of the three sounds, and thereafter clap hands again whenever the sound they find themselves singing is exactly one tone away from its predecessor, but not when it is only a semitone away (Ex. 5.20).

Ex. 5.20

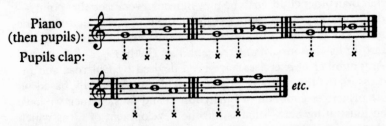

The fact of clapping or not clapping focuses the pupils' awareness on the differences which their automatic vocalizations may fail to bring to their attention, especially when the exercise is carried out in the degrees of a particular tonal scale, in which each sequence of sounds seems to emerge of its own accord—for example, in *C* major (Ex. 5.21)—and affords the teacher an immediate way (without having any exercise books to correct!) of controlling his pupils' aural progress.

Ex. 5.21

2. *The study of whole* (C-to-C) *scales*, that is, learning tonalities by listening to and singing their respective scales, always starting at *C* (whether natural, sharpened, or flattened). The tonic of each scale is thus defined by the order in which tones and semitones occur in the scale from C to C (Ex. 5.22).

Ex. 5.22

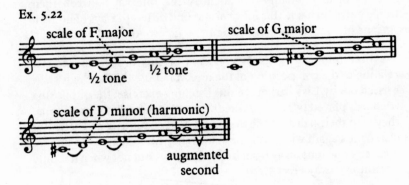

By using this type of exercise, apart from the result that all scales are singable at the written pitch, it is in particular much easier to get the pupil to sense the relations between different tonalities (and between the notes of a given tonality). This is not the case with the teaching of scales all based on the same model, which does not give adequate preparation in passing smoothly from one to another.

Note, too, that if, in the various arrangements of tones and semitones forming the C-to-C major scales, C itself (natural, sharp, or flat) is always regarded as the tonic, scales are obtained which correspond to the *modes* of old. This possible opening into modal music by way of C-to-C scales had already been pointed out by the musicologist Maurice Emmanuel, in an article he dedicated to Dalcroze after reading and appreciating *Le Rythme, la musique et l'éducation* (Emmanuel 1924: 22).[36]

As it is not the purpose of the present work to examine in detail a subject which is really worthy of a book in its own right, I will restrict myself to adding here two remarks of a general nature on the subject of Dalcrozian *solfège*. First, I should like to recall that, in the mind of its founder, rhythmics should be followed at least a year before the latter is begun, and should then be pursued in parallel with it. For the most part, *solfège* exercises consist in adapting rhythmics exercises to the musical voice and ear. In these lessons,

> the teacher . . . having developed the faculties of inner perception of and response to *rhythms* in his pupils, now seeks to create those of internally listening to, physically responding to, and creating rhythmic *sonorities*. (Dalcroze 1914: 67)

Secondly, now that everyone customarily associates the terms *solfège* or *music theory* with the daunting prospect of a grammatical, technical instruction padded out with all sorts of rules and prohibitions, we must also remember to what extent, according to his own definition (1914: 61), Dalcroze attaches primary importance to the pupil's

---

[36] In particular, Emmanuel wrote: 'The way in which you exercise the ear in picking out the semitones *in the study* [sic] *of a single octave* solves the perilous problem caused by confusion between *tones* and *modes*. Thanks to you, it becomes an easy matter to acquire the ability to distinguish between the two.' [*Study (étude)*, above, may be in error for *space (étendue)*]. Today, such Dalcrozians as Marta Sanchez (USA) and Claude Bommeli-Hainard (Berne) also emphasize this aspect by getting their pupils to grasp the difference between a fluctuating tonic (*tonique mobile*), which characterizes *diatonic scales* within the C-to-C octave, and a fixed tonic (*tonique immobile*), corresponding to the lower C, which enables the definition of different *modes* according to the order in which tones and semitones appear in sequence.

sensations, his aural development, his capacity for internal repres—
entation and powers of imagination:

The study of *solfège* awakens a sense of the degrees and relative pitches of
sounds (tonalities) and the faculty of recognizing their timbres. It teaches the
pupils to hear and mentally envisage melodies and all sorts of melodic
combinations, to identify and vocally improvise them, to notate and compose
them.

It is significant that Dalcroze places last in this sequence the
activities of notation and composition, two achievements which presuppose that one can hear and internally perform the music one is
writing. And it may be said that, in the study of rhythmics no less than
in that of *solfège*, there is one order, one sequence of events which both
sums up the Dalcrozian process and constitutes, for anyone who
claims to follow it, the only untransgressable rule, namely: *reacting,
feeling, and hearing; reproducing and envisaging, imagining, performing,
and improvising; identifying, noting, or describing; and finally composing
or creating.*

I will not multiply examples relating to the potential abilities of children beyond 9 years old; rather, to conclude this chapter, I should like
to return briefly to a question I raised earlier but did not dwell upon.

In an area as broad as Eurhythmics, it is important, no matter what
age the pupils are, to *keep referring*, in every lesson, to exercises that
have been done before, whether by repeating them in another form
(using different props, for example), or by devising others which
follow on naturally from them or bear some obvious relation. In
forging explicit links between different exercises—even those separated
by intervening lessons—one proceeds with economy. For the making
of generalizations does not come easily to pupils who do rhythmics
exercises without any possibility of standing back from them. What
children consciously retain (and often adults too) is rather the particular
features of a given exercise: attractive things to use, a nice tune, an
activity they enjoyed, an out of the ordinary experience. Their bodies
often remember better than their minds, for progress is often visible
even in pupils whose horizons do not extend beyond the activities of
the moment. Now it is the teacher's job to make such extrapolations as
may be necessary to ensure that the pupils' level of awareness is raised
to a par with their musical sensitivity and motor performances. For
every time such harmony is reached, Eurhythmics may be considered
to have attained, in a particular field and as to pupils of a given age, that
level of achievement to which it can aspire.

BY WAY OF CONCLUSION: FROM ADOLESCENCE TO EARLY MATURITY, AS RECOLLECTED BY AN ADULT

The reader may perhaps be surprised not to find the foregoing followed by a chapter devoted to the age of adolescence. It was my original intention to write such a chapter, for Eurhythmics nowadays is taught in many secondary-school classes. In the event, I decided not to do so, partly to keep the size of this book within reasonable limits, but also for the same reason that inhibits me from offering chapters on the elderly, the handicapped, and the very young: in each case what is involved is adaptations of Eurhythmics requiring one to take account of the characteristics of a given population in order to identify the best means of access and the types of objective envisaged, at the same time carefully avoiding the gratuitous stereotyping of such and such an age. Adolescence is no exception to the rule, and, in the context of physical or musical education, one must be very wary of the fences behind which the adolescent is sometimes the first to try to hide, especially those fences relating to his likes and dislikes. Without making light of the latter, the rhythmician who wishes to involve adolescents in a course of work that is both structured and directed towards art must guard against the danger of giving way to a facile demagogy aiming at all costs for the tastes of the moment. The distinction introduced above (in Chapter 5) in respect of younger children, that between manifested and latent abilities, is valid for pupils of all ages. We note that it remains so for adolescents when—side by side with those supposedly artistic performances which are nothing but a caricature of the movements and behaviour encountered in discos—we have an opportunity to witness, for example, that performance of Ravel's *Bolero* presented on stage some years ago by the pupils of Danièle Baudraz of Nyon.

For this work, characterized notably by an increasing and continuous tension right up to the final clash, Danièle Baudraz had had the happy idea of giving the pupils a visible support, which, simultaneously, acted as an aid for the expression of their continuous movement and added an important and spectacular dimension to the choreography: each pupil was secured at the waist by a fairly long piece of stretched cord fixed to a central pole, and the progressive tension of the cords, powerfully subjected to muscular control, gave concrete and intensifying form to the music in the spectator's eyes.

Apart from its felicitous artistic result, this experiment bears witness, pedagogically speaking, to a deep understanding of adolescents and young adults. It is indeed often noticeable how well they fall into a natural form of bodily expression free of all stereotyping when their movements are furnished with some sort of material support enabling them from the outset to focus their attention elsewhere than on their own bodies.

With adolescents, as with younger pupils, the experience of the teacher and her understanding of psychological development together make a good guide. If we had had to write a book on musical education as such, we should not have omitted this time of life at which the individual begins to evince a capacity for reasoning not only in respect of concrete data but also in speculating upon the possible, which, in particular, opens up to him the functional employment of the concepts of chance and probability. Counting on these abilities, musical education today can prompt the adolescent into the understanding and exercise of music of all periods by aleatory methods and experimental forms, by listening to and constructing electronic or 'concrete' music, or even by initiating him into serial or dodecaphonic music, both of which are combinatorial in nature. Similarly, through formal analysis of, and an intuitive approach to, works of the past or present, his interest and desire to learn will be quickened far more surely than by starting—as is still so often done—from the simplest phrase-analysis of childish songs and note-learning, far removed as they are from his immediate concerns.[1]

Eurhythmics, furthermore, as far as the applying of its principles is concerned, can be defined without needing to refer it to formal structures of thought which begin to develop from the age of 12. Such considerations certainly occur at the pedagogic level when the question arises of presenting pupils with musical works which they are now

---

[1] In this connection see Maneveau 1977. (Translator's note: On the practical plane, reference is also made to Rainer Boesch of Geneva.)

ready to appreciate, or getting them to undertake a piece of analysis, develop a concept, or achieve a mode of representation suited to their real or presumed capacities. The actual construction of exercises, however, is always carried out by reference to a *concrete support*, namely, bodily movement; the framework suggested by pscyhogenetic theory relative to the development of intuitive and operative thought therefore strikes me as both necessary and sufficient to account for most of the processes which Dalcrozian exercises, by their nature, put into play amongst the pupils to whom they are addressed. This may be verified by going back to the descriptions of exercises for all ages that are scattered throughout this book. Also, the more or less systematic presentation of exercises which I have made in the latter part of this work (often requiring the reader to put his own formal thought structures into operation!) is itself to be better understood as an analysis of the different levels of *integration* possible within the various levels·of rhythmics training rather than as a progressive pedagogic model relating to the ages under consideration. I will recall the distinction, which to me is crucial, made at the beginning of this book (Chapter 2) between the fallacious notion of a type of rhythmics especially *for* children (or for adolescents, or adults, etc.)—a notion illustrated by certain handbooks of a reductionist tendency—and the Dalcrozian notion of an *appeal* to the individual's various component parts with a view to *harmonizing their functioning* by means of musical rhythm.

This is the time to recall finally that the definition of Eurhythmics —'education through music and into music'—which Dalcroze gave, and which is the subtitle of this book, has to be understood on two distinct but complementary levels of meaning. On one level the word 'music' is what anyone would normally mean. But Jaques-Dalcroze often uses it in the enlarged sense of Greek inspiration, seeing in it, that is, the reunited harmony of those three human essentials expressed in French as 'le Geste', 'le Verbe', and 'le Son', which in English we can translate as Gesture (bodily expression), Speech (the expression of logical thought), and Sound (expression of feeling). And exactly what Eurhythmics is and does can be defined in each of the two following statements, whose synthesis leads straight back to the original definition of 'education through and into music':

1. The use of *music*, which has the power (especially as regards musical rhythm) to encourage the harmonized co-ordination of human

physical movement and thereby enlarge every person's capacity both
for resistance to and adaptation to the surrounding world, and for
inner equilibrium.

2. The use of bodily movement in exercises created by imagination
and disciplined by reasoned will-power to stimulate a relationship to
music and inform any apprenticeship in musicality (and, indeed,
more generally, open ways into all art forms which have a basis in the
relationship between movement and form).

'Jaques-Dalcroze' . . . originally a word whose very existence I felt
to be justified by the way it rhymes with 'rose': a name I became aware
of when I was already indebted to it for most of my nursery songs,
learning as I did, in the course of a rhythmics lesson, the one that tells
of 'la maison de la petite Rose'[2]—which to my ear meant rose with a
little 'r' like the flower, and not Rose with a big R like the name, which
didn't belong to anyone I knew myself! On that occasion (a premoni-
tion?) I was only one element of the 'white house', that magic house
which grew bigger and then smaller to the rhythm of the round song
'Dans le doux gazon se pose et se repose | la blanche maison de la
petite rose'. The little friend whom we encircled and gently protected
could never possibly have called herself Rose; it was in fact Marianne,
and she was herself 'the rose'—the prettiest, most golden-haired, and
plumpest of the group; while skinny Anne-Marie, the earnest one
with the long neck, encapsulated the whole farmyard in a single
person: 'Les poules dans la cour vont picorant et gloussent'; and her
sister, the self-possessed Danièle, was so like the cat who 'd'une voix
douce vient nous dire bonjour' that you could hardly tell them apart.
It never surprised me, living as I did in this land of flower-children
and talking cats, to see the little rose turn into the 'nimble farmer's
wife' who 'dampens the ground with her watering-can' and is rightly
rewarded by 'gathering roses by the dozen in her garden'. I was 7 or 8
years old then, and had first-hand—almost day-by-day—experience
of country life. But not for a moment did the solid, down-to-earth
content of the song get through to me (until today, when I find it
imposed by the written word): its opening words, evoking the flower-
house which 'se pose et se repose' (or 'se re-pose', as I heard it then and
hear it still), surely prove that it was written for dreaming to? As too
was its slow waltz speed, subject to sudden flights (Ex. 6.1). As was its

[2] In Dalcroze 1935c, No. 3.

Ex. 6.1

Dans le doux ga - zon se po - se et se re - po-se la

blan -che mai - son de la pe - ti- te Ro - se

ethereal chorus, borne by the breeze of its accompaniment far beyond
the expressive capacity of words, wherein I looked forward with
delight to the moment when a modulation into the mediant would
carry us into another world (Ex. 6.2).

Ex. 6.2

La la_____ La la_____ La

la_____ la la la la la etc. etc.

etc.

At that time there was no question of either 'waltzes' or 'modulations', only of listening and hearing, of moving about and letting oneself be moved. Must she not have been something of a magician, the rhythmician who made such pleasure possible for us?[3]

Later, there came other tunes, other words; my tastes changed; I discovered other sources of aesthetic pleasure—sometimes less conditioned, often inexhaustible—in music written before or after that of Dalcroze, and I sincerely believe that I have Eurhythmics to thank for opening my ear to every one of them. But this association of a name and a flower, 'Dalc-rose', has long remained with me, and I turn to it again now that the moment has come to put an end to so many earnest pages of text, and realize for how long the name Jaques-Dalcroze, rhyme or no rhyme, has remained constant even when the topic has changed (and certainly no end of topics have flowed from the pen of this multiple personality!) And yet I like to think that the name he chose for himself was not entirely foreign to that of the flower which echoes to it, in his capacity as poet and musician: which is why, among his many and many-coloured songs (and they include the dark and the severe) he so often favoured gardens and roses; and why among his many writings (and they include the trenchant, even at times the bitter) he always showed his confidence in the strikingness of beauty, proclaiming from the outset of his pedagogic career (1905: 13): 'There can be no evolution, no progress accomplished without the help of youth!'

I am glad that Dalcroze used the word 'help' where most people would hardly have looked for advice, let alone assistance. The heart of the matter, for the creator of Eurhythmics, lay in the question of how to appeal to youthfulness—and primarily, if one plays with the idea of growing up, how to recall one's own youth. Not in the sense of 'Well, in *my* day'; for 'our own experience is of value only to ourselves, and it is quite wrong to offer it as a model to others who are built differently from ourselves' (1942: 61), but in that spirit of youthfulness which we bear within ourselves—so that it may in its turn come once more to bear us up.

[3] Irène Reichel (now Boghossian-Reichel).

APPENDIX

PROFESSIONAL COURSES IN DALCROZE EURHYTHMICS

The following schools or universities provide full details relating to the contents of the Dalcrozian studies they offer, conditions of admission, length of studies, and qualifications which may be obtained.

AUSTRALIA

SYDNEY: Australian Dalcroze School of Music and Movement, Gerard Street 39, Cremorne, NSW 2090.

BELGIUM

BRUSSELS: Institut Jaques-Dalcroze de Belgique, rue Henri-Waffelaerts 53, Bruxelles 1060.

JAPAN

TOKYO: Kunitachi Music College, 5-5-1 Kashiwa, Tachikawa City, Tokyo 190.

NETHERLANDS

ROTTERDAM: Rotterdam Conservatorium, Pieter de Hooghweg 122, 3024 PJ Rotterdam.

SWEDEN

STOCKHOLM: Dalcroze Institute of Stockholm, State Academy of Music, Vallhallavägen 103–9, 115 31 Stockholm.

SWITZERLAND

BIENNE: Rhythmikseminar Jaques-Dalcroze, Conservatoire, Ring 12, 2502 Bienne.
GENEVA: Institut Jaques-Dalcroze, Terrassière 44, 1207 Genève.

UK

SOUTH CROYDON: The Dalcroze Society (Incorporated), 26 Bullfinch Road, South Croydon, Surrey CR2 8PW.

USA

BOSTON: Longy School of Music, Dalcroze Program, 1 Follen Street, Boston, MA 02138.
ITHACA: Ithaca College School of Music, Dalcroze Studies, Ithaca, NY 14850.
NEW YORK: Dalcroze School of Music, 161 East 73rd Street, New York, NY 10021.
PITTSBURGH: Carnegie Mellon University, Pittsburgh, PA 15213.

The above information was kindly provided by the secretariat of the FIER (Fédération Internationale des Enseignants de Rythmique). It is valid for the academic year 1984–5, but may be subject to modification in subsequent years.

REFERENCES

A. WORKS OF EMILE JAQUES-DALCROZE

Abbreviations:
RME = *Le Rythme, la musique et l'éducation*, 1965 edn.
SNC = *Souvenirs, notes et critiques*, 1942 edn.
MN = *La Musique et nous*, 1945 edn.
1898 'Les études musicales et l'éducation de l'oreille', in *RME* 9–12.
1900*a Le Cœur chante* (Geneva: Eggimann) (Date of publication given by BERCHTOLD 1965: 38).
1900*b Quinze nouvelles rondes enfantines, Op. 37* (Neuchâtel: Sandoz) (*c.* 1900, cf. DÉNES 1965*a*: 516).
1903 *Six chansons de gestes, Op. 58* (Neuchâtel/Lausanne/Paris: Sandoz/ Foetisch/Rouart, Lerolle).
1904 *Chansons d'enfants, Op. 42* (Neuchâtel/Lausanne: Sandoz/Foetisch).
1905 'Un essai de réforme de l'enseignement musical dans les écoles', in *RME* 13–36.
1906 *Dix nouvelles chansons de gestes, Op. 60* Paris/Lausanne/Londres, Jobin/ Sandoz.
1907 'L'Initiation au rythme', in *RME* 37–45.
1909 'L'Éducation par le rythme', *Le Rythme*, 7: 63–70.
1910 'L'Éducation par le rythme et pour le rythme', *Le Rythme*, 2/3: 18–31.
1912*a* 'La Musique et l'enfant', in *RME* 46–56.
1912*b* 'Comment retrouver la danse?', in *RME* 120–31.
1914 'La Rythmique, le solfège et l'improvisation', in *RME* 57–74.
1915*a* 'La Rythmique et la composition musicale', in *RME* 75–84.
1915*b* 'L'École, la musique et la joie', in *RME* 85–95.
1916*a* 'A bâtons rompus', *Le Rythme*, 1: 3–17.
1916*b* 'Le Rythme et le geste dans le drame musical et devant la critique. (1910–1916)', in *RME* 104–19.
1919*a* 'Avant-propos', in *RME* 5–8.
1919*b* 'La Rythmique et la plastique animée', in *RME* 132–51.
1919*c* 'Le Rythme, la mesure et le tempérament'. in *RME* 162–78.
1919*d Action Songs* (4 vols; London: Augener).
1920 'Fragments d'une conférence (1910)', *Le Rythme*, 6: 6–8.
1921*a* 'Définition de la "Rythmique"', *Le Rythme*, 7/8: 1–8 (see also *MN* 155 ff).
1921*b Rythmus, Musik und Erziehung* (Transl. from the French by J. Schwabe; Basle: Benno Schwabe).
1922*a* 'La Technique de la "plastique vivante" (extraits)', *Le Rythme*, 9: 4–11 (Largely reprinted in *SNC* 113–36).

1922*b* 'Devoirs et savoirs du maître de rythmique', *Le Rythme*, 10: 7–10.

1924 'Lettre aux rythmiciens', *Le Rythme*, 13: 1–8.

1926*a* 'La Grammaire de la rythmique (préparation corporelle aux exercices de la méthode', *Le Rythme*, 17: 2–9.

1926*b* 'Quelques recommandations aux professeurs de rythmique', *Le Rythme*, 17: 10–15.

1927 *Cueillons des chansons* (12 songs) (Lausanne/Paris: Foetisch/Jobin).

1930*a* 'Les "hop" musicaux', *Le Rythme*, 28: 14–19.

1930*b* *Six chansons animées pour les enfants* (Paris: Heugel).

1931*a* 'La Rythmique et l'éducation corporelle', *Le Rythme*, 32: 3–5.

1931*b* 'L'Enfant et le sentiment plastique', *Le Rythme*, 32: 10–13.

1932*a* 'Remarques sur l'arythmie', *Le Rythme*, 33: 3–13 (repr. in *SNC* 71–84).

1932*b* 'L'Improvisation au piano', *Le Rythme*, 34: 3–15. (This article was reproduced in full the following year in the *Revue Musicale*, under the title 'L'Improvisation musicale'. It is also largely repeated in certain later works, notably *SNC* 220–4.)

1932*c* 'Le Jardin d'enfants', *Le Rythme*, 34: 21–4. (reprinted in *SNC* 53–6).

1933 'L'Improvisation musicale', *La Revue Musicale*, 136: 344–58.

1935*a* 'Petite histoire de la rythmique', *Le Rythme*, 39: 3–18.

1935*b* 'Causerie à bâtons rompus', *Le Rythme*, 40: 3–17.

1935*c* *Au printemps fleuri* (6 songs) (Lausanne/Paris: Foetisch/Rouart, Lerolle).

1939 'Notes éparses sur la danse artistique de nos jours, *Le Rythme*, 46: 3–26.

1942 *Souvenirs, notes et critiques* (Neuchâtel: Attinger).

1945 *La Musique et nous* (Geneva: Perret-Gentil). (Repr. 1981 by Slatkine, Geneva).

1948 *Notes bariolées* (Geneva: Jeheber).

1965 *Le Rythme, la musique et l'éducation* (Lausanne: Foetisch) (First edn. 1920).

B. OTHER AUTHORS

ANSERMET, E., 'Qu'est-ce que la "Rythmique"?', *Le Rythme*, 12 (1924), 5–8.

——, 'Les Structures du rythme', in *Deuxième congrès international du rythme et de la rythmique* (Geneva: Institut Jaques-Dalcroze, 1965), 156–66.

ARONOFF, F., *Music and Young Children* (New York: Turning Wheel Press, 1979).

ARTAUD, A., 'Ce matin . . .', *84*, 5–6 (Paris, 1948).

BAERISWYL, J., 'L'Éducation pour et par le rythme', *Le Rythme*, 9 (1922), 14–18.

——, 'La Gymnastique rythmique et l'école primaire', in A. Pfrimmer (ed.), *Compte rendu du Ier congrès du rythme tenu à Genève du 16 au 18.août 1926* (Geneva: Institut Jaques-Dalcroze, 1926), 220–4.

BAMBERGER, J., 'Intuitive and Formal Musical Knowing: Parables of Cognitive Dissonance', (Unpubl. manuscript; Boston: MIT, Division for Study and Research in Education, 1978).

——, 'Cognitive Structuring in the Apprehension and Description of Simple Rhythms', *Archives de Psychologie*, 48 (1980) 171–99.

BEAUVAIS, J., 'La Place essentielle de l'éducation musicale dans l'éducation générale', in *Musique en tête: Actes du colloque sur la psychopédagogie de la musique (1979)* (Issy-les-Moulineaux: Éditions scientifiques et psychologiques, 1981), 33–6.

BERCHTOLD, A., 'E. Jaques-Dalcroze et son temps', in F. Martin *et al.*, *Emile Jaques-Dalcroze: l'homme, le compositeur, le créateur de la rythmique* (Neuchâtel: La Baconnière, 1965), 27–158.

BOCHENSKI, I. M., *La Philosophie contemporaine en Europe* (Paris: Payot, 1962).

BOEPPLE, P. (ed.), *Der Rhythmus als Erziehungsmittel für das Leben und die Kunst* (Basle: Helbing & Lichtenhahn, 1907).

BOLTON, T. L., 'Rhythm', *American Journal of Psychology*, 6 (1894).

BRIEGHEL-MÜLLER, G., *Eutonie et relaxation* (Neuchâtel: Delachaux & Niestlé, 1979) (first edn. 1972).

CLAPARÈDE, E. 'La Conscience de la ressemblance et de la différence chez l'enfant', *Archives de Psychologie*, 17 (1918), 67–78 (Cited in GILLIÈRON 1979: 47).

COMBARIEU, J., *La Musique, ses lois, son évolution* (Paris: Flammarion, 1916).

COPLAND, A., *Music and Imagination* (Cambridge, Mass. London: Harvard University Press, 1977) (first edn. 1952).

DÉNES, T., 'Catalogue complet', in F. Martin *et al.*, *Emile Jaques-Dalcroze: l'homme, le compositeur, le créateur de la rythmique*, (Neuchâtel: La Baconnière, 1965), 461–572 (*a*).

——, 'Bibliographie', in F. Martin *et al.*, *Emile Jaques-Dalcroze: l'homme, le compositeur, le créateur de la rythmique* (Neuchâtel: La Baconnière, 1965), 573–80 (*b*).

DUMAURIER, E. (ed.), *Cahiers Recherche/Musique, 6: Le pouvoir des sons* (Paris: Institut National de l'Audiovisuel, 1978).

DUTOIT-CARLIER, C.-L., 'Le Créateur de la rythmique', in F. Martin *et al.*, *Emile Jaques-Dalcroze: l'homme, le compositeur, le créateur de la rythmique* (Neuchâtel: La Baconnière, 1965) 305–412.

Ed. C., 'La Méthode Jaques-Dalcroze à l'exposition internationale de musique (Genève)', *Le Rythme*, 20 (1927), 17–18 (repr. from La Patrie Suisse, 18 May 1927).

EMERY, E., *Temps et musique* (Lausanne: L'Age d'Homme, 1975).

EMMANUEL, M., 'Le Rythme et la musique (lettre ouverte)' (1923), *Le Rythme*, 12 (1924) 21–3.

FAVRE-BULLE, L. and GARO, E., *Prim's: Formulettes, jeux, comptines et chansons pour le premier âge* (Nyon: Editions Prim's, 1976).

GAMPERT, B., *A l'œil nu* (Zurich: Collection de l'Arc-en-Ciel, 1971).

GILLIÈRON, C., 'De la epistemología piagetiana a una psicología del niño de edad preescolar', *Anuario de Psicología*, 21 (1979), 29–49.

GORTER, N., 'La Place de la méthode Jaques-Dalcroze dans les écoles populaires de musique', *Le Rythme*, 3, (1919) 1–5.

HEIDER, F. and SIMMEL, M., 'An Experimental Study of Apparent Behavior', *American Journal of Psychology*, 57 (1944), 243–59.

INGHAM, G., 'The Place of Dalcroze Eurhythmics in the School Curriculum', in A. Pfrimmer (ed.), *Compte rendu du Ier congrès du rythme tenu à Genève du 16 au 18 août 1926* (Geneva: Institut Jaques-Dalcroze, 1926), 162–8.

KLEE, P., 'Credo du créateur', in *Paul Klee* (Martigny: Fondation Pierre-Gianadda, 1980), 33–6.

KOFFKA, K., 'Experimental – Untersuchungen zur Lehre vom Rhythmus', *Zeitschrift für Psychologie*, 52 (1909).

'La Musique vivante', *Le Rythme*, 5 (1920), 27–8.

LAURENDEAU, M. and PINARD, A., *Les Premières notions spatiales de l'enfant* (Neuchâtel: Delachaux & Niestlé, 1968).

LIPATTI, D., 'Une lettre . . .', in *1970: In memoriam Dinu Lipatti (1917–1950)* (Geneva: Labor et Fides, 1970), 107–8.

LUSSY, M., *Le Rythme musical: Son origine, sa fonction et son accentuation* (Paris: Fischbacher, 1884).

MANEVEAU, G., *Musique et éducation* (Aix-en-Provence: Edisud, 1977).

MARTENOT, M., an account of his method in *Musique en tête: Actes du colloque sur la psychopédagogie de la musique (1979)*, (Issy-les-Moulineaux: editions scientifiques et psychologiques, 1981), 146–72.

MARTIN, F., 'La Mesure et le rythme', *Le Rythme*, 19, (1927) 2–6.

——, *Un compositeur médite sur son art: Ecrits et pensées recueillis par sa femme* (Neuchâtel: La Baconnière, 1977).

——, DÉNES, T., BERCHTOLD, A., *et al.*, *Emile Jaques-Dalcroze: l'homme, le compositeur, le créateur de la rythmique* (Neuchâtel: La Baconnière, 1965).

MEUMANN, E., 'Untersuchungen zur Psychologie und Aesthetik des Rhythmus', *Philosophische Studien*, 10 (1894).

MEYER, L. B., *Music, the Arts and Ideas* (Chicago: University Press, 1967).

MOTHERSOLE, A., 'La Rythmique est-elle une lubie?', *Le Rythme*, 5 (1920), 23.

OEHL, M. 'Les Cours d'enfants à l'institut de Genève: Rythmique', *Le Rythme*, 4 (1920), 3–6.

'Opinions et critiques', *Le Rythme*, 12 (1924) (special issue), 36–81.

PIAGET, J., 'Les Méthodes nouvelles: leurs bases psychologiques' (1935), in *Psychologie et pédagogie* (Paris: Denoël, 1969), 199–264.

——, *La Naissance de l'intelligence chez l'enfant* (Neuchâtel: Delachaux & Niestlé, 1959).

——, 'Éducation et instruction depuis 1935' (1965), in *Psychologie et pédagogie* (Paris: Denoël, 1969), 11–195.

——, 'Introduction', in M. Laurendeau and A. Pinard, *Les Premières notions spatiales de l'enfant* (Neuchâtel: Delachaux & Niestlé, 1968), 5–10.

——, *Psychologie et pédagogie* (Paris: Denoël, 1969).

——, *Problèmes de psychologie génétique* (Paris: Denoël, 1972).

——, and INHELDER, B., *La Psychologie de l'enfant* (Paris: Presses Universitaires de France, 1968) (first edn. 1966).

Plan d'études pour l'enseignement primaire de Suisse romande (Office romand des services cantonaux des éditions et du matériel scolaire, 1972).

POINCARÉ, H., 'La Relativité de l'espace' (repr. from H. Poincaré, *Science et méthode*), *Le Rythme*, 1 (1916), 29.

PORTE, D., 'Quelques principes en vue de l'enseignement de la rythmique dans les écoles primaires', *Le Rythme*, Dec. 1966, 3–8.

RUCKMICH, CH. A., 'The role of kinaesthesis in the perception of rhythm', *American Journal of Psychology*, 24 (1913).

SEASHORE, C., *The Psychology of Musical Talent* (1919).

STAMBAK, M., *Tonus et psychomotricité dans la première enfance* (Neuchâtel: Delachaux & Niestlé, 1963).

STANISLAVSKI, K., *An Actor Prepares* New York: Theatre Arts, 1936.

STURGEON, T., 'Le Bâton de Miouhou' (trad. franç), in M. Leconte, *Les enfants de Sturgeon* (anthologie), Paris, Librairie des Champs-Elysées, 1977, pp. 75–137.

SZÖNYI, E., *Quelques aspects de la méthode de Zoltàn Kodály* (French tr. by Jean Gergely; Budapest: editions Corvina, 1976).

TEPLOV, B. M., *Psychologie des aptitudes musicales*, trans. Jean Deprun (Paris: Presses Universitaires de France, 1966) (original Russian edn. 1947; cf. EMERY 1975: 514).

TOFFLER, A., *Future Shock* (London: Bodley Head, 1970).

VERLAINE, P. *Sagesse* (Paris: Gallimard, 1978) (first edn. 1889).

de VERTEUIL, I., *La Rythmique Jaques-Dalcroze: La pédagogie musicale, dans la première moitié du XXᵉ siècle, selon la méthode Jaques-Dalcroze* (Paris: Université de Paris-Sorbonne, 1976).

WILLEMS, E., *Le Rythme musical: Rythme–rythmique–métrique* (Paris: Presses Universitaires de France, 1954).

——, *Les Bases psychologiques de l'éducation musicale* (Bienne: Pro Musica, 1976.) (first edn. Paris, 1956).

ZAZZO, R., 'Stades du développement psychologique de l'enfant', in J. M. Tanner and B. Inhelder (eds.), *Entretiens sur le développement psycho-biologique de l'enfant: Compte rendu du premier congrès du groupe d'étude de l'organisation mondiale de la santé sur le développement psycho-biologique de l'enfant (Genève, 1953)* (Neuchâtel: Delachaux & Niestlé, 1960), 175–96.

INDEX

Printed in the United Kingdom
by Lightning Source UK Ltd.
99750UKS00001B/187